Women and survival
in Mexican cities

Women and survival in Mexican cities

Perspectives on gender, labour
markets and low-income households

Sylvia Chant

Manchester University Press

Manchester and New York
Distributed exclusively in the USA and Canada by St. Martin's Press

Copyright © Sylvia Chant 1991

Published by Manchester University Press
Oxford Road, Manchester M13 9PL, UK
and Room 400, 175 Fifth Avenue,
New York, NY 10010, USA

Distributed exclusively in the USA and Canada
by St. Martin's Press, Inc.,
175 Fifth Avenue, New York, NY 10010, USA

British Library cataloguing in publication data
Chant, Sylvia
   Women and survival in Mexican cities: perspectives on
gender, labour markets and low income households.
   1. Latin America. Society. Role of women, history
   I. Title
   331.40972

Library of Congress cataloging in publication data
   Chant, Sylvia H.
      Women and survival in Mexican cities: perspectives on gender,
   labour markets, and low-income households / Sylvia Chant.
         p. cm.
      Includes bibliographical references and index.
      ISBN 0–7190–3443–4
      1. Women—Employment—Mexico.   2. Sexual division of labor—
   —Mexico.   3. Urban women—Mexico.   4. Poor women—Mexico.   5. Women
   heads of households—Mexico.   6. Women—Mexico—Querétaro.
      I. Title.
      HD6101.C48   1991
      331.4′0972′09173—dc20   90–36942

ISBN 0 7190 3443 4 *hardback*

Typeset in Great Britain
by J&L Composition Ltd, Filey, North Yorkshire

Printed in Great Britain
by Biddles Limited, Kings Lynn and Norfolk

Contents

Figures

Tables

Women and survival in Mexican cities

3.10   Firms in Employer Survey in León: preferred age and marital
        status of male and female workers at time of entry   91
3.11   Firms in Employer Survey in Querétaro showing average frequency
        of advertising for workers and personnel department's
        perception of staff turnover   94
3.12   Assembly-line workers according to sex and rank in a large-scale
        refrigerator manufacturing plant in Querétaro   95
3.13   Firms in Employer Survey in Querétaro showing main modes of
        advertising staff vacancies at worker level   96
3.14   Firms in Employer Survey in Querétaro: preferred age and marital
        status of male and female workers at time of entry   97
3.15a   Firms in Employer Survey in Puerto Vallarta, showing personnel
        manager's perception of sex of workers with higher degree of
        turnover   100
3.15b   Firms in Employer Survey in León, showing personnel manager's
        perception of sex of workers with higher degree of turnover   100
3.15c   Firms in Employer Survey in Querétaro, showing personnel
        manager's perception of sex of workers with higher degree of
        turnover   101
3.16   Personnel managers' perceptions of the positive and negative
        attributes of male and female workers in the three study cities   103
4.1   General characteristics of the study settlements   111
4.2   Breakdown of household types in interview sample by city
        and settlement   112
4.3   Mean age of women according to activity and sex of household
        head   124
4.4   Average age of women according to level of education   125
4.5   Women's activity and educational levels   126
4.6   Mean household size, number of workers and dependency ratios
        according to women's activity   128
4.7   Women's labour force participation and per capita household
        earnings   130
4.8   Women's employment in the study cities   136
4.9   Percentage of women-headed households in the study cities   137
4.10   Family types in household interview sample by city   137
4.11   Households selected for 1986 survey in Querétaro according to
        structure in 1982–3 and change by 1986   138
4.12   Household structure and women's labour force participation   139
5.1   Household structures in sub-sample (1986)   144
5.2   Women's labour force participation and household structure
        in the sub-sample   145
5.3   Women in nuclear households in the sub-sample: some basic
        characteristics   161
6.1   Actual changes in household structure in Querétaro 1982–3 to
        1986   182

Preface

This book represents the culmination of nearly four years' work and grew out of a key area of 'unfinished business' in previous research for a doctorate on women, housing and household survival strategies in Querétaro, an intermediate city in the central highlands of Mexico. One of the major findings of this earlier research was that women's labour force participation among the urban poor varied considerably according to the types of household to which they belonged, with the most marked differences arising in relation to whether a man or woman was head of household, and whether parent(s) not only lived with their own children but other members of their kin groups as well. On the basis of this experience in Queretaro I concluded that household structure (as the joint product of sex of household head and household composition) was a critical variable in understanding the role that women played in household survival strategies. However, the argument could not easily be extrapolated unless there was evidence from other kinds of cities as well. One needed to know, for example, whether household structure would exert the same effect on female labour force participation in cities with different types of economy and different levels of demand for women's labour. There was also the thorny question of the influence that the local economy could have on household formation among the poor. There was clearly a need, therefore, to see what happened to rates of female labour force participation and the balance of different types of household units in areas where the local economy, and *ipso facto*, demand for male and female labour might be different. In order to shed light on this question, the present research explores the question of key determinants of female labour force participation in the context of a comparative study of three intermediate Mexican cities (Querétaro, León and Puerto Vallarta) with very different kinds of economy. As an important feature of this issue the book also addresses the question of whether household structures themselves have different configurations under different economic conditions, how far this relates to the representation of low-income women in the local economy, and in turn how variations in female labour force involvement and household structure shape men's, women's and children's experiences of urban poverty. In short, on the basis of extensive interviews with low-income households and local employers, the study attempts to provide a detailed and integrated analysis of the articulations between women, employment and household survival strategies in contemporary urban Mexico.

Chapter 1 sets out the principal ideas and hypotheses of the study and places them within the context of current debates in the literature. Chapter 2 provides historical, economic and demographic details of the study cities with reference to Mexican development as a whole in the post-war period. Chapter 3 considers labour demand in the three cities by looking at policies and practices of gender recruitment in key sectors of the respective local economies. Chapter 4 examines a range of factors at the household level which influence female labour supply, and Chapter 5 brings the analysis of supply and demand together by taking a much more detailed look at the articulations between female labour force participation and household structure in the different urban contexts. This is taken further in Chapter 6 with analysis of changes in household structure and women's employment in Querétaro between 1982-3 and 1986 based on direct longitudinal research. Chapter 7 considers the implications of women's work and household structure for the survival and welfare of the poor, and Chapter 8, along with a summary of the major research findings and a brief comment on the future for low-income Mexican women, concludes with a few suggestions as to 'ways forward' for the analysis of gender, households and economic development . Two detailed appendices are also provided to clarify terms and to outline the research methodology used in the surveys of households and employers respectively.

The fieldwork for the project took place between January and December 1986 and was funded by the Leverhulme Trust under the auspices of a Study Abroad Studentship. Additional finance and equipment was kindly provided by the Central Research Fund, University of London. During my time in the field I was attached to the Department of Geography, University College London and the Instituto de Geografía, Universidad Autónoma de México and am grateful to Professor Ron Cooke and Dra María Teresa Gutiérrez de MacGregor, Head of Department and Institute Director respectively, for having provided me with their support. I would also like to thank Miss Jane Bennett, Secretary of the Research Awards Advisory Committee at Leverhulme, who handled the processing of the award so efficiently. The book also draws on data gathered in Querétaro during 1982–3 on an SSRC (now ESRC) post-graduate studentship (Award No.D00428125288) linked to the research project 'Public Intervention, Housing and Land Use in Latin American Cities' funded by the Overseas Development Administration and directed by Drs Alan Gilbert and Peter Ward (my former Ph.D supervisor) in the Department of Geography, University College London.

In addition to the above, several friends and colleagues in Mexico deserve mention: thanks to Cilla Connolly for putting me up in Mexico City when I first arrived, to the Vilches family in León, to Arturo Castro Sánchez in Querétaro, and to Pepe and Julieta González for helping me find my feet in Puerto Vallarta; to Alvaro Sánchez Crispin and Victor Montiel for extensive help in translation of questionnaires; to Mercedes González de la Rocha and Agustín Escobar of CIESAS del Occidente for providing unfailing support, advice and help and for inviting me to participate in a most enjoyable conference on 'Mujer y Sociedad' at the Colegio de Jalisco in June 1986; to Brígida García at the Colegio de Mexico; to Angel Bassols Batalla at UNAM; to Ivan Mascoso at SEDUE, Mexico City; to José Manuel Gómez at the Fideicomiso Puerto Vallarta; and for their friendship to Magda Montiel, Juan Carlos Amezcua, Lucero and Agustín Alamán, Ricardo Ugalde, Guille Rodríguez, Astrid Oliveira dos Santos, Patty Jeffs, Laura Pérez, Ismael Aguilar Barajas and Josefina Palomero.

In the work connected with the Employer Survey I am particularly grateful for the advice, help and cooperation offered by Liset Joffa and Manuel Gómez Camacho in Puerto Vallarta, to Ignacio Valderrama and José Luís Monroy in León, and to Marco Antonio Espinosa and María Dolores Guzmán in Querétaro. Regarding the Household Survey I am indebted to the people of the settlements who received me so warmly into their homes, provided me with much of their time and information, and whose goodwill and cooperation were vital to the success of the fieldwork. In particular thanks are owed in Puerto Vallarta to Justino Castillo (leader of Caloso), Ana María Rubio, Rodalinda, Idalia Rodríguez, Rosa Riso, Elba Flores, Lupe Gómez, Fidelina Verduzco, Francisca Joya, Consuelo González, Dolores Castillo and Adolfo and Juana Torres (leaders of Buenos Aires); in León to Celia Hernández, Gerónima Mejía, María Granados and María Luisa Hernández; and in Querétaro to Paula Moya, María del Refugio Martínez, María Cruz González, Lourdes and Miriam Campos, Doña Lupe Paniagua, Guadalupe Ramírez, José Hernández Castillo (leader of Bolaños), and Socorro Juárez.

Back in the UK, I am extremely grateful to all those people who in the course of the two-and-a-half years the book took to write spent their valuable time reading drafts of various chapters and providing comments and suggestions critical to its satisfactory completion: thanks here are especially due to Alison MacEwen Scott, Paul Cammack, Simon Duncan, Steve Dunn, Gerry Kearns, Rory Miller, Colin Murray, David Siddle and Peter Ward. I am also grateful to Mark Schankerman for having drawn attention to the value of different statistical techniques in interpreting some of the data.

On the technical side, the help of colleagues at the LSE is gratefully acknowledged; thanks are particularly due to Mabel Scott in the Geography Department office who worked through several versions of the bibliography and many of the tables, to Christine Gazely who also gave valuable word-processing assistance and stepped in in Mabel's absence, to Pat Farnsworth who helped to speed up production in the final stages, and to Nesta Herbert for help in xeroxing; to Chris Holcroft and Jane Pugh of the Drawing Office who produced the figures; to Dan Salaman and Carlo Faulds of the Photographic Unit who were responsible for turning my frequently poor-quality slides and negatives into publishable black and white plates; and not least to Brian Linneker in the Geography Department who gave very valuable assistance in the final stages of the computer analysis. The help of various staff in the Department of Geography at Liverpool University in the early stages of the book is also warmly appreciated, especially that of Jackie Vellenoweth, Ian Qualtrough, Sandra Mather and Clare Sullivan.

Finally, for their support throughout, I would like to thank my parents, June and Stuart Chant, my sisters, Adrienne and Yvonne, and various close friends who have been consistently encouraging, particularly Pat Treasure, Ceinwen Rowles and Liza Jane Sadovy. This book is dedicated to them and to all those who have assisted in the course of the project both here and in Mexico.

Sylvia Chant
London, March 1990

Glossary

Adornadora   Worker who cleans shoes after the final stage of the production process.

Adorno   Process of cleaning shoes after production, and the penultimate stage before counting and packing. This may involve removing dirty stains, burning off stray threads, polishing or touching up with paint or dye.

Ama de llaves   Hotel housekeeper/person in charge of a department or section, responsible for supervising chambermaids and general cleaners.

Ayuntamiento   Municipal government.

Calzado   Footwear.

Cámara   Chamber.

Cena/cenaduría   Supper/diner. In Jalisco it is common for many low-income households to convert part of their dwellings into an informal diner for the sale of snacks and supper at the weekend and/or some weekday evenings. The clientele are usually friends and neighbours – information about menus and serving times is by word of mouth.

Chile   Chilli pepper (Capsicum Spp.). There are several varieties of *chile* used in Mexican cooking, with the hotter ones such as *chile serrano* (highland chilli) and *chile piquín* (spiky/hot chilli) being used as an important source of flavouring. *Chiles* also provide a cheap source of vitamins.

Ciudad media   Intermediate or secondary city.

Colonia popular   Term to denote low-income neighbourhood of the type exemplified by the study settlements, i.e. peripheral tracts of irregular housing development.

Conquistador   Participant in the Spanish conquest of the New World.

Constancia   Document giving right of temporary usufruct over urban land plot.

Contrato de compraventa   Receipt for land purchase.

Cortador   Cutter of leather.

De planta   Term given to status of worker who is employed by a firm on a regular or long-term basis.

Desebradora   Someone who removes stray threads from shoes. Also known as '*recortadora*'.
Ejidatario   Member of an *ejido*.
Ejido   Tract of land handed over by the state to an agricultural community. Tenure is limited to usufruct.
Escrituras   Title deeds to property.
Estado   State.
Eventual   Term given to worker who is on a short-term contract or working on a casual basis.
Fayuca   Colloquial term for contraband. Usually refers to illegally imported items such as watches, radios, sunglasses and cassette players.
Fideicomiso   Trust fund.
Forrador   Worker who lines, covers and sticks labels on cardboard boxes.
Fraccionador   Literally 'sub-divider'. *Fraccionadores* are individuals who sub-divide and sell land, generally for residential development.
'Ganas de trabajar'   This term literally means 'a will to work'. It was often cited as an important entry requirement for unskilled work.
Gobierno Constitucional de los Estados Unidos Mexicanos   Constitutional government of Mexico.
Gobierno del Estado   State government.
Grapadora   Worker who staples sides and lids of cardboard boxes.
Industria   Industry.
Machetero   Term used in León to describe skilled shoe factory workers who hire out their tools and labour to small-scale enterprises on a part-time basis.
Machismo   Cult of masculine superiority. Manifests itself in a variety of ways, including sexual assertiveness, and promiscuity, heavy drinking, aggression and violence.
Madre soltera   Unmarried mother.
Mestizo   Name given to people of mixed Spanish and Indian blood during the colonial period. Most of the Mexican population are now *mestizo*.
Máquila   Assembly, usually through a sub-contracting arrangement whereby processing work or production for a firm is carried out by smaller firms or individuals working from home. The latter (homework) may be termed '*domestic máquila*' (see Benería and Roldan, 1987: 32). In places in the interior of the country such as Mexico City, most *máquila* production is undertaken for the domestic market, whereas the *maquiladoras* in the northern border free trade area of Mexico represent export-processing activities for large multinational firms (ibid.).
Maquiladora   Assembly plant.
Municipio   Municipality.
Peso   Unit of Mexican currency. In 1986 the value of the *peso* fluctuated widely ranging from a value of between 650 and 1,000 *pesos* per £1.00 Sterling (or between 450 and 690 *pesos* per US dollar at 1986 rates of exchange).
Pespuntador   Leather-stitcher.
Pica   Small-scale shoe-manufacturing enterprise, normally employing family labour.

Sexenio   Six-year presidential term of office.

Sierra   Mountainous or highland country.

Taco   Describes a *tortilla* filled with meat or beans.

Tamale   Foodstuff consisting of ground maize mixed with another ingredient such as *chile* and wrapped in the original maize leaf.

Tejedora   Woman outworker who hand-sews shoes with detailed or specialised stitching, such as moccasins.

Tortilla   Round flat 'pancake' made of maize or wheat flour (usually the former). It is a primary Mexican staple.

Tortillería   *Tortilla* production and retail outlet (most *tortillería*s are small-scale employing between three and five persons.

Union Libre   Free union/common-law marriage.

Vecindad   Group of rented rooms around a central courtyard.

Zapatero   Cobbler.

Abbreviations

CANACINTRA	Cámera Nacional de la Industria de Transformación
CNC	Confederación Nacional de Campesinos
CNOP	Confederación Nacional de Organizaciones Populares
COCODERA	Comisión Co-ordinadora del Desarrollo de la Desembocadura del Río Ameca
CONATUR	Consejo Nacional de Turismo
CROC	Confederación Revolucionaria de Obreros y Campesinos
CTM	Confederación de Trabajadores Mexicanos
DF	Distrito Federal
FAT	Frente Auténtico de Trabajadores
FDN	Frente Democrático Nacional
FOGATUR	Fondo de Garantía y Fomento de Turismo
FONATUR	Fondo Nacional de Fomento de Turismo
GDP	Gross Domestic Product
GNP	Gross National Product
ILO	International Labour Office
IMF	International Monetary Fund
IMSS	Instituto Mexicano de Seguro Social
INFONAVIT	Instituto Nacional del Fondo de Vivienda para los Trabajadores
PAI	Programa de Apoyo Integral
PAN	Partido de Acción Nacional
PARM	Partido Auténtico de la Revolución Mexicana
PEMEX	Petróleos Mexicanos
PNDU	Plan Nacional de Desarrollo Urbano
PNR	Partido Nacional Revolucionaro
PPS	Partido Popular Socialista
PRD	Partido Revolucionario Democrático
PRI	Partido Revolucionario Institucional
PRM	Partido Revolucionario Mexicano
SECOFI	Secretaría de Patrimonio y Fomento Industrial
SECTUR	Secretaría de Turismo
SEDUE	Secretaría de Desarrollo Urbano y Ecología
SHCP	Secretaría de Hacienda y Crédito Público
SPP	Secretaría de Programación y Presupuesto
UNAM	Universidad Nacional Autónoma de México
US/USA	United States (of America)

Where the Rockies meet the northern outliers of the Andes, Middle America rises out of the sea: its plateaus form one of the roofs of the world. Their ground still pulses with the seismic shocks that gave them birth. The great volcanoes rise above the landscape, clad in a mantle of snow as if they had relinquished their dark powers and fallen into eternal sleep. But the crust of the earth is still unstable. It trembles even when asleep, and overnight a fiery monster may burst forth in a man's field . . . The ancient prophets of this land spoke of five great periods of time, each destined to end in disaster. At the end of the first of these periods the sky would fall upon the earth. The second would be destroyed by storms. The third would go up in flames. The fourth would be washed away by flood. The fifth period of time is our own: it will come to an end when the world disintegrates in a cataclysmic earthquake. Thus the people of Middle America live in the mouth of the volcano. Middle America with its twin provinces, Mexico and Guatemala, is one of the proving grounds of humanity where men change themselves by changing their surroundings and labour in defiance of the perennial prophecy.

From *Sons of the Shaking Earth*
Eric R. Wolf, pp. 1–2

Se me han ido las horas en tejer un encaje,
en prender una cinta y en bordar una flor...
Se me han ido las horas en mirar un paisaje,
y en oír una fuente y en copiar un celaje,
y en hacer una rima y en soñar un amor.

Se me han ido las horas enhebrando quimeras,
y tejiendo locuras imposibles de ser . . .
Se me han ido las horas – golondrinas viajeras –
y han pasado los sueños como nubes ligeras,
por mi triste y errante corazón de mujer

Hours have flown while I've made lace,
sewn ribbon and embroidered flowers . . .
Hours have flown while I've gazed at a landscape,
heard fountains, imitated clouds,
invented verses and dreamt of love

Hours have flown threading wild illusions
and weaving impossible fantasies . . .
Hours have flown like migrating swallows
and dreams have swept like fickle clouds
through this sad and wandering woman's heart

From 'Se me han ido las horas'
Margarita Mondragón

I

Introduction: 'sisters of the shaking earth'

Background and key issues

The setting

In the final chapter of his book **Sons of the Shaking Earth**, Eric Wolf (1959) contemplates with some dismay the transition of Mexico from an essentially rural society, in which vestiges of indigenous beliefs and lifestyles have managed to survive since pre-Colombian times, towards a 'modern' North American-oriented urban industrial state dominated by the mestizo majority.[1] Commenting on the way that new ethnic and social relations forged during the colonial period and thereafter wrought dramatic shifts in cultural norms and practices, he notes a polarisation of power and status between men and women:

> To the mestizo, the capacity to exercise power is ultimately sexual in character: a man succeeds because he is truly male (*macho*), possessed of sexual potency. While the Indian strives neither to control nor to exploit other men and women, the mestizo possesses a 'limitless sexual deficit' which feeds merely upon past conquests. While the Indian man and the Indian woman achieve a measure of balance in their relationship, the mestizo male requires absolute ascendance over women. Thus even familial and personal relationships become battlegrounds of emotion, subject to defeat and victory.
>
> (Wolf, 1959: 239–40)

While Wolf's concern was mainly with the male heirs of Middle America, the present book is about their female counterparts – the 'sisters of the shaking earth' (hence this chapter's title). Thirty years ago, Wolf left his readers with a question mark hanging over Mexico's future: 'men still remain torn between yesterday and tomorrow ... there can therefore be no finis to this book nor any prophecy' (Wolf, 1959: 256). With at least twenty of those years characterised by massive rates of economic growth and widespread out-migration from rural areas to towns and cities, there is little doubt that his essentially pessimistic vision of Mexico's transition to a modern urban society has become a reality. This book attempts to explore what these changes have meant for low-income women and their survival in some of the areas of most rapid development. However, although in very broad terms both studies are concerned with the outcome of social and economic change for disadvantaged groups (in Wolf's case ethnic minorities, in this case women), there are major differences aside from the subject of the analysis, particularly in terms of approach. Wolf takes an evolutionary historical perspective pitched at a regional scale (Middle America as a whole), whereas this study focuses on the present, and works with a selective intra-national comparative framework (three Mexican cities with different types of economy). One major reason for so doing is the chequered nature of Mexican development: locally specific patterns of production may give rise to certain variations in social relations (between ethnic groups, between men and women for example).[2] Looking at three very different cities in Mexico means that a range of contemporary local realities may be examined.

A more specific reason for using a comparative approach, however, stems from the principal aim of the study itself: to establish the extent to which women's involvement in the urban workforce is influenced by local patterns of labour demand, as against local conditions of labour supply (primarily household structure).[3] This question arises out of previous research in one of the cities in this study (Querétaro) (see Chant, 1984), where although it was concluded that household structure (a term embracing varying combinations of two main constituents of household form: sex of head and composition – see Appendix 1) appeared to play a critical part in influencing low-income women's participation in the local labour force, it was not possible to generalise that finding on the basis of one city alone. In order to find out how far household structure could explain women's likelihood of entering the workforce, it was necessary to examine patterns of female labour force participation in other urban contexts, and particularly in places where local demand for female labour might be higher. Since it was imagined that all types of household unit found in Querétaro would occur, albeit in varying proportions, in other cities as well, then a comparative framework of three cities with very different economies enabled a 'control' to be placed on household structure that allowed the examination of potential variations arising from wider economic conditions. In addition to exploring the relative strength of household structure (as a major aspect of labour supply) and local labour demand in shaping women's economic activity, it was also hoped that findings about the ways in which specific types of urban household and urban labour market structured female labour force participation would shed light on the broader influences of 'culture' and 'economy' in influencing gender roles among low-income groups in contemporary Mexico. In assuming that to some degree households embodied and/or reflected elements of broader cultural institutions such as family and kinship ideology, and that local urban economies were to some extent the spatially-contingent outcomes of a more general process of capitalist economic development, then detailed study of articulations between the two phenomena as they related to women's role in survival strategies was expected to yield some idea of potential points of tension in gender roles and relations in Mexican society today, notwithstanding that 'culture' and 'economy' themselves are extremely difficult to define, and arguably interrelated to such an extent that it is difficult, if not inappropriate to draw a clear dividing line between the two. Moreover, a third phenomenon, patriarchy, complicates the issue further.

Referring broadly to a complex of male dominance,[4] patriarchy is an element relevant to all major phenomena discussed thus far: gender roles and relations, family and kinship, culture and economy. Part of the problem in empirical studies of issues such as female labour force participation lies in analytically distinguishing patriarchy from these other elements. As Benería and Roldan (1987: 10) point out with respect to examining the interplay of capitalism and patriarchy in affecting women's position:

> The specificity of real life does not present itself in a dualistic manner but as an integrated *whole*, where multiple relations of domination/subordination – based on race, age, ethnicity, nationality, sexual preference – interact dialectically with class and gender relations (their emphasis).

Beyond this and with particular reference to the present study, it is difficult to know where to locate patriarchy in terms of its association with the other phenomena under examination. While there is broad agreement on the fact that the origins of patriarchy are probably rooted in the family, it is also an entity which extends into and derives from several other spheres of social and economic organisation (Barrett, 1986; Lerner, 1986; Lim, 1983; Scott, 1990). In the context of this specific research on women's labour force participation in Mexico, patriarchy as a system of male–female inequality can probably most easily be linked on one hand with culture, kinship and family organisation, and on the other with gender roles and relations, yet there is also much evidence to indicate that it is highly institutionalised within the economy as well. Given the complexity of treating patriarchy as a part or product of any single one of these phenomena, or indeed as a system in its own right, it is treated here as an issue which has relevance under all structural headings but one which also has different manifestations and different consequences in different places and at different times, and which is an intrinsically dynamic entity (see also Scott, 1990).

The three cities chosen for the study are broadly representative of those branches of activity which, in the closing years of the 1950s, Wolf identified as spearheading Mexico's economic transformation: the tourist trade, light 'traditional' industry directed towards the internal market, and 'modern', capital-intensive and/or heavy industry reflecting foreign interests. These activities are still of considerable significance today, despite their varying fortunes during the oil boom of the 1970s and the debt crisis of the 1980s. With this in mind, the following intermediate cities were selected for a research project on which this book is based: Puerto Vallarta, a fast-growing tourist resort on the Pacific coast; León, the most important centre for shoe production in the Mexican Republic; and Querétaro, a major location for large-scale 'modern' industry with several multinational interests (see Figure 1.1)

Puerto Vallarta's economy is dominated by a large and buoyant tertiary sector geared towards the tourist trade; León is a city where several small family-owned

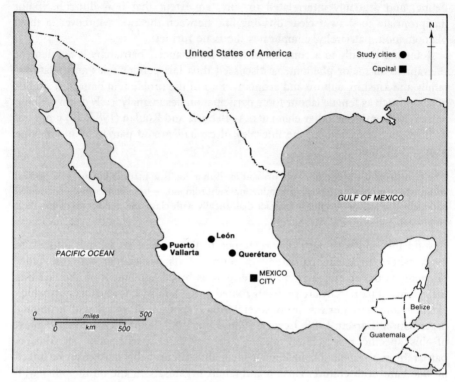

Figure 1.1 Mexico: location of the study cities

enterprises stand alongside larger manufacturing units within a predominantly labour-intensive artisanal production structure; and Querétaro's economy is highly sophisticated and capital-intensive, consisting of large mechanised firms of a type more common in 'First World' countries.

Based on a combination of questionnaire surveys and in-depth interviews with low-income women in irregular settlements[5] and a sample of employers from dominant branches of economic activity in each city (see Appendices 1 and 2), differences between the cities provide a means of evaluating the relative influences of local demand and supply factors on women's labour force participation. In addition this inter-urban comparative approach is also useful in examining three other questions integral to the study: the first concerns the way in which household structures themselves vary according to the local economy; the second involves the specific role played by women's employment in affecting the formation and composition of low-income households, and the third concerns the implications of the interaction between all three variables – economy, household structure and female employment – for the survival and welfare of the urban poor.

Each of the above questions, particularly those concerning the links between household, economy and women's labour, cannot really be answered in isolation and therefore need setting within the framework of a single study. The way in

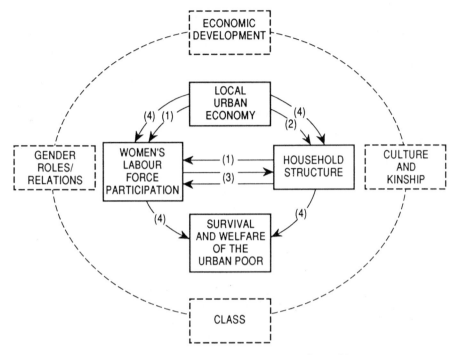

Figure 1.2 Economy, culture and gender: some basic interrelationships

Key
(1) Influences on female labour force participation (labour demand and labour supply)
(2) Effects of economic development on household structure (evolutionary and short-term)
(3) Interactions between household structure and female labour force participation
(4) Effects of local economic development, household structure and female labour force participation on the survival and welfare of low-income groups.

Notes
The inner circle relates to the specific questions of the book; the outer circle contains the broader themes/structures with which they related. Evidently certain 'feedback' arrows in the diagram could be sketched in, such as the implications of household structure for local economic development. However, these are not within the scope of the present study and are only discussed in the final chapter.

which the different elements interrelate and are treated in the book is depicted diagrammatically in Figure 1.2.

The rationale for the study

Having identified the main thrust of the enquiry and the key questions to be addressed, it is important to outline why this research is necessary and to point to its general significance in terms of current work on gender and household formation during economic development.

The principal reason for undertaking a study concentrating on the reciprocal relationships between women's employment and household structure is to answer a set of questions which remain disturbingly under-examined at a general level. A notable gap is apparent in the literature between that concerned with women's work and development, and that which is addressed to the effects of economic change on household form. Apart from a very small number of studies which have broached the links between the two (e.g. Brydon, 1979; Fernández-Kelly, 1983b; González de la Rocha, 1988; Standing, 1985), most of the mainstream analyses of these issues have appeared as largely separate debates, with little attempt at collaboration or synthesis, either in terms of theory or in terms of the focus of specific empirical research. In general, the literature on women's work, while recognising the importance of the 'household', particularly as an expression of wider institutions such as the 'family', has been less concerned with the more precise effects on female labour force participation of specific household structures (e.g. Papanek, 1976; Siraj, 1984; but see also Peek, 1978).[6] At the same time, much of the work on household structure, while occasionally pointing to women's changing economic roles, has seen these as incidental, rather than central, to the evolution of household form (e.g. Das, 1980; Goode, 1963; Mitterauer and Sieder, 1982). Why this should be so is somewhat surprising given a great deal of potential overlap (see below); however, the intention of the present study is not to speculate about why this gap has appeared, but to help to close it, my argument being that the failure to take on board the correspondence between household structure and women's labour force participation has not only led to a weakness in the explanatory power of theories of women's labour force participation on the one hand, and of household evolution on the other, but also, in the case of the latter has contributed (albeit unwittingly) to the general marginalisation of gender issues in mainstream social science research.

Before going on to justify these claims and to point out why it is important to consider the links between women's labour force participation and household structure (and their role in mediating the impact of economic 'development' [and crisis] on the urban poor), it is necessary to define briefly what is meant by the terms 'household' and 'household structure' given their centrality to the questions in this book.

Households and household structure

A household is primarily a unit of social organisation which usually combines shared *residence* and shared *reproduction* (defined here as income-generation, consumption, and domestic activities such as cooking and eating) (see also Brydon and Chant, 1989: 8–10). Although the degree to which residence and reproduction are shared varies in different societies, in Mexico this definition applies to most low-income households, and only those who combined both were included in the survey (see Appendix 1). Having defined households as units who share reproductive activities within a single dwelling environment, however, it is also important to note that participation in the inputs and benefits of household life is by no means equal for all household members; there are often considerable imbalances in labour loads and resource allocation between different individuals within the same domestic unit (see, for example, Benería and Roldan, 1987; Bruce and Dwyer, 1988; Delphy and Leonard, 1986; Harris, 1981; Land, 1977; Murray, 1987; Pessar, 1988; Safilios-Rothschild, 1984; Sharma, 1986).

A second major point about the 'household' is that in many societies it consists of kin, and thus in addition to being a unit of residence and reproduction is also a basic unit of *family* organisation; again this applies to all households in the Mexican survey.[7] When households correspond with units of family organisation, they inevitably to some degree embody values of the wider kinship system, and in a sense, then, are vehicles for what Michèle Barrett (1986: 40) terms 'familial ideology'.[8] With respect to the principal subject of this study – women – key aspects of familial ideology filtered through to household members include patriarchy and a division of labour along lines of gender.[9] Both are very strong in Latin America and conventionally manifested in a sharp normative and often practical demarcation of male and female roles and status. Men are almost invariably allocated the primary responsibility for 'productive' work (income-earning usually outside the home), whereas women's tasks are 'reproductive' (unwaged activities mostly carried on *within* the home which contribute to the daily maintenance and survival of household members, such as child-care and housework). The significance of this division, often expressed in the popular Mexican saying, 'men are for the streets, and women for the home' (de Barbieri, 1982), embodies a wide range of ideological, economic and moral connotations. At the level of the household, most Latin American women are channelled into the roles of housewife and mother, only reluctantly and intermittently allowed to step out of their homes and into the labour market in times of acute poverty (Lomnitz, 1977; Schmink, 1986; but see also Scott, 1990). The household is thus a primary material context for the development and structuring of gendered ideologies, and for resultant patterns of gender roles and relations (Barrett, 1986; Harris, 1981; Townsend and Momsen, 1987).

However, a third relevant point here is that the 'household' (and for that matter, familial ideology) does not exist in a vacuum. It is by no means a 'natural' institution which has the same form and content through time and across space (see Harris, 1981 and Stivens, 1987 for more detailed discussions). Households are dynamic entities, often responding to economic change, even if they are not necessarily determined by it (Banck, 1980). Evidence to support this view comes from a wide variety of sources which demonstrates that in order to survive, households adjust in various ways to wider changes in the economy. Here the term 'household survival strategies' has been used to refer to the general methods by which poor households adapt to and attempt to cope with adverse external circumstances.[10,11] A major element of household survival strategies may include not only the reorganisation of *internal* divisions of labour (e.g. Chaverría *et al.*, 1987; Moser, 1989), but also, and sometimes as a response to changes in internal organisation, the adoption of new *structures* (González de la Rocha, 1988; Safilios-Rothschild, 1984). Marianne Schmink (1986: 142) suggests that the success of household survival strategies is frequently determined by the 'fit' between household composition and the local labour market. While the 'ideal fit' is hard to establish when on one hand households are differentiated into multiple socio-economic strata and a wide range of structures, and on the other when 'local labour markets' are extremely difficult to draw boundaries around and/or to define (see, for example, Duncan and Savage, 1989: 187–91), it appears that certain kinds of economic contexts are more conducive to the emergence of certain household stuctures than others. Evidence to support this idea is discussed later in the chapter, but for explanatory purposes here, evolutionary changes in household form tend to be analysed and explained in relation to shifts in the dominant mode of production (usually from agrarian feudalism to industrial capitalism); whereas short-term fluctuations in household form are generally linked to the economic and demographic vagaries of local economies and their labour markets.

However, while the *preponderant* type of household structure may change in response to external economic trends, it is important to note that there is often a *multiplicity* of forms in the same geographical area, the main ones in the Latin American (and Mexican) case being: the nuclear household (a couple and their children), the woman-headed or one-parent household (a mother and her children), and the extended household (a nuclear family or woman-headed household which resides with other relatives who form a single unit for consumption) (see Appendix 1). This diversity may in part derive from the coexistence at any one time of households at different stages in the 'developmental cycle' (a term used to describe the way in which households evolve with age, see Fortes, 1958, 1970; Goody, 1958; MacDonald and MacDonald, 1978 and Murray, 1987). Differentiation may also result from variations in culture, technology, state legislation, inheritance patterns and class position (Gudmundson, 1986; Harris, 1981; Stivens, 1987; Youssef, 1972). However, whatever the principal reason for household change, different family structures in themselves can place their constituent members in very different relationships to the wider economy: female household heads, for example, may have a far greater need to participate in the labour force than women with a resident male partner with paid work (Anker and Hein, 1986). In this way, it is obvious that the household exerts an important influence on the *supply* of labour. However, it is also important to bear in mind that the changing roles of individuals within a given economic and social context, can also feed back into the form that household structure takes in the first place. The household, then, should be conceived as occupying a pivotal position between the individual and the wider economy, mediating the release of different members into the labour force and at the same time reshaping itself in response to the changing activities of individual members. Having said this, it is now important to consider why in Mexico and elsewhere, one might expect a particularly strong relationship between women's work and household structure, and in turn why this may be relevant to the urban poor.

Reasons for linking the analysis of women's work, household structure and economic development

Over and above the fact that a number of recent investigations in various parts of the Third World have presented convincing evidence to show that women's changing economic roles *are* having a profound effect on household structure (and vice versa) (e.g. Fernández-Kelly, 1983b; Safa, 1983; Standing, 1985), the main reason for expecting a particular correspondence between them is that in Mexico and most other countries, women's roles and status are closely tied to the domestic domain. Since women are usually the cornerstone of household reproduction, their movement into the labour force, particularly if it involves working outside the home and/or full-time, is extremely likely to rebound in some way upon the organisation of the domestic unit. There are of course, various possible scenarios here, two of which may *not* involve changes in household composition *per se*. The first of these is that women simply work more hours to accommodate their entry into the labour force, i.e. they continue with their domestic chores and work a 'double day' (Achío and Mora, 1988; Anker and Hein, 1986; Quiróz *et al.*, 1984; Saffioti, 1980); the second is that working women delegate their domestic chores to other household members, such as children or husbands (Achío and Mora, 1988; Ennew, 1982; González de la Rocha, 1988; Morris, 1988; Moser, 1989; Ramirez Boza, 1987). However, a third possibility, and the most important one in terms of the present analysis, is that changes might be made to household *structure* (increasing membership or fostering out children for example). Evidence from a number of Third World case studies suggests that this last response is not uncommon (e.g. Abu, 1983; Blumberg, 1978; Brydon, 1979; González de la Rocha, 1988; Nelson, 1987; Tienda and Ortega, 1982), however, the general significance of women's labour force participation in shaping household structure has not been incorporated sufficiently into the mainstream (predominantly non-feminist) work on household change.

A casual glance at the general literature on the historical evolution of the European family (e.g. Anderson, 1980; Flandrin, 1979; Wall, Robin and Laslett, 1983), on the contemporary family in a cross-cultural perspective (e.g. Goode, 1963; Hutter, 1981; Lee, 1987; Queen and Habenstein, 1974), and on changing patterns of household organisation in Third World settings (e.g. Bruner, 1982; Das and Jesser, 1980) reveals a notable absence of attention to the issue of women's labour force participation *per se* as a precipitating factor of changing household form, notwithstanding that in the historical literature in particular, considerable emphasis has been placed on the breakdown of the family as a unit of labour (in which women's productive and reproductive tasks were subsumed) in contributing to a nuclearisation of household structure (e.g. Anderson, 1980; Mitterauer and Sieder, 1982). Moreover, in many accounts of contemporary households, mention is made of the role of female labour force participation in influencing age at marriage and family size, although sometimes women's work and other forms of independence are seen to be an *effect* of declining family size rather than a cause of it! (see, for example, Wilson, 1985: 57; but see also Uthoff and Gonzalez, 1978: 43 who maintain that studies of both directions of causality are valid).

However, the idea that women's changing economic roles might be a *linchpin* in the short- and long-term evolution of household composition and headship has not been broached in any significant measure. Micro-level case studies demonstrating clear links between women's labour force participation and household structure tend, in the rare instances that they *are* acknowledged, to be cast to the sidelines of general accounts of household change. The consequences of this are serious. First, it means that in the general (and usually most widely read) literature, an incomplete picture is presented of the range of processes involved in household evolution. Second, it consigns women to a passive role in wider social and economic change, denying them a place as participants or agents in their own right. Third, it means that women-headed households are not effectively incorporated into the mainstream theories of household change, a particularly serious omission given that these units are now around one-third of households worldwide (Bolles, 1986; Moser and Chant, 1985). Moreover, the tendency to exclude women's actual or potential economic independence as a factor contributing to the emergence of these units, means that if and when they are explained as a phenomenon, it is usually as 'victims' of social and economic change, rather than expressions of female initiative and decision-making (see Brydon and Chant, 1989: 145–51). Finally, the analysis of women and gender relations in general is further marginalised from the main body of academic enquiry: the study of women is set apart as something to be done by feminists, rather than as an issue which has relevance to all aspects of social change (see also Lerner, 1986: 3–14 for an illuminating discussion of the separation of 'Women's History' from 'History' in general). The net result of these effects is production of an androcentric view of reality that can have serious practical implications. Failure to recognise the needs of women by planners and policy-makers means their disadvantaged position in Third World countries remains untreated (see, for example, Buvinić and Youssef, 1978; Machado, 1983; Molyneux, 1984; Moser, 1987; Ortíz Monasterio and Schmink, 1986; Resources for Action, 1982b). Thus although it is now a widely confirmed fact in the feminist literature that in most parts of the developing world women and children are usually preponderant amongst the poorest of the poor (Bisilliat and Fiéloux, 1987; Dankelman and Davidson, 1988; Townsend and Momsen, 1987), consistent lack of reference to them in the general literature not only weakens academic arguments, but also has serious ramifications in terms of practical policy measures and prospects for change.

Although similar criticisms of exclusion cannot be levelled in quite the same fashion at the bulk of the literature on women's work and development (carried out in the main by feminist and/or 'gender-aware' researchers), there are still problems in terms of ignoring the importance of *specific* types of household structure on women's work, and in explaining the complexities of the interrelationships between the two in different economic settings. Although evidence from a number of Third World cities suggests that extended and women-headed households are especially numerous among the poor, there is still a tendency to assume that most households are headed by men and conform to a nuclear stereotype (see discussions in Chant and Ward, 1987; Moser, 1987; Moser and Chant, 1985). Inadequate attention to the diversity of household structures inevitably weakens analysis. To cite an example, Singhanetra-Renard's (1984) study of women construction workers in Chaing Mai City, Thailand, shows that access to female employment is tending to raise marrying age and hence to reduce fertility, however there is little discussion about how the number of children women have might also be determined by the type of household structure to which they belong. Indeed high fertility might well not impinge to any great degree upon the working lives of adult women if there are other household members who may take care of them, or relatives to whom they may send their children (see, for example, Brydon, 1979 and Sharma, 1986).[12] Moreover, Singhanetra-Renard's idea that women workers in Chaing Mai now postpone marriage due to the difficulties of combining their productive and reproductive roles in urban environments may also not apply to cases where there are other relatives in the home, or where women are not expected to undertake a major share of the domestic labour as is sometimes the case with women-headed households (Chant, 1984). Failure to incorporate a perspective on the diversity of household structures tends to render studies of women's labour force participation somewhat partial. Furthermore, one also has to take into account here the *type* of employment women have. In cases where they have 'informal', part-time jobs they may be able to reconcile their earning activities with child-care (Peek, 1978; Peil, 1975; Smith, 1981). The above points suggest that explanations of women's work could be improved by considering both household structure *and* the local economy at closer range, in much more detail, and above all, as part of an analysis that combines perspectives on both at the same time.

In terms of a general working hypothesis this study argues that there are critical links between women's labour force participation and household structure, that these variables and the relationships between them are influenced to a greater or lesser extent by the nature of the local economy, and in turn that they can have major effects on the way in which low-income groups survive in urban settings. Inevitably this is a very broad proposition and in order to show how its different elements might break down in the context of the present study, and given the dominant tendency for research on the relevant themes to be somewhat compartmentalised, it is necessary to consider briefly the literature concerned with each major element of the overall question in turn (see also Figure 1.2). In the following sections therefore the hypotheses associated with each stage of the research are discussed first, in relation to the literature on supply and demand factors influencing female labour force participation, second, the impact of economic development on household structure, third, the interactions between women's labour force participation and household structure, and finally the implications of the above for the survival of low-income groups. Each literature review is selective rather than exhaustive and attempts where possible to point to specific evidence on Mexico.

Women's work, household structure and economic development: a review of the literature and major hypotheses

Women's work in Third World cities: evidence and explanations

In terms of ideas about women's employment, various models have been developed to explain its generally restricted and subordinate nature compared with that of men (see, for example, reviews by Beuchler, 1986; Carvajal and Geithman, 1985; Scott, 1986c and Walby, 1985). However, Veronica Beechey (1987: 170) claims that most studies fall into one of two camps: the first main body of explanation is oriented towards a 'familial'-centred analysis of women's sub-ordination in the labour market (encompassing what are broadly designated as 'supply' factors in the present study), the second set of interpretations focuses on what happens in the workplace (here referred to as 'demand' factors). Family-centred explanations tend to take women's reproductive role as a starting point, emphasising the constraints posed by wifehood and motherhood on their movement into the labour force, whereas workplace-centred analyses tend to look at the barriers presented by discriminatory recruitment practices and labour legislation.[13] At a conceptual level, the distinction between these two orientations is not especially obvious perhaps: Marxist–Feminist researchers in particular have long recognised the fundamental interdependence of 'family' and 'economy' in examining women's labour. Maureen Mackintosh (1979) for example, notes that the subordination of women in the labour market is highly interrelated, if not derived from their subordination in the household. However, when it comes to detailed empirical studies, most researchers tend to focus on only one element ('family' *or* 'workplace'), possibly because the kinds of data collection necessary for more comprehensive analyses are often impracticable for reasons of time or finance. In addition, it is often extremely difficult to establish the highly intricate articulations between familial and workplace influences on the ground, without reducing analysis to a narrowly functionalist and mechanistic exercise. However, the need to combine perspectives on both in the context of in-depth investigation of women's employment in specific areas is now being recognised, as Beechey (1987: 176) argues:

Large-scale studies need to be complemented by those of the local labour market which try to unravel the process of interaction between labour supply and the demand for female labour in particular empirical situations.

The main use in my view of detailed local studies based on direct interviews with households and employers is that they can, at a minimum, document immediate personal causes of women's move into the workforce at the level of supply, and at least some of the rationale for recruitment at the level of demand, thereby reducing reliance on aggregate statistics which are not only silent on the question of meaning, but also, especially when it comes to female employment, often inaccurate anyway (see Brydon and Chant, 1989: 99ff.). In many respects interviews with women themselves and key decision-makers in the local labour market provide a relevant starting point in examining the interface between demand and supply actually experienced by the affected parties. In turn this might be expected to yield certain insights into the deeper social and economic processes which underpin them.

Labour supply factors and women's labour force participation

Explanations of women's labour force participation revolving around supply factors have tended to identify three main types of variable:

1 personal characteristics (e.g. age, education, skills);
2 material and demographic characteristics of the household unit (e.g. income levels, ages and numbers of children); and
3 social/ideological aspects of family organisation (e.g. gender relations and the sexual division of labour).

Generally speaking all three sets of variables are seen to combine in shaping the nature of women's work at different stages in the lifecycle. Thus women's ages, their educational achievements, their general levels of 'human capital', and so on interact with the economic and demographic characteristics of the households to which they belong, such as family size, levels of household income, and numbers of children at school or work, to affect in a very direct and practical way their likelihood of entering the workforce (Aguiar, 1986; Anker and Hein, 1986; Bolaños and Rodríguez, 1988; Moser, 1989; Peek, 1978; Quiróz *et al.*, 1984; Ramirez Boza, 1987; Safa, 1986; Standing, 1981; Uthoff and Gonzalez, 1978).

As suggested by the third set of factors in particular, the household is also important in influencing the release of women into the labour force, through its role in transmitting wider cultural and ideological values, and as a decision-making unit (Anker and Hein, 1986). As Gerry Rodgers (1989: 20–21) notes: 'the variation in female labour supply, which is always much larger than that for men, depends considerably on cultural and status factors which vary regionally and internationally'. In Mexico, and in other parts of Latin America, the widely-held belief that women should have primary responsibility for reproductive labour, the idea that the 'proper' place of women is in the home, and the power to control their wives' labour accruing to men through patriarchy, have often translated in practical terms to prevent women from even considering taking a job (Chant, 1984, 1987a; García *et al.*, 1983b).[14] With departures from normative gender roles tending to threaten existing sexual divisions of labour in the home and challenge conventional patterns of familial power and authority (see, for example, Roldan, 1988), it is not surprising that Latin American women often have to ask their husbands for permission to go out to work (González de la Rocha, 1984) and frequently meet with outright refusal. Indeed at one time, Mexican law required women to have formal written permission from their husbands as a precondition for employment, and even today it is estimated that around two-thirds of Mexican husbands have the final say on whether their wives take a job (Elmendorf, 1977). Most low-income Mexican women consider themselves 'lucky' to be able to go out to work, although they usually pay for the privilege by shouldering a 'double day' of labour;

male consent to women's employment is rarely accompanied by a reallocation of gendered responsibilities for housework and child-care. The struggle many women undergo in order to get permission to work, combined with a general absence of relief on domestic tasks, is seriously exploitative, especially given that neglect by husbands is frequently a major factor in women's *need* to go out to work. Substantial proportions of male earnings in Latin American households are siphoned-off for personal expenditure and in this context a contradictory situation emerges in which women and children are condemned to financial privation but at the same time prevented from doing anything about it (Beuchler, 1986; Chant, 1984).

While it is true that material problems are not the only reason that women enter the workforce (García *et al.*, 1983a), another major catalyst of this type is increased poverty arising from wider economic factors such as national recession or draconian structural adjustment packages (see, for example, Bolaños and Rodríguez, 1988; Chaverría *et al.*, 1987; González de la Rocha, 1988; Moser, 1989; Quiróz *et al.*, 1984; Yudelman, 1989). Yet even here women's entry into the labour force is far from straightforward. As Boyle (1986), drawing on evidence from popular drama, points out for the case of the Chilean poor: 'While for women female employment is a logical solution in times of economic hardship, for men it is a further affront to their battered dignity' (Boyle, 1986: 91).

Women's labour force participation poses an even greater psychological threat to men in times of economic crisis and has to be broached extremely sensitively. Boyle, for example, notes how women often subscribe to the ritual of asking their un- or under-employed husbands for permission to work, even where household income is so low that there is effectively no room for a negative response. However, despite these difficulties, it would be wrong to think that women were unable or unwilling to face up to change. As Alison MacEwen Scott (1986a: 23) points out, 'women are not passive incumbents of socially-ascribed gender roles, but individuals who make choices in the context of conflicting pressures'. Women experiencing extreme poverty may resort to actions (taking a job with or without their husbands' permission for example) which have potentially draconian implications for the organisation of their households and the particular form of gender roles and relations operating within them. While at a symbolic level, therefore, the patriarchal family, as an institution, may be left intact, at the material level of the household unit, social norms and practices may be considerably modified (see also Scott, 1990). Michèle Barrett (1986: 186) encapsulates the thrust of these ideas in stating that:

the gender divisions of social production in capitalism cannot be understood without reference to the *organisation of the household* and the ideology of familialism. This area represents the primary site of relations between men and women, of the construction of gendered individuals, and is closely related to the organisation of social production. (emphasis added).

However, as I pointed out earlier, what is *unclear* in much of the above is what happens with *alternative* household structures. Much work generated on the 'supply' side of female labour force participation has conflated 'family' (specifically the normative/'ideal' model of the nuclear unit) with the actual reality of a diverse range of household structures, possibly as a result of insufficient empirical evidence. Despite the persistence of assumptions about the predominance of nuclear households in Third World cities, large numbers of poor families are not male-headed, nuclear and/or governed by a rigid sexual division of labour, and these alternative structures are often characterised by alternative roles for women.[15] For example, although numbers of women workers in Mexico are generally low, female heads of one-parent families usually have high rates of labour force participation, particularly if they are the only potential earners in the family unit (Chant, 1985a; García *et al.*, 1983b; Moser and Chant, 1985). Moreover, extended households comprising several adults engaged in multiple-earning strategies and shared reproductive labour often have higher levels of female employment than less flexible nuclear structures (García *et al.*, 1982). 'Familial ideologies' may thus be subject to modification, or even outright rejection when they go against the practical needs, objectives or possibilities of specific residential units. The household is not a passive entity therefore, but has two-fold status reflecting extra-domestic phenomena on the one hand, and generating internal forces important for domestic, economic and social formation on the other (González de la Rocha, 1984). In the context of the present study, and on the basis of the findings of the above research, it is imagined that women's labour force participation will be higher in women-headed and extended households. However, it is also the case that conjectured variations in female employment may well be contingent upon, or mediated by, local variations in labour demand.

Labour demand factors and women's labour force participation

Explanations of 'demand' constraints on women's labour generally revolve around issues of discrimination by employers, the need for 'skills' in certain kinds of manual jobs (which women by virtue of their lower education and vocational training do not possess, or are imagined not to possess as a result of general assumptions and/or prejudices), legislation which artificially raises the costs of employing women relative to men, and exclusionary practices by male-dominated trade unions (see Anker and Hein, 1986; Benería and Roldan, 1987; Garro, 1983; Gonzalez, 1980; Heyzer, 1981; Joekes, 1985; LACWE, 1980).

However, the relative importance of these demand factors is likely to vary in different settings. In cities dominated by large-scale capital-intensive mechanised production, for example, employers tend to recruit men rather than women. In Latin America this is seen to particularly apply to import substitution industrialisation (Joekes, 1987: 129). Several authors have noted that women factory workers are relegated to labour-intensive branches of the manufacturing process, such as garment-making and textiles, and tend to get squeezed out when their skills are replaced by machinery, which is usually operated by men (Elmendorf, 1977; Joekes, 1987; Pearson, 1986; Saffioti, 1986), a fact perhaps best summed up in Neuma Aguiar's (1980: 112) statement that 'machine technology crystallises the differential status of the sexes'. However, while an inverse relationship generally obtains between the degree of technology used in production processes, and the participation of women, it is not really known how the association between men and machinery arose in the first place nor how it is sustained (Scott, 1988a). Nevertheless, the widely observed existence of this pattern not only excludes women from skilled sections of the industrial labour force, but also makes the rewards for entry far inferior to those of men. For example, although the overall participation of women in the labour force in Mexico has risen over the years, from 4.6% in 1930, to 13.6% in 1950, 19.2% in 1970 (LACWE, 1980) and 21% in 1980 (Seager and Olson, 1986), women's earnings are generally only 40% of men's (Elmendorf, 1977). The widely-held assumption that women's employment is secondary and their earnings merely supplementary to those of an assumed male household head is a significant element in determining their wage rates in manufacturing and other employment, and access to jobs and promotion in general (Anker and Hein, 1986; Heyzer, 1981; Papanek, 1976). In terms of the cities in the present study, Querétaro is closest to a capital-intensive industrial economy and as such likely to display lowest rates of female labour force participation compared with the other two.

On the other hand, where local industrial growth is based almost exclusively on labour-intensive manufacturing, women tend to predominate among manual workers. This is particularly the case with transnational assembly plants or 'world market factories' established in peripheral regions of the world economy since the 1970s in a bid by international capital to reduce labour costs. Here, up to 70% of the workforce are women (Bisilliat and Fiéloux, 1987; Cunningham, 1987; Hein, 1986; Pearson, 1986; Safa, 1981; Sassen-Koob, 1984; Townsend and Momsen, 1987). Female workers are recruited for a combination of reasons, principally because their wage rates are usually 20–50% less than those of men, but also because of their supposed 'docility'; their unlikelihood of joining unions or creating political conflicts in the workplace; their capacity to perform tedious and repetitive tasks over long periods; their visual acuity and manual dexterity (reflecting gender-specific childhood training in detailed handiwork) and as a consequence, the probability that they will cause less wear-and-tear on machinery; and finally, their 'natural' disposability on account of marriage and child-birth, both of which can be manipulated to coincide with factory production cycles (Benería and Roldan, 1987; Elson and Pearson, 1981; Fernández-Kelly, 1983a; Harris, 1983; IBG, 1984; Iglesias, 1985; Lim, 1983 Safa, 1981).

Women are also likely to form a large component of the labour force where outworking is common (Benería and Roldan, 1987; Bisilliat and Fiéloux, 1987: 60–4). In areas of labour-intensive industrialisation or where parts of the production process depend on manual skills, women outworkers fill in the gaps where capital and machinery have been thus far unable or unwilling to penetrate. Some writers have drawn attention to the fact that flexible part-time outwork sits more comfortably with women's domestic routines than full-time factory employment and allows them to combine their reproductive and productive roles (Benería and Roldan, 1987; Smith, 1981). As June Nash (1986: 6) asserts:

'Women engaged in piece work and putting out systems in their homes, weave together the production schedules of highly-capitalised and mechanised firms with their familial chores in the home.'

However, the emphasis sometimes placed on the advantages for women arising from the flexibility of outwork, should not be mistaken in any circumstance as a kind of 'autonomy' which is often derived from self-employment, since as Allen (1981) argues, 'autonomy' under these circumstances is a myth since the employer always determines supply. Furthermore, outwork may well be the only type of employment available to women (Barrett, 1986). In terms of the cities in this study, León is most likely to have large numbers of outworkers and as such to have higher rates of female employment than Querétaro. Footwear production is labour-intensive and seasonal fluctuations in demand give rise to the need for a casual workforce outside the plant which may be drawn upon in times of peak production and discarded when demand is slack (see also Benería and Roldan, 1987: 38–9 on the general logic and structure of sub-contracting in Mexico).

Towns with a large service economy, however, are likely to employ most women given that in Mexico and Latin America on the whole women are heavily represented in the tertiary sector (Albert, 1982; LACWE, 1980). There are few detailed urban case studies here, but García *et al.*'s (1983a) study of two Brazilian cities, for example, finds women's employment to be higher in Recife (predominantly a service centre) than in São José dos Campos (a more industrial city). Women's employment is likely to be higher still in towns dominated by tourist services where large numbers of jobs are gender-typed as 'female' due to their association with reproductive tasks generally carried out by women in the home such as bed-making and laundry work. For example, high levels of female labour force participation have been found in Ixtapa-Zihuatanejo, another Mexican tourist resort by Kennedy *et al.* (1978). In terms of the study cities, therefore, Puerto Vallarta, as a tourism-based economy may be expected to employ larger numbers of women than the other two centres.

While the tendency for different types of economy to influence the recruitment of women in the workforce may have been recognised, little is known about how different levels of demand for female labour intermesh with the local-level determinants of supply (particularly household structure). Owing to the 'control' in this study provided by a comparative framework, we can at least begin to examine these two sets of factors in such a way as to evaluate their relative importance in explaining women's labour force participation at specific points in time. If women's involvement in the workforce is consistently higher in certain types of economic context than others, regardless of household structure, then we may assume (for a given moment at least) that female employment is led primarily by demand or factors external to the household, bearing in mind that national-level changes such as recession may well forge additional sets of consequences. If, on the other hand, certain types of household appear to keep women in the home, regardless of local employment conditions, or even national economic crisis, then we may assume that supply factors (individual and household characteristics) constitute a more significant obstacle to female employment. However, intrinsic to this analysis is also the need to discover the extent to which household structure itself is influenced by the nature of local economic activity, which brings us to review the literature on the next major element of the question.

Household structure and economic development

Given that extended, nuclear and women-headed households are the most common structures in Mexican cities, analysis here is confined to these alone. The first section deals with extended and nuclear households which are the focus of most of the general literature on household evolution, the second looks at women-headed households which have been studied for the most part only by feminist writers.

Extended versus nuclear families

Generally speaking, nuclear families have been thought to replace extended households with urbanisation, industrialisation and economic development (Barrett, 1986; Bock, Iutaka and Berardo, 1980; Brambila, 1986; Chant, 1985a; Das, 1980; Durrani, 1976; García *et al.*, 1983b; Goode, 1963; Lee, 1987). This view is shared by writers working with both 'modernisation' and 'Marxist' perspectives, albeit for different reasons – the former tend to view the process as one of rational individual responses to economic development, whereas the latter largely regard it as a bid by capital to guarantee the exploitability of labour. However, whatever theoretical framework is used, the trajectory is the same. The shift from a subsistence to an exchange economy is supposed to divert the bulk of production (except that of the production of labour power) away from the sphere of the household into the hands of capitalist producers or the state. The accompanying break-up of the family as a unit of labour and the individualisation of the wage contract negate the rationale for living with kin (Barrett, 1986; Goode, 1963; LACWE, 1980; Leacock, 1972; Peil and Sada, 1984; Seccombe, 1980; Vatuk, 1982). In part the trend towards a more minimal family structure has also been viewed as a functional response to the fact that extended families are too large or unwieldy to cope with the economic and demographic requirements of a free labour market (see Lee, 1987: 62–3). Moreover, the demands placed on wage earners by dependent kin are seen to run counter to the rise of individualism associated with the development of the capitalist mode of production (Brambila, 1986; Carter and True, 1978; Hutter, 1981). Extended households are regarded as placing a brake on the individual's or minimal (nuclear) family's potential for upward socio-economic mobility (Bock, Iutaka and Berardo, 1980; Cross-Beras, 1980; Das and Jesser, 1980; Jules-Rosette, 1985; Lee, 1987).

However, one of the major problems with these mainstream ideas of household change, as with approaches to women's labour force participation, is that 'economic development' has often been treated in too generalised a way. More detailed case studies have pointed to a range of trends in different types of economy. For example, Lowell Gudmundson's (1986) research on early nineteenth-century Costa Rica demonstrates that the great majority of rural households were *not* extended, but nuclear or women-headed, mainly because most people did not own the means of production but instead cultivated common village lands or worked on the estates of the elite. Another study of economic change in eighteenth- and nineteenth-century São Paulo, Brazil has shown that with the shift from a subsistence to a commercial export economy, households tended to move from a nuclear to an extended form due to the need for emerging family enterprises to incorporate workers (Kuzesnof, 1980). In addition to this historical data from Latin America,[16] there is also a wealth of evidence from contemporary studies of urban areas in the continent, as well as those in Africa, Asia, the Middle East and the Caribbean, which shows a high incidence of familial extension of various types ranging from combinations of relatives living in the same dwelling, to kin who maintain strong ties across the boundaries of their individual households (Banck, 1980; Brambila 1986; Ennew, 1982; Lobo, 1982; Lomnitz, 1977; Merrick and Schmink, 1983; Peil and Sada, 1984; Roberts, 1985; Sharma, 1986; Smith, 1988; Vatuk, 1982). Here Mexico is no exception. In Mexico City between one-fifth and one-quarter of low-income households are extended (García *et al.*, 1982); a similar proportion was found in previous work carried out by the author on low-income communities in Querétaro (Chant, 1984).

Large numbers of extended households in Third World cities have often been explained in terms of a general framework of spatial and social inequality arising with underdevelopment: thus at least the differential experience of 'economic development' of different groups of people has been recognised, if not the effects of particular types of production in given areas. For example, among the poor, extended households are seen to develop with urbanisation and migration; hosts provide migrant relatives with food, board, job contacts and emotional security in the early stages of their move to the city (Arizpe, 1978; Bruner, 1982; García *et al.* 1983b; Kemper,1977; Peil and Sada, 1984; Stivens, 1987). Large extended households which at various times of the year are dispersed across different regions and different economic sectors may be the only types of household capable of minimising risk of destitution by diversifying their sources of earnings (Arizpe, 1982b; Roberts, 1985). In addition extended families are seen to form as a response to housing shortages for low-income groups; people moving to cities where land supply is scarce may not be able to afford their own accommodation so they continue to stay with kin (García *et al.*, 1983b). These kinds of ideas reflect an assumption that the extended family tends to take up the slack in situations where the 'transition' to industrialisation is not quite complete and there is insufficient provision of social welfare (Pasternak, 1976).

However, although extended households are often associated with extreme poverty, in recent years, greater emphasis has been placed on the idea that there is a considerable degree of positive and conscious calculation behind the formation of such units, and that several are financially better-off than their nuclear counterparts (Banck, 1980; Chant, 1984). The incorporation of relatives into the residential unit is one way of permitting the entry of several wages into the household, to economise on consumption, and to lead to greater socialisation of reproductive work in peripheral and isolated shanty towns (Chant, 1984, 1985a;

Padilla, 1978). Extended formations are also seen to provide more flexibility for women-headed units (Pollard and Wilburg, 1978; Tienda and Ortega, 1982). So rather than being a marginal or disadvantaged category of family structure in Latin America, instead extended households seem to be an enduring and viable domestic unit among low-income urban groups, and particularly perhaps where the nature of local production is organised on family lines (see Kuzesnof, 1980). In terms of the cities in the present study it is imagined that they will be most numerous in León for the reason that small-scale domestic-based labour-intensive enterprises may operate most effectively on the basis of extended units.

Having said that, it is also likely that in situations of grave national economic crisis, which in peripheral regions of the world tend to strike modern industrial cities such as Querétaro particularly severely, they register an increase. At the beginning of the period of the earlier study in Querétaro (1982), before the worst effects of recession were felt, most households were nuclear. In some respects this bears out the predictions of the models which associate nuclear families with modern capital-intensive industrialisation. However, longitudinal work on other Mexican cities since 1982, such as that of Mercedes González de la Rocha (1988) on Guadalajara, shows that one-time nuclear households are now retaining their married sons and daughters in order to keep multiple sources of income within the family. One major focus of interest in this study is to find whether similar processes have been happening in Querétaro over three to four years of economic decline.

Women-headed households

Another major problem with the 'extended-to-nuclear' theories and often with the ideas which have followed them is their gender-blindness, a fact that has resulted in little or no attempt to account for women-headed households, despite their rise in recent years to 30% in the Third World as a whole, and up to 50% in some cities of Latin America and the Caribbean (Bolles, 1986; Moser and Chant, 1985; Rogers, 1980) (see Appendix 1). However, although women-headed households have often been marginalised and/or excluded from the mainstream theories, various analyses of their formation has been carried out within the context of regional or country case studies (see, for example, MacDonald and MacDonald, 1978 for an excellent review of matrifocality among black families in the Americas). In many respects this has been positive; closer examination of the regional or national context has allowed for the analysis of several factors other than economic development *per se*.

Women-headed households in Latin America

Of the various factors seen as contributing to female household headship in Latin America, two demographic issues figure prominently. One is that female life expectancy is greater than that of men; this leads to early widowhood in many parts of the continent, such as Mexico and Brazil and therefore a high incidence of women household heads (García *et al.*, 1983b; Kemper, 1977). A second is the fact that women tend to predominate in permanent city-ward migration due to their relative difficulty in obtaining work in rural areas compared with the towns (Butterworth and Chance, 1981). While men often move permanently to cities as well, it is more common for them to return on a periodic basis to rural small-holdings or to hire themselves out for seasonal work on large farms. The overlaying of a permanent excess of women in towns, by a constant rotation of male labour between urban and rural areas means that a great number of sexual unions in cities are both fragile and temporary, with the outcome that women are left as *de jure* or *de facto* heads of household (García *et al.*, 1983b; Papanek, 1976; Quiróz *et al.*, 1984; Rogers, 1980; Townsend and Momsen, 1987) (see Appendix 1).

A number of other analyses have related the emergence of women-headed households in Latin American cities to the failure of men to live up to cultural expectations of provider and protector of the family unit in situations of extreme poverty. Un- or under-employed men on low wages have difficulty fulfilling their normative role of breadwinner. This marginal position in the family is often such that men desert their wives and children, thereby leading to the break-down of 'conventional' male-headed structures (Arizmendi, 1980; Blumberg and García, 1977; Bridges, 1980; Pescatello, 1976; Queen and Habenstein, 1974; Safa, 1964, 1981).

Some studies have also emphasised historical factors: women-headed house-holds have been viewed in part as the outcome of a legacy of concubinage dating back to the early days of the Spanish conquest, where *conquistadores* fathered many children of indigenous women but left them unprovided for (Youssef, 1972). This of course tends to contradict the previous point that men leave their families when they are unable to fulfil their marital and parental responsibilities, however the apparent contradiction is perhaps easier to understand if set within the context of another dominant cultural trait: *machismo*. Broadly defined as a system of patriarchy (see Scott, 1990), the term derives from the Spanish word '*macho*' meaning male, and is often associated with male control (both ideological and physical) of women, virility, sexual prowess, courage and competition between men (Cubitt, 1988: 103–4). The roots of *machismo* are generally traced to the colonial period when long-standing circum-Mediterranean opinions of male superiority were overlain with the idea that indigenous New World women were racially inferior (ibid.). Given that these women were also victims of conquest, the groundwork was laid for the development of an exaggerated male supremacy, which was undoubtedly reinforced by the patrilineal kinship system and ideology of female domesticity, chastity and fidelity set down by Church and State (Scott, 1986b, 1990). In contemporary Latin America, *machismo* contributes to the polarisation of gender roles and is often invoked as a cultural legitimation for the abuse of women (Arizpe, 1982a; Bromley, 1982; Stevens, 1973). Abuse may take the form of physical, economic, psychological and/or emotional cruelty, with domestic violence, financial privation and sexual infidelity being particularly common where men have to contend with low status in the labour market and a marginal role in the family (Chant, 1985b; Harris, 1982; Moser, 1989). In the light of this cultural framework, poverty inevitably places considerable strain on domestic units and couples often separate, leaving women as household heads

(Chant, 1985b). Thus although there appears to be an inherent contradiction between man as social being (prescribed by the family system) and man as sexual being (prescribed by *machismo*), poverty seems to blur the lines between them to such an extent that they are not only more or less compatible, but mutually reinforcing. When men resort to '*macho*' behaviour (heavy drinking, gambling, promiscuity and/or wife-beating for example) to overcome a sense of inadequacy as husbands or fathers, these kinds of actions in turn remove the likelihood of men (re)gaining the respect of their families. However, just because women suffer as wives or partners in this setting of gender conflict and opposition, does not necessarily imply they are unable to experience close and satisfying relationships with other male relatives. As Beuchler (1986: 179) points out from her case study of Bolivian women workers:

It would ... be misleading if one analysed the subordination of and dependence of women in Bolivian families engaged in petty commodity production from the perspective of marital relationships alone. The women described ... are also daughters, sisters and mothers. Thus Inez, who suffered at the hands of her father and her husband, enjoys the warm support of her godfather, brother and oldest son.

Nevertheless, given the frequent problems of marital relationships, together with the other factors identified, women-headed households are extremely numerous in Latin American cities, ranging from between 20 and 25% in Venezuelan urban communities (Blumberg and García, 1977; MacDonald, 1979; Peattie, 1968), to one-third in Honduran towns (Resources for Action, 1982a), to around 50% in Managua, Nicaragua (Vance, 1985). In Mexico, women-headed households are usually between 15 and 20% of the total in urban areas (Chant, 1984; García *et al.*, 1982).

Despite the importance of regionally-specific cultural, historical and demographic factors in explaining the emergence of women-headed households, some authors, recognising the global increase in female-headed units, are concerned with setting these explanations on a more general footing. Perhaps the most systematic work here is that of Rae Lesser Blumberg (1978) who proposes five conditions for the evolution of women-headed households. These include, first, that the unit of compensation, labour and property accumulation should be the individual, regardless of sex. Second, that women must have access to the means of subsistence, be this personal access to waged employment, or access to the earnings of children, and/or state welfare and the right to inheritance. Third, that it is possible to reconcile income-generation or subsistence with child-care. Fourth, that women's opportunities for subsistence must not be dramatically less than those of men, or in such a case, that a fifth and final condition is met, namely that the state either supports women-headed households explicitly (via the provision of welfare for example) or implicitly (via lack of legal prohibition to women as titular household heads) (ibid.: 529–39).

In varying degrees, at least the first three (and in some respects the fifth) of these conditions are fulfilled in Latin America, and the relevance of the economic prerequisites in particular appear to be borne out by empirical evidence: the fact that women-headed households are more numerous in towns than in the countryside is undoubtedly linked in some way with the fact that urban women have greater access to employment than their rural counterparts. However, the specific importance of economic factors is open to a considerable amount of doubt, since to date there have been few (if any) genuinely comparative studies of household structures and women's work in *different* economic situations within the *same* cultural, or at least national, context. By examining three highly contrasting urban economies in Mexico, the relevance of the conditions suggested by Blumberg may be clarified further.

What is likely in the context of the present study is that women-headed households are most prevalent in Puerto Vallarta. Here women's greater opportunities for paid work may give them a greater margin of choice in deciding whether to reside with a man or not. As Helen Safa (1981: 428) comments:

It is possible that a job contributes to a woman's sense of economic autonomy and the ease with which she may dissolve a marital relationship; that is, working women may be more likely to end an unsatisfactory relationship since they have the possibility of supporting their families on their own.

On the other hand, female-headed households might be expected to be less common in León, where although women may have employment, it is not likely to be of a type conducive to the establishment of independent households. Many women may work as unpaid labourers in small family businesses, yet not *own* the means of production, as indicated by other studies of artisanal enterprises (see Goddard, 1981 on Naples, and Padilla, 1978 on Guadalajara). Alternatively, if women engage in outwork for large shoe firms, it is unlikely that their earnings will be sufficiently high or regular to support their own households. In Querétaro, women-headed households are perhaps likely to be rarer still due to the conjectured difficulty of women finding work in large capital-intensive manufacturing plants.

Obviously in this last section we have broached not only the question of general economic influences on household formation, but also issues relevant to the third main element of the study which concerns the possible effects of female labour force participation on household structure. In the following discussion we take this further and review the literature on reciprocal linkages.

Women's work, household structure and the economy:
evidence for linkages

Studies concerned specifically with the interactions between household, economy and women's work are somewhat disparate, having not benefited from inclusion in the general overviews of household change, but several important points can be drawn-out.

A first major issue is that patterns of female labour force participation and household structure appear to vary systematically according to the nature of the local economy. Garcia, Muñoz and de Oliveira (1983a) in their study of two

Brazilian cities cited earlier found that proportions of extended families and rates of women's employment (both shown to be related) were slightly higher in Recife, where services predominate, than in São José dos Campos which is rather more industrial.

In another study by Mercedes González de la Rocha (1988), the Mexican economic crisis is seen to have affected low-income households in Guadalajara (a city dominated by the production of consumer goods for the domestic market and characterised by a mix of small- and large-scale enterprises) in two main ways: first there has been a notable increase in the labour force participation of 'secondary' earners in the household (especially women and young boys), and second, there has also been a tendency towards the *extension* of household units. Again the fact that these trends run parallel with one another appears to suggest links.

Second, in addition to the studies already discussed in the previous section, it has also been stated categorically by some authors that one major reason for changes in household structure stems from female labour force participation itself. Longitudinal work by Lynne Brydon (1979) among the Avatime in Amedzofe, Ghana, for example, demonstrates how increasing job opportunities for women and growing consumerism have resulted in a drift away from the broadly stable nuclear family system. Women's increased labour force participation is made possible at the household level by intensifying a pattern of fostering which had roots in pre-colonial Avatime culture. Nowadays, children are increasingly taken care of by grandparents and other kin while their mothers engage in wage-earning activities in the town. Here there is a clear relationship between women's changing roles and household formation.

Another study pointing to the significance of women's work for household structure is that of Hilary Standing (1985) on Calcutta. Here the author demonstrates that increased opportunities for female employment are also leading to changes in household structure, concluding that 'the entry of women into the labour market is affecting the dynamics of household formation' (Standing, 1985: 254). Girls are now retained to support their ageing parents (a responsibility once borne by their brothers), thereby delaying their own marriages and the establishment of neolocal nuclear units.

Third, these links between female labour force participation and household structure have in some instances been interpreted as mutually reinforcing. Perhaps the most appropriate case study here is that of Maria Patricia Fernández-Kelly (1983b) on the industrial cities of the US-Mexican border where women work in transnational assembly operations and have far higher rates of employment than men. Fernández-Kelly (op. cit.) strikes at the heart of the major concern of this book by concluding that women's labour force participation in northern Mexico is a function of both supply and demand. Demand for female labour derives from foreign capital's objectives to recruit as cheap a workforce as possible, which in turn has repercussions on labour supply. Since many men cannot find work, households *must* deploy women into the labour force. At its logical extreme, because men cannot find jobs and/or jobs that command high enough wages, they frequently cross the border as illegal immigrants; this leaves women to fend for themselves and their children, making female participation in the labour force even more imperative (ibid.). Similar observations have been made elsewhere. Helen Safa's (1983) study of Puerto Rico, for example, also shows that because women generally have greater access to work in the multinational labour-intensive industries on the island, male out-migration has risen steadily since the 1960s with a resultant increase in women-headed households (ibid.). However, the influence of the local economy on household structure and women's work does not stop there: once women become heads of household, the composition of their households is frequently subject to further change. Since female rates of pay are so much lower than those of men's, and women have a multiplicity of familial roles which make it difficult for them to enter the workforce full-time, many extend their households, as in Mexico and Jamaica, in order to survive (Bolles, 1986; Chant, 1985b; Safa, 1983; Tienda and Ortega, 1982). This is also noted by Deborah Bryceson (1985) in her study of Tanzania, where she notes that female heads of household often have to rely on the domestic labour of other female members in order to work (which of course in turn restricts the employment of other women) (see also Teresa Quiróz *et al.*, 1984 on Costa Rica, and Caroline Moser, 1989 on Ecuador).

The above case studies demonstrate clear links between household structure, women's roles and labour demand in various settings, however as yet the dominant sequence of events is not well-documented. We are nowhere near being able to establish in any conclusive way whether women's entry into the labour force is motivated primarily by 'demand' or 'supply' factors, nor how connections between the two are articulated. Although it is hard to disaggregate these associations and it is unlikely that there is any general 'law', by addressing the relative importance of local conditions of labour demand and supply in the context of a detailed comparative national study, the present work hopes to shed light on how they interrelate in different circumstances, and hence to move the basis of the analysis of women, households and urban economies a little further forward.

Implications of and women's work and household structure for household welfare

The final objective is to explore the implications of household structure and female labour force participation for the welfare and survival of low-income groups. Here the issues are more straightforward. Those who have looked at this question have often noted how working women tend to devote more earnings than their husbands to family needs as opposed to personal expenditure (Bruce and Dwyer, 1988; Chant, 1984, 1985b; Huston, 1979; Kishwar and Vanita, 1984; Mencher, 1988; Quiróz *et al.*, 1984; Rogers, 1980; Smith, 1978). Thus in situations where women are able to work, especially in women-headed and extended households, it might be expected that individuals in these fare better economically. It is also the case that such households, particularly women-headed households, might be less emotionally conflictive than male-headed nuclear units (see Chant, 1985b).

However, the persistent belief that nuclear households are preponderant in urbanising areas of the developing world, and by implication, appropriate to the tenor of progress, means that non-nuclear households are often considered in some way as 'deviant' (see Chant, 1985a; Chester, 1977; Murray, 1987; Smith, 1988). This is especially the case with women-headed households (see MacDonald and MacDonald, 1978).[17] Even where matrifocal households are not regarded as particularly negative because they are *headed* by women, many have noted that women have such a disadvantaged labour market position compared with men that women-headed households are unable to cope with survival to the same degree as two-parent nuclear units and *ipso facto* suffer greater poverty (Bolles, 1986; De los Ríos, 1989; Elmendorf, 1976; Folbre, 1988; Merrick and Schmink, 1983; Quiróz *et al.*, 1984; Schmink, 1986; Selby *et al.*, 1981). I have contested these views elsewhere (e.g. Chant, 1985a, 1985b) and one major point of the present study is to challenge, with further empirical evidence, some of the

Table 1.1: Key hypotheses of study: links between local economy, female labour force participation, household structure and household welfare

A	B	C	Household structure		E
City	Economic base	Likely level of female labour force participation	D(a) likelihood of female household heads	D(b) likelihood of extended composition	Likely level of household well-being
Puerto Vallarta	Tourism Services	High (due to B)	High (due to C)	Medium/High (due to C, D(a))	High (due to C, D(a), D(b))
León	Labour-intensive small-scale domestic-based industry	Medium (due to B)	Low/Medium (due to C)	High (due to B)	High (due to D(b))
Querétaro	Capital-intensive, large-scale factory-based industry.	Low (due to B)	Low (due to C)	Low (due to B, C, D(a))	Low (due to C, D(a), D(b))

Key
A = City
B = Economic base
C = Female labour force participation
D = Household ⎱ (a) female household heads
    Structure ⎰ (b) household composition
E = Household welfare

Note: The table has been greatly simplified for purposes of clarity. Causal/relevant factors cited in brackets refer to principal influences only.

assumptions on which the idealisation of the nuclear family is based. The findings of the present research suggest that non-nuclear household structures are often of very considerable benefit to women, their children, and ultimately to men as well.

Organisation of the book

The main aim of this introductory chapter has been to raise the objectives, key questions and major hypotheses of the research, and to place them in context of current literature. A summary and synthesis of the main hypotheses are presented in tabular form as a means of recapping the main arguments and for purposes of reference as the text unfolds (see Table 1.1).

Chapter 2 sets the scene of the research by outlining Mexican economic development since World War Two and discussing the historical, economic and demographic characteristics of the three study cities.

Chapter 3 considers the issue of women's labour force participation from the point of view of *demand* in each of the study cities Here interviews carried out with personnel managers provide the basis for analysis of levels of female employment in major types of enterprise, the attitudes and behaviour of key decision-makers in the local labour market, and their rationale for employing men and women workers.

Chapter 4 introduces the settlements in which interviews with low-income families were carried out and, on the basis of quantifiable data gathered in the questionnaire survey, looks at factors operating at the household level which might be expected to influence women's entry into the labour force such as age, fertility, migrant status, family size, education, income and household structure. This chapter provides a counterpoint to Chapter 3 by stressing *supply* factors in the urban labour market. It also looks at variations in household structure between the cities.

Chapter 5 takes an in-depth look at how women's work roles mediate, and are mediated by the type of household to which they belong and hence considers the extent to which women's position is a product of interaction between the supply and demand factors discussed in the previous two chapters. Which category of factors, if either, is more important? Is household structure (as a reflection of lifecycle, cultural norms, familial ideologies and so on) the primary determinant of female labour force participation? Or, does the overall structure of the local economy exert a more important effect by influencing the very organisation of the household itself – not only through a mediation of the demographic characteristics of the local population, but also by drawing women into the labour force? The data here are drawn from life histories compiled during in-depth interviews with a sub-sample of female respondents. From these we can establish the extent to which changes in household form precede or postdate women's entry and exit from the labour force.

Chapter 6 looks at the effect of national economic crisis on women and their households. Here data gathered from Querétaro during two time periods are compared to analyse the effects of economic recession on household structure and women's labour force participation. Having a large-scale industrial sector with many foreign interests, Querétaro's economy was severely hit by the deepening of the recession in 1982–3. What happens to low-income families, and particularly women's role within them, when the foundations of the local economy are shaken by crisis? This chapter allows us to consider the issue of women–household linkages in a cross-temporal as well as a cross-spatial context.

Chapter 7 considers the implications of women's work for the level and quality of survival for the Mexican urban poor, and examines the potential effects of rising female labour force participation during the crisis years on the probable future organisation of household survival strategies, on the configuration of household structures, and on the productive and reproductive behaviour of other groups of household members such as sons and daughters.

Chapter 8, the conclusion, brings together the principal findings of the book, evaluates their significance in terms of current debates and identifies pointers to future research. It also returns to Wolf's concern with the impact of economic change on Mexican society. Thirty years ago, Wolf's speculations about what the future held for the 'sons of the shaking earth' were bleak to say the least. To what extent should this pessimism shroud the prospects for their female counterparts in the 1990s?

Notes

1 'Mestizo' is the term given to people of mixed Spanish and Indian origin and applies to around 90% of the Mexican population.

2 See for example Urry and Warde (1985) on the significance of 'locality' for studies of class and gender in Britain. See also Duncan (1989) and Duncan and Savage (1989) for deeper discussions of spatial variations in social behaviour and the problems in using 'locality' as an analytical concept.

3 Use of the terms 'labour supply' and 'labour demand' in no way implies adoption of a neoclassical theoretical framework. 'Supply' is used here to refer simply to factors which are largely internal to households (such as income, family size, domestic divisions of labour) and 'demand' to broader external factors (local production, national recession and so on), notwithstanding, as argued in the text, that these are highly interactive.

4 The term patriarchy originally derived from Greek and Roman law where the adult male of the household had legal and economic power over dependent household members (both male and female). In its more general sense (as used in this book), Gerda Lerner (1986: 239) describes it as the 'manifestation and institutionalisation of male dominance over women and children in the family and the extension of male dominance over women in society in general'.

5 The term 'irregular settlement' denotes an area of self-help housing in which initial occupation of land was illegal. Irregular settlements generally house low-income people and are the most common form of popular housing in Mexico, as in many other parts of the Third World. There are three main types of irregular settlement in Mexico:

1 *Squatter settlements*: these arise out of invasion of either public or private land.
2 *Low-income or clandestine subdivisions*: here land is sold off illegally for residential develoment by private owners who not only lack planning permission but who also fail to provide official minimum levels of services and infrastructure.
3 Ejidal *urban settlements*: an *ejido* is an area of land handed over by the state to an agricultural community. Tenure is limited to usufruct and the land may not be sold or in any other way alienated. However, despite this, many members of these communities (*ejidatarios*) sell land to urban settlers for which they are ultimately compensated by government. Tenure is awarded to the urban inhabitants once a presidential decree makes possible expropriation.

6 While not exclusively concerned with women, Lydia Morris's (1988) paper on employment, the household and social networks in which she emphasises the importance of studying the household as a residential unit, its responses to economic change, and its utility as a focus of research, notes the difficulties of finding a literature that encompasses the links between households and various social and economic phenomena:

> The potential field is so broad that it is rare to find all possible aspects of the perspective combined in one study. Rather there exists a collection of non-comparable studies which tend to focus on specific areas of interest within the household – domestic labour, household finance, power and decision-making, self-provisioning and labour market position – but are in no way cumulative, or even mutually informing. The result is not 'a literature' on the relationships between the household, employment and social networks, but rather distinctive pockets of material. The work required to bind them together has only relatively recently begun (Morris, 1988: 378).

In many respects the problems of a sectoralised literature also face the study of links between gender, households and the economy, the latter which itself is likely to represent an important contribution to the area of enquiry identified by Morris.

7 Given that all households in the survey consist of kin, the term 'family' is sometimes used in the text to describe residential household units. However, it should be remembered that 'family' is also a broader concept, embracing kinship and ideology (see, for example, Ennew, 1982 and Smith, 1988 on kinship and the household). I attempt to make it clear in what sense term is used in different places in the book. Interestingly, all households in Benería and Roldan's survey of women outworkers in Mexico City were also based on kinship relations (see Benería and Roldan, 1987: 112).

8 The term 'ideology' might convey the impression here of 'non-material' factors, but while ideologies of family, of gender and so on may well develop through cultural processes that are not necessarily derived from mode of production, Barrett (1986: 40) is careful to stress that 'no clear separation can be made between the economic and ideological'. However, she continues with the proviso that 'relations of production, grounded as they are in a deeply ideological division of labour, cannot be investigated through economic categories alone'. Hence the need to explore factors over and above the economy when examining familial organisation and the position of women.

9 A 'division of labour along lines of gender' (Mackintosh, 1981: 2) refers to the social construction of men's and women's roles. A more common term, also used in the book, is 'sexual division of labour'.

10 The term 'livelihood strategies' is preferred by some authors (e.g. Clarke, 1986; Radcliffe, 1986). Sarah Radcliffe (1986: 30) defines household livelihood strategies as the 'decisions, actions and goals of household members which ensure their reproduction'. Another term is 'household work strategy' defined by Ray Pahl (1984: 20) in connection with his discussion of pre-industrial households in England as a method for making 'the best use of resources for getting by under given social and economic conditions'. However,

Gerry Rodgers (1989:20) cautions against indiscriminate use of the term 'strategy', especially in situations of economic crisis, observing that: 'the term strategy may itself be misleading, implying a well worked-out plan for the allocation of family labour resources. While this may sometimes be accurate, it is probable that the strategy will more often consist of attempts to obtain additional income by any means available'.

11   While there is a general concern with the 'adaptive' nature of household structures and survival/livelihood strategies in the literature on Third World urban kinship, this is not to suggest that people looking at these issues subscribe to a narrow functionalist viewpoint whereby any phenomenon (household structure, for example) is seen as functional or adaptive because it exists (see Bruner, 1982, for a fuller discussion of the theoretical impasses in post-war literature on the family). On the contrary, concern with 'household survival strategies' goes far beyond analyses of the superficial logic of various household responses to wider economic change, to embrace the cultural, political and ideological substance, meaning, and significance of those actions.

12   Or indeed if there were state facilities and/or socialised alternatives, but these are rare in most market economies.

13   At a general theoretical level Marxist–Feminists have tended to view women's position in the labour market as a result of varying combinations of capitalism and patriarchy. In turn these are usually studied empirically through the phenomena of home and workplace, with various references to the state, familial/social ideologies and so on. Other approaches in a neoclassical vein have tended to set-up a dichotomy between, for example, 'human capital' (i.e. the pre-labour market endowments of women) and 'sex discrimination' (see Carvajal and Geithman, 1985). Various levels of analysis confuse the issue, and as Sylvia Walby (1985: 145) suggests:

The key issues on which approaches to women's unemployment and employment divide do not coincide with the theoretical divisions between neoclassical economic, institutional labour-market analysis, Marxism and radical feminism. The main difference is rather the degree of centrality which is accorded to the family or to labour market structures in explaining women's movements into and out of paid work. It is on the question of whether the family is seen as the chief determinant of women's participation in paid work, or whether structures within the labour market are held to be the key, that the most significant differences emerge.

14   Despite the fact that women's primary identification is usually with consumption/reproduction and men's with production at both normative and practical levels, this should not be taken as a fixed and universal norm. Alison MacEwen Scott's (1990) detailed study of women's employment and the family in Lima, Peru, for example, stresses that neither men nor women are precluded from one another's spheres. In working-class households in Lima women are expected to contribute to household income-generation just as much as men are expected to collaborate in various aspects of domestic work.

15   It is of course dangerous to assume that only non-nuclear households are capable of, or characterised by, less rigid sexual divisions of labour. Scott's (1990) work on Lima identifies how male-headed nuclear households can often exhibit considerable flexibility in gender roles and relations that diverge substantially from normative ideologies of family relations.

16   Comparable historical evidence for households in Europe during the eighteenth and nineteenth centuries may be found in Flandrin (1979), Laslett (1972), Mitterauer and Sieder (1982) and Wall, Robin and Laslett (1983).

17   MacDonald and MacDonald (1978) concentrate on the literature on black families in the Americas. The idea that one-parent families (headed by women) are 'deviant' or 'dysfunctional' is also persistent in work done on families of other racial minorities in the United States (see, for example, Gongla and Thompson, 1987; Macklin, 1987).

Economic development in Mexico: comparative perspectives on three intermediate cities – Puerto Vallarta, León and Querétaro

Introduction

This chapter examines the growth and development of Puerto Vallarta, León and Querétaro within the context of the national economy. The first section provides a brief overview of Mexican development and urbanisation since 1940. The second section presents a detailed profile of the demographic, economic and social evolution of each of the study cities and their labour markets.

Mexican economic development: an overview

Since 1940 Mexico has undergone a rapid, intense, albeit uneven, process of economic transformation. Growth was particularly marked in the thirty years up to 1970 when GNP grew by an annual average of 6% (Reyna, 1977; Villareal, 1977), and industry by 8.0% (Villareal, 1977; Ward, 1986). Only in the last fifteen to twenty years has growth declined to a more modest average of 2.6% per annum. (World Bank, 1988: 223), mainly as a result of the drastic slumps in world oil prices in the 1980s. Even then Mexico still ranks as an upper middle-income economy and in 1986 had a per capita GNP of $1,860 US.

In terms of industrial development, Mexico has pursued two main types of strategy: first, import substitution aimed at stimulating and diversifying production for the domestic market, and second, export-oriented manufacturing. Import substitution industrialisation (ISI), by far the more important strategy and preceded by massive agrarian reform and nationalisation of strategic sectors of the economy such as oil and the railways, was initiated during World War Two when shortages of foreign manufactured goods gave automatic protection to infant Mexican industries. By the end of the 1940s, the first stage of ISI (substitution of consumer goods) was virtually complete. The index of import substitution of non-durable consumer goods fell from 0.22 to only 0.07 between 1940 and 1950, against an overall fall of 28% of imports in the total supply of manufactured goods in the same period; by 1950 consumer goods represented only 17.6% of total imports (Villareal, 1977). Between then and 1970 a range of protectionist measures including currency devaluations in 1949 and 1954, and tariff increases on imports in 1958, 1962 and 1968, allowed ISI to pass into its second, and to a lesser extent, its third stages (substitution of intermediate goods and substitution of capital goods respectively). The Law for New and Necessary Industries (*Ley de Fomento de Industrias Nuevas y Necesarias*) also gave domestic industries access to subsidies and tax concessions. Between 1950 and 1969 the import substitution index of intermediate goods fell from 0.42 to 0.22, and that of capital and durable goods from 0.74 to 0.51, and overall, the participation of imports in the total supply of manufactured goods declined by 25% between 1958 and 1969 (ibid.). Although excessive protectionism ultimately generated inefficiency, and ISI became associated with a range of problems including widespread unemployment, and increasing reliance on foreign capital and technology, there is no doubt that it set Mexico on the road to industrialisation and economic growth, especially up to 1970.

Export-oriented manufacturing, on the other hand, was less important in the early stages of industrialisation, but since the 1960s has risen to prominence, especially with the inauguration of the Frontier Industrialisation Programme (*Programa de Industrialización Fronteriza*) in 1965 (Carrillo and Hernández, 1981; Cockcroft, 1983a; Sklair, 1988). This established a tariff-free 20-kilometre strip on the Mexican side of the US–Mexico border where multinational firms were allowed to set-up branch plants for the assembly of export products. These 'in-bond' or '*maquiladora*' plants may be up to 100% foreign-owned and are entitled to import duty-free parts from the United States provided that all goods assembled within them are exported. By confining these operations to the border area it has been argued that Mexico's import substitution regime to the south is thus protected (Harris, 1986: 79). However, more recent reports indicate that the establishment of *maquiladoras* is now being allowed in the interior of the country (Sklair, 1988: 292). Most of the factories concentrate on the assembly of electronic or electrical goods and garment-making and include several well-known international firms such as Ford, Chrysler, General Electric, RCA and Dow Chemical (Cockcroft, 1983a). The *maquiladora* industry is currently the second most dynamic sector of the economy after oil (earning almost $2 billion US in foreign exchange in 1985), and contrary to ISI, generates a considerable amount of employment (Cornelius, 1986; Rivas, 1985). From 1983 onwards, the rate of job creation in *maquiladoras* stood at between 8 and 12% per annum (Cornelius, 1986), and by the end of 1987, border plants were providing employment for between 250 and 300,000 people (Kouyoumdjian, 1988; Sklair, 1988).

Although post-war development was most pronounced in the manufacturing sector, agriculture also played an important role in the expanding Mexican economy, with production increasing six-fold between 1940 and the mid-1970s (Cockcroft, 1983a). However, the prioritisation of industry (in terms of investment, protection and so on) at the expense of agriculture led to a widening disequilibrium (Villareal, 1977) and by the mid-1960s agriculture in Mexico had become 'crisis-ridden' (Philip, 1988: 2). Between 1955 and 1965 agricultural output grew by 4.2% p.a., but declined to 2.1% p.a. in the following decade (Harris, 1986); moreover, by 1981 agriculture contributed only 8% of value of the national product, compared with 18% in 1955 (ibid.). Inevitably declining growth has reduced labour opportunities in agriculture, but losses in rural employment are also attributable to the nature of agricultural development itself, consisting in the main of drives to promote large-scale export-oriented production. Investment and new technology associated with the 'Green Revolution' have been channelled into the capital-intensive production of export crops such as cotton and coffee at the expense of subsistence crops such as maize that traditionally employed large numbers of Mexican farmworkers (Cockcroft, 1983a; Ward, 1986). Over the period 1940 to 1960, the amount of land under maize cultivation dropped from 65% to 53% (Cockcroft, 1983a), and between 1960 and 1980, agriculture's share of total employment fell from 55% of the total economically active population to only 36% (Harris, 1986). Currently there are between 4.5 and 6 million landless labourers in Mexico, employed for only one-third of the year or less (Cornelius, 1986). Rural out-migration has been one response to this decline in agricultural employment, helping to account for Mexico's rapid transition to an urban–industrial state. Nevertheless, it should also be remembered that since ISI has been characterised by the increased use of capital-intensive technology, unemployment is also a serious problem in urban areas (Villareal, 1977; see also Cornelius and Craig, 1988: 523).

Economic growth and urbanisation

Against a background of relatively sustained economic growth until the mid-1970s, Mexico's population leapt from 19.6 million in 1940 to an estimated 73 million in 1982, to around 82 million in 1986. Most of this growth was in urban areas, fuelled both by rural out-migration and by comparatively high rates of natural increase in the towns. Indeed while the population as a whole grew by an average of 3.2% a year between 1960 and 1980, in urban areas this was 4.5% (World Bank, 1988). Urban–rural wage differentials played a key role in prompting population movements. For example, in Querétaro state in the early 1980s, minimum wage levels between countryside and town revealed a 20% discrepancy and were a major reason cited by migrants for having moved to the state capital (Chant, 1984). With progressive and selective urban bias in industrial investment, inter- and intra-regional inequality became prominent hallmarks of Mexican development (see Aguilar-Barajas and Spence, 1988; Stern, 1982). Rates of rural out-migration were such that the urban population doubled from one- to two-thirds of the national population between 1940 and 1978, and while in 1960 only 36% of the population lived in cities with 500,000 or more inhabitants, this had grown to 48% by 1980 (World Bank, 1988: 285). Demographic movement tended to follow the concentration of manufacturing investment and was regionally biased to the urban centres of the Federal District, Nuevo León and the United States border area (Keren, 1982).

In Mexico City alone, the population grew from only 4.7 million in 1950, to 8.5 million in 1970, 13.2 million in 1980, 14.8 million in 1985 and an estimated 19 million in 1988, accompanying its disproportionate concentration of resources. Mexico City's share of national manufacturing employment, for example, increased from 35% in 1950 to 47% in 1975 (Gilbert and Gugler, 1982), and in 1979 the Federal District received 58% of all private investment in the country (Ward, 1986). Presently the metropolitan area contains only 24% of the national population, yet contributes 43% of Mexico's total manufacturing product and 36% of GDP (see Ward, 1989: 308). The city's annual rate of demographic growth from the 1940s has been close to 5%, although since 1960 natural increase has been more important in accounting for its expansion than migration (Butterworth and Chance, 1981; Schteingart, 1989). Other major areas of urban development have been Monterrey, Guadalajara and Puebla (Garza, 1980; Stern, 1982), however, compared with the capital their growth has been relatively small. Mexico City in the mid-1980s was still over four times the size of Mexico's second largest city, Guadalajara. This concentration has inevitably resulted in huge regional imbalances and diseconomies of scale, which as we shall see a little later in the chapter have been a major reason for government drives to promote the development of 'secondary' or 'intermediate' cities.

The political economy of Mexican development

The so-called 'Mexican Miracle' of economic development was set on a stage dominated by one political party – the Institutional Revolutionary Party (PRI), which under various guises (the National Revolutionary Party [PNR] 1929–38; the Mexican Revolutionary Party [PRM] 1938–45) has held power since the Revolution of 1910–17. The party has won all presidential and most state elections since its inception, although at the same time it is strongly dominated by the executive (Eckstein, 1977; Hansen, 1971). The extent of interdependence between state and party is such that the government and the PRI are often indistinguishable in the minds of the Mexican public (Cornelius, 1975). Indeed as Paul Cammack (1988) notes this has been central to the way the system functions: the state needs the party to mobilise the support of the electorate and to keep potential opposition at bay; at the same time, state-backing for the PRI affords the party a degree of legitimacy, if no significant access to resources, and also sometimes allows up-and-coming party officials to ascend to government positions. The PRI is able to manage a broad cross-section of the population through three major affiliated organisations: the Confederation of Farmworkers (CNC), the Confederation of Labour (CTM) and the Confederation of Popular Organisations (CNOP).

The political system in Mexico has been described variously as 'populist corporatist' (Reyna, 1977), 'imperfectly democratic' (Scott, 1959), 'authoritarian–corporate' (Kaufman Purcell, 1975), and 'bureaucratic–authoritarian' (Kaufman, 1977), yet common to most interpretations is an emphasis on the fundamentally authoritarian nature of the regime and recognition that 'an ongoing, systematic suppression of electoral competition underlies its democratic and constitutional façade' (Kaufman, 1977: 193).

The management and containment of opposition has been one of the keys to the long-standing stability of the regime; legislation passed in 1963, 1972 and 1977 guaranteeing successively larger numbers of seats in the Chamber of Deputies for opposition parties allowed Mexico to maintain the appearance of an operative democracy that reinforced the regime's legitimacy (see Cammack, 1988, for a more detailed discussion of this legislation). Until 1988, the large majority of the PRI meant that most government legislation could be passed, but with decline over the years of voting turnout, along with the share of the vote going to the PRI (see below), the opening of opportunities for the opposition which originally helped to validate the regime, began to backfire: the inconsonance of creating space for political opponents at the same time as denying them access to major positions of power eventually undermined the system's credibility (Cammack, 1988). In these circumstances, various members of the PRI themselves saw the need for change. Mid-1986 saw the development of the '*Corriente Democrática*' headed by the party's president, Porfirio Muñoz Ledo, and Cuahtémoc Cárdenas (son of former Mexican president Lázaro Cárdenas) whose principal objectives were to relax methods of internal selection of candidates and to reform economic policy, especially vis-à-vis external debt (Cornelius and Craig, 1988; Loaeza, 1988; Smith, 1989). Forming the core of a subsequent coalition of left-of-centre opposition groups – the 'Frente Democrático' – which gained the support of two parties that had formerly backed the PRI (the Authentic Party of the Revolution [PARM] and the Popular Socialist Party [PPS]), a serious challenge was presented to the offical candidate Carlos Salinas Gortari in the 1988 elections, with Cardenas polling 31% of the total vote (Carr, 1989; Philip, 1989). Salinas's slim electoral victory (50.36% of the vote) together with the emergence of the *neocardenista* Revolutionary Democratic Party (PRD) has placed major question marks over Mexico's political future.[1]

Until the PRD emerged in 1988, the PRI's most important rival was the National Action Party (PAN) – a conservative grouping founded in 1939, supported by private business interests (especially in the north of the country), the urban middle and upper classes, and the Catholic Church (Hamilton, 1986; Loaeza, 1988). Although the PAN regularly captured most of the opposition's votes, until recently this was only a very small proportion in relation to the total vote; for example in 1976 only 15% of all votes in the presidential election went to the PAN (Gilbert and Ward, 1982) and in 1982 still less than 17% (Loaeza, 1988).[2] However, in the 1980s, and especially in the northern cities, the PAN continued to attract progressively greater support in response to dissatisfaction with the incumbent regime's management of Mexico's economic crisis. For example, PAN won twelve of the municipal elections which took place in five states in June 1983 (Hamilton, 1986), and in various elections for state governor in Nuevo León and Sonora (1985), and Chihuahua and Durango (1986), PAN candidates were so popular that the PRI had to resort to open fraud in order to maintain its control.[3] In turn, somewhat inevitably, this fraud proved highly destabilising (Cammack, 1988; Loaeza, 1988). The share of votes going to the PAN however, was not wholly attributable to the growing unpopularity of the PRI; in part it derived from the fact that urbanisation and industrialisation had progressively reduced the proportion of voters in rural areas from where the PRI traditionally drew most of its support (ibid.; see also Cornelius and Craig, 1988: 38; Kaufman Purcell, 1988: 11).

Aside from successful manipulation (until recently) of political opposition, the Mexican regime's stability over fifty years of capitalist economic development was also sustained through the legitimacy derived from its historic revolutionary victory and frequent recourse to populist rhetoric thereafter, its avoidance of explicit and/ or obvious alliances with particular class groups, and the early incorporation of the working class and the peasantry into different sectors within the party structure (Cammack, 1988; see also Ronfeldt, 1988: 57). By incorporating strategic class groupings into separate parts of the state apparatus, the government has been able to give the appearance of being representative at the same time as demobilising these groups, and also to prevent the emergence of broad class-based alliances forming outside the system (Reyna, 1977). The hierarchical structure of grassroots party organisations means that mass demand-making is kept to a minimum and allows for co-optation of key individuals. The regime is able to keep a tight rein on the outflow of resources by maintaining a 'distended bureaucracy' (Ward, 1986: 38): a complicated nexus of multiple and overlapping agencies and/or functions turns demand-making into a diffuse and long drawn-out process involving substantial personalistic negotiation and delay (Cammack, 1988). When demands go unmet, blame is apportioned to individuals rather than the party or the state as a whole. In extreme circumstances, when piecemeal concessions are unable to co-opt the leaders of mass movements or to head off open confrontation, the government turns to repression (Reyna, 1977). A final major factor accounting for the long-term stability of the system is the regular turnover of personnel (Garrido, 1989; Smith, 1979). Each *sexenio* (six-year non-renewable presidency) replenishes the system, and provides scope for the new leader to pass the political buck onto his predecessor(s). Within this structure, each president tends to make a distinctive stamp on his term of office.

In the wake of the events of 1988, the system described here entered into a period of fundamental restructuring. However, for an understanding of the context of the present research it is necessary to briefly outline the principal characteristics of economic development (and crisis) in the presidential periods of Luís Echeverría Alvarez (1970–76), José López Portillo (1976–82) and Miguel De La Madrid Hurtado (1982–88).

Politics, economy and the crisis

By the late 1960s, the Mexican economy was showing severe signs of strain, particularly in terms of rising unemployment, increased concentration of income, inefficiency of several home industries, dependence on foreign capital and a growing balance-of-payments deficit (Villareal, 1977). These kinds of trends had led to sporadic outbreaks of social and labour unrest in the 1950s and 1960s, the most notable being the student uprising in 1968, which was met with severe repression by the state (Enriquez, 1988; Reyna, 1977; Sheahan, 1987). Concerned to salvage political legitimacy, Echeverría embarked upon his presidential term in 1970 with the prime objective of appeasing political disquiet, broadening state–class alliances and moving away from a 'stabilising development model' to one of 'shared development' aimed at spreading the benefits of economic growth to a broader cross-section of the population (Aguilar-Barajas and Spence, 1988; Enriquez, 1988; Looney, 1983; Ward, 1986). In an effort to stimulate the economy, public expenditure as a proportion of GDP increased to around 28% in the mid-1970s compared with only 12.5% a decade earlier (Harris, 1986), and the share of public investment in GDP increased from 6.8% in 1960 to 10.9% in 1975 (Villareal, 1977). Echeverría also established numerous welfare and development agencies to enact his redistributive policies (Ward, 1986). Most expenditure was fuelled by borrowing from abroad, thus increasing Mexico's foreign debt. In 1970 Mexico's external debt was only $3.6 billion US (Keren, 1982), but by 1975 it had climbed to $20.6 billion US (Ros, 1987). The balance in the current account began to deteriorate after a brief improvement in 1971–2, and in 1974 stood at $3,010 million US, nearly three times its level in 1970 (Villareal, 1977). In the latter half of the *sexenio* inflation began to escalate, income from exports declined (owing to an overvalued exchange rate), and capital flight began mounting as big business, distrustful of Echeverría's policies and revolutionary rhetoric, began to withdraw its accounts to foreign banks; these trends led finally to an unavoidable devaluation of the Mexican currency in 1976, the first in over 20 years (Hamilton, 1986; Twomey, 1989). As Rosario Enriquez (1988: 29) puts it: 'In retrospect the 1970–1976 period shows a government that tried to do too much, too fast and without the necessary resources to succeed.'

However, despite the problems inherited from the previous *sexenio*, Echeverría's successor, López Portillo, had a major trump card: oil. The discovery and exploitation of new oil reserves promised not only to avert further economic crisis but to usher in a new era of economic development and equality; massive government investment was thus poured into the development of the oil industry as a means of increasing exports and invigorating the industrial sector (Hamilton, 1986; Sheahan, 1987). The years 1978–81 witnessed a phenomenal upturn in growth: GDP climbed at a rate of between 8–9% per annum, and oil production grew at an annual level of 19.4%, receiving an additional boost from the oil price rise of 1979–80 (Ros, 1987). By 1980 oil had become the country's largest generator of export-earnings, accounting for two-thirds of the total value (Hirschman, 1986).

However, far from proving to be the salvation of the economy, oil instead paved the way for unprecedented deterioration, usually attributed to three main factors. First, in order to exploit its oil reserves, the Mexican government stepped-up public expenditure to the extent that the foreign debt (public and private) leapt from $29 billion US in 1977 to $75 billion US in 1981 (Ros, 1987). The international banking system was only too ready to lend money to Mexico believing that oil wealth would offer 'solid guarantees of repayment' (Hirschman, 1986: 24). Between 1978 and 1981, the value of international bank loans to Mexico rose by 146% (approximately twice the rate in the rest of the developing world) (Ros, 1987). At the same time, the tripling of interest rates in the US and UK increased interest payments on Mexico's debt from 6% to 18–19% (Hamilton, 1986). Rising indebtedness was exacerbated by the fact that much of the equipment and technology needed for rapid exploitation of petroleum resources had to be imported from abroad (Hamilton, 1986; Ward, 1986); in addition Mexico failed to develop a petrochemical industry of its own and remained largely dependent on exports of crude oil, thereby stifling its chances of building a more secure basis for future development.

Second, selective state investment in the oil industry (which by 1981 absorbed nearly one-half of all public investment), and a shift of private investment away from manufacturing into services and distribution, brought torpor to the manufacturing sector; between mid-1979 and 1980–1 manufacturing output declined from 10% to 7% with direct implications for reduced revenue from non-oil exports; imports of foreign goods, on the other hand, grew at an annual rate of 30% during the same period (Ros, 1987). As a result, despite the increase in foreign exchange derived from oil during the boom years, exports never managed to exceed imports thus aggravating Mexico's ever-widening balance-of-payments deficit (Hirschman, 1986; Ros, 1987). By 1981, imports cost the Mexican government $4 billion US more than earnings derived from exports (Hamilton, 1986). In order to extricate itself from growing indebtedness Mexico had to rely on raising levels of oil production which reduced still further its scope for lessening dependence on this one resource. Depite having set an initial production limit of 1.5 million barrels per day in the early 1980s (so as not to dissipate valuable reserves), by 1982 daily production stood at 2.7 million barrels (Ward, 1986). In addition, backed into a corner by US threats to withold credit, Mexico soon overshot its ceiling of not more than 50% of production going to any one country; four-fifths of national production by 1981 went to the United States (ibid.). Over-reliance on a single commodity and a single customer thus increased perilously throughout the late 1970s and early 1980s.

However, the final blow was dealt by the slump in world oil prices in 1981, at a time when dependence on oil was at its peak, representing 72% of total exports (Ros, 1987). This caused a wave of panic among creditors and business interests, and gave rise to a renewed bout of capital flight and profit repatriation (Hamilton, 1986). In February 1982 a major devaluation cutting the value of the peso by about half, doubled the costs of imported inputs for industry, and led to further speculation and capital flight, the latter becoming by far the most important factor in the widening trade imbalance (Ros, 1987). By August 1982, Mexico's reserves of foreign exchange were at the point of exhaustion, and on 1 September 1982 in his final presidential address to the nation, López Portillo announced the nationalisation of the private banks as a last desperate bid to keep reserves of hard currency in the country and to guarantee private-sector foreign debts (Harris, 1986). Some also viewed it as an attempt to curry favour among the Mexican populace whose standards of living had dropped considerably (Ward, 1986). Indeed, among the left, the unions, peasant organisations and students, the move was extremely popular (Hamilton, 1986). However, all it really did was to buy time before an even worse period of hardship; the final months of the López Portillo administration witnessed the arrival of the IMF on the scene and the start of negotiations over the procedure for a drastic programme of structural adjustment.

Miguel De La Madrid's term of office thus began on 1 December 1982 with a three-year IMF stabilisation plan ahead, inflation running at about 100%, and no access to external finance (Ros, 1987). The 'Austerity Programme' implemented in the early part of the administration included cuts in public spending, the reduction of subsidies, the 'rationalisation' of public-sector enterprises, fiscal reforms and rigid import controls (Hamilton, 1986; Ros, 1987). The effects on the workforce were devastating, with wages in industry falling by about one-third between May 1982 and November 1985 (Roxborough, 1988: 110), and minimum wages in general dropping by 44% between 1980 and 1986 (Gilbert, 1989b: 159–60) In order to revitalise the economy the Mexican government stepped up its programme of foreign investment in the border industries and also returned 34% of the nationalised bank's shares to former clients, workers and a number of local state organisations (Hamilton, 1986). By August 1983 some compensation had been received for bank personnel for their losses with the nationalisation. The above measures helped to restore some private-sector confidence in the government, and even if austerity did little for the poorer classes, the Mexican example was heralded by the IMF as a successful adjustment to the debt crisis (Ros, 1987). By 1983 inflation had dropped to 80% (from a level of 98.8% in the previous year) (Kouyoumdjian, 1988), and in 1984, with the best growth rate of the *sexenio* (3.7% in real terms), Mexico once again appeared to be on the road to recovery. However, this optimism proved to be short lived (Cornelius and Craig, 1988; Kouyoumdjian, 1988).

Slight relaxation in the austerity programme at the end of 1984 (probably in order to win the support of the electorate prior to the 1985 state and municipal elections) led to another upturn in inflation and capital flight (around $5–6 billion US in 1985 alone); these problems were exacerbated by the earthquake in September 1985 and yet another decline in oil prices the following year (Cornelius, 1986; Hirschman, 1986).[4] Oil prices fell 55% in value between November 1985 and February 1986 (Cornelius, 1986). Economic growth in 1985 was as low as 2.7%, only marginally ahead of national population growth (2.6%), and inflation, while lower than its 1982 levels, was still high at 63.7% (ibid.).

However, the major problem was foreign debt, which continued climbing along with rising interest rates on the US market. Mexico's external debt in 1986 was around 100 billion US dollars, involving the government in debt service expenditure of 700 million US dollars a month (Cornelius, 1986) – equivalent to 7.3% of GNP compared with 2% in 1970 (World Bank, 1988). This represented an intolerable drain on the economy, especially since Mexico had received no new credits since 1985. In July 1986 a deal was made between Mexico and a consortium of three international lending agencies (the IMF, the World Bank and the Inter-American Development Bank) whereby Mexico received a new 3.6 billion loan package for industrial restructuring on which repayment, for the first time in any IMF agreement, was linked to the price of their major export commodity, oil (Cornelius, 1986; Duran, 1988). Despite the provision of some new finance however, De La Madrid's presidency, and the period of fieldwork on which this study is based, were characterised by deep economic crisis. With the partial exception of Puerto Vallarta, prospects for the poor in all cities in the study have been decidely bleaker since the advent of recession. These are discussed in more detail later in the chapter after a brief look at the implications of post-war economic development for low-income groups in Mexico as whole.

The consequences of development: employment and income

Ismael Aguilar-Barajas and Nigel Spence (1988: 192) point out that 'The period 1940-1970 was one in which Mexico experienced a high rate of growth, but also one in which the adverse social effects of this process were largely ignored.' Among the most pronounced social inequalities underlining Mexican development was that of widening disparities in the distribution of wealth (Ward, 1986). In 1977, the top 5% of income earners in Mexico received forty-seven times more salary than the bottom 10% (Cockcroft, 1983a), and Susan Kaufman Purcell (1988: 3) goes as far to say that by the 1980s 'Mexico's distribution of resources was one of the most highly skewed in the hemisphere.' In addition to social there were also spatial inequalities such as marked unevenness in regional development (Cornelius and Craig, 1988).

In the more rapidly expanding urban centres, population increase far outstripped local capacity to provide employment, forcing many of the poor to create their own income opportunities in order to survive (see for example, Arizpe, 1977). This led to the emergence of a broadly two-tiered or 'dualistic' labour market structure noted in several other parts of the developing world, where alongside a 'formal' sector consisting of large-scale firms using 'modern' mechanised production techniques, and in receipt of large inputs of foreign capital and technology, there exists an 'informal' sector comprising self-employed or casual workers, and small-scale labour-intensive family businesses characterised by rudimentary production techniques and low levels of indigenous capital (Bromley, 1982; Moser, 1978; Raczynski, 1977; Rodgers, 1989; Schaefer, 1976). In the 'formal' sector, employees are generally unionised, protected by minimum wage legislation and have access to social security; whereas in the 'informal' sector, workers operate outside of social and labour regulations (Gugler, 1982; Lailson, 1980; Moser, 1978). In reality the boundaries of each sector are often crudely drawn and open to a wide variety of interpretation, with each sector covering such a wide range of different occupations, that a simple two-fold distinction has frequently been seen as inadequate (Connolly, 1981; Hart, 1973; Rodgers, 1989; Sinclair, 1978). Furthermore, the rather arbitrary division of the labour market into two sectors tends to obscure the numerous interchanges of products, services and labour between them, when often the so-called 'informal sector' functions in a subordinate and directly beneficial way for accumulation in the formal sector (Escobar, 1988; Moser, 1978; Raczynski, 1977). However, despite the finely-tuned nuances of the theoretical debate, many of the poor themselves distinguish between two main types of employment in the city – that which is 'protected' and that which remains outside the framework of government legislation.

One of the most significant problems for workers outside the 'formal' sector concerns the absence of minimum wage legislation. Only a small minority of the population are protected by the minumum wage, defined by the National Commission of Minimum Wages as an amount which should cover the 'social, material and cultural necessities' of a head of household and to provide education for his children (Comisión Nacional de los Salarios Mínimos, 1975: 5). In reality this does not take into account the number of dependents belonging to a head of household, and the fact that wages consistently fall behind price increases. For example, in 1980 it was estimated that 'the legal minimum wage was less than half what a working class family of five needed simply to maintain itself' (Cockcroft, 1983b: 93). The annual or bi-annual establishment of minimum salaries is the responsibility of an amalgam of regional and national bodies comprising workers, employers and government officials. Given each group's respective interests, mutually satisfactory wage settlements are rarely achieved. In no case was this more apparent than in 1983 when against a background of inflationary cost-of-living increases of up to 200% in certain items, workers on minimum salaries were only granted a 23% emergency pay rise (Chant, 1984). Indeed, between 1975 and 1985–6 it is estimated that the purchasing power of the minimum wage declined by between one-third and one-fifth (González de la Rocha, 1988). While minimum wages are increasingly inadequate for basic survival, to remain unprotected by any wage legislation at all has even graver consequences for the poor's ability to ride out the crisis, even though some informal workers appear to earn more than those in the formal sector. In June 1986, it was estimated that 62% of the economically active population in Mexico as a whole earned sub-minimum wages (Cornelius, 1986). Financial penury has serious ramifications for several other aspects of survival, such as diet, health (see for example Cornelius and Craig, 1988: 48) and, perhaps most obviously, shelter.

The consequences of development: housing and the urban poor

Massive urban growth, coupled with widespread income deficiencies, has put severe pressure on urban land and housing markets. Relatively few of the urban poor qualify for a subsidised public-sector dwelling, which would be the alternative in most advanced industrial countries. The Mexican state institution INFONAVIT (the National Workers Housing Fund) is geared to providing low-cost homes for workers at 'social interest' rates. But this is inadequate; not only does the need for proof of formal employment disqualify many of the poor from even applying for government housing schemes, but there are simply too few dwellings built to meet demand. The major alternatives are low-budget rental accommodation and self-help housing.[5]

In the period up to the 1970s, most rental housing was in the inner city, but as populations have grown and stock has deteriorated in terms of quality and availability, tenants have increasingly had to move out to the intermediate and even peripheral areas of the city to rent in former 'irregular settlements' (see below) (Gilbert, 1983; Edwards, 1982). Recent expansion of proportions of the poor housed in rental accommodation has been most apparent in the larger cities.

In most of the intermediate cities, however, by far the most important form of low-income housing continues to be what the poor construct for themselves in 'irregular' settlements. Access to a plot of land in a peripheral irregular settlement is gained through illegal means only and there are a variety of ways in which it can be obtained (Gilbert and Varley, 1989; Gilbert and Ward, 1985; Ward, 1982). People squat, buy land in unauthorised sales engineered by *ejidatarios* (members of state-owned agricultural cooperatives), or purchase it from private individuals or government personnel acting in an unofficial capacity (Gilbert and Ward, 1985). Irregular settlements are generally unserviced and their residents have to wait a number of years before they receive legal title at a price from a relevant agency. However, the fact that the Mexican government has actually tolerated illegal settlement and, more recently, intervened to provide services and regularise tenure represents in itself an implicit recognition that self-help housing, despite its limitations, is a viable answer to the shelter problem. All governments face the dilemma of having to reconcile the contradictory objectives of accumulating capital at the same time as providing the labour force with at least some means of survival (Roberts, 1978). As in other parts of the world, self-help housing in Mexico has represented a mechanism for housing the poor at minimal cost to the state. However, despite this '*laissez-faire*' attitude towards housing, other effects of rapid and uncontrolled development, including massive illiteracy, malnutrition and poor living conditions, made for a change in general policy direction in the late 1960s towards greater intervention by the government in national economic affairs (Ward, 1986).

Industrial decentralisation and intermediate cities

When President Echeverría came to power in 1970 he was not only concerned with *sectoral*, but also *spatial* inequalities in the distribution of wealth (Unikel, 1982). Indeed in Echeverría's view, regional inequalities were not only 'unjust', but also a 'serious limitation to further economic growth' (Aguilar-Barajas and Spence, 1988: 195). As a result, the federal government began offering financial incentives to induce industry away from the capital and thereby counteract an excessive concentration of resources and increasing diseconomies of scale. In the early 1970s, over 50% of manufactured goods in the country were produced in Mexico City (SHCP/SEDUE, 1982). The bid to spread the process of economic development through the regions was continued through the administrations of López Portillo and De La Madrid (see also Aguilar-Barajas and Spence, 1988, for a detailed review of industrial decentralisation and regional policy between 1970 and 1986).

Incentives for industrial decentralisation have taken the form of free licences, low rents, cheap prices of energy and basic petrochemical products, and low tariffs for public services. One element of this programme has been a commitment to designating certain secondary towns and cities, otherwise known as '*ciudades medias*' or 'intermediate cities', as centres for industrial investment and regional growth. Intermediate cities may contain anything between 100,000 and one million inhabitants (IAP Querétaro/SEDUE, 1986). In the National Urban Development Plan (*Plan Nacional de Desarrollo Urbano* or PNDU) of 1984–88, fifty-nine intermediate cities were ear-marked as priority areas for economic incentives, and sub-divided into three grades of importance. Both Querétaro and León fell into the top category of priority (IAP Querétaro/SEDUE, 1986). The decentralisation programe involves the coordination and cooperation of a number of different federal agencies with state and municipal governments to promote deconcentration of capital and infrastructure. While Puerto Vallarta is defined under the PNDU as an intermediate city it is not listed as a target area for regional policy, possibly because its growth has long been high enough not to warrant special government assistance.

Women in the Mexican labour force

Before proceeding to a detailed discussion of the three intermediate cities in this study, it is important to briefly note how men and women have been affected by the Mexican development process at the national level.

Theoretically equality of opportunity on the grounds of sex in formal employment has been part of Mexican law since the presidency of Lázaro Cárdenas (1934–40), reinforced more recently by the Federal Labour Law (*Ley Federal de Trabajo*) of 1970 (Cobos, 1974). Yet even in 1970, Mexico still had one of the lowest rates of female labour force participation in the world, at around 19% of the total economically active population (LACWE, 1970). Part of this is due to the fact that a number of regulations and restrictions ostensibly designed to protect female labour, in practice exclude them from the workforce. For example, Mexican women are not allowed by law to do night shifts, or to undertake 'dangerous' or 'arduous' work (Canton Moller, 1974; Cobos, 1974; Gonzalez, 1980). There are also certain stipulations regarding the employment of pregnant women or those nursing young children. For example, a creche should be provided in all establishments employing certain numbers of female workers, but employers often evade these obligations by recruiting men (LACWE, 1980). Similarly some factories do not employ women in order to save expenditure on maternity pay.

Despite these restrictions, by the early 1980s, women's labour force participation had reached one-quarter of the economically active population in urban areas (Cockcroft, 1983a; Pedrero and Rendón, 1982). However, jobs for women thus far have tended to be confined to a narrow range of activities. As in other Latin American countries, over two-thirds of women workers are involved in the tertiary sector (LACWE, 1980). Even the one-million women employed in Mexican industry in the early 1980s were employed in a limited number of branches, notably textiles, food-processing, electronics and assembly plants (Cockcroft, 1983a). Indeed in the border areas, where most transnational assembly operations are situated, women constitute up to 70% of the industrial labour force (Fernández-Kelly, 1983a; Pearson, 1986). As in other parts of the developing (and developed) world, women's jobs are not only concentrated in a restricted range of economic activities, but also tend to be low-status and low-paid (Anker and Hein, 1986; Arizpe, 1977; Moser, 1981). Inequalities and sexual segregation in the 'formal' sector are, not surprisingly, replicated in the 'informal' sector. In the former, discrimination by employers often presents the major barrier to female entry and promotion; in the latter the inferior level of women's wages and working conditions is also interwoven with a range of constraints operating at the level of the household. In the informal sector women's work is generally household-based with a low profit margin compared with men's activities in the same (Bromley, 1982; Moser and Young, 1981). This is due to the fact that the very 'flexibility' of informal employment implies that women often have to continue playing a major part in running the home, and women who have to balance mothering and housework responsibilities with income generation obviously have less time to devote to paid work than men. Furthermore, the scope for women taking up certain kinds of trade or business is limited by their comparatively poor access to training, skills and capital (Scott, 1990). Women may also be forbidden by their husbands to engage in certain types of self-employment.

Puerto Vallarta

Growth and development

Puerto Vallarta is capital of the fastest growing of the 124 *municipios* which make up Jalisco state in western Mexico, and itself is the most rapidly growing tourist resort on the Mexican Pacific (COCODERA, 1980). It lies in the country's largest natural bay, the Bahía de Banderas (see Figure 1.1).

Puerto Vallarta was originally founded in 1871 as a small fishing village under the name of 'Las Peñas', but it was not until the 1960s that its growth as a major centre for national and international tourism took off following John Huston's filming of Tennessee William's *'The Night of the Iguana'* in 1963.[6] During the 1970s the town's population grew at an average annual rate of 11.9%. This intensified during the period 1980–83 to 12.3% per annum at a time when the corresponding growth rate for the state of Jalisco was only 2.7% (Fideicomiso Puerto Vallarta, 1985). In 1984 the population was officially estimated at 132,554 inhabitants (SEDUE/Gobierno del Estado, 1985), and more recent figures suggest around 160,000 for 1986. A large number of Puerto Vallarta's inhabitants are first- and second-generation migrants who have mainly come from rural areas within Jalisco itself, and from Nayarit, one of the poorest states in Mexico which lies to the north of the River Ameca, the state boundary of Jalisco, some ten kilometres up the coast from Puerto Vallarta. However, a number of people have come from as far afield as Mexico City, Guanajuato and Veracruz. In 1976 it was estimated that 60% of Puerto Vallarta's inhabitants were migrants (SEDUE/ Gobierno del Estado, 1985).

Puerto Vallarta stands out as an example of extremely rapid urban development, not only within Jalisco itself, but also within Mexico as a whole, where in the past such growth has tended to be restricted only to major industrial cities such as Mexico City and Monterrey. Indeed within Jalisco, Puerto Vallarta has been the only municipal centre to attract migrants on a scale approaching that of the state capital, Guadalajara, the second-largest city in the Mexican Republic (Alba, 1983; De la Peña, 1986).

Perhaps the most striking aspect of Puerto Vallarta's development is that its growth as a tourist centre has been largely unaided by the national government tourist agency, FONATUR, an organisation which has played a major role in the financing of other important Pacific resorts such as Ixtapa-Zihuatanejo, Puerto Escondido and more recently Santa Cruz Huatalco; and other centres such as San Jose del Cabo/Loreta in Baja California, and Cancún in the Yucatan peninsula (Stansfield,1980). One possible explanation for this is that the development of Puerto Vallarta was already underway by the time FONATUR was created in 1974, and because FONATUR's policy was to take the benefits of tourism to the poorest regions it thus favoured new rather than old-established resorts (Stansfield, 1980). Puerto Vallarta had also missed out on direct investment from various forerunners of the cabinet-level agency which emerged from the mid-1960s onwards such as FOGATUR and CONATUR (Jud, 1974; Stansfield, 1980). However, it could be suggested that this lack of formal intervention has not in fact jeopardised so much as enhanced the attractiveness of the town in national and international circles. Its image is that of a sedate resort with a certain old world charm, as opposed to the modern and rather functional appearance of planned tourist developments. This is also reflected in the somewhat exclusive nature of hotels; two-thirds of the establishments offering accommodation to tourists are in the three- to five-star range, many of which are modelled on a picturesque colonial style of architecture (SEDUE/Gobierno del Estado, 1985).

Despite lack of federal funding Puerto Vallarta plays a crucial role in national tourism, which is currently the third largest generator of foreign exchange in the Mexican economy after oil and in-bond manufacturing (Cornelius, 1986; Rivas, 1985). Until the oil boom of the late 1970s, tourism was actually the country's most important source of export income (Hirschman, 1986; Stansfield, 1980), but by 1980 receipts were only covering one-third of the national trade imbalance (Cockcroft, 1983a). Notwithstanding its eclipse by other sectors of the economy, in absolute terms tourism still brings in significant amounts of export earnings, and Puerto Vallarta is undoubtedly one of the major centres, with annual visitors to the resort growing over 50 times in the period 1966–80, and quadrupling again in the first half of the 1980s (SEDUE/Gobierno del Estado, 1985). This recent dynamism is in fact probably attributable in large part to the crisis, with earnings from tourism displaying a more or less inverse relationship with overall economic decline. In times of national recession, activities heavily dependent on foreign exchange such as tourism and in-bond manufacturing usually benefit from deterioration of the currency (Harris, 1986). In the words of Jud (1974: 23) the demand for tourist services in Mexico is 'highly income- and price-elastic'; the cheaper the country is for those with foreign exchange, the more attractive it is to international tourists.

In 1985, an estimated total of 1,600,145 people visited Puerto Vallarta, staying on average for a two-week period (Fideicomiso Puerto Vallarta, 1985). Thus at any one time, the town's resident population increases by about one-third of its normal size creating a high demand for services. Numbers of non-residents are likely to be greatest during the 'high season' which lasts from November to April, and is dominated by foreign tourists, primarily from the United States and Canada. During the 1970s and 1980s over 80% of all revenue derived from tourism as a whole in Mexico has come from the US market (Lea, 1988; Stansfield, 1980). However, national tourism, which is estimated to constitute 47% of the total number of visitors (SEDUE/Gobierno del Estado, 1985) tends to take up the slack of business in the so-called 'low season' over the hot and rainy summer months.

Most foreign tourists arrive by air via direct flights from places such as Houston, Vancouver, Los Angeles and Dallas, with the building of the airport in 1970 making a significant contribution to Puerto Vallarta's 'take-off' as an international tourist resort (SEDUE/Gobierno del Estado, 1985). An increasing number of Mexican tourists are also beginning to fly to Puerto Vallarta via internal flights not only from Mexico City, but also from secondary centres such as León, Monterrey and Guadalajara. Several package deals have become available in recent years in order to encourage use of Mexican airlines. However, because air travel is still very expensive for the average Mexican visitor, most national tourists still come by road. This is rather problematic since there is only a single-lane carriageway linking Puerto Vallarta with Guadalajara, the nearest large city. The road winds through the extreme western section of the Sierra Madre, taking a detour into the southern part of the state of Nayarit, and while Puerto Vallarta is only 340 kilometres from Guadalajara, the journey takes up to seven hours by bus and five by car. Plans for a motorway have been under discussion for some years now and if realised will undoubtedly increase the volume of national tourist traffic.

Employment structure

Puerto Vallarta's character as a major tourist centre is clearly reflected in a marked dominance of tertiary employment in hotels, restaurants, entertainment establishments and commercial outlets. The tertiary sector has been growing steadily over the last decade and a half, employing 53% of the workforce in 1970 and a record 73% of the economically active population by 1980 (Fideicomiso Puerto Vallarta, 1985). Growth in the service sector has inevitably been accompanied by relative decline in both agriculture and industry over the same period; agriculture's share of the total labour force fell from 25% in 1970 to 11% in 1980, and industry from 22% to 16% (Fideicomiso Puerto Vallarta, 1985). Employment figures for 1984 indicate that while agriculture continues on its relative decline, industry is beginning to show signs of resurgence (Fideicomiso Puerto Vallarta, 1985). The latter is largely linked to the growth of the tourist trade, with most plants in the area concerned with the processing and packing of food products geared to local consumption, such as beans, maize, tomatoes, water melons and dairy produce (SEDUE/Gobierno del Estado, 1985; Fideicomiso Puerto Vallarta, 1985). However despite recent upward trends in industrial employment, by the year 2000 it is estimated that 76.9% of the projected labour force will be involved in tertiary activities (SEDUE/Gobierno del Estado, 1985).

What does the marked predominance of the tertiary sector imply for the gender composition of the workforce? Official estimates suggest that men constitute 67.8% of the total, and women, 32.2% (SEDUE/Gobierno del Estado, 1985). Women's employment is thus very high compared with other Mexican cities, including the ones in the present study, suggesting that tourism generates significant demand for female labour (Kennedy, Russin and Amalfi, 1978; SEDUE/Gobierno del Estado, 1985), and bearing out results of other studies of Latin America which show women to be disproportionately represented in tertiary activities (Arizpe, 1977; LACWE, 1980; Pedredo and Rendón, 1982). Women tend to enter service occupations on account of their acquired gender character-istics, with several jobs utilising skills associated with their domestic roles of caring, providing food and drink, cleaning and so on (Babb, 1986; Jelin, 1977; Safa, 1980). In many respects women are seen to be 'naturally' or 'traditionally' predisposed to a wide range of tertiary activities, and in Puerto Vallarta, as pointed out in the next chapter, there are often strong links between employer assumptions about women's characteristics, the jobs into which they are placed, and the reproductive responsibilities assigned to them through the sexual division of labour. However, these high figures of female labour force participation may also reflect certain basic demographic factors concerning the balance of labour demand and supply in the city-wide economy.

Tourism is a labour-intensive industry and as such probably has far greater capacity to provide employment for both men and women than other forms of enterprise such as large-scale manufacturing, albeit if many occupations are at the lower end of the skill and productivity spectrum (see McKee, 1988). Not only does tourism absorb large numbers of workers, but in areas where it is the dominant sector of the economy, significant numbers of the temporarily resident population purchase local goods and services, but do not form part of the labour force, hence resulting in higher than average ratios of consumers to producers. Moreover, on the basis of figures produced by the Mexican Tourism Ministry, David Stansfield (1980) points out that jobs in this sector are up to two-thirds cheaper to create than in other industries. It is not perhaps surprising then that in the 1980 census a total of 36.4% of the the population over twelve years in Puerto Vallarta were recorded as economically active compared with only 31% in Querétaro and 33.6% in León. While the buoyancy of Puerto Vallarta's economy has led to rapid population growth in the last two decades, demand for labour can often exceed available supply. During the high season in particular, certain enterprises face labour

Figure 2.1 Beach trader, Puerto Vallarta

shortages (a fairly unique phenomenon in Mexican cities), and in this respect it could be argued that women's high rates of economic activity reflect a situation in which they are filling gaps that might otherwise be filled by men. For example, many restaurant managers in Puerto Vallarta prefer an all-male staff, but women are employed as dishwashers and cooks when men are unobtainable.

On a related note, women's participation in the city-wide economy may also reflect differential sex-selectivity in long- and short-term migration to the area. Women generally move to Puerto Vallarta as permanent residents, whereas a number of men divide their time between the city and the surrounding countryside. Rural impoverishment in Jalisco state has long generated a considerable amount of seasonal out-migration, not only to cities and towns in other parts of the country, but also to the United States (Alba, 1983; De la Peña, 1986; Escobar, González and Roberts, 1987). Thus it is not uncommon for men to live and work alongside their families in Puerto Vallarta during the high season, but to return to rural areas in leaner months to work their own plots, to help on relatives' farms, or to hire themselves out as day labourers on large land-holdings. The relative permanence of women in the city may therefore be regarded favourably by those employers, particularly in the 'formal sector,' who need a skeleton workforce all year round.[7]

Another aspect of Puerto Vallarta's economy which deserves mention is the scope for informal and self-generated activities to develop in a situation where there is high demand for a wide range of commercial and personal services,

Figure 2.2 Kerbside refreshment stall, Puerto Vallarta

underlining the point made by Lea (1988: 46) that in less-developed countries tourism is vitally important in terms of both direct and indirect job creation. McKee (1988: 423) for example has stressed the importance of 'support-businesses' to larger tourist operations. This is also the case in other parts of the world: Pahl's (1984: 55) work in the Isle of Sheppey, Kent, shows that casual employment tends to flourish in holiday areas where people from outside have money to spend on leisure and entertainment. In Puerto Vallarta, many of the poor develop income-generating activities which in themselves do not enter the formal accounting of local labour statistics. Such activities include making clothes or handicrafts for souvenir shops and/or direct sale to tourists, refreshment-selling from barrows or makeshift street stalls, running errands for people on the beach (particularly among children), and taking in tourists' laundry from hotels and holiday apartments (see Figures 2.1 and 2.2).

Beyond this, it should also be emphasised how the large number of people in work related to the tourist trade tends to create a second tier of 'informal' entrepreneurial activity in the sense that secondary business may also be established to cater specifically for the town's workers. This is especially relevant for women who might not engage directly in tourism themselves, but perceive an opportunity to make money by providing a service for other families where wives and daughters are out of the home much of the time. This may include charging a fee to look after other people's children, taking in a neighbour's laundry, hiring themselves out for part-time cleaning, selling *tacos, tamales* and other types of staple prepared foodstuff from their front porch or kitchen and so on. Thus where the 'formal', large-scale sector within the urban economy is labour-intensive itself, as is the case with tourism, opportunities for income generation appear to be multiplied at a number of points further down the employment hierarchy. The kinds of service activities geared to provisioning workers involved in tourism directly are unlikely to be recorded in official figures, but are vitally important for those on low incomes.

Socio-economic implications of Puerto Vallarta's development

Large-scale generation of service employment and the concomitant flood of in-migration has resulted in extreme pressure on Puerto Vallarta's housing, education and health services, which even before the tourist boom had limited capacity (SEDUE/Gobierno del Estado, 1985). Despite the city's large 'formal sector' of employment, in 1980 32.8% of the population earned less than the minimum wage (SEDUE/Gobierno del Estado, 1985), although tipping in hotels and restaurants helps to counteract low basic wages. Poverty combined with high demographic growth rates is reflected in widespread deficiencies in shelter and infrastructure, with around one-third of the population living in neighbourhoods lacking sewerage, piped water and other basic services. In 1970 for example, only 47.6% of Puerto Vallarta's inhabitants had drainage in their homes, and 73.8%, electricity (SEDUE/Gobierno del Estado, 1985). Insanitary living conditions constitute a major health risk and are mirrored in locally prevalent causes of mortality: around 30% of deaths each year in Puerto Vallarta are from preventable parasitic intestinal infections commonly associated with unhygienic environments (SEDUE/Gobierno del Estado, 1985).

Most of Puerto Vallarta's low-income population are located in about twelve irregular settlements on the outskirts of the city, with populations ranging from 500 to nearly 4,000 inhabitants (see Figure 2.3). These settlements nestle into the hills which run parallel to the coastline behind the town. One other area of low-income settlement is El Pitillal, a kind of dormitory town to the north east of the city, which now forms part of the built-up area (see Figure 2.3). About one-third of irregular settlements began forming in the mid to late 1960s, settling initially in the lower reaches of the Cuale River in the older part of town. As land became scarce the settlements nudged back into the hills. Hillside settlement involved a major work of colonisation, including the clearance of dense palm forest and the levelling of steep terrain.

Prior to the 1970s, most of this low-income residential development, as well as other types of construction, was built on *ejidal* land (communal farmland) sold off by members of agricultural communities whose tenure was limited to usufruct.

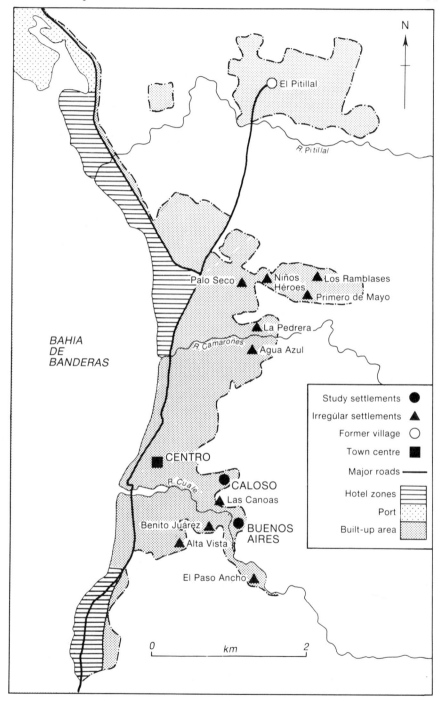

Figure 2.3 Puerto Vallarta: major areas of low-income housing and location of study settlements

Commercial transactions of *ejidal* land were not only illegal, resulting in a large number of people lacking authorised title, but also produced a rather chaotic pattern of settlement. In addition the poor came to occupy potentially valuable sites. In 1970 a trust under the name of the 'Fideicomiso Traslativo de Dominio' was set up by the federal government as a means of organising and regularising the land problem and coordinating development in the Bahía region as a whole (covering the coasts of both Jalisco and Nayarit.) This body achieved little other than mapping out the area now covered by the city and designating tracts of land where title was contentious or non-existent. In 1973, recognising the impossibility of achieving any major action from a single body charged with such a large and complicated brief, a presidential decree split the organisation into two separate entities: (1) the Fideicomiso Bahía de Banderas centred in Nayarit: and (2) the Fideicomiso Puerto Vallarta. The new streamlined Fideicomiso Puerto Vallarta was given specific powers to provide services, to draft approriate criteria for awarding land tenure and to keep some land in reserve for future development or conservation for scenic reasons. However, the Fideicomiso has not been particularly effective in achieving these aims. Soon after its inception it caused widespread resentment among the inhabitants of the long-established *colonias populares*. Residents were unhappy about the agency for two main reasons: first, they objected to paying the Fideicomiso for land title, since this appeared to constitute an unwarranted second payment on their plot. As far as the residents were concerned, they had already paid in full to the original 'owner'. Second, their reluctance to pay was compounded by a largely justified lack of confidence in the organisation actually providing them with the services it was supposed to deliver following regularisation. Most people who paid for official land title in the mid to late 1970s are still without basic services, and some do not even have *escrituras* (legal title deeds). Furthermore, in the absence of alternative housing options and given the high price of plots in the conventional land market, at least seven settlements have been forced to occupy tracts within the Fideicomiso's reserve between 1973 and the present (SEDUE/Gobierno del Estado, 1985). Although these recently established communities have been reluctantly tolerated in the interim absence of alternative forms of low-income housing or suitable land sites, the Fideicomiso is unable to guarantee tenure and many of these people fear they may get moved on at a later date.

However, comparatively speaking Puerto Vallarta has a high proportion of owner-occupiers or quasi owner-occupiers compared with other Mexican cities. The 1980 Census records 71.3% of the population as residing in their own homes. With the exception of Mérida, Culiacán and Chihuahua, most other intermediate cities have smaller proportions than this, even if owners are usually in the majority (see Gilbert and Varley, 1989: 4). The city also enjoys a relatively low residential density with only 5.2. persons per dwelling (SEDUE/Gobierno del Estado, 1985), compared with a national average of 5.5.

León

Growth and development

León de los Aldamas, the major industrial city of Guanajuato state, lies in the fertile valley of the Gómez River about 320 km north-west of Mexico City and has a population of around 1,200,000 inhabitants.[8] (see Figure 1.1). Located in the heart of the Bajío, the most productive farming region in Mexico, it is the seventh largest city in Mexico and the most important centre for national shoe production in the Republic (Estrada, 1980; SECOFI, 1980). León produces around 37% of national shoe output, specialising mainly in childrens' and teenagers' footwear, and high-quality boots and shoes for men, most of which is destined for the domestic market (De la Peña, 1986). The other main areas of shoe production in Mexico are Mexico City and Guadalajara, the latter specialising in fashion footwear for women (Estrada, 1980).

León was originally founded in 1576 under the name of Villa de León (Gobierno del Estado de Guanajuato/H Ayuntamiento del Municipio, 1981). From the eighteenth century onwards its economy was closely integrated into the agricultural-mining complex of the Bajío. León supplied Guanajuato, the state capital, with grain, animals, saddles, textiles and leather. The town had a nascent shoe industry by the turn of the twentieth century which until the 1930s and 1940s remained largely in the hands of small-scale producers. However, when World War Two created a high demand for shoes, the profile of the Mexican footwear industry began to change from one consisting almost entirely of small enterprises to one characterised by concentration of a significant segment of production in the hands of a few large-scale firms (Arias, 1980). During the war, bulk buyers from North America flocked to León looking for merchandise (Calleja, 1984). This attracted much investment and by the 1950s a small group of large employers emerged in León to lead local development. In this decade shoe production gradually supplanted the textile industry as the most important branch of local manufacturing (ibid.).

In the 1960s there was an unprecedented expansion of footwear firms, both horizontally, in terms of opening up new factories, and vertically in terms of forging linkages with leather tanneries and manufacturers of other related products such as cardboard boxes, wooden moulds and linings (Calleja, 1984). Traditional small family workshops, known locally as '*picas*', did not disappear in the face of this competition but endeavoured to adapt to the market by reducing costs and moving into a kind of small-scale 'mass' production, making greater quantities of shoes out of cheaper materials (ibid.). At the time of this 'boom' in footwear manufacturing, León's growth was at its highest, with much in-migration from rural areas in other parts of Guanajuato state, and from impoverished communities in neighbouring states, such as the highlands of Jalisco (Gobierno del Estado de Guanajuato/H Ayuntamiento del Municipio, 1981; Salazar, 1984). León's population grew at 6% per annum between 1960 and 1970 (Gobierno del Estado de Guanajuato/H Ayuntamiento del Municipio, 1981). However, growth is now slowing down as in-migration has declined, and during the period 1970–80, the average annual growth rate, while still high, had fallen to 3.9% (Salazar, 1984).

The most recent published migration figures available for León are those of the 1980 census which suggest that only 12% of the population were born outside the municipality. However, there is probably a good deal of under-recording here; the proportion of migrants to native-born inhabitants is probably nearer 40 to 50% since the random survey carried out by the author in 1986 in two low-income settlements in León shows that 69.6% of the total number of female household heads or spouses are migrants. This is low compared to the survey data on migration for Puerto Vallarta (where migrants constitute 88% of the total of interviewees), but still indicates that migrants in low-income areas in León are in the majority, at least for women aged around twenty years or more (see also Chapter 4).

Employment structure

Reflecting the historical process of specialisation in shoe production, and its contemporary role in providing footwear for a large segment of the domestic market, León's economy is so heavily dominated by the shoe industry that it has been described as a virtually 'mono-industrial' city (Gobierno del Estado/H Ayuntamiento del Municipio, 1981). During the 1970s, León's shoe and leather industry together absorbed 60% of the increase in industrial output in the city, with the local economy leaning even more towards footwear over that period (Garza, 1980). Calleja (1984) cites an assertion made in 1976 by the Guanajuato Chamber of Footwear (*Cámara Guanajuatense de Calzado*) that the activities of 95% of the economically active population in León over twelve years of age were in some way related to the shoe trade. While this is perhaps an inflated estimate, it indicates the extent to which the principal element of local production extends into other aspects of the city-wide economy such as wholesale and retail commerce, finance and other branches of manufacturing. The commercial importance of footwear in León, for example, is reflected in entire streets of shoe shops, a special precinct for the sale of best-quality local production called the '*Plaza del Zapato*' ('Shoe Plaza'), and the fact that footwear is by far the dominant commodity in all the major permanent and periodic markets in the city. In the case of manufacturing, several branches of local activity are related to shoe production, such as the curing and tanning of leather, buckle-making, the chemical manufacture of thermoplastic sheets for soles, and box-making, which together contribute to the high overall proportion of people employed in the city's industrial sector (Estrada, 1980).

While figures on sectoral employment in the city vary widely amongst other things on account of differing definitions, it is generally estimated that around two-thirds of León's economically active population are involved in industry, and only one-third in commerce and services (Salazar, 1984). In 1979, official statistics indicated that only 4.3% of the labour force were engaged in primary activities, 62.3% in secondary activities (although this figure apparently included commerce along with manufacturing) and 30.4% were involved in the tertiary sector comprising transport, services and government (Gobierno del Estado de Guanajuato/H Ayuntamiento del Municipio, 1981). According to these figures it appears that the secondary sector has been stable in relative terms for some time, since in 1960 it already occupied 59.1% of the labour force. The major changes have thus occurred in the primary and tertiary sectors; agriculture declined from employing 27% in 1960 to less than one-quarter of this amount in 1980, whereas the service sector doubled its share of the labour force over the same period from a proportion of 15.5% in 1960 (Gobierno del Estado de Guanajuato/H Ayuntamiento del Municipio, 1981).

Regardless of the above trends however, the majority of the economically active population in León are involved in manufacturing, and the bulk of these are in footwear, with an estimated 1,270 enterprises in the city exclusively concerned with shoe production (Cámara de la Industria del Calzado del Estado de Guanajuato, 1985). Even then, this is probably a conservative estimate since up to 30% of the total number of businesses consist of small family workshops not generally registered in the census (SECOFI, 1980) (see Figure 2.4). Indeed the tendency towards concentration of industry in larger-production units does not necessarily stop the proliferation of small manufacturing enterprises (De la Peña, 1986). This is particularly true of the leather trade which demands a number of specialised skills. Activities such as shoe production, belt-making, saddle-making and hand-tooling of craftwork are often carried out in labour-intensive family enterprises (Padilla, 1978). Persistence of manual skills within the shoe trade has been argued to arise from the fact that certain aspects of the production process cannot be mechanised (Estrada, 1980). Indeed even within large firms at least 10–20% of the production process is carried out by hand, including the stitching of straps and buckles, cutting, the hand painting of leather and so on. (Calleja, 1984). Sometimes these activities are carried out in the factories themselves; at others they are farmed out to small workshops, which thus perform a dual function of producing either for their own distribution or on contract from large-scale firms.

Aside from benefiting from the artisanal sector's capacity to undertake specialised, manual tasks, Calleja (1984) argues that the expansion of larger manufacturing units is intrinsically related to the existence of the small family workshops in a number of other ways. Large firms offset their own vulnerability by using the 'informal' sector as a means of probing the market, as a source of cheap components such as inner soles and laces, to execute tasks insufficiently profitable to warrant permanent factory installations, and by paying low piece rates for skilled outwork from the *picas* (see also Benería and Roldan, 1987: Chapter 3 for a more general discussion of sub-contracting). Aside from this, small-scale enterprises are an effective instrument of social organisation and absorb much labour, thereby taking pressure off the state to cope with open unemployment (Alba, 1983). They also equip workers with a range of skills which may subsequently be used directly in large manufacturing establishments who thus avoid having to subsidise training and apprenticeship. These ideas find parallels with studies supporting the theory of 'petty commodity production' in urban labour markets, whereby 'informal'

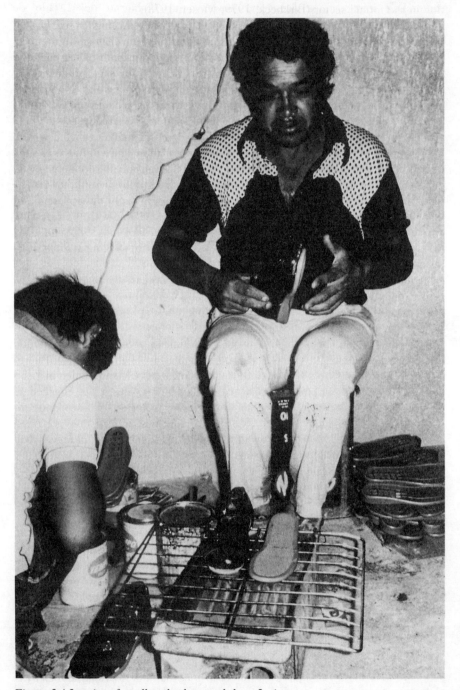

Figure 2.4 Interior of small-scale shoe workshop, León

activities are regarded as highly integrated into the dynamic of capital accumulation in the formal sector (Birkbeck, 1979; Moser, 1978).

Another aspect of small-scale workshops is that they are highly sensitive to national economic trends and often act as an adjustment mechanism in the local labour market (Calleja, 1984). This observation is relevant both to seasonal and cyclical patterns of demand. For example, peak seasons for shoe production in León are spring (March to May) and autumn (late August to November–December) in anticipation of holidays and the start of the school year/Christmas period respectively (ibid.). Cyclical demand patterns alternatively, tend to accompany the contraction and expansion of the domestic market which above all hinges on the purchasing power of the national population, since only 2% of shoe output in Mexico is exported. Frequently *picas* disappear only to re-emerge again at a later date, with heads of household finding interim employment (if they can) as temporary operatives in large factories (ibid.). The permanent disappearance of *picas*, however, is perhaps especially likely at the present time with the recession causing a major contraction of the internal market. In June 1986 one daily newspaper argued that the shoe industry in Leon was only working at 70% of its installed capacity.[9]

In terms of labour force composition in this footwear-dominated economy, census figures indicate that women made up 29.2% and men 70.8% of the total economically-active population in 1980. Women's employment had obviously been growing in the previous decade since in 1970 they only constituted 21% of León's labour force. These figures suggest that female labour force participation in León is lower than in Puerto Vallarta, but again, just as in the case of Puerto Vallarta, there is probably a good deal of under-recording. Many women in León work, often unpaid, as labourers in small family businesses, or are engaged as outworkers on piece-rate payments from large factories. These kinds of occupations are not likely to enter the official statistics; indeed they are often deliberately disguised in order to avoid legal sanctions against lack of registration and/or absence of social security protection.

Within the small-scale sector, women rarely participate in the supervisory aspects of production, nor indeed are heads of family workshops, features which are also characteristic of the leather trade in Guadalajara (Padilla, 1978) and southern Italy (Goddard, 1981). The issue of divisions of labour within the footwear industry will be discussed in more detail in later chapters, but suffice to say that women in León play a critical role in shoe production and distribution, especially at the level of small and medium-scale workshops. However, they are inserted into the local economy in rather different ways to the female workforce in Puerto Vallarta, and generally occupy an even more inferior and 'hidden' position in the labour market.

Socio-economic implications of León's development

Despite the fact that León has a far longer history than Puerto Vallarta, the city is extremely deficient in basic services and housing. Around one-third of dwellings

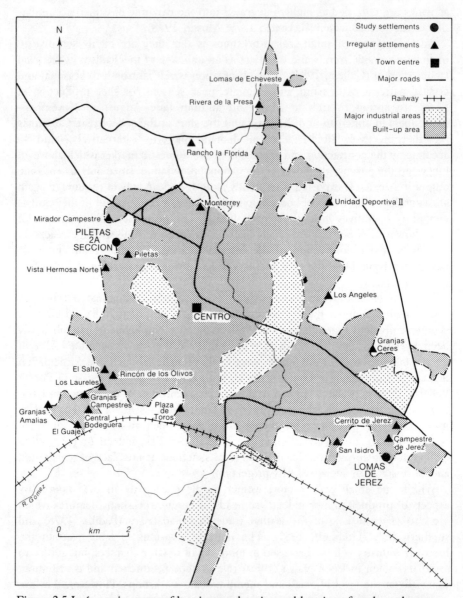

Figure 2.5 León: major areas of low-income housing and location of study settlements

in the city lack drainage, and one-sixth of the population lack access to a piped domestic water supply (Gobierno del Estado de Guanajuato/H Ayuntamiento del Municipio, 1981). As many as 38% of the population in 1979 were forced to rent accommodation. Density per dwelling is far higher than in Puerto Vallarta at 6.7 people per house. In part this may reflect the lack of well-remunerated job opportunities. For example, in 1979, 36.8% of León's population earned sub-minimum wages. Aside from a large rental sub-market, many of the poor occupy land in irregular settlements. There are presently well over twenty irregular settlements in León, most of which are clandestine sub-divisions where land has been sold off illegally for low-income residential development by private owners of agricultural small-holdings (see Figure 2.5). The predominant mode of land acquisition is different to the other cities since there are very few *ejidos* around León.[10] Most settlements began forming about twenty years ago when León underwent its period of greatest expansion, the bulk of which are located in rocky terrain in the north and western parts of the city. However, recent years have seen the appearance of new settlements in unproductive farmland to the south east and south west of the built-up area.

The sub-dividers (*fraccionadores*) of low-income settlements pass privately-held agricultural land into the urban market where general scarcity allows for an exaggerated subdivision of plots and therefore makes good returns despite sale to poor clients. Land is sold without planning permission and does not comply with minimum norms of building, servicing and infrastructure. The purchasers of lots in these illegal subdivisions are not therefore awarded with a legal title deed from the *fraccionador* but merely receive a certificate of proof of purchase (*contrato de compraventa*). In order to obtain legal title, residents either have to persuade the *fraccionador* to intervene on their behalf to the authorities, or put pressure on the relevant bodies themselves to regularise tenure (in this case the State Planning Commission in Guanajuato and the Municipal Urban Development Division). After regularisation, services should theoretically be easier to obtain. Having said that, one striking feature about many of the irregular settlements in León, including those now legalised, is that they remain without streets and pavements after twenty years of existence. This makes them extremely dangerous for vehicles, and even impassable in the rainy season.

Querétaro

Growth and development

Querétaro, capital of the state of the same name, lies on the eastern edge of the Bajío about 200 kilometres north of Mexico City, and is one of the leading industrial centres in the Republic (see Figure 1.1). Founded in 1445 by the Otomí Indians, it came into the hands of the Spanish in 1531 and was an important agricultural and mining centre in colonial times (Chant, 1984). However, it was not until the 1960s and 1970s that Querétaro came to be a major focus of economic development within the country.

By 1981, despite being only twenty-ninth in the republic in terms of population, Querétaro ranked fifth nationally in terms of fixed capital investment in industry, following close behind the other leading centres of Mexico City, Monterrey, Guadalajara and Puebla (Nacional Financiera, 1981: 12–15). Querétaro's rapid ascent to the status of one of the leading industrial centres of the republic is largely attributable to its strategic position in the geographical centre of the country, its

Figure 2.6 Industrial zone, Querétaro

good road and rail connections particularly to the north/south and west, its abundant natural resources, and its proximity to Mexico City. With an accessibility that led Selby (1979: 37) to describe it the 'crossroads' of the republic, Querétaro has not suprisingly been one of the major beneficiaries of incentives offered under national industrial decentralisation schemes aimed at inducing firms away from the overcrowded Federal District (Chant, 1984; see also Aguilar-Barajas and Spence, 1988).

Industry in Querétaro is dominated by food processing, chemicals, and the manufacture of industrial machinery and electrical products (CANACINTRA, 1984). Many firms are subsidiaries of foreign companies and include Singer, Gerber, Black and Decker, Kelloggs, Carnation, Clemente Jacques, Tremec, Massey-Ferguson and Fords (Selby, 1979). The first multinational located in Querétaro in 1956 setting a precedent for other factories to move onto the city's large, well-planned, low-cost greenfield sites (Keren, 1982) (see Figure 2.6). Production units in Querétaro are larger than in León, with an average workforce of at least ten more operatives, greater amounts of mechanical infrastructure, and higher rates of capital investment. In 1970 for example, Querétaro had 436 industrial enterprises employing 11,113 people with a total aggregate value of $55,643,000 US; whereas León, despite having a population three times larger, only had 21,077 people employed in 1,385 enterprises representing a total aggregate value of $42,832,000 US (Garza, 1980: 141–2).

Progressive relocation and concentration of large-scale industrial enterprises in

Querétaro has engendered rapid and massive rates of demographic growth. The city's population grew from around 75,000 in 1960, to 140,000 in 1970, to 293,586 in 1980 and to 442,903 in 1985, with an average annual growth rate of 4.1% in the 1970s and 6.1% in the 1980s (Gobierno Constitucional de los Estados Unidos Mexicanos/Gobierno del Estado de Querétaro, 1986)

Most migrants to Querétaro have come from rural areas in other parts of the state, especially from the *sierra* around Jalpan and Peñamiller in the north east, or from rural areas in the neighbouring states of Michoacán and Guanajuato. According to the census, around one-quarter of the population were migrants in 1980, but again this figure appears low compared with the author's survey where 58% of the total number of women heads of household and spouses interviewed in three low-income settlements in 1982–3 were recorded as having been born outside the entity.

However, despite high growth rates over two decades, in the early 1980s industry in Querétaro underwent drastic decline in the face of national economic crisis. Dependence on components from abroad, shortages of foreign currency arising from the nationalisation of the private banks, and reduced markets meant that many factories could not continue operating on a regular basis. The Carnation factory, for example, had to lay off around half its workforce in the latter part of 1982 because production was almost entirely based on imports which the company could not afford (Chant, 1984). By December 1982 industry in Querétaro was working at only 20% of its installed capacity compared with a level of 60% only two months earlier. Between 1982 and 1983, around 25% of the total industrial workforce in Querétaro lost their jobs, mainly in construction (due to state cut-backs on public works programmes) and in the metal-mechanical industry (ibid.).

However, despite this bleak scenario, ten firms sought permission to locate in Querétaro between January and June of 1983 when the crisis was at its height (Chant, 1984). Subsequently, preferential exchange rates for industrial dollars and relaxation of currency controls have helped revive the local economy to a limited extent. However, future industrial growth looks like being a good deal more constrained than it was in the past, especially in the light of catastrophic events of the 1980s such as the earthquake and the precipitous fall in oil prices. In order to reduce the city's future vulnerability to fluctuations in the international terms of trade and to general economic decline, a limited amount of credit has recently been injected into Querétaro via the Programme of Integral Support (PAI), a fund geared towards the encouragement of medium- and small-scale labour-intensive workshops in an attempt to diversify local production and to stem open unemployment (Chant, 1984; Gobierno Constitucional de los Estados Unidos Mexicanos/Gobierno del Estado de Querétaro, 1986). No doubt Querétaro should continue to follow its plan of strengthening local sources of employment if it is to withstand further shocks from the wider economic system.

Employment structure

The rapid transformation of Querétaro's economy over twenty-five years is reflected in the massive decline of the primary sector which fell from employing a

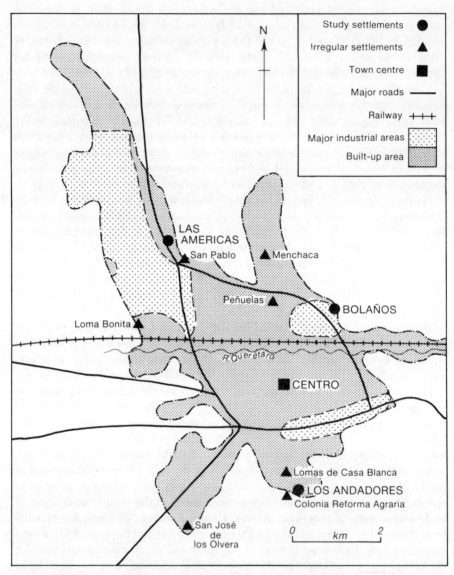

Figure 2.7 Querétaro: major areas of low-income housing and location of study settlements

total of 39.7% of the economically-active population in 1960 to half that amount in 1970, to less than half that again (7.5% of the labour force) in 1980. Industry on the other hand moved from employing 24.5% of the workforce in 1960 to 31.8% in 1970 and to 38.2% in 1980 (Chant, 1984). Querétaro's level of manufacturing employment is very high compared with most cities in the developing world where services are by far the dominant sector (Browning and Roberts, 1980; Hall, 1985). Indeed only one-seventh of the population of developing urban centres are normally estimated to be directly engaged in 'productive activities' (Hackenberg, Murphy and Selby, 1981). Proportions of the economically active population employed in Querétaro's tertiary sector remained relatively constant over the period at around 40% between 1960 and 1980 (Chant, 1984).

Some maintain that industrialisation in Querétaro has created greater job opportunities for women (Meza, 1982; Selby, 1979). According to census data, the proportion of the workforce made up by women rose from 21% in 1970 to 28.3% in 1980. However, on closer examination the figures reveal that less than one-quarter of the female labour force are employed in industry, with most engaged in services and commerce. Numbers of women in manufacturing may well decrease as recession continues given their general tendency to be slotted into the more precarious and casual positions of industrial employment.

Socio-economic implications of Querétaro's development

As in León and Puerto Vallarta, a substantial number of Querétaro's poorer inhabitants have been forced to house themselves in the absence of state-provided alternatives, with an estimated one-third of the popuulation residing in ten irregular settlements around the edges of the city (see Figure 2.7). Two dominant modes of land acquisition have characterised the self-help housing process in Querétaro: illegal *ejidal* transactions and the fraudulent promotion of unauthorised sales by government officials. The Commission for the Regularisation of Land Tenure (CORETT) opened an office in Querétaro in the mid-1970s to settle tenure problems, and only three communities in the city, including one or two which formed as late as the early 1980s, are currently without legal title. However, several settlements still lack basic services, and in 1980, when one-quarter of the total urban population did not have street lighting, almost half were without a domestic water supply (Chant, 1984).

Despite this rather pessimistic scenario, settlement thus far at least has been low-density. The number of inhabitants per hectare in Querétaro is only 51 (SAHOP, 1980), compared with 160 in León a year earlier (Gobierno del Estado de Guanajuato/ H Ayuntamiento del Municipio, 1981) and 120.91 per hectare in Puerto Vallarta in 1983 (Fideicomiso Puerto Vallarta, 1985). Only 30% of the population were renters in 1980, and the overall rate of occupancy was only 5.9 persons per dwelling.

Conclusion

This chapter has attempted to set the scene of the research by describing first, the general trends of Mexican development since the 1940s, and second, by presenting a socio-economic profile of each of the study cities.

By way of conclusion and to lead us onto the next chapter on labour demand, it is important to note that female employment, as per the 'official' statistics in 1980, is highest in Puerto Vallarta (32.2%), which in the light of dominant sources of employment in the city suggests that services and commerce are more conducive to the entry of women into the labour force than industry. Regarding the industrial cities, there is in fact very little difference between rates of female employment in León (29.2%) and Querétaro (28.3%), although the nature of the former's production structure, consisting as it does of large numbers of family workshops and considerable amounts of outworking, is such that there are probably far more women working in León than official statistics would lead us to believe. However, these overall differences may not only be due to the type of employment available in the local economy; at another level it could be suggested that the higher proportion of women employed merely results from a higher relative demand for labour in general, remembering that a total of 36.4% of the population over twelve years is economically active in Puerto Vallarta, compared with 33.6% in León and only 31% in Querétaro. Perhaps the most viable conclusion to draw at this stage is that women's employment is likely to be greatest both where there is a high demand for labour and where tertiary activities predominate. Indeed it is possible that these two features are inextricably interlinked, since services and commerce generally absorb more labour than manufacturing, especially when the latter is of a large-scale, capital-intensive nature. Nevertheless I think there is still a strong case to be made for employment-*type* being a key issue, especially given that clear disparities between rates of female employment in each city are apparent from the results of the employer and household questionnaire surveys which form the basis of the next two chapters. However, thus far, we can see that women's employment ranges from highest in a tertiary urban economy to lowest in a large-scale capital-intensive industrial city, with an intermediate proportion employed where the local economy is characterised by substantial numbers of small-scale manufacturing units. Interestingly, the cities where women's labour force participation is higher are those which are probably best able to withstand the shocks associated with the national economic crisis. As mentioned earlier in the chapter, international tourism is actually likely to grow when the value of national currency is low, hence Puerto Vallarta's relative immunity to the more deleterious effects of the Mexican recession. Further to this, cities like León specialising in the manufacture of a basic consumption good such as footwear, for which demand is reasonably stable, are less vulnerable than urban economies such as Querétaro dominated by the production of more specialised, large-scale and/or luxury capital or consumer goods, especially those that rely heavily on large injections of foreign capital and components.

As far as other indicators are concerned, Puerto Vallarta, as a tourist centre, also appears to have fewer housing and infrastructure problems than the other cities, and to display less un- and under-employment in general. In addition the city is built on an extremely attractive site, with a good deal of tropical vegetation and a healthy climate. However, optimism about encouraging tourism as a widespread and intrinsically viable development alternative should be tempered on a number of counts. Although Stansfield (1980: 229) suggests that besides being an agent of development for lagging regions, tourism is a vital source of foreign exchange, a high generator of employment, and an industry that can draw upon rely upon 'infinitely renewable resources' such as climate, scenery and culture, it is important to remember that the expansion of tourism can itself engender unwelcome changes in the local environment that might ultimately render its original attractions obsolete. Moreover, although in Mexico's case, tourism during the 1960s and 1970s was subject to less fluctuation than other types of export-oriented activity such as manufacturing, it is highly prone to 'fad and fashion' (Jud, 1974: 34), and thus potentially equally vulnerable to the vagaries of the world economy as other sources of export-earnings (see, for example, McKee, 1988). The critical point here is that none of the cities in the present study is ultimately immune to national, or indeed international, crisis. Having said that, in the current economic climate it appears that for the local labour force and for women in particular, a labour-intensive service economy such as that of Puerto Vallarta holds most benefits if one accepts the premise that it is desirable for women to have an opportunity to work if they wish and/or need to do so. In the next chapter we explore the validity of these generalisations by examining more specific patterns of gender recruitment in a range of firms in the different urban contexts.

Notes

1   In their overview of political change and alternative futures for Mexican politics, Cornelius, Gentleman and Smith (1989: 1–2) point out that until recently:

there were no big unsettled debates about the Mexican system. It was one of the quintessential 'living museums' of Latin American politics – a system whose principal actors and rules of the game were well known to all, and eminently predictable ... [but] ... since the elections of July 6 1988, many of the supposedly axiomatic, unshakeable truths about the Mexican system have been demolished or seriously shaken.

See also Garrido (1989) and Knight (1989) for discussions of potential political futures for Mexico.

2   The PAN candidate for the presidency in July 1988, Manuel Clouthier, received just over 17% of the total vote (Philip, 1989: 82).

3   Municipal and state elections occur every three and six years repectively and are staggered at various mid-term intervals during the presidential *sexenio*.

4   It is estimated that the earthquake of 1985 cost Mexico, in material terms, around 2.7% of Gross Domestic Product – more or less equivalent to the loss of one year's growth for the country (Duran, 1988: 99).

5   See Gilbert (1989a) for an up-to-date overview of low-income housing in urban Mexico.

6   Richard Burton co-starred in the film with Ava Gardner and was visited on location in Puerto Vallarta by Elizabeth Taylor. This brought certain air of mystique and notoriety to the town, enhancing its appeal to North American tourists (*Nuevo Día*, 17 March 1986, p. 1).

7   The interview survey in Puerto Vallarta was carried out between February and April 1986 which covered the peak tourist period. Thus figures for the presence of men in households are possibly higher than they would have been if the survey had been carried out during the summer months.

8   Estimate on population of León in 1986 from the Dirección de Desarrollo Urbano, Presidencia Municipal de León, Guanajuato. (The most up-to-date published plan available at the time was that of 1981.)

9   *El Heraldo de León* 16 June 1986, p. 1.

10   Information from Dirección de Desarrollo Urbano, Presidencia Municipal de León.

3

Gender and local labour demand

Introduction

Having sketched a general profile of the economies of Puerto Vallarta, León and Querétaro in the previous chapter, the present one concentrates on a more specific analysis of male and female labour demand in each city. Labour demand is evaluated on the basis of two main factors; (1) current composition of the workforce in locally-preponderant sectors of the respective urban economies; and (2) attitudes and policies towards gender of key recruiting personnel therein. Data is drawn from a sample survey of employers in the major types of industrial, commercial or service establishment in each city (see Appendix 2). While Harris and Morris (1986: 93) point out that personnel recruitment is rarely the direct result of 'formal rational and public procedures on the part of either worker or employer', assumptions and attitudes of key decision-makers at managerial and/or supervisory levels undoubtedly contribute to determining whether or not women are employed in particular enterprises and why they are inserted into specific occupations within them (see also Benería and Roldan, 1987: 50–53). Examining the attitudes of a variety of employers in different firms and their rationalisations for current patterns of gender composition is important not only in examining how and why female labour demand varies in different types of employment (why *are* women usually found in services rather than industry for example?), but also from the point of view of interrogating prevailing conceptualisations of gender. To what degree is gender-typing and/or discrimination generalised across a broad cross-section of employers and how might this contribute in broader terms to the entrenchment of patriarchal structures in local labour markets? In addition to the attempt to answer these general questions, the chapter also makes extensive use of detailed case study material to illustrate the range of behaviour and responses arising from different scales of enterprise, different types of economic activity and gender differences among recruiting personnel.

In Puerto Vallarta, a total of twenty-one employers related in some way to the

Table 3.1a: Firms included in Employer Survey, Puerto Vallarta, showing total numbers employed, percentage of women in the workforce and sex of personnel manager

Type of firm	Total number of employees	Percentage of women employed (absolute nos in brackets)		Sex of personnel manager or equivalent
Commerce (sub-total)	*68*	*66.2%*	*(45)*	
Jewellery store	4	0%	(0)	Male
Jewellery store	4	50%	(2)	Male
Tourist shop	3	66.6%	(2)	Female
Tourist shop	8	75%	(6)	Female
Department store	28	75%	(21)	Male
Supermarket	21	66.6%	(14)	Male
Hotels (sub-total)	*709*	*38.5%*	*(273)*	
1-star hotel	11	54.5%	(6)	Male
2-star hotel	11	54.5%	(6)	Female
2-star hotel	4	75%	(3)	Female
3-star hotel	65	46.2%	(30)	Male
4-star hotel	138	55%	(76)	Male
Gran turismo[a]	480	31.7%	(152)	Female
Restaurants (sub-total)	*220*	*25%*	*(55)*	
Snack-bar[b]	4	75%	(3)	Female
Snack-bar	5	60%	(3)	Male
Fast-food restaurant	8	62.5%	(5)	Male
Small family restaurant	6	83.3%	(5)	Male
Small restaurant	5	80%	(4)	Female
Medium-sized restaurant	8	12.5%	(1)	Male
Medium-sized restaurant	24	8.3%	(2)	Male
Large exclusive restaurant	68	36.8%	(25)	Female
Large exclusive restaurant	92	7.6%	(7)	Male
Total	*997*	*37.4%*	*(373)*	

Notes
[a] Gran turismo is the term given to hotels which are classified as luxury establishments by international standards. Gran turismo is therefore equivalent to 5-star status or over.
[b] The term 'snack-bar' is used as a catch-all for establishments which sell fresh fruit juices (*jugos*) and light snacks such as sandwiches, hamburgers and cheesecake (*lonches*). In Mexico they are known as *jugerías* or *loncherías* depending on their primary function.

Source: Employer Survey, Puerto Vallarta, 1986.

tourist trade were selected for interview, notably hotels, restaurants and commercial enterprises (see Table 3.1a).[1] In León, interviews were held in fourteen firms related to the footwear industry including shoe manufacturers, sole-makers and cardboard-box makers (see Table 3.1b). In Querétaro, a sample of fourteen factories were selected from the most important branches of local

Table 3.1b: Firms included in Employer Survey, León, showing total numbers employed, percentage of women in the workforce and sex of personnel manager

Type of firm	Total number of employees	Percentage of women employed (absolute nos in brackets)		Sex of personnel manager or equivalent
Shoe manufacturers (sub-total)	1,256	31.2%	(393)	
Pica[a]	3	0%	(0)	Male
Pica	5	20%	(1)	Male
Pica	9	22.2%	(2)	Male
Medium-scale	32	15.6%	(5)	Male
Medium-scale	62	32.2%	(20)	Male
Medium-scale	100	50%	(50)	Male
Large-scale	175	30.3%	(53)	Male
Large-scale	210	28.6%	(60)	Female
Large-scale	660	30.5%	(201)	Male
Cardboard-box makers (sub-total)	60	46.6%	(28)	
Small-scale	7	28.6%	(2)	Male
Medium-scale	53	49%	(26)	Male
Sole-manufacturers (sub-total)	95	24.2%	(23)	
Medium-scale leather	17	52.9%	(9)	Male
Medium-scale PVC	78	17.9%	(14)	Female
Rubber-sheet producer (sub-total)	190	8.9%	(17)	
Large-scale	190	8.9%	(17)	Male
Total	1,601	28.7%	(460)	

Note
[a] *Pica* is a term used in León to describe a small-scale shoe manufacturing unit which operates clandestinely and generally employs family labour.

Source: Employer Survey, León, 1986

industrial production: food and drink manufacturers, metal-mechanical concerns, chemical and para-chemical firms, and producers of capital goods (See Table 3.1c.) The Employer Survey consisted primarily of interviews with decision-makers in so-called 'formal' establishments, namely registered businesses whose workforce is normally protected by social security legislation. Although in the following chapter it will become obvious that many people in low-income settlements are engaged in 'informal' activities, analysis of the labour demand characteristics of 'formal' enterprises still provides an idea of the relative ease of access of male and female workers into major sectors of the local economy. In most cases the manager or deputy manager of the personnel department was interviewed; in firms which were small and had no personnel department as such, interviews were held with the owner or general manager.[2]

Table 3.1c. Firms included in Employer Survey, Querétaro, showing total numbers employed, percentage of women in the workforce and sex of personnel manager

Type of firm	Total number of employees	Percentage of women employed (absolute nos in brackets)		Sex of personnel manager or equivalent
Food and drink manufacture (sub-total)	*2,285*	*37.3%*	*(852)*	
Bottling factory (small-scale)	18	11.1%	(2)	Male
Baby foods (large-scale)[a]	621	30%	(186)	Female
Cereals (large-scale)[a]	776	17.3%	(134)	Male
Canned fruit and vegetables (large-scale)[a]	870	61%	(530)	Male
Metal-mechanical (sub-total)	*1,617*	*34.1%*	*(552)*	
Steel products (small-scale)	30	23.3%	(7)	Male
Refrigerators (large-scale)	751	18.3%	(137)	Male
Electrical household goods (large-scale)[a]	836	48.8%	(408)	Female
Capital goods (sub-total)	*1,261*	*8.4%*	*(106)*	
Machine tools (medium-scale)	90	17%	(15)	Female
Agricultural machinery (large-scale)	352	9%	(32)	Male
Sewing machines (large-scale)[a]	653	7.3%	(48)	Male
Turbines (large-scale)	166	6.6%	(11)	Male
Chemical and parachemical (sub-total)	*2,345*	*5.1%*	*(121)*	
Plastic shapes and moulds (small-scale)	5	20%	(1)	Male
Fertilisers (large-scale)	978	9.5%	(93)	Male
Synthetic materials (large-scale)[a]	1,362	2%	(27)	Male
Total	*7,508*	*21.7%*	*(1,631)*	

Note

[a] Denotes multinational enterprise.

Source: Employer Survey, Querétaro, 1986.

Before going on to examine the results of the interviews in detail for each city, it is important to identify the main questions it is hoped the data will help to answer.

Key questions relating to labour demand

First, under what kinds of labour market conditions are women most likely to be employed? Specifically to what extent do numbers and types of jobs available in the different economic contexts influence the relative share of women in the labour force? As suggested in the previous chapter, women are most likely to be taken on in situations where there is a permanent or temporary shortage of labour. Thus in Puerto Vallarta, where the local economy is expanding at a high rate relative to population growth, women may get jobs which in other circumstances are the domain of men. However, to what degree is this simple demographic equation complicated by the nature of the skills and characteristics required for different types of employment, and in turn mediated by employers' assumptions of men's and women's suitability for various kinds of post? Related to this, to what degree are women recruited into traditional 'female' occupations or sectors? A likely hypothesis is that firms which have customarily employed women may have larger than average female workforces. This point is relevant not only to women entering at lower levels of the occupational hierarchy, but also to those at administrative and managerial levels.

The above point leads onto a second question, namely the extent to which firms employing a relatively large proportion of women in higher-status supervisory positions, and especially those with a woman personnel manager, are likely to recruit higher than average numbers of women at other levels of the enterprise. A positive relationship between the two has been observed in the tertiary sector of Ixtapa-Zihuatanejo, another Mexican tourist town, by Kennedy *et al.* (1978), and may well apply not only to Puerto Vallarta, but also to the other two cities.

Third, what is the nature of sexual segregation *within* firms? In accordance with a widely observed *vertical* (hierarchical) division of employment on the basis of gender (see, for example, Anker and Hein, 1986), we might expect to find men occupying better-paid and more 'skilled' jobs than women.[3] To what extent is this also accompanied by a *horizontal* (sectoral/departmental) segregation of the labour force, both by enterprise and within the firms themselves, and what is the rationale behind it in the context of the study cities?

Finally, on the basis of the above three sets of questions, to what degree does women's access to primary branches of formal-sector employment vary both within and between cities? This issue is critical when we come to review the principal determinants of women's labour force participation later in the book.

Having identified the key questions, a resume follows of employment patterns in various firms in each city paying particular attention to the extent and nature of women's work, and the existence and implications of gender-specific recruitment policies. Each city is discussed individually in some detail to provide the reader with an overall impression of local employment structures. Following this an attempt is made to analyse the general findings more systematically in relation to the questions identified above.

Puerto Vallarta

Women in Puerto Vallarta constitute a large segment of the local tourist workforce, and on the whole are considered quite positively by employers. Having said this, they tend not to be employed in high-status, managerial or supervisory positions, unless the owner and/or manager of the firm is female.[4] Moreover, women entering at lower levels of tourist-related employment often stand less chance of internal labour market promotion than men; those who start work in hotels as chambermaids, for example, are unlikely to be able to move vertically or even horizontally within the firm, whereas it is much more common that men entering

Table 3.2: Firms in Employer Survey in Puerto Vallarta showing average frequency of advertising for workers and personnel department's perception of staff turnover

Type of firm	Average frequency of advertising vacancies	Personnel department's perception of staff turnover
Commerce		
Jewellery store	every 6 months	average
Jewellery store	every 2–3 months	high
Tourist shop	once a year	low
Tourist shop	once a month	high
Department store	every 4 months	average
Supermarket	every 6 months	average
Hotels		
1-star hotel	once a year	average
2-star hotel	every 2 years	low
2-star hotel	every 4 years	average
3-star hotel	every 2 weeks	high
4-star hotel	every 3 days	high
Gran turismo	permanent advertisement	high
Restaurants		
Snack-bar	every week	high
Snack-bar	once a month	high
Fast-food restaurant	–	–[a]
Small family restaurant	never	low[b]
Small restaurant	once a month	high
Medium-sized restaurant	every 4 months	high
Medium-sized restaurant	once a month	high
Large exclusive restaurant	once a year	average
Large exclusive restaurant	every 2 months	high

Notes

[a] This firm had only been open for one month and the owner-manager felt it was impossible to make a meaningful statement about the rate of staff turnover.

[b] Being a family firm which does not employ outside workers, vacancies are never advertised. It should also be noted that the family labour force is highly stable.

Source: Employer Survey, Puerto Vallarta, 1986.

as general cleaners or kitchen hands end up as head waiters or even bar managers (see below).

Of the total workforce in the firms sampled in Puerto Vallarta, 37.4% were women, a figure which compares favourably with the proportions in León (28.7%) and Querétaro (21.7%). (See Tables 3.1a – 3.1b.) Within tourist-related enterprises women are most commonly employed in commerce (66.2%), followed by hotels (38.5%) and finally snack bars and restaurants (25%). (See Table 3.1a.)

Commerce

Most commercial establishments in Puerto Vallarta are small, privately owned and independent, although some have another branch in the same town or other tourist resorts.

Several shops operate a system of split shifts, from 9am to 2pm, and 4pm to 8pm, six days a week. Most shop assistants earn the legal minimum salary which at the time the employer survey in Puerto Vallarta was carried out in April 1986, was 9,380 pesos a week (about $19 US). The majority are protected by social security which guarantees benefits such as access to state health care, paid holidays and so on. Despite the fact that wages in commerce are generally low, those working in specialist tourist handicraft shops may earn up to one-third more out of commission (5–10% of retail prices) on weekly sales. However, additional earnings vary greatly over the course of the year. They are highest during the period of international tourism over the winter and early spring, and drop considerably during the summer, not only because the numbers of tourists decline, but also because the nationals that form the bulk of low season visitors spend less on tourist goods and souvenirs. Turnover of staff in commercial enterprises is not, however, particularly high compared with turnover in other branches of the tourist trade in Puerto Vallarta, with staff changes occurring only twice a year on average (see Table 3.2).[5]

It is comparatively easy for low-income people to enter shop work since formal educational qualifications are generally deemed less relevant than personal qualities such as honesty and trustworthiness. The value set on personal integrity is reflected in the manner in which new salespeople are recruited – usually via the existing staff or through acquaintances/contacts of the owner/manager (see Table 3.3). However, the continued expansion of international tourism in the resort means that foreign language skills (especially English), and previous sales experience are increasingly becoming prerequisites for such jobs.

Language requirements present more of an obstacle to women entrants than men, since the former are far less likely to have secondary schooling or to have had the opportunity to travel to the United States as migrant workers. Languages are most valued in specialist tourist shops, particularly those selling jewellery and silver-ware.[6] Two silver retailers formed part of the survey and only 2 women appeared among their joint total of 8 employees (25%) (see Table 3.1a). In one of these, the manager was not only unwilling to recruit women, but also felt it was not worthwhile to train them. Here female applicants were consistently turned away in the belief that they had greater difficulty with English, little aptitude for saleswork and were less patient than men. The same manager also felt that men were more likely to be successful in selling jewellery to what was a predominantly female clientele, with flattery and flirtation reckoned to be vital ingredients of good sales strategy for this type of merchandise. However, it is interesting to note that while men were used in jewellery retail, they are rarely employed to sell other 'feminine products' such as clothing or cosmetics, in Puerto Vallarta or elsewhere.

In the other jewellery shop in the sample, 2 women were employed alongside 2

Table 3.3:Firms in Employer Survey in Puerto Vallarta showing main modes of advertising staff vacancies at worker level

Type of firm	Main mode of advertising					
	Through present staff/ personal contacts	In the window/ firm itself	Newspaper	Radio	Trade union[a]	Rarely has to advertise[b]
Commerce						
Jewellery store	X					X
Jewellery store						X
Tourist shop	X					X
Tourist shop	X					
Department store		X				
Supermarket	X	X	X			
Hotels						
1-star hotel	X					
2-star hotel	X					X
2-star hotel		X				
3-star hotel	X			X		
4-star hotel		X		X	X	
Gran turismo	X		X			
Restaurants						
Snack-bar		X				
Snack-bar	X	X				
Fast-food restaurant						X
Small family restaurant[c]						
Small restaurant		X				
Medium-sized restaurant						X
Medium-sized restaurant	X					X
Large exclusive restaurant	X				X	
Large exclusive restaurant	X		X			

Notes
[a] The unions to which workers in Puerto Vallarta are generally affiliated are the CTM (Confederation of Mexican Workers) or the CROC (Revolutionary Confederation of Workers and Peasants). Membership of a union requires one to have worked or to be working in 'formal' employment i.e. registered legal employment.
[b] Some firms get several people coming in and asking for work and keep files of applicants which they consult when vacancies arise. Therefore they rarely need to advertise for staff.
[c] Since this firm used family labour only there was no need to advertise.

Source: Employer Survey, Puerto Vallarta, 1986.

men (one being the owner), mainly because women had been found to be more readily disposed to take-on multiple duties in their jobs – a factor which came up in several rationalisations for using female labour. Here the owner declared that women were far more willing to clean and polish the stock in the moments when they were not actually serving customers, whereas male assistants regarded such work as 'beneath them'. However, despite this stated advantage, female applicants were still subject to very stringent (and often blatantly sexist) entrance requirements: women sales assistants had to be well-presented (*'tener buena presentación'*), attractive and young (preferably between 15 and 30 years of age), yet no such stipulation applied to men (see Table 3.4).

In general tourist souvenir shops, which sell a variety of merchandise ranging from confectionery and drinks to Mexican handicrafts and clothing, women tend to make up a significant proportion of the workforce. Here 8 out of a total of 11 workers (72.7%) were women (see Table 3.1a). To gain employment in tourist shops again usually involves knowing someone already in the business, and often having an elementary knowledge of English. Of the two establishments of this type in the survey, an interesting case was presented by the manageress of the larger one, which was part of a chain of resort shops. The woman in question was physically handicapped and had experienced considerable difficulty getting work in the past. The only reason she had obtained her present post was because her brother-in-law belonged to the parent company (see Note 4). The manageress preferred on the whole to have female assistants because they were cooperative and easily disciplined; men, on the other hand were unhappy about taking orders from a woman. The issue of male resistance to female authority is extremely important in recruitment decisions and helps to explain why women managers are more likely to employ greater numbers of women. However, an additional factor in this particular case was that the manageress was a single-parent and keen to help those in similar positions. She knew only too well that the welfare of the children of unmarried or abandoned mothers depended heavily upon women getting access to employment; in addition these women often needed work so badly that they were usually more committed to their jobs. The only problem with exercising positive discrimination for this group was that if and when husbands returned, they would often force their wives to leave work, thereby posing problems in finding replacements.

Moving on to the largest shops in the survey – notably a department store and a supermarket – here women workers were also in the majority (71.4%) (see Table 3.1a). Most employees were protected by social security and were paid slightly above the minimum wage. In the department store, women and men were placed in different departments according to gender-typing of assumed knowledge and characteristics; male staff were employed in men's clothing and furnishing, whereas female staff predominated in women's clothing, drapery, glassware and fancy goods. At the administrative level women were employed as secretaries and clerks, but not as managers or accountants. The personnel manager declared that positions of responsibility would be wasted on women due to their inability to exercise authority, particularly over male workers. In the supermarket, greater numbers of women were employed at intermediate supervisory levels, but again were absent from the upper echelons of the administrative hierarchy.

Table 3.4: Firms in Employer Survey in Puerto Vallarta: preferred age and marital status of male and female workers at time of entry

Type of firm	Age (years)	Women marital status	Age (years)	Men marital status
Commerce				
Jewellery store	– no women workers –		18+	n.i.[a]
Jewellery store	15–30	n.i.	15–50	n.i.
Tourist shop	n.i.	n.i.	n.i.	n.i.
Tourist shop	16–25	single/separated	16–25	n.i.
Department store	18–30	single	18+	married
Supermarket	19–25	single	16–25	married
Hotels				
1-star hotel	n.i.	n.i.	n.i.	n.i.
2-star hotel	n.i.	n.i.	n.i.	n.i.
2-star hotel	n.i.	n.i.	n.i.	n.i.
3-star hotel	18–35	n.i.	n.i.	n.i.
4-star hotel	18–35	n.i.	16–45	n.i.
Gran turismo	15–35	n.i.	15–35	n.i.
Restaurants				
Snack bar	18–40	single	– no men at worker level –	
Snack-bar	16–30	n.i.	16–30	n.i.
Fast-food restaurant	16–32	n.i	16–32	n.i.
Small family restaurant	– family labour –			
Small restaurant	18–30	n.i.	– no men at worker level –	
Medium-sized restaurant	25–60	n.i.	16–60	n.i.
Medium-sized restaurant	18+	n.i.	18+	n.i.
Large exclusive restaurant	20–60	n.i.	20–60	n.i.
Large exclusive restaurant	– no women at worker level –		18+	n.i.

Note

[a] n.i. = not important/no preference.

Source: Employer Survey, Puerto Vallarta, 1986.

In large stores, marital status is a significant factor in recruitment and differs acording to gender. As far as women are concerned, single status is preferred because it is imagined that unmarried or childless women are less prone to absenteesim or resignation as a result of family problems. Men, on the other hand stand a better chance if married; husbands and fathers are thought to have more of an incentive to work than single men because of responsibilities to dependants (see Table 3.4).

Hotels

There are many different types of hotel in Puerto Vallarta, ranging from a number of small, cheap establishments to large exclusive ones belonging to international chains. Entrance requirements for hotel work tend to vary according to the size and nature of the establishment. Generally speaking, the more exclusive the hotel, the likelier it is that people going into un- or semi-skilled jobs as cleaners, chambermaids and waiters need a primary education. However, in most cases, the requirement of an educational certificate is waived if people are introduced personally by someone who already works for the establishment; indeed even the largest enterprises advertise vacancies by word-of-mouth through their existing workers (see Table 3.3). Experience or simply *'ganas de trabajar'* ('a will to work'/ enthusiasm) also constitute adequate entry qualifications for a number of hotel jobs.

Hours of work and type of shift vary considerably, both among hotels and among different departments within the enterprises, although most people work a five-and-a-half day week. Chambermaids generally work a straight shift from 9am to 5pm with an hour's break for lunch; kitchen, restaurant and bar staff also tend to work straight shifts but starting earlier or later than those in the housekeeping department, usually from 7am to 3pm, or 3pm to 11pm respectively; reception and office staff tend to work a split shift from 9am to 1pm and then 4pm to 8pm. Many women prefer a split shift, especially if they live nearby and can get back home to provide the main meal for their husbands and children between 2 and 3pm. However, the disadvantage with this arrangement is that late shifts do not finish until after dark and many husbands object to their wives being out alone at night.

In the high season (November to April), around half the un- or semi-skilled hotel staff such as chambermaids and bell-boys, are recruited on a short-term basis and are known as *'eventuales'*. If they have formal contracts they are entitled to social security and must be paid at least the minimum wage, although many remain unregistered. The rest of the staff are *'de planta'* (permanent or long-term employees). Long-term workers receive not only legal minimum or above-minimum wages but also the full benefits of social security which include maternity leave, paid holidays, a Christmas bonus, access to state health care and rights to double or triple time on public holidays. Nevertheless, turnover among so-called permanent workers tends to be fairly high, especially in the larger hotels (see Table 3.2).

Although men and women are usually segregated into different types of occupation in the hotel trade, (women in housekeeping, men in portering, maintenance and catering and so on), salaries are broadly similar, and in some cases, legal minimum wages for 'female' occupations are even higher than those of men (see Table 3.5).

However, the wages cited in the above table are not an accurate representation of what workers take home at the end of the week; differentials in basic wage rates are partly due to disparities in tipping between jobs. Bell-boys and waiters, for example, are much more visible to clientele and in many of the larger hotels received up to 30,000 pesos a week in tips. Chambermaids, on the other hand, are often the victims of forgetfulness, especially if guests vacate their rooms out of working hours. Most were were lucky to take home 6,000 pesos a week in gratuities.

Another important issue in hotel work concerns differential promotion

Table 3.5: Selected legal minimum weekly wages for hotel staff in Puerto Vallarta, January–June 1986

Occupation	Minimum legal weekly wage (in pesos)	Usual sex of worker
Minimum general wage[a]	9,380	
Bell-boy	9,380	Male
General cleaner	9,380	Male
Groundsman	9,380	Male
Chambermaid	11,851	Female
Laundryworker	12,500	Female
Waiter/ress	9,380	Male
Bar attendant	9,380	Male
Dishwasher	9,380	Male or female
Kitchen assistant	12,000	Male or female
Cook	13,000	Male or female

Note

[a] At the time the survey was carried out in Puerto Vallarta in April and May 1986, there were around 495 pesos to the US dollar. This was equivalent to around 19 US dollars.

Source: Employer Survey, Puerto Vallarta, 1986.

prospects for men and women. A woman entering an hotel as a chambermaid is very restricted in her chances for career advancement; not only is there limited promotion opportunity within housekeeping departments themselves, but horizontal segregation by gender means that there are only remote prospects of moving 'sideways' into other areas of work with more multi-layered structures. The only potential opening after several years of service as a chambermaid is to move into the position of *ama de llaves* (housekeeper). Such supervisory posts are few in number, with generally only one *ama de llaves* in charge of twenty chambermaids in the larger hotels. Men entering as bell-boys, corridor cleaners or dishwashers, on the other hand, can frequently find themselves within a few years as cooks, waiters, head waiters and sometimes even in supervisory or managerial posts in catering or maintenance. In part, male promotion relates to vacancies created by the constant rotation of male staff, but it also has to do with specialisation within the departments which employ them and the fact that men can move more easily between different areas of activity. Therefore, while women stand a good chance of being recruited into hotel work due to the existence of a large 'traditional' female niche in housekeeping, it is important to remember that there is little career structure in this area, and after ten or fifteen years they are likely to still be in the same post.

Women constitute a large percentage of the workforce in smaller establishments (57.6%), although here they tend to be segregated into traditional 'feminine' occupations such as those of laundryworker or chambermaid. In the larger hotels, on the other hand, women are admitted into a greater range of jobs despite the fact that they make up a smaller proportion of the workforce (see Table 31.a). However, there appears to be no consistent policy or rationale for the distribution of men and women in different types of hotel work at different scales of operation. For example, in one small hotel women were not employed as reception clerks because it was felt they would suffer unwanted attentions from clients or present a security risk, whereas in another, female receptionists were preferred because they showed willing to do all manner of tasks and were more patient with guests. Differences in policy might be explained by the clientele different types of hotel are likely to attract. The former establishment was mainly frequented by Mexican tourists, many of whom were young men who tended to harass female staff; the latter, on the other hand, attracted greater numbers of foreign visitors who did not appear take a similar 'interest' in the women workers.

Despite the fact that certain hotel jobs have no clear gender association, the majority do, and substitution of men and women between them is rare. Despite the fact certain personnel managers, especially women, indicated that they would be very willing to consider employing men as chambermaids or kitchen assistants, men never turned up for vacancies. A common reason cited was that Mexican men felt it beneath their dignity to do a 'woman's job'.

The placement of women in 'male' posts however, was somewhat more common, especially where there was a specific rationale for so doing. One reason involved the need to economise; one small hotel, for example, employed a female accountant because she did not demand overtime rates. Another reason for employing women relates to the fact that certain managers felt they were more *reliable* than men, both in terms of general punctuality and commitment to staying some time in their jobs. In the one medium-sized hotel in the sample where rooms were full most of the year, women not only made-up nearly half the labour force (46%) but were also employed as bar attendants. Conventionally, women in Mexico are not employed in jobs dealing with the public, especially bar and restaurant work with its connotations of hostessing and prostitution; female bar attendants are said by many to 'lower the tone' of a place, or give it a 'bad name'. Being a barmaid is also difficult for the women themselves who are frequently subject to lewd comments and propositions from customers. In this particular hotel, however, women had been recruited in order to counteract high turnover resulting from the low-season out-migration of men, and also to reduce the incidence of drunkenness on the job (an almost exclusively male phenomenon). In addition the hotel had a 'family atmosphere' and as a general rule women workers suffered little sexual harassment. Following the success of this strategy, the manager was also thinking of training a number of women as waitresses.

Another reason for employing women in traditionally 'male' occupations stems from highly specific job requirements. In the largest hotel in the sample, where one-third of the workforce is female, women had been taken on as security officers because guests had objected to men entering the ladies' toilets, searching handbags and so on. In the same hotel, a number of women also worked in the bar. A critical factor here was that the personnel manager, herself a woman, believed that with the exception of very heavy work, women were perfectly capable of doing the same jobs as men. As a result she resisted segregation and placed both male and female workers in several of the same departments. The only restriction was that married couples should not work together, mainly because husbands objected to male superiors scolding their wives. The general readiness to employ women in 'male' occupations possibly also derives from the fact that the hotel was always desperate to get staff and indeed had a permanent advertisement of vacancies in the local press (see Tables 3.2 and 3.3).

The marital status of women is not really taken into account in hotel recruitment, unlike that noted for some of the commercial establishments (see Table 3.4). This is possibly because a percentage of hotel workers taken on during the course of the year, by larger establishments in particular, is laid off at the end of the high season. In this way 'natural' turnover does not present a major problem.

Snack-bars and restaurants

Snack-bars and restaurants constituted one branch of the tourist industry where women were least likely to be employed; in the nine establishments which formed part of the survey, women only made-up an average of around one-quarter of the workforce. (See Table 3.1a).

Entrance requirements for catering jobs are generally similar to those required in shops and hotels: willingness to work, work experience, and personal acquaintance with present or former employees are much more highly-valued than formal education. In the larger and more exclusive restaurants, however, waiters and barmen need some knowledge of English. Restaurant and kitchen-staff usually work a six-day week on straight shifts beginning either at 8am or 4pm and finishing at 4pm or 11pm respectively. In the smaller restaurants the workforce is generally long-term, whereas in the larger ones as many as one-third of workers are employed as *eventuales* during the high season. Even then turnover is fairly high for all sizes of restaurant, with the smaller ones suffering most from labour instability (see Table 3.2).

Most long-term workers supplement their basic minimum wage with tips. Theoretically gratuities should be shared equally among restaurant and kitchen workers, but frequently waiters retain a large amount for themselves and in the most exclusive restaurants were taking home up to 50,000 pesos a week, nearly six times the legal general minimum wage for the region.

Women workers were in the majority in both snack-bars in the sample. These were small relatively informal establishments and here the sex of the worker did not appear to be an important issue in recruitment. In both enterprises the age of the workers was very young, usually under twenty years old and there was a high turnover of staff; in one of them the average length of time worked was only one week (see Table 3.2). Both firms were constantly having to find new employees, which they did by advertising in the window or through their regular staff (see Table 3.3) (see Figure 3.1). Labour scarcity was undoubtedly a major reason for lack of concern about whether men or women were employed. Having said this, the eighteen-year-old manager of one of the snack bars declared a preference for

Figure 3.1 Advertisement for job vacancies, Puerto Vallarta

hiring young girls because they tended to attract male customers (see Table 3.4).

Women were also in the majority in a slightly larger fast-food enterprise with both a take-away and an eat-in service. Here wages and conditions were the same for both male and female workers and there was little segregation; indeed women even waited on the tables. As noted previously, attendance at table is usually a male preserve. However, here the manager felt that men and women were equally capable for the work, and was not particularly concerned with the fact that the 'image' of his enterprise might appear somewhat 'downmarket' as a result of employing female staff. He also stressed that a major advantage of hiring women derived from the fact that they not only had more experience of domestic skills useful in the restaurant trade, but also tended to be more willing to help each other out and exchange duties if necessary. For example, when the kitchen was short-staffed his waitresses would help with the cooking and wash dishes. Again this reinforces the point that female workloads may be 'stretched' far more readily than those of men.

Moving on to the restaurants *per se*, the two smallish, cheap restaurants in the sample were basically family concerns serving traditional Mexican dishes (see Table 3.1a). One was run by a man who had had several years of experience as a chef in various hotels throughout Mexico and had decided to set up his own business when he reached his early forties in 1975. This restaurant, named after his home town in central Mexico, was shabbily but gaily decorated and contained about twelve tables covered with plastic cloths. Aside from managing the business, he also handled the ordering of food and drink, did the accounts and waited on table, while his wife and three teenage daughters shared the cooking, washing-up, taking money and cleaning. None of them received a formal wage, but instead, according to the interviewee, were given what money they needed for new clothes, shoes, entertainment and so on. When the family was younger the owner had employed outsiders, but found it too problematic, particularly with respect to the payment of statutory overtime and public holiday rates. The use of family labour was not only more profitable, but also reduced the problem of absenteeism.

The other small restaurant also employed more women than men, although here there were two permanent contracted workers. This restaurant was slightly larger than the previous example and belonged to a married couple who also had another restaurant in León, their home town. The Puerto Vallarta branch was managed mainly by the wife who had given her sister the job of head waitress. Although there were twenty tables in the restaurant, the place was rarely full, and if extra help was needed then the owner-manageress herself or one of the kitchen workers stepped in to assist. Once again, as was found in other firms, female workers appeared quite willing to take on different tasks if required, and their flexibility and cooperative disposition were cited as key factors in their recruitment. The fact that a woman was in charge also contributed to the greater readiness to employ an all-female labour force. The manageress felt not only that a single-sex labour force was more efficient than a mixed one, but also had the attitude that men were less trustworthy than women, were more likely to steal from the till, and had also observed that male workers tended to get drunk either on the job or outside work hours and to arrive late and tired in the morning as a result. Moreover, she had had trouble in the past with men who refused to pay her due respect as manageress or to take orders.

In contrast, positive discrimination for women was non-existent in the two medium-sized restaurants in the survey, with the only apparent explanation being that they both had male managers. Here the average share of female employment was only 12.5%; in one of the restaurants there was only 1 woman worker out of 7 who was employed as a cook; and in the other there were only 2 women out of 24 who worked as cashiers. In the former case, the owner-manager had very rigid ideas about the 'proper place' of women; women belonged behind the scenes in the kitchen and should not be seen in the restaurant or bar area. In the latter, it was argued that restaurant work was heavy and hectic and required strength and speed – qualities seen as belonging to men rather than women. The reason that women were at the cash desk was that this was 'female work' and also the only place in the establishment where they could sit apart and be safe from harrassment by male staff, or indeed 'provoke' the male workers. The manager argued that it was impossible in Mexico for men and women to work together because of the likelihood of sexual and emotional attachments. In his belief that '*el hombre es el fuego, la mujer es la broza*' (loosely translated as 'man is fire and woman is the brushwood'), mixing the sexes was a certain recipe for disaster. This perceived need to desexualise relations in the workplace was a major factor in rationalising and operating policies of gender segregation, and was also cited as important in several other firms, especially in the industrial cities.

In the largest two restaurants, which offered a combination of traditional Mexican food and international cuisine, women made up only 20% of the labour force. In the bigger of these two there were only 7 women out of a total of 92 staff, employed as secretaries and cashiers. In the other one, 25 out of 68 employees were women who in this case worked alongside men in the kitchen, primarily as dishwashers and general assistants. Here the owner and personnel manager were female.

In the former enterprise, one of the most exclusive restaurants in Puerto Vallarta, there were two main reasons cited for women not being employed in the kitchen and restaurant area; the first of these was the common argument that a mixed workforce would lead to sexual relations; the second was that men were thought to improve the 'status' of the restaurant – the widely-travelled personnel manager had observed on his journeys to various parts of the world that the most exclusive restaurants employed male waiters.

In the other large restaurant, although women were by no means in the majority, the juxtaposition of male and female workers was not regarded as problematic. One contributory factor might have been, as in the case of some of the shops in the sample, that many of the male kitchen staff were homosexual and there was not therefore the same risk of sexual relations arising among male and female workers. (Interestingly the potential for homosexual relationships developing between men in all-male working situations was never cited as a problem.) The other key factor is probably the existence of a woman in charge of personnel recruitment. Female managers are far more willing to give women the opportunity to work than their male counterparts, and also much less concerned about the potential consequences of placing men and women together.

Indeed, referring back to Table 3.1a and calculating the mean percentage of women employed in the 8 firms in which there was a female personnel manager, and in the 13 firms where a man was in charge of recruitment, it appears that that in commerce, women workers averaged 72.7% of the workforce in firms with female personnel managers, compared with 64.9% where personnel departments were run by men. Corresponding figures were 41.5% and 16.0% in the restaurant trade, and only in hotels was the proportion of women actually higher, at 52.4%, under male personnel managers than it was under women (32.5%). So with the exception of hotels, where there is a large 'traditional' area of female employment in housekeeping anyway, and significantly, less need for direct communication between management and workers which in many cases appears to be facilitated where they are of the same sex, it seems that in Puerto Vallarta at least, if women are in charge of recruitment, more women at lower levels will be taken on.

It should also be noted that women personnel managers in Puerto Vallarta are far more common than in the other cities: here, eight out of 21 firms (38%) employed a female personnel manager, compared with 3 out of 14 (21.4%) in Querétaro, and only 2 out of 14 (14.3%) in León (see Tables 3.1a–3.1c).

León

The León survey consisted of 9 shoe firms, 2 enterprises specialising in the production of soles, 2 cardboard box firms and 1 factory producing rubber sheeting for sole manufacture (see Table 3.1b). In none of these firms were women in the majority and in virtually all of them women had lower occupational status than men. In part this relates to horizontal segregation by gender; as in Puerto Vallarta there were reasonably large sectors of female employment, but opportunities for upward mobility within them were very limited.

Shoe firms

Three of the shoe factories in the sample were what are known in León as *picas* (small clandestine workshops). Each of these produced an average of 300 pairs of shoes a week, mainly relied on family labour and utilised between 3 and 9 persons in production. All three *picas* were situated in the neighbourhood of Piletas in the north west of the city.[7] A further three of the shoe factories can be described as medium-scale concerns, bearing in mind there was considerable variation within this category. For example, one of the medium-sized firms produced 600 pairs of shoes a week, whereas another produced 3,500. These firms employed between 32 and 100 workers. Finally there were three large-scale factories in the survey, producing between 5,000 and 25,000 pairs of shoes per week and employing between 175 and 660 workers. Table 3.6 provides data on the mean number of pairs produced per worker in each category of enterprise and identifies the top and bottom of the range. Interestingly medium-scale firms tend to have the lowest apparent productivity, but this is because they tend only to make leather shoes, whereas both *picas* and large factories also work with mass-produced synthetic materials which require less labour-intensive handiwork.

Table 3.6: León: Weekly per capita production of footwear according to size of firm

Size of firm	Mean no. of pairs of shoes produced per worker per week	Range of weekly per capita shoe production
Small (*picas*) (n=3)	58.6	33–83
Medium (n=3)	30.3	18–38
Large (n=3)	63.3	31–119

Source: Employer Survey, León, 1986.

Conditions of work and entry requirements for footwear enterprises tend to vary according to size of the firm. In the small-scale *picas*, hours of work are fairly flexible, especially for family labour, although on the whole days begin at around 9 or 10am and finish around 7 at night, with two or three hours break for lunch. The smallest *pica* in the survey worked a 4-day week, the next one up, a 5-day week and the largest one, a 6-day week. Usually the owner of the *pica* markets the shoes as well.

There is no system of fixed wages in the *picas* and minimum salary legislation is not observed since there is no formal registration of either enterprise or workforce. Generally workers are paid by piece rates according to what they produce. Some of the more skilled workers, particularly *zapateros* (fully-trained cobblers), earn between 15,000 and 20,000 pesos a week (an average of 25 US dollars at the time the survey was carried out in August 1986). However, there are huge disparities in rates of pay between these and other workers, especially women and juveniles. For example, 2 out of the 3 *picas* employ a young boy – in one case to put hems on leather uppers, and in the other to provide general assistance; both work 3 to 4 days a week and earn only 2,000 pesos. Both boys were related by kin or friendship ties to the owner. Two out of the 3 *picas* employ women; in two cases these were wives of the owner, and in the other, a family friend. As with the youths, women were in the least skilled branches of production such as packing the shoes or working in *adorno* (cleaning and polishing the finished product). Women are also paid on piece rates but earn only about half that of men because unit rates are so much lower. In one of the *picas* the owner's wife, an *adornadora*, was supposed to receive a weekly wage of 13,000 pesos, but often went unpaid if her husband had not made sufficient profit to cover all his outgoings.

The larger the *pica*, the greater was the division of labour, however regardless of the degree of specialisation, all *pica* owners prefer to recruit fully trained cobblers in order to cover in periods of absence. Hence experience and skill are key entry requirements at this level of production. In the largest *pica* the *cortador* (cutter) and *pespuntador* (stitcher) were both *macheteros* (skilled craftsmen generally employed by large factories who hire out their tools and labour to *picas* on a part-time basis one or two days a week, occasionally doing the work from their own homes).

In all except the largest *pica*, staff turnover was very low, suggesting that a labour force comprised mainly of family members is far less likely to fluctuate than one consisting of contracted workers (see Table 3.7). On the whole the personalised nature of labour relations means that most jobs are filled by contacts of the owner himself or existing staff and are rarely advertised formally (see Table 3.8). Fully-trained female cobblers are rare and this helps to explain why *pica* workforces are predominantly male; women rarely apply for *pica* work and are also unlikely to get it (see Table 3.9).

Table 3.7: Firms in Employer Survey in León showing average frequency of advertising for workers and personnel department's/manager's perception of staff turnover

Type of firm	Average frequency of advertising vacancies	Personnel department's perception of staff turnover
Shoe manufacturers		
Pica	–	low[a]
Pica	never	low
Pica	once a month	high
Medium-scale	every 4 months	average
Medium-scale	every 6 months	low
Medium-scale	once a year	low
Large-scale	every 2 months	average
Large-scale	every week	high
Large-scale	every week	high
Cardboard box-makers		
Small-scale	–	–[b]
Medium-scale	every 10 years	low
Sole manufacturers		
Medium-scale: leather	once a year	average
Medium-scale: PVC	every 2 months	average
Rubber sheet producer		
Large-scale	every 3 months	average

Notes

[a] This enterprise had only been open for three months. While the present workforce appeared stable the owner felt it was impossible to make a meaningful statement about the rate of staff turnover in the longer term. However, so far no one had left and high turnover was unlikely since the workforce was largely comprised of family and friends.

[b] This firm had only been open for a month and it was therefore impossible to say what turnover would be like in the long term.

Source: Employer Survey, León, 1986.

Table 3.8: Firms in Employer Survey in León showing main modes of advertising staff vacancies at worker level

| Type of firm | Through present staff/ personal contacts | In the window/ firm itself | Main modes of advertising | | | | |
			Newspaper	Radio	Trade union	Rarely has to advertise	Other firms
Shoe manufacturers							
Pica	X						
Pica	X						
Pica	X	X					
Medium-scale	X	X	X				
Medium-scale	X		X				
Medium-scale	X	X	X				
Large-scale	X	X	X				X
Large-scale			X				
Large-scale	X	X	X				
Cardboard box-makers							
Small-scale			X				
Medium-scale	X						
Sole manufacturers							
Medium-scale leather	X					X	
Medium-scale: PVC	X					X	
Rubber sheet producer							
Large-scale			X			X	

Source: Employer Survey, León, 1986.

Table 3.9: Women's employment in footwear production in León according to size of firm

Size of firm	Average proportion of women in labour force %	Absolute range for firms in group %
Small (*picas*) (n=3)	17.6	0–28.5
Medium (n=3)	38.1	15–50
Large (n=3)	29.9	28.5–30

Source: Employer Survey, León, 1986.

In contrast to the *picas*, applicants for work in medium-sized factories are not necessarily required to have prior experience except for skilled posts such as those of cutter or stitcher. Un- and semi-skilled workers are trained on the job during which time they are paid the minimum general wage. The apprenticeship period in a medium-scale factory may last from one week to one month depending on the complexity of the task. Thereafter most workers are paid according to what they do. A production quota is tied to the minimum wage which means a certain quantity has to be produced in order to receive even this amount. Since registered employers are legally obliged to pay at least the minimum wage, workers unable to meet stipulated production levels are thrown out. 'A will to work' is generally an adequate pre-requisite for entry into a middle-sized establishment, with one firm making the additional specification that applicants should not have prior involvement in labour conflicts and another requesting a certificate of completed primary education.

The middle-sized firm in this category employed its workers from 9am to 7pm with an hour's break for lunch for five-and-a-half days a week; the other two operated a system of split shifts and were only open five days a week. Interestingly although most of the workers employed in medium-scale factories were long-term, none belonged to unions. Medium-scale factories in León tend to be paternalistic, foster frequent contact between management and workers, and often explicitly forbid union affiliation on the grounds that they cannot afford to have labour conflicts.

Piece rates vary according to the task at hand. Since men predominate in the more skilled areas of stitching, cutting and moulding they earn more than women who generally work as packers and *adornadoras*; average weekly wages were around 25,000 pesos a week in the former jobs and 16–17,000 in the latter.

A youthful workforce is generally preferred in the medium-scale factories, with most applicants older than thirty-five years being turned away. Although the marital status of men is deemed unimportant, among women, single applicants are given preference because it is thought they will be more reliable than those with family responsibilities (see Table 3.10). In the smallest firm in this group women were excluded from all areas of production except for *adorno* (cleaning and polishing), mainly because it was not considered worthwhile to put them in skilled areas of production where they might less easily be replaced in the event of absence or permanent departure due to pregnancy or family problems. However, in the largest firm in this group, the personnel manager was keen to see women entering as many areas as possible, and even replacing men, since he had found the latter to be far more prone to absenteeism as a result of heavy drinking and hangovers. In order to execute this plan some women in the factory were already being trained to use specialised machinery.

This largest firm in the medium-sized group had casual arrangements with between 5 and 10 women *tejedoras* who did outwork for the factory in their own homes. The job of *tejedora* consists of hand-sewing leather uppers (usually of moccasin-style footwear) (see Figure 3.2). This is extremely labour-intensive work and most women sewed 100 pairs a week in return for a sum of 5,000 pesos calculated on a piece-rate basis. The situation of domestic outworkers is generally unfavourable compared with staff based in the plant itself: women who did manual stitching jobs in the factory earned a fixed minimum weekly wage which at the time was 11,725 pesos (about $16.3 US) and are also guaranteed regular employment, whereas *tejedoras* do not know from one week to the next if they will have work. In

Figure 3.2 Women outworkers, León

two out of three medium-scale firms, evidence of formal education was not
required, although it is preferred that workers have basic numerical ability to keep
a check of their own production totals. Absence of requirements for formal
education and the relatively high level of labour-intensive production methods in
medium-sized firms help to account for the fact that in these establishments
women represent a higher share of the labour force than in the other two
categories (see Table 3.9).

It is in the largest shoe factories where male–female differentiation of job status
and wages is most apparent. Here there is an even greater specialisation of labour,
with different departments broken down into numerous sub-sections. Within the
female-dominated *adorno* sector for example, there is a highly intricate division of
labour; some women work as *desebradoras* whose sole responsibility is to remove
stray threads from shoes, some count, some match pairs, some polish, some pack,
and others embellish shoes with special paints, varnishes and dyes (see Figure 3.3).
In the area of *pespunte*, aside from mechanised stitching which is done by men,
several women are also involved as '*preliminares*' doing intricate jobs by hand such
as sewing buckles on straps or making decorative accessories such as patent leather
bows (see Figure 3.4).

Workers in the large firms worked a five-and-a-half day week on straight shifts,
either from 9am to 6pm with 45 minutes for lunch, or from 8.15am to 6pm with an
hour for lunch; those who wished to increase their wages were entitled to stay late
into the night. In two of these large firms workers were unionised, but highly

Figure 3.3 Women *adornadoras*, León

screened before formal acceptance – generally the personnel departments would telephone their previous employers to verify that they had no history of trouble-making, union activity and so on. As in the small- and medium-scale shoe firms, wages are usually paid on a piece-rate basis, with a different unit value being attached to jobs in different departments. In the largest firm *adornadoras* were paid only 2.5 pesos per pair, and generally cleaned, polished or touched up 7,000 pairs of shoes a week for an average wage of 17,000 pesos. Whereas *pespuntadores* (all male in this factory) were paid at a rate of 56 pesos a pair and would only have to machine-stitch 440 pairs of shoes for an average take-home wage of 25,000 pesos. One highly-skilled *pespuntador* in this firm who regularly worked a 16-hour day, earned around 200,000 pesos a week, apparently more than the manager himself.

All these larger firms had a number of outworkers, some who carried out the complete *adorno* process in their home, especially of limited leather lines; some who sewed linings into leather uppers and some who stitched moccasins. As in the medium-scale firms, outworkers earned far less than those in the plant itself.

Gender-segregation in large-scale firms is not only rationalised on the basis of skills and aptitudes but is also tied in with considerations noted earlier in the chapter about the sexual and moral implications of men and women working in close proximity. The personnel manager of the largest firm explained how his fears on this front had been confirmed when he placed a woman in a section of the cutting department with a five-member male staff: she became pregnant after only four months, resigned shortly afterwards and left him in a state of considerable

Figure 3.4 Female strap-cutter, León

Table 3.10: Firms in Employer Survey in León: preferred age and marital status of male and female workers at time of entry

Type of firm	Women		Men	
	Age (years)	Marital status	Age (years)	Marital status
Shoe manufacturers				
Pica	– no women at worker level –		n.i.[a]	n.i.
Pica	– no women recruited outside family –		n.i.	n.i.
Pica	n.i.	n.i.	n.i.	n.i.
Medium-scale	18–35	single	18–35	n.i.
Medium-scale	16–50	n.i.	16–50	n.i.
Medium-scale	15–38	single	15–38	n.i.
Large-scale	16+	single	16+	married
Large-scale	16+	n.i.	16+	n.i.
Large-scale	16–38	single	16–38	n.i.
Cardboard box-makers				
Small-scale	– no women at worker level –		n.i.	n.i.
Medium-scale	18–45	n.i.	18–45	n.i.
Sole manufacturers				
Medium-scale: leather	15–18	single	15–18	n.i.
Medium-scale: PVC	16+	single	16+	married
Rubber sheet producer				
Large-scale	– no women at worker level –		n.i.	n.i.

Note

[a] n.i. = not important/no preference.

Source: Employer Survey, León, 1986.

indignation for having 'wasted' valuable time and training. Quite apart from the fact that this kind of occurrence was often used as cast-iron proof for justifying the continued exclusion of women from key areas of production, one also got a sense that the 'moral laxity' of women, rather than men, was accorded an unduly large (and very likely unwarranted) share of the blame.

In contrast to large 'modern' factories elsewhere in Mexico and Latin America, proof of education was required in only one of these factories. Two also requested prior experience in the shoe trade. Amongst women, young single girls from the age of sixteen years upwards were preferred, particularly if they had been able to gain a certain amount of knowledge and training from previous experience in small-scale family workshops (see Table 3.10). As far as men were concerned, one firm preferred to recruit older, married men because they were thought to be more responsible, reliable and skilled than youths, however another preferred taking on young boys because they were relatively cheap to train – receiving only the minimum wage until they had learned the job properly – and were also less disposed to cause trouble over demands for better conditions or earnings, due to lack of union and work experience.

Footwear-related firms

Sole manufacturers
In one sole-manufacturing firm making leather soles, women made-up 52% of the labour force; here the work was extremely labour-intensive and women were employed on account of their putative dexterity. In the other firm, which was far more mechanised and made soles out of PVC, women employees were concentrated in administration and in only one section of production: quality control. Quality-control workers were paid 13,000 pesos a week, whereas male general operatives (with fewer skills) received 14,500 pesos a week. The personnel manager was unable to account for the differential.

Cardboard-box makers
In one of the firms producing cardboard boxes, women constituted 28.5% of the labour force, and in the other, 49%. In the former, female employees were only found in administration as the production process was highly mechanised and women usually lacked the relevant technical experience for manual jobs. However, in the other more labour-intensive factory which employed 53 workers, women and men worked alongside each other in various departments, albeit with a degree of segregation. Only men were employed in the cutting section because this was particularly heavy work requiring the ability to lift ten massive sheets of cardboard at one time. The same principle applied to loading and despatch work. However in the lighter occupations such as those of *grapadora* (stapler) and *forradora* (liner/coverer), women were in the majority since it was thought they were more dexterous. The owner-manager of this firm had never experienced problems with a mixed workforce, possibly because he anticipated that there might be trouble and always gave new male workers a brief chat about the necessity for respecting their female colleagues when they started.

Rubber-sheet production
In the factory producing rubber sheeting, only 8.9% of the total labour force were women, all of whom were in administration. In part this is because the work was extremely heavy and highly-mechanised, but it is also attributable to the fact that the firm's union, FAT (Frente Auténtico de Trabajadores or Authentic Workers Front) made it their policy not to admit women to the enterprise.

One general point about the data from León is that it seems the sex of the personnel manager was of far less importance than in Puerto Vallarta in influencing levels of female recruitment. Overall there were only two firms with women personnel managers, and in these the average percentage of women workers was 28.1% compared with 29.1% in the case of firms with a male owner or manager. This finding suggests that the sex of the personnel manager in footwear-related enterprises is unlikely to be important, possibly because many jobs in this sector require considerable technical skills and experience and consequently cannot absorb people without previous training. Women are discriminated against as a result of their limited skill endowments, as opposed to their gender *per se*, and as such it is of little consequence whether recruiting personnel are male or female.

Querétaro

In Querétaro a total of fourteen firms of different sizes from the four most important branches of local industry were selected for the survey (see Table 3.1c). In all cases the firms were registered and may be classified as 'formal' enterprises. Among the four branches of industry analysed, women formed a significant part of the labour force in food and drink processing and the metal-mechanical sector, but were largely absent from the capital goods and chemical firms, one major reason being that the former industries tended to be more labour-intensive than the latter.

Food and drink processing

In the smallest food and drink firm, a soft-drink factory employing only 18 workers, 2 women were employed in administration and none in manual work. At one time the firm had employed women operatives, but had had to get rid of them due to conflicts of an emotional and/or sexual nature which developed between male and female staff. This had also been the case with the large multinational cereals factory in the sample, which in 1979 had laid off women, first because of personal attachments forming between staff, and second because male workers resented taking orders from female supervisors. In 1980, the firm began to employ women again, but this time restricting them to 'female-only' departments such as packing where they would not come into frequent contact with men. In the multinational baby foods and tinned fruit and vegetable factories, however, women formed a far greater part of the workforce (see Table 3.1c). Aside from technical staff such as electricians, mechanics and forklift truck operators, most workers were women whose activities in both firms ranged from selecting, cleaning, peeling and preparing the produce, and canning, packing and bottling. Women workers in these factories were paid less than their male counterparts basically because the jobs were non-technical and unskilled. Wage differentials reflect the low status of female-dominated occupations. Most general women workers earned only 11,725 pesos a week in the baby foods factory (the legal minimum wage at the time which was about $14 US) whereas forklift truck operators took home an average of 30,065 pesos a week (about $35 US).

Metal-mechanical manufacture

In the metal-mechanical firms in the survey, again women in the smallest firm constituted a minimal proportion of the workforce, and also appeared in the least-skilled areas of the production process. The owner-manager rationalised this in terms of the fact that small-scale firms are less able to cope with high staff turnover and women were more likely than men to be absent due to family problems,

Table 3.11: Firms in Employer Survey in Querétaro showing average frequency of
advertising for workers and personnel department's perception of staff turnover

Type of firm	Average frequency of advertising vacancies	Personnel department's perception of staff turnover
Food and drink manufacture		
Soft drink factory (small-scale)	every 3 days	high
Baby foods (large-scale)[a]	every 3 months	low
Cereals (large-scale)[a]	every 3 months	average
Canned fruit and vegetables (large-scale)[a]	every 2 weeks	high
Metal-mechanical		
Steel products (small-scale)	every week	high
Refrigerators (large-scale)	once a year	low
Electrical household goods (large-scale)[a]	every 3 months	low
Capital goods		
Machine tools (medium-scale)	once a year	low
Agricultural machinery (large-scale)	once a year	low
Sewing machines (large-scale)[a]	every 2 months	average
Turbines (large-scale)	once a year	low
Chemical and parachemical		
Plastic shapes and moulds (small-scale)	every 2–3 years	low
Fertilisers (large-scale)	once a month	high
Synthetic materials (large-scale)[a]	every 10 months	average

Note
[a] Denotes multinational enterprise

Source: Employer Survey, Querétaro, 1986.

pregnancy and so on (see Table 3.11). In the large-scale refrigerator factory,
although women made up only 18.3% of the total workforce, their distribution in
the production hierarchy was notably different to the usual pattern: not only were
they interspersed with male workers but a disproportionate number received
higher salaries (see Table 3.12).

One of the reasons for the fact that there were more male operatives than
women overall was that some of the work required a good deal of physical strength;
another was that male workers were able to do night shifts which women were
rarely allowed to do by over-protective and/or suspicious husbands and fathers.
However, despite these constraints, the personnel manager observed that women
were very conscientious, tended to be far less troublesome than men, and were
anxious to get ahead. This perhaps helps to explain how proportionally more
women had achieved category A and B status than men.

Table 3.12 Assembly-line workers according to sex and rank in a large-scale refrigerator manufacturing plant in Querétaro

Category of worker	Weekly wage (in pesos)	Women workers	Men workers	Women workers %
Category 'A' (machine operators)	24,360	31% (30)	19% (82)	26.7
Category 'B' (general workers)	21,189	20% (20)	14% (61)	25.9
Category 'C' (helpers)	18,900	29% (28)	67% (290)	8.8
Total		100% (98)	100% (433)	22.6

Source: Employer Survey, Querétaro, 1986.

In the other metal-mechanical firm, a multinational factory producing electrical domestic goods such as irons, microwave ovens and drills, again men and women were not especially segregated, particularly at lower levels of the production process. However, at higher and more specialised levels, women were notably absent with the exception of one female mechanic. One reason for the absence of women in the higher-paid, higher-skilled positions of truck operator, electrician and so on was because applicants needed to have previous experience or technical training and women rarely arrived with these kinds of qualifications. Except in the smallest firm in this branch of the industry, a certificate of completed primary education was a prerequisite for un- or semi-skilled manual work. Modes of advertising vacancies were similar in these branches of industry to others, namely via trade unions or newspapers (see Table 3.13). On the whole young people are preferred but among women the issue of being single does not appear to be quite so important as in León (see Table 3.14).

Capital goods production

In contrast to the above branches of industry, capital goods and chemical firms employ only very few women. In the medium-scale machine tools plant, only ten women, aside from a female cleaner, were employed in production – in this case in high-precision quality-control work. According to the personnel manager, herself a woman, the rest of the production process was too heavy for female workers. Again wages reflected the inequality of male and female occupations. In this factory the cleaner (female) earned only 16,000 pesos a week, whereas the highest-skilled of the machine operators (male) earned 44,835 pesos a week; most of the women in quality control earned towards the bottom of this range, although they still earned well above the minimum wage.

In the large-scale agricultural machinery plant which specialised in tractor production, there were no women operatives at all, (1) because the work was extremely heavy; (2) because it was thought that a mixed labour force would lead to

Table 3.13: Firms in Employer Survey in Querétaro showing main modes of advertising staff vacancies at worker level

Type of firm	Through present staff/ personal contacts	In the window/ firm itself	Newspaper	Radio	Trade union	Rarely has to advertise
Food and drink manufacture						
Soft drink factory (small-scale)			X			
Baby foods (large-scale)[a]	X				X	
Cereals (large-scale)[a]	X		X		X	
Canned fruit and vegetables (large-scale)[a]					X	
Metal–mechanical						
Steel products (small-scale)		X			X	
Refrigerators (large-scale)	X		X			
Electrical household goods (large-scale)[a]			X	X	X	
Capital goods						
Machine tools (medium-scale)			X		X	X
Agricultural machinery (large-scale)	X		X		X	
Sewing machines (large-scale)[a]					X	
Turbines (large-scale)	X		X			
Chemical and parachemical						
Plastic shapes and moulds (small-scale)	X					
Fertilisers (large-scale)			X		X	
Synthetic materials (large-scale)[a]	X				X	

Note
[a] Denotes multinational enterprise.

Source: Employer Survey, Querétaro, 1986.

sexual relations and conflicts between workers; and (3) because women were usually unable to do overtime and at times of peak production the factory stayed open all night. In the multinational sewing-machine factory, the only women at production level were in quality control and spent their entire time testing out sewing machines. They were not recruited into other areas of production for want of requisite technical skills. In the turbine plant, again women were absent from production because the work was heavy and highly mechanised. In addition, this

Table 3.14: Firms in Employer Survey in Querétaro: preferred age and marital status of male and female workers at time of entry

Type of firm	*Women*		*Men*	
	Age (years)	*Marital status*	*Age (years)*	*Marital status*
Food and drink manufacture				
Bottling factory (small-scale)	– no women at worker level –		18–40	n.i.[a]
Baby foods (large-scale)[b]	17–40	n.i.	17–40	n.i.
Cereals (large-scale)[b]	16–40	n.i.	16–40	n.i.
Canned fruit and vegetables (large-scale)[b]	16–30	n.i.	16–30	n.i.
Metal–mechanical				
Steel products (small-scale)	18+	n.i.	18+	married
Refrigerators (large-scale)	16–35	n.i.	n.i.	n.i.
Electrical household goods (large-scale)[b]	18+	n.i.	18+	n.i.
Capital goods				
Machine tools (medium-scale)	18+	single	18+	single
Agricultural machinery (large-scale)	n.i.	n.i.	n.i.	n.i.
Sewing machines (large-scale)[b]	18–25	single	18–25	married
Turbines (large-scale)	– no women at worker level –		n.i.	n.i.
Chemical and parachemical				
Plastic shapes and moulds (small-scale)	– no women at worker level –		n.i.	n.i.
Fertilisers (large-scale)	– no women at worker level –		18–50	n.i.
Synthetic materials (large-scale)[b]	– no women at worker level –		18–45	n.i.

Notes

[a] n.i. = not important/no preference.

[b] Denotes multinational enterprise.

Source: Employer Survey, Querétaro, 1986.

firm had even had to get rid of their woman cleaner because she was subjected to so much sexual harrassment by the male workers.

Chemicals and parachemicals

In chemical firms, the same kinds of principles applied, namely that women lacked the necessary technical skills, were unable to do nightwork, did not have the requisite physical strength, and also in one case because the admission of female workers was against union rules.

As far as the influence of personnel managers in Querétaro is concerned, there appears again (as in Puerto Vallarta), to be a correspondence between the gender composition of the managerial and manual labour force. In the 3 firms in the sample which had a female personnel manager women represented 39.3% of the workforce, compared with an average of only 17.1% in the remaining 11 firms with a male personnel manager. However, since a number of firms did not employ any women at worker level, these aggregate figures do not mean very much; instead the data needs to be broken down by branch of activity. If we do this, then the employment of women in two sectors appears to be substantially higher in firms with women in charge of hiring labour: 48.8% of the workforce in the metal-mechanical industry were female under women personnel managers, compared with 18.4% under men, and the corresponding figures were 17% and 7.2% respectively in capital goods production. However, in food and drink processing, women constituted only 30% of the workforce in the one firm where there was a woman personnel manager, compared with an average of 40% in the firms with a male personnel manager, although it is obvious that this latter figure is brought to a high level by the particularly large number of women in the fruit and vegetable canning factory (see Table 3.1c).

Observations on labour demand in the three study cities

It is obviously difficult to derive general conclusions from the data presented for the three cities, given the wide-ranging extent and nature of women's employment in individual firms. Furthermore, there are too few cases in the sample to be fully representative of formal economic activity as a whole in the respective cities. Nevertheless, an attempt is made below to summarise the data in relation to the questions posed at the beginning of the chapter.

Gender recruitment in different labour market conditions

The first question concerned the types of labour market conditions under which women will be taken on, bearing in mind that this would probably be associated with the relative balance between local labour supply and demand in general, the type of jobs available – particularly the existence of sectors of traditional gendered employment, and the extent to which employers associate the characteristics appropriate for certain kinds of work with assumptions about the qualities and abilities (socialised or otherwise) of male and female workers.

Labour shortages and turnover

Referring to the first part of this question, the higher numbers and proportions of women employed in Puerto Vallarta indicate that women are recruited where there is a high ratio of labour demand relative to labour supply, not only because the tourist industry here is growing extremely rapidly, but also because men tend to leave town in the low season.[8] Small establishments catering for both Mexican and foreign tourists require some continuity in the workforce and in response to greater male turnover arising from seasonal out-migration women are now being taken on in various 'male' jobs within them. The problem of high seasonal male turnover is exacerbated by the fact that once men have gained a little experience in one aspect of the tourist trade they often move on to another job. Not only is there a wider variety of opportunities for men in Puerto Vallarta, but also considerable potential for upward mobility in terms of higher earnings or promotion. Therefore, men are not particularly likely to remain long in the lowest-paid posts. In contrast, women, who have relatively restricted opportunities for career advancement, stay longer in their first jobs; they are thus seen as more attractive by those establishments less able to absorb the costs of a constantly rotating labour force (such as advertising vacancies, training new staff and so on).

Having said this, a slightly greater number of firms in Puerto Vallarta felt that despite periodic out-migration and more frequent job-change among men, their female workforce was still likely to be more unstable as a result of marriage, pregnancy or family problems: seven firms stated women were more likely to leave their jobs, five felt this was more likely to be the case with men, and three firms observed that there was no real difference between the sexes (see Table 3.15a). Interestingly, the general feeling about gender and turnover appeared to be the reverse in León and Querétaro, despite the fact that fears of greater instability among the female workforce represented one of the major justifications for excluding women from key areas of manufacturing in the first place. In León, out of 9 firms in which managers were in a position to make a statement about turnover and employed both men and women at worker level, 6 felt men were more likely to leave, and 3 said there was no difference, i.e. in no single case were women workers cited as the more unstable (see Table 3.15b). In Querétaro, 5 firms suffered from greater turnover of male staff, only 2 from women, and 1 employer stated there was no difference between the sexes (see Table 3.15c). The above findings tend to reinforce Anker and Hein's (1986:24) conclusion that: 'for a number of Third World countries, sex differentials in turnover may not be great and are not a critical variable in explaining employer preferences for male workers'.

Nevertheless, *perceptions* of female labour instability are often so strong as to draw a complete veil over reality. An intervening factor here is probably that turnover is likely to be greater in low-level dead-end jobs; as such real or imagined high female turnover may due more to the kinds of *occupation* women are in, than any 'inherent' 'female' characteristic (Baron and Norris, 1976, cited in Anker and Hein, 1986: 11). Even then, a number of case studies, such as that of John Humphrey's (1985) in Brazil, suggests that employers feel that women are likely to stay longer *despite* their being in dead-end jobs, a fact which seems to borne out in all three of the Mexican study cities. Over and above this it must also be added that high turnover may be *functional* to certain firms which need to cut back temporarily on staffing; in this respect employing women can be very advantageous.

Areas of gendered employment
Moving on to the second and third parts of the question, which concern the types of jobs available in the three cities, the types of skills necessary for these jobs and

Table 3.15a: Firms in Employer Survey in Puerto Vallarta, showing personnel manager's perception of sex of workers with higher degree of turnover

Type of firm	Sex of workers with higher (perceived) degree of turnover
Commerce	
Jewellery store	– (only male workers) –
Jewellery store	No difference
Tourist shop	Female
Tourist shop	Female
Departmental store	Male
Supermarket	Female
Hotels	
1-star hotel	Female
2-star hotel	Female
2-star hotel	Female
3-star hotel	Male
4-star hotel	No difference
Gran turismo	Female
Restaurants	
Snack-bar	– (only women at worker level)
Snack-bar	Female
Fast-food restaurant	– (only open one month)
Small family restaurant	– (no turnover – family labour)
Small restaurant	– (only women at worker level)
Medium-sized restaurant	No difference
Medium-sized restaurant	Male
Large exclusive restaurant	Male
Large exclusive restaurant	– (only men at worker level)

Source: Employer Survey, Puerto Vallarta, 1986.

Table 3.15b: Firms in Employer Survey in León, showing personnel manager's perception of sex of workers with higher degree of turnover

Type of firm	Sex of workers with higher (perceived) degree of turnover
Shoe manufacturers	
Pica	– (only open three months)
Pica	– (no turnover since *pica* opened)
Pica	Male
Medium-scale	No difference
Medium-scale	Male
Medium-scale	Male
Large-scale	Male
Large-scale	No difference
Large-scale	No difference

Cardboard-box makers
Small-scale — (only open one month)
Medium-scale No difference

Sole manufacturers
Medium-scale – leather Male
Medium-scale – PVC Male

Rubber sheet producer
Large-scale — (only men at worker level)

Source: Employer Survey, León, 1986.

Table 3.15c: Firms in Employer Survey in Querétaro, showing personnel manager's perception of sex of workers with higher degree of turnover

Type of firm	Sex of workers with higher (perceived) degree of turnover
Food and manufacture	
Bottling factory	— (only men at worker level)
Baby foods (large-scale)[a]	No difference
Cereals (large-scale)[a]	Male
Canned fruit and vegetables (large-scale)[a]	Male
Metal-mechanical	
Steel products (small-scale)	Male
Refrigerators (large-scale)	Male
Electrical household goods (large-scale)[a]	Female
Capital goods	
Machine tools (medium-scale)	Female
Agricultural machinery (large-scale)	— (only men at worker level)
Sewing machines (large-scale)[a]	Male
Turbines (large-scale)	— (only men at worker level)
Chemical and parachemical	
Plastic shapes and moulds (small-scale)	Male
Fertilisers (large-scale)	— only men at worker level)
Synthetic materials (large-scale)[a]	— (only men at worker level)

Note
[a] Denotes multinational enterprise.
Source: Employer Survey, Querétaro, 1986.

prevalent assumptions held by employers about men's and women's differential suitability for various kinds of work, certain general conclusions may be drawn. One point is that areas of gendered employment do exist and there seems to be litle penetration by men into jobs which have traditionally been the domain of women or *vice versa*. Employment designated as 'feminine' includes such posts as chambermaid and laundrywoman in the tertiary sector, and labour-intensive unskilled work in industry, particularly that which requires a high degree of manual dexterity such as the hand sewing of shoes in León, or the preparation and processing of foodstuffs in Querétaro. These occupations draw upon the skills women characteristically acquire in the context of a rigidly differentiated sexual division of labour, and indeed many jobs have a distinctly 'domestic' character. One reason for high rates of female employment in Puerto Vallarta, for example, is undoubtedly the existence of extensive areas of employment which are associated with women's 'home-making' skills.

Men, on the other hand, tend in tourist employment to be placed in more visible, 'public' roles of waiter or barman; in industry they are overwhelmingly concentrated in skilled mechanised or technical aspects of the production process; in both industry and services they also tend to predominate in jobs which require physical strength such as despatch workers or porters. Men's comparatively greater formal and informal training in mechanical and technical skills has undoubtedly been a major factor in their recruitment into more specialised industrial jobs, though their involvement in certain types of tertiary activity is harder to explain without reference to social, ideological and moral norms (see below).

Only few sectors of employment in the Mexican survey may be classified as 'gender-neutral', notably commerce. Here employers generally feel that men and women are more readily substitutable for one another, again contributing to a higher than average rate of female employment in Puerto Vallarta. Even then, there are still several instances of discrimination against women, particularly in terms of their exclusion from the merchandising of certain high-value products such as jewellery, and their relegation to non-supervisory positions.

The rationale for gendered employment
Undoubtedly to some degree, current patterns of recruitment of men and women into specific sectors – especially the tertiary sector – or into certain kinds of jobs, is derived from skill differentials. Most employers welcome workers they do not have to train from scratch and accordingly base their decisions on real or conjectured 'male' and 'female' abilities. Moreover, once an association is established, jobs tend to become 'masculinised' or 'feminised' and lead to self-perpetuating patterns of gender-typing in recruitment. Another major factor in segregation, however, is the whole ideology of gender roles and what it is deemed appropriate for men and women to do. Because 'women's jobs' are usually *similar* to domestic chores, subordinate, unskilled, secondary and often hidden from view, they conform to widely held social stereotypes about what work it is 'proper' for women. The rationale for gendered employment therefore, goes beyond a simple reference to skills, and relates also to the content, status and identification of different types of work with wider social and cultural mores. As Alison MacEwen Scott (1986b: 183) observes: 'The gender embeddedness of the division of labour is thus an outcome of the wider structure of gender inequality and of the institutional linkages which shape the divisions of labour'.

Moreover, the insertion of women into lower-skilled occupations with a 'domestic' character is not only symbolic, but also tends to reinforce gender ideologies in society as a whole (Humphrey, 1985). A third major reason, linked in with gender ideology is that employers often have very fixed ideas about male and female characteristics, many of which relate to ideas about the inherent 'nature' of men and women, as well as to skills they are likely to possess. Regardless of whether these ideas are positive or negative, verified in practice, and no matter how much they vary, the key issue is that Mexican employers often feel there are quite pronounced differences between men and women workers, and these perceptions go on to inform the decisions they make about who to recruit and in which jobs they are placed. (See Table 3.16.)[9]

Table 3.16: Personnel managers' perceptions of the positive and negative attributes[a] of male and female workers in the three study cities

| *Positive* | |
Men	Women
Greater work experience	Docility
Greater physical strength	Reliability
Foreign language skills/experience	Punctuality
Willingness/ability to work overtime	Flexibility (in extra work they take on in
Speed	their jobs)
	Willingness to take orders (from both
	male and female supervisors/managers)
	Domestic skills
	Diligence
	Patience
	Cooperative disposition
Negative	
Men	Women
Drunkenness on the job	Neurotic/temperamental
Greater rates of absenteeism (due to	Greater rates of absenteeism (due to
idleness/heavy drinking)	family problems/pregnancies)
Trouble-making (through union activity)	Unwillingness/inability to work overtime
Dishonesty	Lack of education/work experience
Impatience	Physical weakness
Inflexibility (especially in terms of doing	Lack of authority
extra duties in their jobs)	
Unwillingness to do demeaning (often	
'feminine') work such as cleaning	
Demanding (e.g. of higher wages)	
Resistance to authority (especially from	
female supervisors)	

Note
[a] Terminology/evaluation of attributes based diectly on employer's own wording/ interpretations.

Source: Employer Surveys, Puerto Vallarta, León and Querétaro, 1986.

In some cases 'positive' assumptions about female characteristics have led women to be substituted for men – especially in tourist enterprises in Puerto Vallarta, and to a lesser extent in certain areas of manufacturing in León and Querétaro. However, in the latter cities gender substitution has been more problematic since many manufacturing jobs require technical training, experience, and/or physical strength, which are clearly difficult for low-income Mexican women to acquire.

One point which should also be added here is that positive evaluations of female workers tend to revolve around their passivity, productivity and ultimately their *exploitability*. Women often accept less pay, are less demanding, more malleable, harder-working and so on. Managers recruiting large numbers of female workers, especially male ones, are arguably not so much enlightened as shrewd. In this respect those firms beginning to come round to the idea that they should employ more women and in more areas, may not really be described as 'pro-feminist'; instead it is likelier that wider economic pressures in Mexico at present are leading to general strategies to dampen labour costs, of which the recruitment of women plays a vital role (see also Benería and Roldan, 1987: 49).

A further dimension to the issue of employers' assumptions about men and women concerns restrictions placed on the entry of women workers into many firms on account of age and marital status (see Tables 3.4, 3.10 and 3.14). In several firms, particularly industrial concerns, young single women are preferred, mainly because employers feel that married women are more likely to get pregnant, which not only involves them paying a part of their maternity leave, but also in finding temporary or permanent replacements (see also Benería and Roldan, 1987: 98 on Mexico City factories). In addition, many employers feel that single women concentrate better on their work because they do not have family responsibilities to distract them. This point was also found by Safa (1986) in her study of the Puerto Rican garment industry, and constituted a major reason for the predominance of young single female workers; other reasons included the fact that employers felt that younger women represented a more docile labour force, having less labour or political experience than old-established workers; they were rarely absent, and furthermore had greater energy (Safa, 1986). Bolaños and Rodríguez (1988) make similar observations for the Costa Rican flower industry, and Pearson (1986) for women workers in world market factories on the Mexico–US border, although the latter also draws attention to the way in which perceptions vary: in some cases older women are preferred because it is thought they will have greater levels of maturity and responsibility towards to their work (ibid.). This was also found in a study of export-processing firms in Mauritius where married women were often deemed more conscientious (Hein, 1986).

While older women are rarely favoured in the firms in the Mexico survey, older men often are, especially married ones, primarily because it is felt that obligations to wives and children mean they will work harder than single men. Having said this, on the whole men face far fewer restrictions in gaining employment than women in terms both of age and marital status, and for married women over the age of thirty in all cities, access to employment drops considerably.

Gender composition of management: its influence on labour recruitment

Moving on to the question of how the sex of personnel managers may influence female recruitment, I noted in earlier sections how this was particularly apparent in Puerto Vallarta where women managers were usually more favourably disposed in theory and in practice to taking on women workers. On one hand this may be due to the fact that women who attain management level posts have greater confidence in women's abilities generally, but on the other I think there is also a very practical consideration which often enters the calculation. Where enterprises are small and there is frequent contact between management and staff, a woman personnel manager appears to find it easier to exercise authority over female than male staff. This is particularly true in small-scale catering and commercial establishments in Puerto Vallarta, and is highly relevant in a social context in which *machismo* normally dictates that women are subordinate to men and should defer to male authority both at home and in wider society. When men have to take orders from women, this produces an uncomfortable and conflictive departure from ideological norms, and as a result women personnel managers often prefer to employ female staff (see also Anker and Hein, 1986; Purcell, 1988) (see also Table 3.16). However, it must be stressed that this point is probably only relevant for small-scale establishments. The generally larger size of firms in the León sample was probably one of the reasons why here the sex of the personnel manager appeared to have little impact on recuitment – there being little vested interest since managers did not have to deal directly with workers on the shopfloor. In Querétaro, alternatively, we noted that there was a relationship, irrespective of size of firm, in two sectors – notably metal-mechanical production and capital goods. However, overall there were very few women personnel managers in the industrial cities and this in itself could help to explain why women here represent a far smaller proportion of the local workforce.

Internal segregation of the labour force

Moving onto the third main question, namely the degree to which jobs *within* various enterprises are segregated on the basis of sex, it is true to say that in most instances there is not only a vertical, but also horizontal segregation of the workforce, with women usually occupying the lowest-level, lowest-paid posts in peripheral or 'background' departments. On one hand this pattern relates again to kinds of skills and characteristics employers believe male and female workers are likely to possess. In industry, gender-based occupational differentiation is particularly apparent because men tend to have greater work experience or monopoly over technical skills. However, in the tertiary sector particularly, where ostensibly technical abilities or physical strength are not especially relevant, we can identify another major reason for sex segregation especially at the horizontal level: namely that the juxtaposition of men and women in the same department is frequently thought to undermine efficiency by bringing a 'Pandora's Box' of sexual complications into the workplace. Many employers felt that the inevitability of sexual relations between male and female workers would not only disturb operational efficiency, but also corrupt staff morality and even give their enterprises a 'bad name'. Research on gender and employment in other countries indicates that this phenomenon is not unique to Mexico (see, for example, Durrani, 1976 on Tunisia; Hein, 1986 on Mauritius; Weiss, 1984 on Pakistan; Dex, 1988 and Purcell, 1988 on Britain; see also Benería and Roldan, 1987: 176–7n. on Mexico City), and certainly is a major factor accounting not only for occupational segregation by gender, but also for the fact that some firms have deliberately recruited an entirely single-sex workforce. Employers most likely to pursue this latter policy tend to be male. An interesting aside is that several firms which employed both women and men suffered few problems in practice. However, the attitude that men and women working in close proximity will lead to a destabilising invasion of personal and/or sexual issues into the workplace is extremely persistent and has far-reaching implications.[10]

Major differences in female labour demand between the cities

Finally, to what degree does labour demand in the formal sector vary between the cities? On the basis of both the census data and the survey it is clear that of the three, Puerto Vallarta employs by far the greatest proportion of women, followed by León and then Querétaro. Although women's work is not of a particularly high status in any of the firms in all three cities, in Puerto Vallarta, low-income women lacking skills and employment experience may still quite easily find a job in several of the tourist-related enterprises. In addition many of these jobs are comparatively well-paid by standards in other cities. Greater female work opportunities in Puerto Vallarta result from the fact that in hotels for example, certain departments such as housekeeping have traditionally employed only women; in shops, women often find they are in an equal if not more favourable position than men due to an absence of specific technical skill requirements or physical abilities; and even in restaurants, where many posts are designated as 'male', especially those involved in dealing with the public, women can still find jobs, especially in small-scale establishments or behind the scenes in larger ones.

However, this does not mean that women are excluded by any means from possibilities of gaining employment in the industrial cities. In León, for example, low-income women can usually find some kind of job in shoe manufacturing, mainly because of the persistence of labour-intensive, feminised areas of production such as *adorno*, and also because of the need for domestic outworkers, especially by large firms (see also analysis of women's concentration in *adorno* in the Guadalajara shoe industry by Hernández-Aguila, 1988). The case of Querétaro is slightly different since here the situation is one of recent manufacturing development of which there is little historical precedent in the local context. In a sense one might expect that maybe new, and especially multinational, industry would be more 'gender-neutral' or even biased in favour of women workers as a means of keeping wage costs down, as in the case of the world market factories on the Mexico–US border (e.g. Fernández-Kelly, 1983a, 1983b;

Pearson, 1986). However, the fact that much industry in Querétaro is heavy, mechanised, skilled and capital-intensive means that men predominate, with women confined to the few labour-intensive aspects of the production process. Some managers expressing a personal ideological commitment to the principle of gender equality, declared considerable difficulty in putting their beliefs into practice: several social and cultural constraints experienced by Mexican women, such as restrictions on overtime or nightwork, frequent pregnancies, sole responsibility for child-care and domestic labour and so on, means they cannot easily adapt to the demands of modern manufacturing employment.

As we shall see in the following chapter, the broad impressions derived from the Employer Survey of women's differential access to employment in the three cities, filter down to the community level. In Puerto Vallarta, for example, low-income women felt they could always get employment if and when they wanted, albeit if not of a 'formal' nature. Indeed many women had migrated to Puerto Vallarta precisely because opportunities were imagined to be greater here than in cities with a more industrial economy. Certainly women in León and Querétaro had no illusions about it being easy to find a job and recognised that they would stand far less chance of obtaining employment than men. These perceptions and realities of women's ease of access to work in the different cities appear to have quite pronounced effects on local patterns of household organisation and women's role within that as we now go on to see in Chapters 4 and 5.

Notes

1 Names of firms are not disclosed in the text or tables for reasons of confidentiality (see also Appendix 2).

2 The term 'manager' is used throughout this chapter to refer to both male and female managers.

3 The issue of defining skills is very complex. Authors such as Anne Phillips maintain that jobs performed by men are often defined as 'skilled', whereas the reverse is true for women workers: 'It is not just that women do unskilled jobs – the jobs *become* unskilled because women do them' (Phillips, 1983: 17 – her emphasis). Phillips also notes that pay levels usually reflect the sex of the worker rather than the 'skills' involved – for example manual dexterity is supposedly a 'female' characteristic so it is accorded a low value, whereas physical strength, because it is a 'male' preserve, is given higher prestige and pay (ibid.). Once an area of work has become 'feminised', i.e. filled by women, it loses its status. From this concept has developed the idea that jobs are 'bearers of gender' (Elson, 1982).

4 In their study of tourism employment in Ixtapa-Zihuatanejo on the Mexican Pacific, Kennedy *et al.* (1978) found that the sex of hotel managers often corresponded with the sex of owners, with women personnel managers more common in female-owned firms. The same is generally true of the sample of firms in Puerto Vallarta, although sometimes personal/kin relationships could also have an effect. For example, in two male-owned firms, women were placed in positions of authority through being relatives of the owner.

5 No distinction was made in the Employer Survey as to whether staff changes were forced or voluntary, but on the whole, except at the end ot the high season (April) when some workers finish fixed-term contracts, most departures are voluntary.

6 Most Mexican tourist resorts have a large number of outlets selling a variety of silver goods such as jewellery and ornaments. The bulk of Mexican silver handiwork comes direct from Taxco, the principal silver-mining town in the country, situated about 100 kilometres south-west of Mexico City in the state of Guerrero.

7 Since *picas* are generally located inside domestic premises it is extremely difficult to identify them from the street. Therefore the *picas* selected for the employer survey were chosen from a sample of workshops identified during the household survey in the community of Piletas.

8 Purcell (1988:165) also notes the importance of gender differentials in labour supply in laying the groundwork for the subsequent emergence of gender segmentation: 'the initial conditions which generate gender segmentation may be shortage or availability of male or female labour, but once the job becomes identified with one sex, perception of it as a potential job for members of the other sex is less likely and its gendered character is consolidated by custom'.

9 See also Benería and Roldan (1987: 47–9) on assumed characteristics of women workers in their survey of employers in Mexico City.

10 In her discussion of research on sexuality in the workplace, Purcell (1988: 174) observes that while its survival can signify resistance to employer domination and allow the men and women involved to fight back against the 'tedium and depersonalising straitjacket of bureaucratic control', at the same time, 'expression of and reference to sexuality and gender differences in the workplace more often indicate male attempts to control and restrict women'. Purcell concludes that 'whether gender interaction at work is characterised by hostility and harassment or by chivalry and flirtation, the net effect is to remind women of their subordinate gender and, usually, occupational status and, in the case of women in 'male' environments or occupations, of their essential marginality and vulnerability in 'male' territory'.

4

Gender and local labour supply

Introduction

Having considered demand for female labour in Puerto Vallarta, León and Querétaro in the previous chapter, the present one goes on to examine the extent to which actual rates of women's employment in low-income settlements reflect general inter-urban variations in labour demand, and to explore a range of 'supply' factors at the household level which impede, precipitate and/or favour women's participation in remunerated work. 'Supply' factors selected for consideration include key individual characteristics of women such as age, education and migrant status, and household-level characteristics such as family size, household income and dependency ratios. In varying combinations and degrees these kinds of factors have been invoked in other studies to explain women's entry into and position in urban labour markets. To this spectrum of variables is added household structure, which, in the final analysis, appears to be the critical overriding determinant of women's involvement in paid work. General socio-economic data gathered in questionnaire surveys with a total of 189 households in Puerto Vallarta, León and Querétaro in 1986, and 244 households in Querétaro in 1982-3 provide the bulk of empirical material in this chapter. A more detailed in-depth analysis follows in Chapter 5 of the interrelationships between household composition and female labour force participation on the basis of qualitative case-study material from a sub-sample of households (see Appendix 1). The focus in the present chapter is exclusively upon female spouses and female household heads; that is, the adult woman at the core of the household unit, with or without a male partner.

Before proceeding with the analysis, it is important to briefly outline the characteristics of the settlements in each city from where the sample populations were drawn, and to identify general socio-economic and demographic aspects of their inhabitants.

Characteristics of the study settlements

Puerto Vallarta: Caloso and Buenos Aires

Two settlements in Puerto Vallarta were selected as study areas: Caloso, a community dating back to 1968 which began as an *ejidal* urban zone, and Buenos Aires, a more recent squatter settlement originating in 1979 (see Figure 2.3). Both these neighbourhoods lie south of the city centre, wedged between the banks of the Cuale River and the hills behind. The slopes on which the settlements are located were originally covered with thick palm forest, but much has now been felled in the process of land clearance and/or to provide materials for the construction of inhabitants' dwellings.

Caloso contains a population of around 1,800 persons and has a wide variety of tenure arrangements, housing conditions and household types, bearing out a common observation that older settlements tend to be more heterogeneous than younger ones. The majority of households in Caloso (65.2%) are owner-occupiers, most of whom have paid for legal land title even if they have not yet received official documentation from the Fideicomiso Puerto Vallarta, nor the services promised on receipt of payment for their lots.[1] As a consequence the few services possessed by the community have been negotiated for directly with individual servicing agencies, as was the case with electricity, and for the few households which have a piped water supply (see Table 4.1). All other households in Caloso use the River Cuale or its tributary streams and local springs for water. The settlement as a whole has no access to the city's sewerage network, lacks paved roads and has no form of public transport. To get to the town centre one has the choice of crossing a precarious rope bridge over the River Cuale to get a bus on the other side, or taking a twenty minute detour over dry land on foot. In the initial house count it was discovered that almost one-third of households (78) did not conform to the major types I wished to interview (namely nuclear households, one-parent families, extended households and childless couples) and were therefore excluded from the survey (see Appendix 1). This was a fairly large number of 'non-standard' households and reflects a far greater diversity of household forms than in the other cities; rejected households included single-person units, households consisting of adolescent siblings whose rural parents had sent them to work in the town, and even two male-headed one-parent families – a category of household which was not found in either of the other two cities (in both cases the men were widowers).

Sixty-nine households were interviewed in Caloso, randomly selected from within the stratified sample universe (about 30% representation) (see Table 4.1). Although the single most important category of family unit was nuclear, nearly one-third of the sample were extended households (see Table 4.2) Altogether 20.3% of household heads were women, who, with an average age of 45.5 years, were about 15 years older than male households heads (30.3 years) and 12 years older than their female spouses (33.6 years). Average family size in Caloso was 5.8 and the great majority of the sampled population (89.7%) were migrant households.[2]

Table 4.1: General characteristics of the study settlements

| City | Puerto Vallarta | | | León | | Querétaro* | |
Settlement	Caloso	Buenos Aires	Piletas	Lomas de Jerez	Bolaños	Los Andadores	Las Américas
Population							
Households	313	136	261	59	435	502	256
Inhabitants	1,815	966	1,958	400	2,948	3,418	1,740
Sampling universe	235	115	227	59	368	340	192
Sample households	69	23	54	23	100	92	52
Services							
Legal land title	X		X		X	X	
Electricity	X		X		X	X	X
Piped water	P		P			X	O
Street/side-walk paving			P			X	
Sewerage			P			X	
Rubbish collection	X		X			X	
Market			X			X	
Bus service		X	X		X	X	X
Health-centre						X	
Schools							
Kindergarten	X		X		X	X	X
Primary	X		X		X	X	X
Secondary			X			X	

Key
X = Service exists for majority of inhabitants
P = Partial coverage only (minority of inhabitants have access to service)
O = Public standpipes

Notes:
[a] The 1982–3 survey of Querétaro is represented here rather than that of 1986, mainly because the former was large and random, whereas the latter involved a non-random follow-up study of only 20 households. Certain changes in access to services and infrastructure had occurred in the settlements over the three-year interval, and are identified in Chapter 6. It is important to note that while all tenure categories are represented in the 1986 three-city survey, only owner-occupiers were interviewed in the earlier survey in Querétaro.

Source: For Puerto Vallarta and León, Household Questionnaire Survey, 1986. For Querétaro, Household Questionnaire Survey, 1982–3.

Table 4.2: Breakdown of household types in interview sample by city and settlement

	Nuclear	One-parent	Household types Male-extended	Female-extended	Childless couple	Total
Puerto						
Vallarta	51.1%(47)	9.8%(9)	22.8%(21)	9.8%(9)	6.5%(9)	92
Caloso	55%(38)	8.7%(6)	17.4%(12)	11.6%(8)	7.3%(5)	69
Buenos Aires	39.1%(9)	13%(3)	39.1%(9)	4.4%(1)	4.4%(1)	23
León	63.6%(49)	5.2%(4)	22.1%(17)	5.2%(4)	3.9%(3)	77
Piletas	62.9%(34)	5.6%(3)	24%(13)	5.6%(3)	1.9%(1)	54
Lomas de Jerez	65.2%(15)	4.4%(1)	17.4%(4)	4.4%(1)	8.7%(2)	23
Querétaro						
(1982–3)	68.5%(167)	9%(22)	18%(44)	4.5%(11)	–	244
Bolaños	72%(72)	10%(10)	13%(13)	5%(5)	–	100
Los Andadores	63%(58)	8.7%(8)	22.8%(21)	5.5%(5)	–	92
Las Américas	71.1%(37)	7.7%(4)	19.2%(10)	2%(1)	–	52

Note: Percentages may not add-up to 100 exactly because of rounding.

Source: Household Questionnaire Survey, Puerto Vallarta and León, 1986 and Querétaro, 1982–3.

Buenos Aires, the second study settlement in Puerto Vallarta, is far more uniform in terms of housing conditions and inhabitants. Squatters had tried to take land three times in the area on which the settlement now stands and only on the final occasion were officially allowed to stay by the Fideicomiso on condition that they could be moved at any time in the future. All households in Buenos Aires could be classified as 'owners' despite the fact that they lacked formal title to land. However total insecurity of tenure in this tiny community of less than 1,000 persons has meant that few have bothered to invest in durable housing materials. The settlement also lacks every conceivable service apart from a collective minibus route (see Table 4.1). A total of 23 households were interviewed in Buenos Aires providing about 20% representation (only 21 were rejected from the sampling universe through not meeting selection criteria). The single most important category of households in the sample were extended families (43.5%) (see Table 4.2). A total of 17.4% of household heads were women whose average age was 40.3 years; the corresponding mean age of male household heads was 36 years and of women spouses, 39.3 years. Average household size was 7.1 persons, and as in Caloso the great majority of households (86.2%) were migrants.

León: Piletas and Lomas de Jerez

In León, two different types of settlement were also chosen. The older one, Piletas (Segunda Sección) in the north east of the city arose out of the illegal private sale of lots by the son of a person who had sub-divided an adjacent area (the original neighbourhood of Piletas) in 1967 (see Figure 2.5). Most residents have had legal title since 1976–7. Lomas de Jerez, the younger settlement also resulted from an illegal sub-division which began in 1983. This latter settlement is in the extreme south-east of the city and as yet its inhabitants have no guarantee of land tenure (see Figure 2.5).

Piletas, the older settlement, has a far greater mix of housing, tenure and socio-economic characteristics than Lomas de Jerez. It covers a large area and contains 261 households (nearly 2,000 people), a number of whom have converted parts of their dwellings into small footwear workshops. From 1978 onwards the community received water and sewerage, but water supply is intermittent and can only really be relied upon for two hours in the evening. The residents of Piletas also have electricity, rubbish collection and a number of bus routes, the latter owing to their proximity to the busy market of San Juan de Dios (see Table 4.1). However, residents still lack paved streets, kerbs and sidewalks and in the rainy season, torrential downpours often make the roads impassable. Here a total of 34 households were rejected from the sample universe and of the remainder, one-quarter (54 households) were interviewed (see Table 4.1). Within the sample 72.2% of households owned, 25.9% rented and 1.8% shared with kin. A total of 62.9% of sampled households were nuclear, the rest were mainly extended (see Table 4.2). Only 11% of household heads were female; their average age was 50.2 years, substantially older than male household heads (39.7 years) and their spouses, (40.7 years). Average family size was 7.5 persons and a total of 66.6% of households were migrants.

Lomas de Jerez is less heterogeneous than Piletas. As yet the settlement contains only 59 households (about 400 people), and is notable for its low density; plots are ample and dwellings are separated by wide tracts of empty scrubland. A total lack of roads and large amount of open space provides one major advantage in that children may play safely, however, this is probably the only positive feature of the neighbourhood; Lomas is also very far from the city centre and involves at least 15 minutes walk to get a bus and a further 40 minutes ride into town. Given that the community lacks all basic services and possesses only two small commercial outlets women are involved in making a shopping trip at least every other day which results in a considerable expenditure of time, energy and finance (see Table 4.1). Due to its recent origin and lack of services, there is scarcely any small-scale enterprise in Lomas de Jerez, and unlike Piletas, it does not possess a single shoe workshop. Here 23 households were interviewed, providing about 39% representation.

No inhabitant of Lomas de Jerez has legal tenure but since the authorities have not yet threatened residents with eviction, there is a cautious sense of optimism about the likelihood of being able to stay. Of the interview sample, 95.6% were 'owners' and 4.4% were renting accommodation; 65.2% of households were nuclear, the rest were mainly extended households or recently married couples (see Table 4.2). Only 8.7% of all household heads are female with an average age of 48.5 years. Male household heads have a mean age of 34.4 years and their spouses, 34.5 years. Average household size is 6.5 and a total of 69.6% of households are migrants.

Querétaro: Bolaños, Los Andadores and Las Américas

In Querétaro in 1982–3, three settlements were selected for study. The first Bolaños, was a former *ejidal* urban community dating back to 1968, with a population of about 3,000 people. It lies on a hillside to the north east of the city (see Figure 2.7). Most people had legal land tenure by the time of the interviewing period, but despite its age the settlement was very poorly serviced (see Table 4.1). A total of 100 interviews provided 27% representation of the sample universe. Only owner-occupiers were interviewed in Bolaños, but within this category there was a great variety of housing standards. There was also a mixture of household structures, although the majority of the sample (72%) were nuclear households (see Table 4.2). A total of 13.5% of household heads were female, with an average age of 42.8 years. The average age of male household heads was 30.9 years, and of women spouses, 33.7 years. Average family size was 7.1 persons and only 47% of households in 1982 were migrants.

The second settlement, Los Andadores containing nearly 3,500 people lies on flat land in the extreme south of the city on the edge of a much larger settlement, Lomas de Casa Blanca (see Figure 2.7). Here 92 households were interviewed (27% of the the total sampling universe). In contrast to Bolaños, Los Andadores was a 'planned' settlement, resulting from a fraudulent sale by government officials in the mid-1970s. Lots are all the same size although housing conditions are far from homogeneous. Due to its origins and proximity to Lomas de Casa Blanca, one of the largest and longest-settled low-income communities in Querétaro with a wide range of amenities, Los Andadores has access to most basic services and to a number of facilities in the adjacent neighbourhood (see Table 4.1.). It also has a mixture of household types, with nearly 30% in 1983 being extended households. The majority (63%) however, were nuclear (see Table 4.2).

A total of 14.2% of household heads were female with an average age of 41 years. The average age of male household heads was 32.9 years, and of their spouses, 35.3 years. Average family size was 6.7 persons and a total of 66% of households were migrants. Between 1983 and 1986 one household selected for follow-up interview had sold their house in Los Andadores in order to rent a flat above their photographic business in the neighbouring community, Lomas de Casa Blanca.

The final settlement, Las Américas, contained a population of 2,500 people in 1983, was at the time still unregularised and had only very few services (see Table 4.1). It lies on a hillside towards the north west of the city overlooking one of Querétaro's major industrial zones (see Figure 2.7). Here 52 households were interviewed (27% of the sample universe).

Households again were mixed, although the majority (71.1%) were nuclear (see Table 4.2). A total of 9.7% of households were female-headed. The average age of female household heads was 45 years, about 12 years older than male household heads (33.2 years) and their spouses (33.3 years). Average family size was smaller than in the other 2 settlements, at 6.4 persons, and 66% of households were migrants.

Before going on to examine the extent to which women's labour force participation is related to various personal and household characteristics, a brief overview is presented of employment and income patterns in the study settlements, with particular regard to gender differences both *within* and *among* the cities.

Employment and income in Puerto Vallarta

Gender differences in occupation

The majority of male household heads in the two settlements in Puerto Vallarta were employed as construction workers (35.1% of the total), followed by waiters or barmen (13.5%). Most of the remainder were independent workers, such as owners of seafront or kerbside refreshment stalls, ambulant tradesmen or self-styled tourist guides. Many also worked as sales assistants. Only 2 out of 74 male household heads were unemployed in Puerto Vallarta. As for women, the most common occupations of the 54 female heads and spouses who had paid work (58.7% of the total) were domestic service (14.5%) or taking in washing or sewing (14.5%) (see Figure 4.1).[3] Another major occupation for women was commerce: 10.9% of the total number of women workers had their own shop or sold soft drinks, home-made fruit juices, confectionery or snacks from the front room of their dwellings (see Figure 4.2). Another 14.5% of female workers were employed directly by the tourist industry as waitresses, kitchen assistants and chambermaids.

Few women left the household for work

Figure 4.1 Washerwomen, Puerto Vallarta

Figure 4.2 Home-based commerce, Puerto Vallarta

Despite high demand for both male and female labour in the 'formal' tourist industry as we noted in the previous chapter, around half of all workers in the settlements were self-employed or in small-scale 'informal' concerns.

Gender differences in earnings

Earnings varied considerably between men and women in Puerto Vallarta; the average pay of a male worker (for those whose income was known and declared by their wives) was 23,403 pesos a week, compared with 9,584 pesos for women, although this latter figure includes both full- and part-time workers.[4] Even then, although the average weekly wage of the 28 full-time women workers in Puerto Vallarta was 13,344 pesos, well above the weekly minimum wage of 9,380 pesos and over twice as much as the average earnings of the 27 part-time workers (5,577 pesos), this was still only just over half that earned by men.

Earnings of men in self-employment did not differ greatly from those who worked for a firm or someone else: the 18 men in self-employment (whose income was known) earned an average of 23,822 pesos a week, slightly more than the 53 who worked for a firm (23,261 pesos). This was partly due to the fact that men employed by tourist firms were able to supplement relatively low basic wages with tips. For women the remunerative differences between self-employment and 'formal' employment were far greater; in the latter they earned an average of 16,391 pesos a week, compared with as little as 6,344 pesos in the former. As far as the 'semi-formal' workers are concerned, the eight domestic servants earned an average weekly wage of 7,928 pesos, and the two outworkers, 7,250 pesos. Families in Puerto Vallarta have an average of 2.5 workers, a mean household size of 6.2 members, and mean earnings per capita (total household income divided by household size) of 7,714 pesos a week.

Migrant status, dependency ratios and incomes

Altogether, 88% (81) of households in Puerto Vallarta were migrants. Nearly one-third of women migrants (30.8%) had come to Puerto Vallarta as a child with their parents; another quarter (24.7%) had moved on their own account because there was no work in their previous place of residence; 16.1% came to find *better* work than in their previous place of residence and 11.1% came to join relatives in the city. Aside from those who came with their parents, nearly 10% of the total number of women migrants had moved to Puerto Vallarta alone (at an average age of around 20 years), the rest came with relatives or spouses. Aside from two migrants who arrived in the city in the pre-war period, 5% arrived in the 1950s, 19.7% in the 1960s, 46.9% in the 1970s and 22.2% in the 1980s, suggesting that the bulk of migrants arrived during the tourist boom of the last two decades.

Migrant households tend to be slightly larger (6.2 persons) than non-migrant households (5.5 persons), and to have somewhat higher levels of dependency, with one worker in a migrant household supporting an average of 2.6 dependants, compared with 2.2 in native households. Per capita earnings in migrant units are also lower, at 7,428 pesos a week, compared with 9,369 pesos in native households. Nevertheless, in absolute and relative terms, most low-income households interviewed in Puerto Vallarta were in 1986 far better off financially than their counterparts in León and Querétaro.

Employment and income in León

Gender differences in occupation

By far the most important branch of activity for male heads in León, employing just over half the sample (N=69 cases), was shoe manufacture. Of the 36 un- or semi-skilled workers in footwear production, 38.9% worked in large factories (20.2% of the overall total), a further 33.3% in small-scale workshops (17.3% of the overall total) and 27.8% had full or partial ownership of a shoe production unit (14.4% of overall total). Other men were involved in transport, commerce (often involving the retailing of footwear) and streethawking. Three male heads in León were retired and another two were unemployed. In contrast, only just over half (50.6%) the 77 female household heads and spouses in León had work, and of this number, only one was employed as a full-time worker in a shoe factory. One-quarter of the total number of women working were engaged in piecework for large shoe factories in their own homes. A further 17.9% of working women heads and spouses had their own shops or sold soft drinks from their front rooms, 10% took in other people's washing or sewing, and 7.7% were domestic servants. Two women also worked as unpaid helpers in family shoe workshops. Men's and women's work is thus very clearly differentiated in León, and over half the women worked from home.

Gender differences in earnings

Nowhere is the differentation between male and female activities more apparent than in wage disparities: male heads (for whom wages were recorded) earned an average of 19,616 pesos a week (well above the minimum wage of 11,725 pesos), whereas women workers (excluding two unpaid workers in the sample) earned only 4,581 pesos. In contrast to Puerto Vallarta there was relatively little difference between the mean weekly wage of full-time women workers (6,420 pesos) and part-timers (4,050 pesos), Full-time women workers earned only two-thirds of the general minimum wage and barely one-third of average male earnings.

Regarding remunerative differences between self-employment and working for an employer, there was little difference among men: the 17 men in self-employment earned an average of 21,159 pesos a week, and the 47 men employed by firms, 19,058 pesos. Among women, however, the differences were more marked: the five women working in relatively 'formal' enterprises earned an average of 9,940 pesos a week, only half that of their male counterparts in the same, but nearly double that of the 19 self-employed women (4,717 pesos). Self-employed women earned less than one-quarter of that earned by self-employed men. The 3 domestic servants earned an average of 6,667 pesos and the 10 factory outworkers, 3,083 pesos. Households in León had the highest average number of workers of all cities, at 2.8, yet a large mean family size (7.2 persons), and in per capita terms household earnings were lower in both the other cities at only 5,279 pesos a week.

Migrant status, dependency ratios and incomes
Altogether 67.5% (52) of households in León were migrants. Reasons for
migration varied slightly in proportional terms compared with Puerto Vallarta;
almost one-third (32.7%) of women migrants had moved to León because there
was no work for their households in their place of origin or previous residence, and
a further 11.5% had come to the city to *improve* their work prospects, 28.8% had
migrated as children and 9.6% of migrants had moved to join their husbands or
fiances in the city. Aside from those who had moved to the city as young girls with
their parents, nearly 10% had come alone (around the age of 17 years), and
another 10% with friends or siblings (at an average age of 15 years). The time
span over which migrants have arrived in León is much broader than that of
Puerto Vallarta; here 7.5% of migrants arrived in the 1940s or before, as many as
one-quarter (26.9%) in the 1950s during which time León was beginning to
consolidate its position as a major Mexican footwear centre, another 26.9% of
migrants arrived in the 1960s, and 26.9% in the 1970s, but only 11.5% had come
in the 1980s, reflecting León's waning importance as a centre of in-migration.

As in Puerto Vallarta, migrant households in León tend to be larger (7.5
persons) than non-migrant households (6.7 persons). However, in contrast to the
other cities, migrant households in León seem to be relatively better-off than non-
migrants, having an average of 3 workers (compared with 2.5 in native
households), and a corresponding dependency ratio of 1: 2.5 (as against 1: 2.7 in
native households). Not only are migrant dependency ratios lower in León, but per
capita earnings in migrant families are noticeably higher (at 5,386 pesos a week)
compared with non-migrants (5,051 pesos). The relative wealth of migrants in
León is possibly due to the fact that many arrived earlier than in the other cities,
and have therefore had more time to establish businesses and/or relevant job
contacts.

Employment and income in Querétaro

Gender differences in occupation
In Querétaro in 1986, 3 out of 12 (25%) male household heads were construction
workers, two (17%) were factory operatives, another two were owners or partners
of small family businesses, one was a clerical worker, one a petty trader, one a
soldier, one an assistant in a dry-cleaning firm, and the other was temporarily
unemployed. This distribution is somewhat different to the pattern in 1982–3,
where 22% of men were working in factories and only 17% in construction. In
other words, the situation had become reversed, possibly because while factory
jobs in general had become harder to get during the peak years of crisis, a certain
amount of construction work had been stimulated by a government programme
started in 1983 to involve local builders in human settlement upgrading.
Moreover, in 1982–3, 1 in 10 men in the settlements had been unemployed.
However, these apparent differences in occupational patterns may also be due to
the fact that the 1986 sample was non-random.

As for women, 11 out of the 20 (55%) female heads and spouses interviewed in

Figure 4.3 *Tortilla*-maker, Querétaro

1986 were working which is notably higher than that recorded in 1982–3 when only 30.7% (75 out of 244) had jobs (see Chant, 1984). There has also been a significant change in the type of work in which women were involved. In 1986, 4 (36.3%) of the working women were roadsweepers or office cleaners (protected by a formal contract), 2 (18%) were home-based food producers (see Figure 4.3), one (9%) was a factory operative, another a domestic servant, another ran a breakfast business outside a large factory, and another had her own shop. One woman counted as employed was temporarily laid off from her post as cook in a large hotel. Having been injured at work she was receiving compensation of 5,000 pesos a week (about half her normal salary). In 1982-3, by contrast, the largest single occupational category of female households heads and spouses had been domestic service (employing 32% of the total), with another 55% involved in commerce or the food trade (generally small-scale home-based production and sale), and only 4% in industry. The reasons for these changes in Querétaro are examined in more detail in Chapter 6, but suffice to say that there has been a general increase in women's work in the city, with a rise in both the range and 'formal' status of their jobs.

Gender differences in earnings
In 1986, working male heads of household in Querétaro earned an average of 25,645 pesos a week (more than double the minimum general wage of 11,725 pesos), while women workers earned 14,840 pesos – a much narrower differential than in the other cities, possibly because more women in Querétaro were in 'formal sector' work than in León or Puerto Vallarta, and indeed, none of the women in the 1986 sample worked on a part-time basis. The 3 men in self-employment earned an average of 30,000 pesos a week, whereas the 8 employed by others earned 24,012 pesos. In Querétaro, the 5 women who worked in 'formal' employment earned only marginally more (11,980 pesos per week) than those in self-employment (11,333 pesos). Again, as in León and Puerto Vallarta, there is a pattern for men to earn more in self-employment than in formal sector work, but for women to earn less – possibly because women's forms of self-employment are more casual and less-capitalised. The domestic servant, however, earned only 4,500 pesos. Households interviewed in Querétaro in 1986 had the lowest average number of workers of all the cities, at 2.3, yet the highest mean household size (7.6 members). In per capita terms household earnings were 6,037 pesos a week, substantially lower than in Puerto Vallarta, but higher than in León.

Migrant status, dependency ratios and income
Seventy-five per cent (15) of all households in the 1986 survey were migrants. Half the women migrants (53.3%) had come to Querétaro as a child with their parents, 26.7% to join relatives in the city, 13.3% because of lack of work in their place of origin or previous residence, and 6.7% to *improve* household work prospects. Aside from those women who had come as children to the city, one-fifth had moved to Querétaro alone as adolescent girls, and the rest came either with a spouse or relatives. Although one-quarter of the migrants had arrived prior to or

during the 1940s, another quarter had come in the 1950s, 12.5% in the 1960s, and most (37.5%) in the 1970s, indicating that the bulk arrived following Querétaro's consolidation as a major industrial centre during the late 1960s and early 1970s. No migrants appear to have arrived in the 1980s, but this probably reflects research design; all households interviewed in 1986 were selected from the original survey of 1982–3, and *ipso facto* households which may have arrived after that date were excluded.

As in the other cities, migrant households in Querétaro are larger (8.1 persons) than non-migrants (6 persons). The average number of workers in migrant units is only 2.1 workers, compared with 3 in native ones, despite their larger size. This produces dependency ratios of 1: 3.9 and 1: 2 respectively. Weekly per capita earnings are also far lower in migrant households (at 4,865 pesos) than in city-born families (9,322 pesos).

As a postscript to this section it is important to note that in none of the cities did women workers (mothers *or* daughters in fact) earn the highest salary in the family in more than 10% of cases. It is also important to take into account the fact that in all cities female economic activity rates are far higher than those suggested by either the census or the Employer Survey, undoubtedly because so many women are engaged in self-employment or unprotected casual work which escapes the net of official data collection or remains undeclared by firms engaging part-time female employees or outworkers.

Female labour supply in Puerto Vallarta, León and Querétaro: household determinants of women's labour force participation

Having now provided some idea of settlement characteristics and employment profiles of the sampled population in the three cities, this section considers the effect of various economic and demographic variables such as age, education and family size which operate at the level of the individual or household to influence the 'supply' of female labour (see, for example, Anker and Hein, 1986; Carvajal and Geithman, 1985; Peek, 1978; Standing, 1981; Uthoff and Gonzalez, 1978). As suggested earlier, household structure appears to be the most important single determinant of female labour supply, but is is obviously related to some degree to other facets of family life such as stage in the lifecycle, fertility and so on. As such these other factors must also be considered, albeit briefly.

All 'supply' variables *other* than household structure are analysed on the basis of aggregate data for the three cities in order to maximise the possibility of drawing out general trends, yet even then there seem to be only very weak influences exercised by those variables conventionally invoked to explain female labour force participation. In the final part of the chapter, where household structure is examined, we return once more to consider inter-urban variations in household structure and women's employment – household composition and headship themselves appear to be so strongly influenced by the nature of the local labour market that it seems more appropriate to examine their interrelationships with female labour force participation on the basis of a comparative analysis of the three cities.

Individual factors in female labour supply

Age

In considering the effect of age on female labour force participation it is important to remember that we are *not* dealing with a fully representative sample of women of working age; all interviewees in the questionnaire survey were either *married* and/ or *mothers*, and *ipso facto* data on young single women are not included at this stage of the analysis (instead they are discussed in some detail on the basis of the semi-structured interviews in Chapters 5 and 7). Nevertheless, among adult women it appears that increased age is associated with higher rates of labour force participation, despite the fact that data from the Employer Survey in Chapter 3 indicates that demand for female labour tends to drop markedly after the age of 30 years. Statistically speaking differences in age groups of women according to whether they work or not are reasonably significant with chi-square values significant at a 95% level of confidence.[5] The average age of the 81 full-time housewives is 36.5 years, as against the 101 women with a full- or part-time job whose mean age was 39.1 years. Four women who were unemployed through sickness had an average age was 54.5 years and the remaining three women who provided unpaid assistance to a family business, 29.6 years. Interestingly the 63 full-time workers were actually *younger* (38.7 years) than the 38 women with part-time work (40.5 years), although this does not detract from the fact that both categories of worker are older than full-time housewives. Another interesting finding emerges when women heads and spouses are considered separately; here it seems that increased age only appears to be correlated with higher rates of female labour force participation in *male*-headed families, with no notable relationship in women-headed households, indeed as far as the latter is concerned, the data point to a possible reverse pattern (see Table 4.3).

Table 4.3: Mean age of women according to activity and sex of household head

Occupation of female spouse or head	Male-headed households	Mean age	Female-headed households
Full-time houseperson	35.5 years (71)		43.5 years (10)
Full-time worker	37.0 years (45)		42.9 years (18)
Part-time worker	38.8 years (35)		60.6 years (3)
Unemployed (through sickness)	66.0 years (1)		50.6 years (3)
Unpaid helper	29.6 years (3)		
Mean age of women spouses:	36.8 years (155)	women heads:	45.4 years (34)

Note: Number in brackets refers to number of cases.

Source: Household Questionnaire Surveys, Puerto Vallarta, León and Querétaro, 1986.

Although the age differences between 'working' and 'non-working' women in both male- and female-headed families are quite marginal, they could suggest that women heads of household, especially those who work full-time, have no choice *other* than to work when their children are young, whereas when they are older they may be able to delegate income-earning to sons and daughters and therefore withdraw from the labour force (see Chapter 5). In male-headed families, by contrast, younger women with greater numbers of dependent children are probably in a position where they *can* and *do* devote more time to child-care at earlier stages in the lifecycle because economic support is provided by a male partner; only when children reach adolesence do they have more time to take on paid work. Much obviously also has to do with the type of work in which women engage and the pool of reproductive helpers within the family (Peek, 1978; see below).

Education
Education is another important 'supply' characteristic often argued to influence labour force participation. In accordance with the precepts of human capital theory one might expect to find a positive relationship between levels of schooling and rates of female economic activity and remuneration.[6]

The range of educational levels achieved by women in the three cities varies widely and follows a broadly similar pattern to that of men although overall men tend to have slightly higher levels of educational attainment.[7] A full one-quarter (26.4%) of women heads and spouses had no education at all; nearly one-half (47.6%) had an incomplete primary education (66% of these having 3 years or less), 20.6% a completed primary education, only 3.7% a completed secondary education or equivalent (such as a primary leaving certificate plus a secretarial qualification), 2 women had taken an adult literacy course, and only 1 woman had finished a course in higher education (a post 'A'-level teaching diploma). The data show that younger heads and spouses are more likely to have higher levels of education than older women (see Table 4.4).

Table 4.4. Average age of women according to level of education

Level of education	Mean age of women
No education	56.0 years (50)
Incomplete primary (1–5 years)	37.7 years (90)
Completed primary (6 years)	31.1 years (39)
Completed secondary or equivalent (9 years)	27.2 years (7)
Higher education (15 years)	22.0 years (1)
Adult literacy qualification	37.5 years (2)

Note: Number in brackets refers to number of cases.

Source: Household Questionnaire Survey, 1986.

Interestingly fewer migrant women (28.4%) had never been to school than native women (43.9%), despite their older average age (39.4 years as against 34.8 years). This might appear odd if we remember that older women tend to have less education. However, while as many as one-third of native women had a completed primary education, the corresponding figure was only 16.9% for migrants. Thus despite the fact that many native women are uneducated, they appear to have a greater chance of attaining higher levels of education if they *do* get an opportunity to go to school in the first place.

Given that older women in general are more likely to work than younger women, the finding that they are also likely to be the least educated means that there might *not* be any distinct relationship after all between levels of educational attainment and involvement in waged work. Table 4.5 bears this out, indicating that there is no notable difference between levels of education achieved by women in different categories of activity.

Table 4.5: Women's activity and educational levels

Women's activity	None	Incomplete primary	Complete primary	Complete secondary	Higher education	Literacy course
Housewife (N=81)	25.9%(21)	53.0%(43)	16.0%(13)	4.9% (4)	–	–
Full-time worker (N=63)	30.1%(19)	42.9%(27)	25.3%(16)	–	1.6%(1)	–
Part-time worker (N=38)	21.0%(8)	44.7%(17)	23.7%(9)	5.3%(2)	–	5.2%(2)
Unemployed (through sickness)(N=4)	50.0%(2)	50.0%(2)	–	–	–	–
Unpaid worker (N=3)	33.3%(1)	–	33.3%(1)	33.3%(1)	–	–

Note: Number in brackets refers to number of cases.

Source: Household Questionnaire Survey, 1986.

Looking at the data from another angle, of all those women who had no education, 42% were housewives while 54% had paid work of some description; of all those with incomplete primary schooling, 45% were housewives and 48% had paid work; and of those with completed primary education, 33% were housewives compared with 64% in paid work. The two women who had taken an adult literacy course were also working, albeit part-time. In all cases, then, more women work than stay at home, regardless of education. The only stage at which schooling seems to make an appreciable difference to women's activity, is at the level of completed primary education, where the proportion working to that staying at home is markedly greater compared to those with lower levels of attainment. However, the possibility of identifying a general trend is counteracted by the fact that 57% of those with secondary education or equivalent were housewives, compared with only 28.6% of similarly qualified women who had paid work; this tends to refute the idea that greater educational attainment leads to higher rates of female economic activity. Chi-square analysis on the data also showed there to be no statistically significant differences in whether women work or not arising from levels of education.

Absence of a clear relationship between education and labour force participation is compounded by the fact that the amount of money earned by women bears little relationship to their years of schooling (see also Anker and Hein, 1986: 34). Although working women who had never been to school earned far less on average (8,428 pesos a week) than those with a completed primary education (10,932 pesos), women with between one and five years of primary schooling earned less than those with no education at all (7,271 pesos).

Migrant status
Just as there is no identifiable pattern of age or education with women's economic activity or weekly earnings, neither are there any significant differences according to migrant status.

Although it might be expected that women born in the city have a greater tendency to work than newcomers, because of generally higher levels of education, knowledge of the local job market, more contacts and so on, differences in the activity patterns of migrant and native women are generally negligible. Among non-migrants, 41.5% are housewives and 58.5% workers; among migrants, 43.2% are housewives and 54.1% workers, and chi-square analysis found no statistically significant variation in women's activity according to migrant status. None the less, migrant status does seem to have a relationship with remuneration. Migrant women working full-time earned slightly less (10,833 pesos) than native urban residents (11,860 pesos). This differential is also apparent between native and migrant part-timers, the former earned an average of 5,375 pesos a week, whereas the latter earned 5,020 pesos. This might go some way to supporting the hypothesis that native women have more job contacts and better work opportunities in the respective cities, but again definitive conclusions are elusive.

Household level factors in labour supply

Fertility, family size and dependency ratios
Moving on from individual characteristics of women which might be expected to influence labour supply, to their household characteristics, it seems there are only marginal differences in fertility between women who are currently working and those who remain in the home; the average being 5.9 children for housepersons, 6.0 for 'workers' (5.9 for full-time workers, 6.3 for part-time workers and 4.3 for unpaid workers).[8] The four women who were unemployed through sickness had given birth to an average of 8.2 children. However, more relevant than fertility itself is the actual number of co-resident children and other dependants in the household at time of interview; in cases where these are high we might expect to find women at home, rather than in the labour force.

As far as family size itself is concerned, there appears to be a slight tendency for women with larger families to enter the labour force than women with smaller ones. The average size of households where women were full-time housepersons is 6.5, for all households where women 'worked' (in full-, part-time and unpaid production) 6.8, and in families where the woman head or spouse was too sick to work, 8.3 persons. However, breaking these activity categories down, it seems there are only marginal differences in family size between housewives (6.5) and women with part-time work (6.4). Families with women working full-time however, contained an average of 7.1 persons and where women were unpaid helpers, 7.7. Overall there was no statistically significant difference in household size according to categories of women's activity, neither did chi-square analysis find a significant difference in numbers of children at home and women's activity, partly because some co-resident children have left school and are working full-time. However, there was a statistically significant result when it came to cross-tabulating women's activity and numbers of dependants in households – classified here as schoolchildren (albeit if a small proportion of them have part-time jobs), people who are too old, too young or too ill to work, and unemployed persons. Chi-square found this association to be reasonably strong, with a 95% level of confidence that women would work if there were more dependants in the home. On average the number of dependants in households where women worked was 3.9, and 3.5 where they were full-time housewives.

In order to examine the idea of dependency more closely, however, we also need to take into account the existence of other members of the household with remunerated work and set the total number of household income-generators against household size to produce a 'dependency ratio' (number of non-workers per worker) However, it seems there are only marginal differences in dependency ratios among households except that if women did *not* work in those families in which they presently do have a full- or part-time occupation, then dependency ratios would be higher than those units in which they are currently full-time housewives (see Table 4.6).

Table 4.6: Mean household size, number of workers, and dependency ratios according to women's activity

Occupation of female spouse or head	Household size	No. of workers	Dependency ratio
Full-time housewife	6.5 (81)	2.2	1:2.9
Full-time worker	7.1 (63)	2.8	1:2.5
Part-time worker	6.4 (38)	3.1	1:2.0
Sick/permanently unemployed	8.2 (4)	2.7	1:3.0
Unpaid worker	7.6 (3)	2.6	1:2.9

Note: Number in brackets refers to number of cases.

Source: Household Questionnaire Survey, 1986.

The data in Table 4.6 suggest that *need* may be an important factor in influencing women's work, but it is impossible to verify this without reference to income as well.

Head of household's earnings and total household income
In considering women's labour force participation and household income characteristics, we need to take into account two main factors: first, the income earned by male heads of household, and second, the total earnings of all household units. Regarding the issue of male heads' earnings, where these are low we might imagine that women take-up paid work in order to compensate. However, the data suggest that there is little difference in male wages between those households in which women are in remunerated work and those in which they are not; the weekly pay of the male head is 20,886 pesos in cases where women spouses do not go out to work, only marginally higher than the average earned (20,529 pesos) where women have some kind of employment, be this full-time, part-time or unpaid. However breaking down this latter category, according to whether women's employment is full- or part-time, it seems that the pay of male household heads is markedly lower in families where wives work full-time (19,143 pesos) than in housewives' families, although in cases where women have a part-time job, the mean weekly wage of the household head is in fact higher, at 22,106 pesos; it is higher still (25,000 pesos a week) where women work as unpaid assistants to a family business, although obviously women's work in this latter case is written into their husbands' profits. Overall then, there are only tenuous relationships between weekly average pay of the male household head and women's entry into the labour force, suggesting that 'insufficiency' of the male wage cannot really be cited as a critical variable (bearing in mind of course that wages earned might not reach the family as a whole [see Chapters 5 and 7]). To add to this, chi-square tests did not find the money earned by male heads (grouped into earning bands) to be in any way significant in explaining whether or not their wives worked.

Even taking total earnings into account for all households there does not seem to be any consistent pattern between levels of family income and women's involvement in paid work, although overall families which utilise the labour power of their female heads or spouses to generate income have higher mean levels of per capita earnings (see Table 4.7). As might be expected, per capita earnings of households where women work (as full-, part-time or unpaid helpers) is higher (6,803 pesos a week) than that where they are full-time housepersons (6,285 pesos).[9] However, families where women work part-time have a higher average weekly per capita earnings (7,371 pesos) than that of households where women are full-time workers (6,498 pesos), although the households of unpaid women workers have weekly per capita earnings of only 4,833 pesos. Although the data show generally that families which utilise the labour power of the female head or spouse in economic activity are better-off economically, the relationships between per capita household earnings and women's involvement in income-generating activities seem somewhat anomalous. On the one hand, low per capita earnings in households where women work full-time suggests that if they were *not* working, their families would be far worse-off financially than other households, and therefore that *need* may be a critical factor here. Yet on the other, where women work part-time, they appear to be maximising already relatively high levels of household earnings. However, another important point to bear in mind is that the total amount of income *earned*, is often no real indicator of the *disposable* income of a family unit; this is often contingent upon household structure and is explored in some detail later in the text.

Table 4.7: Women's labour force participation and per capita household earnings[a]

Occupation of female head or spouse	Mean family size	Mean per capita earnings per week (pesos).
Full-time houseperson	6.5 (81)[b]	6,285
Worker (full/part-time or unpaid)	6.8 (104)	6,803
Sick/permanently unemployed	8.3 (4)	7,202

Notes:
[a] Figures rounded up to nearest whole peso (earnings) and to one decimal point (family size).
[b] Number in brackets refers to number of cases.

Source: Household Questionnaire Survey, 1986.

The above set of results suggests that factors often cited as significant in accounting for differential rates of female labour force participation at the point of 'supply' are not particularly meaningful in the present context.[10] Women's employment does not, in other words, appear to be affected by education, migrant status, fertility, family size, numbers of resident children, husbands' earnings or total household earnings, with only age and numbers of dependants being statistically significant in any way. Abstracted from household structure and women's role within it (as head or spouse), even these latter two variables have little meaning: it is only when women's activity is plotted against household structure and sex of household head that some sense may be read into the survey results. Tabulating women's work with sex of household head and household structure respectively produces chi-square values significant at extremely high confidence levels (99.9%). Also important is the city in which women live (a 'demand' factor), although this is less significant statistically (with a chi-square value significant only at a 90% level of confidence). Nevertheless, studied in conjunction with household structure, inter-city differences in rates of female workforce participation provide a major route into understanding variations in women's employment in the present study. In the remainder of this chapter therefore, analysis is focused upon the nature of household structure and its interrelationships with women's labour force participation in the individual cities, outlining *why* household structure is important and relating the findings of the questionnaire survey back to general ideas set out in the Introduction. This investigation is followed up in Chapter 5 with reference to the qualitative data and case study material gathered from the three cities in 1986, and in Chapter 6, by looking at changes in household structure and women's work through time in the city of Querétaro.

The role of household structure in influencing women's labour force participation

Aside from the general case study evidence presented in Chapter 1 which indicates the significance of household structure and particularistic translations of familial ideology in determining the 'supply' of female labour, it is important to note that similar findings were also made in the author's study in Querétaro in 1982–3. As such brief reference to this earlier research is necessary in order to set the stage for discussion of results in the present comparative project. Indeed much of the rationale for the present study grew out of questions arising from the earlier work.

Household structure and female employment: Findings from Querétaro 1982–3

An overriding impression of female labour force participation in Querétaro was that many women remained at home, not because they could not *find* a job, but principally because in cases where they resided with a male partner, they were not *allowed* to work, and it was on this front that family structure appeared to be a critical issue (see Chant, 1984, 1987a). In making this statement, it must be realised that the assertion is based on a 'snapshot' of different family structures at a particular moment in time (1982-3) when in reality family structure is a dynamic and fluid entity changing constantly over the course of the lifecycle and in response to external pressures.

The fieldwork in Querétaro indicated that there were a number of reasons why men were unwilling to let their wives out to work, aside from a straightforward practical concern about the probems involved in managing housework and child-care if women entered paid employment. One reason concerned a frequently unwarranted supposition on the part of men that their partners might earn more than them and 'get ahead'. A second major reason was the fear that others might think that a man who let his wife work was (1) incapable of sustaining the family on his own income, despite the fact that many men are negligent of their domestic responsibilities anyway; and (2) and perhaps more importantly, that the man was failing to exercise authority over his spouse, it being popularly thought that any man allowing his wife 'onto the streets', was weak or 'under her thumb'. A third reason was that certain kinds of work, by bringing women into contact with members of the opposite sex, was seen to threaten female fidelity to their husbands. A final major reason was the fear of women gaining economic independence and therefore effective control over their own lives (see also Roldan, 1988, for similar findings in Mexico City).

The rationale behind male restrictions over women's economic activities, as noted in Chapter 1, is complex; on one hand it has ideological roots – Mexican men are victims of a culture which regards the conquest and control of women as a vital expression of manhood; on the other hand, as low-income men they are victims of an exploitative situation of class relations, with few opportunities to exercise power except within the home; if women work this privilege and status is threatened. However, whatever reasons lie behind male control of women's work, the implications are serious; women's experience of poverty is often filtered through attachment to individual men which in many cases condemns them to a gratuitous intensification of physical, emotional and economic hardship. Those who are 'lucky' enough to obtain permission to work outside the home are usually forced into low-status, demeaning jobs, and also have to pay for the privilege by devoting all their spare time to housework in order that they are not subsequently withdrawn from the labour force through failing to execute their domestic duties. However, while this is a general impression of the poor in Querétaro, the research also showed that household structure played a critical role in determining the translation of these wider norms into practice at the level of daily family life. In particular there appeared to be marked variations in rates of female labour force participation among different types of family which in the 1982–3 survey consisted of the following proportions: nuclear households (68.5% of the survey); one-parent families (9%); male-headed extended families (18%) and female-headed extended families (4.5%).

The most obvious disparity in rates of women's economic activity occurred between *households headed by women* and *households headed by men*: in the former, rates of women's labour force participation were well over twice as high (79%) as in the latter (34%). Inevitably this is in part a response to the fact that in the absence of a man, women have to take on a breadwinning role, although necessity is not always the key determinant: women heads of single-parent and extended families tend to be older (around early middle-age) than spouses in male-headed households and their wage is not generally, therefore, the sole income of the family unit since at least one of their children is usually working. Indeed the average number of family members working in Querétaro in 1982–3 was 1.6 in each one-parent family (with an average size of 5.4 persons), compared with 1.2 in each nuclear family (with an average size of 6.2 members) (Chant, 1985b). Given that need *per se* is not a particularly relevant factor, another important reason explaining the fact that women heads of one-parent families were so much more likely to hold jobs as their counterparts in nuclear households, appeared to be their relative *freedom* in choosing whether or not to work: the decisions of women household heads were not subject to scrutiny or veto by a male partner. Neither were female household heads restricted in the kinds of work they applied for, unlike women in other types of family. These factors undoubtedly helped to explain why more women heads of household were involved in full-time paid employment in factory work and commerce than their counterparts in male-headed units (Chant, 1984, 1987a).

Another major difference was obvious between *nuclear* and *male-headed extended households*, with greater proportions of women in extended households having paid work (44% as opposed to 32%). Here contributory factors were more complex. At a practical level, women in extended households generally had more time to devote to income-earning activities since these units frequently contained female kin who shared domestic labour and child-care; whereas women in nuclear families were often exclusively responsible for household duties, receiving little help from husbands or younger children (Chant, 1984). These findings have been echoed by work carried out in urban Mexico and Brazil by García, Muñoz and de Oliveira (1983a, 1983b), where nuclear households are argued to have lower rates of female involvement in wage-earning because of their scarce labour supply i.e. there are too few adult members to take on major productive and reproductive tasks (see also Peek, 1978, on Chile). Extended households, on the other hand, with greater numbers of adults and sharing of workloads, are able to release more women into the labour market.[11]

In addition to the above, the interviews in Querétaro pointed to other, less tangible reasons for higher rates of female labour force participation in extended units. One is the fact that in extended families multiple-earning strategies require people to pool their wages[12] or the greater part of their wages in order that the unit functions as a viable entity; where there is limited financial cooperation extended households almost inevitably disband.[13] The cooperative income-generation and allocation which residence in an extended unit implies means that there is a vested interest in maximising earning potential; as a result as many people as possible are encouraged to enter the labour force, including women (Chant, 1987a).

This pattern is quite the reverse in nuclear households where there is often only one earner – the male household head. Unlike in extended households where multiple-earning and resource-sharing is generally a prerequisite and a norm, in nuclear households men tend to monopolise the generation and distribution of finance. Exclusive provision of income by male heads allows them considerable freedom in deciding how to allocate their wages; as sole breadwinners they are not not necessarily accountable to other family members as to how their income is spent and often withold a substantial portion of their salaries for personal use. In these cases men have little to gain from letting their wives out to work, except perhaps to justify retaining even more of their own wage. On the other hand, there is probably much to lose: working women may gain sufficient financial independence to leave their husbands altogether – anathema to men who wish to retain the privilege of determining the future of the family unit. In nuclear households therefore, permitting the labour force participation of wives is potentially destabilising not only in terms of the conflict it sets up regarding the gender division of productive and reproductive tasks, but also insofar as it may erode a key element of male control over their womenfolk (see also Chant, 1985a).

A final factor leading to greater labour force participation among women in extended families is that the existence of more than one adult woman contributes to female solidarity and strength, thereby allowing them to challenge conventional male restrictions on their lives; women in nuclear households, alternatively, do not have recourse to support from other women in facing up to male control. Moreover, sharing of workloads in extended families seems to attenuate the rigid sexual division of labour characteristic of nuclear households. It is difficult for one man within the domestic unit to argue that his own wife should not work if another woman in the household has paid employment.

These kinds of findings led to the conclusion that the labour force participation of women related very much to the operation of the sexual division of labour at the household level, and particularly to the degree of control of male heads over wives. Obviously in women-headed households this barrier is removed and is un-doubtedly a major reason why many female heads work, even if they do not actually *have* to. In extended families a combination of the fact that domestic labour is shared, income pooled, that women have recourse to female support, and are not subject to the exclusive authority of husbands but involved in a much more democratically organised survival strategy predicated on higher levels of household cooperation and consensus, means that it is far more difficult for individual men to forbid their wives to work, especially when it runs counter to the rationale of maximising family income. However, in nuclear households where women are isolated and controlled by male monopoly over wage-earning, freedom to enter the labour force is far more limited (see Chant, 1985a, 1987a, 1987b).

However, two major obstacles stood in the way of converting this conclusion into an argument which could be applied in other contexts (see also Preface and Chapter 1). First, there was no basis for comparison. To what extent was it valid to attribute the main cause of limited female employment to male decision-making in nuclear household structures, when Querétaro was unlikely to provide women with major employment opportunities? As a modern manufacturing city dominated by capital-intensive industry and few openings for women in the 'formal sector', it was entirely possible that men felt their was little point in letting their wives go out to work, Would the paltry economic benefits gleaned from part-time, casual or self-employment in the 'informal' sector justify releasing women from the home where arguably they were better placed to manage income more efficiently? In other words, was a rational trade-off being made against the relative costs and benefits of keeping women in full-time 'expenditure-reducing' strategies as opposed to entering them into 'income-generating' strategies?

Second, it was also possible that nuclear families were to some degree more likely to occur in cities such as Querétaro due to the nature of the local productive structure. Certainly an association has been drawn between the rise of 'modern' manufacturing development and a growing preponderance of nuclear families (Das, 1980; Durrani,1976; García *et al.*, 1983b; Goode, 1963). To what extent however, is the classic nuclear structure with breadwinning husband and home-bound wife an adaptation to situations where women are unlikely to get work?[14] In areas where women may obtain employment more easily, nuclear households might be less common. As such were the immediate restrictions placed on wives at the level of the household in Querétaro in some sense 'residual' conflicts determined structurally by the nature of city-wide patterns of labour demand? In other words, were wives apportioning the blame for their non-participation in the workforce to husbands, when in fact there was really no question about them working in the first place in a city unlikely to provide them with reasonable employment opportunities, and in turn to favour the preponderance of small household units governed by a rigid sexual division of labour? In this respect it was possibly misleading to attribute undue importance to 'supply' factors, when those self-same factors were perhaps more properly a secondary outcome of predetermining conditions of local labour demand. Further data from other areas were needed in order to clarify the importance of these variables and their interconnections.

The significance of the 1986 comparative study then, lies in its scope to provide some answers to the above questions, and to strengthen the basis for more generalised ideas. Interestingly its findings confirm many of the discoveries made in Querétaro in 1982–3 regarding the control exerted on female labour supply by household structure, and the speculation that household form would vary according to local economic circumstances. Broadly speaking women's labour force participation is higher in cities with less 'modern' large-scale industrial economies; non-nuclear households are also more common in such contexts within the 1986 study, and finally there are clear relationships between the two – women's labour force participation is significantly higher in non-nuclear units. A brief outline is presented of these associations in the final section of the chapter.

Inter-urban variations in variations in women's labour force participation 1986

As hypothesised in the Introduction, and drawing on data from this and the preceding two chapters, it seems that women's employment is highest in Puerto Vallarta whichever source is used: census data, interviews with managers in key enterprises in each city (the author's Employer Survey), and with women in low-income communities (Household Questionnaire Survey) (see Table 4.8). For all cities estimates of women's employment are highest on the basis of the Household Questionnaire Survey because this captures a wide variety of informal income-generating activities not usually recorded in official statistics. Although it seems that by 1986 women in Querétaro are more economically active than women in León, this should be treated cautiously since the 1986 sample was very small and non-random, notwithstanding the rise in women's employment in Querétaro in the intervening three year period. Given the additional evidence from the census and author's employer survey, it is likely that female labour force participation in León lies somewhere between that of Querétaro and Puerto Vallarta, and whatever, the results in general suggest that *demand* or *opportunity* for female economic activity *does* vary according to the nature of the city-wide economy and this in turn reflects in actual rates of female labour force participation. Certainly chi-square analysis found the differences in participation rates among cities to be statistically significant (at a 90% level of confidence).

Table 4.8: Women's employment in the study cities

	Puerto Vallarta	León	Querétaro
Percentage of women in labour force (Census data 1980, city as a whole)	32.3%	29.2%	28.3%
Percentage of women in labour force (Employer Survey 1986)	37.4%	28.7%	21.7%
Percentage of women with work in low-income settlements (Household Questionnaire Survey, 1986)[a]	58.7% (N=92)	50.6% (N=77)	55.0% (N=20,1986)[b] 30.7% (N=244,1982–3)[c]

Notes:
[a] This figure includes all women who had some form of income-generating activity
[b] Non-random sample, 1986.
[c] Random sample, 1982–3.

Source: Mexican Census, 1980; Employer Survey, 1986; Household Questionnaire Survey, 1986 (and Querétaro, 1982–3).

Inter-urban variations in household structure

Sex of household heads
Turning now to the question of household structure, this also seems to vary substantially among cities. Regarding first, sex of household heads, female heads are most common in Puerto Vallarta on the basis of both the household survey and 1970 census data (see Table 4.9).[15] The link between this particular dimension of household structure and the urban economy undoubtedly relates in part to higher degrees of female labour force participation in Puerto Vallarta.[16] The significance of the results (cross-tabulation of sex of household head and city) were confirmed by chi-square at a 99% level of confidence.

Household composition
However, in terms of composition, extended families are *not* as expected, highest in León, the total being 32.6% (both male- and female-headed) in Puerto Vallarta, 27.3% in León, 22.5% in Querétaro (1982–3 – random) and 60% in 1986 (non-random) (see Table 4.10). The relatively low overall proportion of extended families in León is possibly influenced by the fact that Lomas de Jerez was only a very recently established settlement, containing virtually no local enterprise, and having a very low proportion of extended households (21.7%) compared with Piletas which was far older, and contained several small family-owned footwear workshops many of which employed and resided with kin; here extended families constituted 29.6% of the total. The only single settlement which had a higher proportion of extended families than Piletas was Buenos Aires, the younger

Table 4.9: Percentage of women-headed households in the study cities[a]

	Puerto Vallarta	León	Querétaro
Percentage of women-headed households (Census data, 1970)	17%	13%	10%
Percentage of women-headed households (Household Survey, 1986)	19.6% (N=92)	10.4% (N=77)	40% (N=20)[b] 13.5% (N=244)[c]

Notes:

[a] Married couples in the 1986 Household Survey were defined as male-headed households.

[b] Non-random sample, 1986.

[c] Random sample, 1982–3.

Source: Mexican Census, 1970; Household Questionnaire Survey 1986 (and Querétaro, 1982–3).

settlement in Puerto Vallarta which had originated in the early 1980s. Here large numbers of extended households (43.5%) appear to be attributable not to the existence of domestic-based production, but to the fact that many women with young children are working outside the home: such units often become extended because women have to organise permanent help in child-care and domestic labour from female kin. In part, however, it may also be due to the fact that there has been an extreme shortage of land for low-income housing in Puerto Vallarta since the late 1970s and people have probably been under greater pressure to set

Table 4.10: Family types in household interview sample by city

	Puerto Vallarta	León	Querétaro 1982–3[a]	Querétaro 1986[b]
Family types				
Nuclear	51.1%[c] (47)	63.6% (49)	68.5% (167)	30.0% (6)
One-parent	9.8% (9)	5.2% (4)	9.0% (22)	10.0% (2)
Male-extended	22.8% (21)	22.1% (17)	18.0% (44)	30.0% (6)
Female-extended	9.8% (9)	5.2% (4)	4.5% (11)	30.0% (6)
Couple	6.5% (6)	3.9% (3)	–	–
Total	*100.0% (92)*	*100.0% (77)*	*100.0% (244)*	*100.0% (20)*

Notes:

[a] Random sample.

[b] Non-random.

[c] Percentages may not add up to 100 due to rounding.

Source: Household Questionnaire Survey, 1986 (and Querétaro 1982–3).

up more communally based living arrangements in more recent settlements. Chi-square analysis indicated that the overall relationship between household structure and city was significant, but only at a 95% level of confidence, not quite as high therefore as sex of head of household alone.

Changes in household structure over time: Querétaro 1982–3 to 1986
Regarding the issue of changes household composition over time; in Querétaro in 1986 a sub-sample of respondents from the 1982-3 survey was selected that more or less accorded with overall proportions of different family types in the earlier period, i.e. greater numbers of nuclear families were chosen than female-headed extended households and so on. However, considerable changes in the structure of these selected households had taken place in the intervening three years (see Table 4.11). In absolute terms, 9 out of the 20 households had changed their structure (see also Table 6.2), and in proportional terms (as per Table 4.11), there had been an overall tendency towards a reduction in nuclear and one-parent families and a rise in extended units, particularly female-headed ones. These trends are probably attributable to the effects of crisis and recession which as a modern manufacturing city heavily dependent on imported components, Querétaro felt particularly severely. Kin have had to pool resources and labour in order to ride out a period of extreme vulnerability and privation. Similar findings have been made by Mercedes González de la Rocha (1988) in her longitudinal study of Guadalajara in the 1980s and are discussed further in Chapter 6. The figures also suggest that trends towards the formation of non-nuclear units are likely to be related to rising numbers of women with paid work over this period (see Table 4.8).

Table 4.11: Households selected for 1986 survey in Querétaro according to structure in 1982–3 and change by 1986

Family type	Household structure in 1982–3	Household structure in 1986
Nuclear	40% (8)	30% (6)
One-parent	25% (5)	10% (2)
Male-extended	25% (5)	30% (6)
Female-extended	10% (2)	30% (6)
Total	100% (20)	100% (20)

Source: Household Questionnaire Survey, Querétaro, 1986.

Household structure and female labour force participation: intra- and inter-urban variations

Finally, in considering the relationship between household structure and female labour force participation, the results confirm the findings of the 1982–3 survey in Querétaro; namely that women's labour force participation is lowest in nuclear structures, with the single exception of Puerto Vallarta where a greater proportion of nuclear family spouses have an income-generating activity than female heads of extended structures (see Table 4.12).[17] On the whole, however, women are usually more active economically when they head their own households (see Table 4.12). Indeed chi-square found both sex of head of household on its own, and household structure to be statistically significant in interpreting women's economic activity at 99.9% levels of confidence. Sex of head of household has a relatively greater chi-square value than household structure however, and is therefore probably more strongly related to women's employment than when composition is taken into account as well.

Table 4.12: Household structure and women's labour force participation[a]

	Percentage of women with some form of income-generating activity, 1986			
	Puerto Vallarta	*León*	*Querétaro*	*Total*
Nuclear	55.3%[b](N=47)	42.9%(N=49)	16.7%(N=6)	47.0% (N=102)
One-parent	77.8%(N=9)	50.0%(N=4)	100.0%(N=2)	73.3%(N=15)
Male-extended	61.9%(N=21)	70.5%(N=17)	66.7%(N=6)	65.9%(N=44)
Female-extended	44.5%(N=9)	75.0%(N=4)	66.7%(N=6)	57.9%(N=19)
Couple	66.7%(N=6)	33.3%(N=3)	–	55.5%(N=9)
Total	*58.7%(N=92)*	*50.6%(N=77)*	*55.0%(N=20)*	*55.0%(N=189)*

Notes:
[a] Labour force participation here refers to all women who are involved in an income-generating concern, even if they are unpaid (3 cases).
[b] Percentages might not add-up to 100 exactly because of rounding.

Source: Household Questionnaire Survey, 1986.

Conclusions

Recapping the main findings of this chapter briefly, the single most important determinant of female labour force participation among the urban poor in the survey appears to be:

1 sex of the household head; followed closely by;
2 household structure;
3 age of women (which is closely tied in with both the previous factors: women household heads are usually older than those who have husbands, and women in extended households are older than those in nuclear structures);
4 numbers of dependents in the household (though not dependents per worker); and finally,
5 city of residence.

In turn city and sex of head household are highly interrelated, and so too are city and household structure though to a lesser degree than sex of household head alone. However while these results demonstrate the existence of multiple and overlapping relationships among women's work, household structure and local economies, they do not actually *explain* the nature of the associations. Thus in the next chapter an attempt is made to unravel the links between household structure and the nature of specific urban economies as they influence, and indeed in the case of household structure, are influenced *by* women's labour force participation, using in-depth qualitative data gathered in a detailed sub-sample survey including reconstructions of women's employment and family histories. The key objective of Chapter 5 then is to find out why such interrelationships exist, and to illustrate more precisely how, in practical terms, these interrelationships between women's employment, household structure and the local economy are articulated.

Notes

1 'Owner-occupier' is used here in a rather broad sense to describe households which may or may not have legal title to land, but are not paying rent or living on land loaned by another person (see also Appendix 1).

2 Only the migrant status of the woman head or spouse in the core household unit was recorded in the questionnaire survey. Accordingly this is the basis on which households are classified as migrants or non-migrants, notwithstanding the fact that many children of migrants have been born in the study cities themselves.

3 The terms 'work', 'employment', 'labour force participation' and so on are used in this chapter to describe involvement in income-generating activities of all kinds, including informal domestic-based work and also, direct participation in a family business, although in the latter category two or three women did not actually receive individual payment. In this way the use of the term 'work' as a synonym for income-generating activity in no way implies that women who devote themselves entirely to housework and childcare do not work, indeed these so-called 'reproductive' activities are an integral and critical part of household survival; even when they do not generate income directly, they often reduce expenditure and create surplus income for household use (see, for example, Brydon and Chant, 1989: 10–12).

4 Average wages in each city need to set against the minumum general wage at the time of interviewing. In Puerto Vallarta interviews were carried out between January and May 1986 at which time the minimum general weekly wage was 9380 pesos. However, on 1 June 1986 the minimum general salary was raised to 11,725 pesos until the end of the year, thus in León and Querétaro this is the yardstick against which actual wages should be evaluated. Trying to express these wages in 'hard currency' such as the US dollar is difficult since the peso devalued at a fluctuating rate throughout the year, but if 490 pesos per dollar is taken as a mean value in the first half of 1986, then the average minimum wage in Puerto Vallarta was $18.94 US. If the rate of 720 pesos to the dollar over the summer is used then the minimum wage was equivalent to about $16.28 US in León. However, by the time interviewing was carried out in Querétaro in the autumn of 1986, there were around 850 pesos to the dollar making the minimum weekly wage about $13.79 US.

5 'Chi-square' is a non-parametric statistical test which compares observed distributions with an expected (random) distribution (parametric tests use continuous data, for

example, per capita income, whereas non-parametric tests deal with discrete variables where a distribution takes on a few distinct values, for example, women's activity category, sex of household head etc, or, where data is continuous, for example, age, one groups this data into classes such that one has *groups*: e.g. 15–19 yrs, 20–24 yrs and so on). Chi-square allows one to test whether the difference between observed and expected numbers is greater than could reasonably be due to chance alone. In terms of the present analysis it asks whether women's age groups and their category of activity (houseperson or worker – greater subdivision of categories into full-time, part-time worker and so on would not have satisfied the requirements of the test for specified minimum frequencies of observation in the cells) are linked in any systematic way. The chi-square result produced is then compared with a table of critical values which tells one whether the result is such that the null hypothesis (i.e. there is no difference in women's labour force participation according to age group for example) may be rejected. In addition it also tells one how likely it is that one variable relates to the other by giving levels of confidence which range from 90% to 99.9%. If one has a high level of confidence, for example 99%, then there is far less likelihood that the variables are randomly linked, i.e. one is 99% sure that links are non-random.

Ideally 'multiple regression' (a parametric statistical test which measures how much of the variation in a dependent variable is explained by various independent variables) would have been used to examine the major influences on female labour force participation so that the relative influence of all supply variables could have been examined together. (Chi-square's major limitation is that it can only examine the associations between two things at a time.) However, since female labour force participation is a discrete (and qualitative) variable it was not possible to carry out multiple regression on a dependent variable of this nature: athough independent variables entered on the 'right-hand' side of the equation may be qualitative, the dependent or 'left-hand' variable may not have discrete values. However, multiple regression proved most useful in the analysis of continuous data such as per capita earnings and budgetary income (see Chapter 7).

6   Human capital theory is derived from neoclassical economic theory and suggests that women earn less than men because they have lower 'productivity'. Lower productivity is seen to result from women's comparatively low levels of education, training, skills and work experience (see, for example, Anker and Hein, 1986 and Carvajal and Geithman, 1985).

7   Although 24% of all male household heads in the cities had no education either, only 32.9% of men had not completed primary schooling, compared with 31% who had, and a further 8.4% with secondary education or equivalent. One man had completed higher education and four had taken an adult literacy course.

8   Benería and Roldan (1987: 10) note that although marriage and/or childbirth means a period away from the labour market for the majority of women who have worked when single, this is fairly short-term, with women returning to work quite soon afterwards. Rather than preventing women's reincorporation into paid work, childbirth tends to change the nature of employment women undertake. In their study of Mexico City, it was found that women often move into industrial homeworking after marriage because this particular job can be combined with domestic responsibilities.

9   Table 4.7 shows that families where women are unemployed through sickness have the highest average per capita household earnings (7,202 pesos). This is probably because sickness tends to be more of a problem among older women who tend to be able to rely upon the earnings of adolescent and adult children. This sub-group are treated separately here in order to compare more directly the incomes of households where women work and do not work but are potentially economically active.

10   It is interesting to note that Scott's (1990) work on women in Lima also found no

clear correlation between female labour force participation and similar supply variables such as numbers of children, stage in the lifecycle and so on.

11   Similar observations have been made in rural contexts. See for example Ramirez Boza (1987) on Costa Rica.

12   Inevitably, 'pooling' is a highly variable phenomenon and is discussed further in Chapter 7. For interesting reviews of different pooling arrangements see Fapohunda (1988), Benería and Roldan (1987) and Roldan (1988).

13   Relationships between appended units and core units within extended households in Mexico appear to be generally harmonious, possibly because in cases where relationships have been strained, households have subsequently separated. Susan Lobo on the basis of her work in Lima, Peru, for example suggests that there is often conflict and ambivalence in extended households (albeit beneath the surface), especially regarding in-laws who may have divided allegiances between their families of procreation and affinal kin in their current place of residence.

14   The 'discouraged worker' effect discussed by Gerry Rodgers (1989: 21) may be relevant here. While not directly concerned with women, Rodgers notes that secondary household members in general may abandon job search in the face of the unlikelihood of finding employment.

15   The 1980 Mexican Census does not include data on sex of household heads, unlike that of 1970.

16   Particularly the fact that working women are more likely to leave their husbands and form their own households – a phenomenon also noted in studies of 'First World' countries. See Teachman *et al.* (1987: 12).

17   This inconsistency in the general pattern could be explained by the fact that one woman head of an extended household had been out of work for some time because of illness and was therefore categorised as a 'non-worker' . If she had been employed as she normally was, then the rate of female labour force participation for women-headed extended households in Puerto Vallarta would have been 55.5%, bringing it much more into line with female-headed extended households elsewhere, and making participation marginally higher than in nuclear households in the city. Nevertheless, it is also the case that women spouses in nuclear households in Puerto Vallarta are much more active economically than their counterparts in the other areas. This largely results from the nature of local labour demand and is explored further in Chapter 5.

5

Women's employment and household structure

Introduction

The preceding chapter noted a broad correspondence between rates of female labour force participation and household structure; generally speaking, female labour force participation is lower in nuclear units than in non-nuclear structures.[1] In this chapter an attempt is made to unravel the nature of this association in more detail by examining case study material gathered in in-depth interviews with a sub-sample of households in the three cities (see Appendix 1).

Discussion revolves around two main questions. First, how is the relationship between household structure and female labour force participation articulated? Second, and related to this, is women's labour force participation influenced to a greater extent by demand (i.e. the nature of job opportunities in the local economy) or supply (i.e. factors operating at the level of the household, particularly household structure). These issues are explored on the basis of recent work histories of women in the three cities. Perhaps the most appropriate way of examining the first question is to focus on *moments of transition and change* (in either female labour force participation or household structure) and the *sequence* in which related events occur. In other words, in those cases where a relationship between female labour force participation and family structure is apparent (i.e. where the two factors are closely linked in time or there is some explicit acknowledgement of links by interviewees) does women's entry into the workforce *precede* or *postdate* modifications in household structure? More specifically, to what degree can we establish if changes in household structure arise as a *response* to women's movement into the labour market, or if are there certain conditions within the household which have to be fulfilled *before* women can even consider taking a job? While somewhat mechanistic this line of analysis provides a guide to the source, sequence and direction of labour force moves and household changes. In turn it helps to some degree in answering the second question concerning the relative influence exerted by demand and supply factors on women's labour force participation. Possibly where local demand for female labour is high and rates of female employment correspondingly greater, this acts as a major catalyst of household change in the sense that women's involvement in waged work engenders certain adaptations in household structure: in other words, a key element determining the formation of households in such localities is the actual or potential participation of women in the labour force. In less favourable employment conditions on the other hand, women may only work if the structures of their households require or facilitate it; under these circumstances it may be suggested that female labour force participation is more strongly influenced at the level of supply, occurring primarily as a response to family needs and/or capabilities. Intrinsic to this investigation is obviously the way in which general patterns of household structure vary according to the local economy.

Although reference is made here to all three cities, analysis is slanted most heavily towards Puerto Vallarta and León, given that the next chapter concentrates exclusively on Querétaro between 1982–3 and 1986. In-depth interviews were carried out in all three settlements in Querétaro, and in one in both Puerto Vallarta (El Caloso) and León (Piletas).

Interrelationships between female labour force participation and household structure

At the outset it is important to identify the range of the sample, and the numbers of cases in each city, each category of household structure and so on. Interviewees in the sub-sample were selected from the list of questionnaire interviewees and a breakdown is provided in Table 5.1.[2] With such a small sub-sample, it is obviously not possible to generalise to any great degree about interconnections between household structure and female labour force participation nor to draw any definitive conclusions. Nonetheless scope exists to identify and illustrate dominant patterns of linkages, and to provide an idea of the range of ways in which they operate in practice. Before going on to examine the various interrelationships it is also important to consider women's labour force participation rates in this sub-sample of households (see Table 5.2). As in the questionnaire survey, the sub-sample also reveals that greater numbers of women tend to have remunerated work in non-nuclear households, except in Puerto Vallarta.[3]

Table 5.1: Household structures in sub-sample (1986)

	Puerto Vallarta	León	Querétaro
Male nuclear	8	2	6
One-parent	2	1	2
Male-extended	5	3	6
Female-extended	2	1	6
Couple	3	–	–
Total	20	7	20

Source: Sub-sample Household Interview Survey, 1986.

Table 5.2: Women's labour force participation and household structure in the sub-sample

	Puerto Vallarta			León			Querétaro		
	A^a	B^b	C^c	A	B	C	A	B	C
Male nuclear[d]	4	3	1	–	1	1	–	1	5
One-parent	2	–	–	–	–	1	2	–	–
Male-extended	3	1	1	–	3	–	4	–	2
Female-extended	1	–	1	1	–	–	4	–	2
Couple	2	1	–	–	–	–	–	–	–
Total	*12*	*5*	*3*	*1*	*4*	*2*	*11*	*1*	*9*

Notes
[a] A = Full-time job or remunerated work is main activity.
[b] B = Part-time/casual work (spends more time in home undertaking housework/child-care).
[c] C = No income-generating activity at all e.g. full-time houseperson, permanently sick etc.
[d] In Querétaro, unpaid casual helper in family business classified as houseperson (in male-nuclear group); and woman on sick pay due to industrial injury (in female extended group) classified as employed since in receipt of regular transfer payments.

Source: Sub-sample Household Interview Survey, 1986.

Analysis of recent work histories of the women in the sub-sample suggests that female labour force participation (or lack of) is frequently related in some way to household structure. The household characteristics of around three-quarters (25 out of 33) of women in the sub-sample with some type of paid work had changed prior to, or fairly soon after women had entered the labour force (usually within 12–15 months),[4] *or* household structure was being deliberately retained in its present form to facilitate their participation. Indeed the majority of those women whose entry into the labour force had almost certainly been precipitated in part by family circumstances *explicitly acknowledged* the significance of household form and organisation in their decision to do so. This is important given that although people's own accounts of why they enter the job market are extremely complex, and in several cases reflect a *post hoc* rationalisation of events that might have not been apparent at the time, and/or occurred for other reasons as well, it does suggest that household structure is a relevant variable, especially in the minds of women.

Establishing and analysing the nature of these linkages is inevitably problematic. Across the three cities as a whole it appears that slightly greater numbers of women have entered the labour force as a result of changes in household structure, as those for whom changes in household structure have occurred subsequently; however, conferring undue significance to chronological sequence is obviously dangerous. Separation in time, for example, does not necessarily mean that events are conceived or planned separately (if of course there is any conscious planning at all). Indeed the fact that there is often so short an interval between female entry into the workforce and household change possibly implies that families only take action on one front when they know they can rely on corresponding changes in another. In the case of compositional shifts for example, households which have some idea that kin will come and live with them in the near future may deploy adult women into the labour force in advance of actual extension; conversely, households may extend with the objective of putting women into the workforce, yet some time may elapse before women actually find a job. Another important set of qualifications relates to transitions in household headship: although many women take jobs only *after* they have separated from their partners, in conflictive cases of marital breakdown there is frequently a period prior to separation where women have to go out to work (albeit secretly in some instances) in order to counter dwindling financial support from husbands. Again an uncritical acceptance and/or interpretation of *de facto* chronology assists little in pinpointing the primary catalyst of female labour force participation. In some cases, of course, household structure and female employment behaviour are so inextricably linked that there is no way of identifying the precipitating factor. Having said this, an attempt is made in the following sections to review dominant patterns and interrelationships between the two variables.

Household structure: effects on female labour force participation

As far as women whose entry into the labour force has been precipitated or made possible by a change in household circumstances are concerned, two features stand out from the in-depth interviews and life-history data: one concerns household headship (specifically the absence or departure of the male head), the other relates to composition and its implications for internal divisions of labour and household management. Both these findings bear out conclusions of the earlier work in Querétaro (see Chapter 4).

Sex of the household head

Departure of the male head, for whatever reason – to find work elsewhere, as an outcome of separation or divorce and so on – is in almost all cases a catalyst for female entry into the labour force. Indeed many women-headed households, especially non-extended units, evolve directly out of male nuclear households where they were not previously in paid work. It is hardly surprising therefore that in the great majority of female-headed households in the sub-sample (72%), adult women engage in some kind of income-generating activity, and in most cases have little choice but to do so, especially if in sole charge of young dependent children. Indeed the labour force participation rate of female heads of *one-parent* families in the sub-sample is 80% compared with 67% in extended households where there is greater likelihood of income-earning by other members. In the broader questionnaire survey these figures were 73.3% and 57.9% respectively)

The case of Lupe, 34-year old head of a one-parent household in Puerto

Vallarta clearly demonstrates the significance of household headship for women's workforce involvement.[5] Born in San Luís Potosí in the central highlands, Lupe spent most of her childhood and adolescence in Guadalajara and at the age of 15 met and married the father of her first two children (she now has three). Lupe's short-lived marriage was a bid to escape a desperately unhappy home life. Her own father had deserted her mother and younger sister when she was only 3 years old. Taking casual jobs in restaurants and private houses, first in Mexico City and then in Guadalajara, Lupe's mother was often forced to leave her daughters locked-up at home all day or occasionally (when she could afford it) with a paid child-minder, until she remarried and retired once again to the home just after Lupe's sixth birthday. Although the second partnership lasted over 10 years and gave rise to the births of a further five children, it was highly conflictive. Her new husband was extremely authoritarian and particularly aggressive towards his step-daughters. Although this would not appear to have been a very satisfactory arrangement for her mother to enter into, Lupe feels that in the past it was much more difficult for a woman with children to survive alone; as such there was little choice in the matter. Lupe only had a brief spell at school, entering at the age of seven and completing three grades by the time she was withdrawn at 8 years old to assist her mother in the home. A long and particularly unhappy period ensued in which Lupe's entire days were devoted to repetitive household chores, ministering to the needs of her step-brothers and sisters, and suffering at close quarters the animosity of her step-father and his constant quarrels with her mother. Lupe was continually thinking of ways to escape and seized her chance at 15 when she met a man 20 years her senior who asked to her to move in with him. They married almost immediately under pressure from both families and had two children in the three years their union 'lasted. Although Lupe was obviously busy with child-bearing and child-rearing, she was keen to become involved in productive work and on several occasions tried to persuade her husband (a travelling salesmen dealing in medicines and pharmaceutical products) to let her help out. However, her husband was even more restrictive than her stepfather; not only was he totally opposed to the idea that his wife should work, but also resented her meeting people and going out alone. So, far from marriage providing an escape route out of a claustrophobic and limited upbringing, instead it made Lupe feel even more confined. Frustration, bitterness and quarrels were an inevitable result. By the time she was 18 and her mother and stepfather had finally parted, Lupe decided to leave her own husband and return to her mother. With her children now in the care of their grandmother, Lupe embarked on a career in the buying and selling of '*fayuca*' (colloq. 'contraband') using various of her ex-husband's business contacts. Within a few years she established a lucrative trade and began travelling all over the country. At the age of 26 she met the father of her third child and lived on and off with him for a couple of years, finally abandoning the relationship in the face of various restrictions he attempted to impose upon her, including the demand that she should give up work. In 1982, a few months after her mother had died and there was no longer anything to tie her to Guadalajara, Lupe decided it was time for a change of scene and moved to Puerto Vallarta where she thought she would not only stand a better chance of making a living but also have an opportunity to acquire a 'real' skill and to engage in an 'above-board' occupation (dealing in contraband was financially worthwhile, but also quite dangerous). She is now working as a trainee in one of the numerous photographic laboratories in the city and supplements her earnings by renting out a couple of rooms on her lot in Caloso. The two eldest children, a son and a daughter, both studying at institutions of further education, also contribute with earnings from part-time occupations. Lupe herself has also recently started a return-to-study course in order to complete her primary education.

In this example, Lupe obviously had little choice *but* to work having taken the decision to leave her first husband. Nevertheless it is also apparent that she felt a need to explore other avenues than looking after children and the only way she could do that was to extricate herself from marriage. Indeed the other main reason why absence of a male head is so critical in influencing whether women work is because only on their own are women completely at liberty to do so. This issue is explored further when we come to examine the situations of women not presently in employment.

Changes in composition and internal divisions of labour

The second major way in which household structure influences women's entry into the labour force is through changes in composition. Many women embark upon paid work, albeit on a part-time basis, following extension of the family unit. This is most apparent in male-headed households where the incorporation of additional kin, especially adult women, permits a sharing of domestic duties and thereby removes a major barrier to wives' employment. Under this heading, we must also include instances where male-headed nuclear households have reached a stage in the lifecycle when a significant share of housework and child-care may be taken over by one of the children (almost invariably a daughter).[6] In several respects these 'late-stage' nuclear households are very similar to extended units in that an older daughter may fulfil the same kinds of duties as those of female kin in the latter. It is important to note however that although we might use the term 'late-stage', there is no discernible pattern of age composition reached by households before they pass on domestic tasks to children.[7] In some cases daughters as old as 15 or 16 years are not regarded sufficiently capable to take over from mothers, whereas in others the delegation of domestic responsibilities occurs when girls are still quite young, even pre-adolescent (see also Beneria and Roldan, 1987: 130 on Mexico City). Generally speaking however, daughters are usually in their mid-to-late teens before mothers work full-time; keeping an eye on a toddler for a few hours is all the younger ones are usually required to do.

A case in point here is that of Celia, 28-year-old mother of three and native of León who works part-time selling clothing and footwear from home. Celia's husband is a sales assistant for a large electrical firm, who while earning an above-minimum wage, in 1984 consented to Celia's request to take-up small-scale retailing in order to counter inflationary rises in the costs of living. This was only possible however because her daughter (then aged 9) was thought sufficiently mature and sensible to take care of Celia's youngest child of 3 years. Until then Celia stressed that she could not have entertained the prospect of taking on any paid work at all, partly because her husband would not have been happy about it. Celia devotes about 3 hours a day to her commercial activities, occasionally travelling to nearby villages to pick up cheap shoes and clothes, during which time her daughter minds the younger child before or after her shift at school.

Stage in the lifecycle is also important for women's ability to enter the labour force in those households where the extended appendage is formed of *male* rather than female relatives. For example, Guadalupe R. in Querétaro, is 30 years old and lives in an extended household consisting of her husband, four daughters (aged between 4 and 14 years) and a 17-year-old brother-in-law. Given the sex of Guadalupe's in-law and the fact that he has a full-time job, extension in this case was not particularly beneficial to Guadalupe, in fact if anything, it gave her extra to do – more shirts to wash and iron, an extra breakfast to prepare and so on. However, in 1983 when times were getting particularly hard in Querétaro, and her eldest daughters (then 10 and 11 years) had reached an age where they were able to be left in charge, Guadalupe managed to convince her husband (who had always been against the idea) to let her take a job. Obtaining full-time work on the assembly-line in the local Volkswagen plant has meant that the bulk of the housework has now been passed on to her daughters, although Guadalupe still plays a key managerial role in domestic matters and tends to take over completely at weekends.

As it is however, households extended exclusively with male kin are relatively uncommon. The majority of extended households in the sub-sample (10) contain female kin only, a further 7 contain relatives of both sexes, and only 6 comprise men alone. Generally speaking where both sexes of relatives are involved, extension is vertical (as opposed to lateral) i.e. relatives are of a different generation to the adult woman and/or man, consisting for example of a son or daughter-in-law and their children, or a father and mother. Where relatives are of one sex only, about equal numbers of households are laterally (i.e. same generation as the household head and/or spouse) and vertically extended. Four households containing male kin only were headed by men and without exception were the husband's rather than the wife's relatives (it is rare that men allow their wives to bring their own male kinsfolk into the family). In the case of female kin in male-headed extended households, however, 4 were relatives of the wife, 1 of the husband and 1 was related to both. Obviously in female-headed extended households, all kin are related to the female head. In those households with female kin of some description (17 in all), 12 female heads or spouses had jobs. In the remaining 6 households extended with male relatives, 4 out of 6 women were work-ing, although only 2 of these households with working women were actually headed by men. In only one case in the sample of extended families was a female relative working in place of the female spouse, possibly because women in appended units tend to be older and therefore unlikely to get a job as easily, or much younger and have new-born babies they need or want to attend to (see also Note 6).

So far we have discussed cases where a change in household structure or progression through the 'developmental cycle' has helped to prompt women's entry into the labour force; certainly in male-headed households extension or moving through the lifecycle increases women's bargaining power. If wives can demonstrate that the housework will still be done and the children will not suffer undue neglect, there are stronger grounds for persuading husbands to let them take a job. In female-headed households, economic necessity and/or freedom from male control appear to be the critical precipitants.

Childless couples

A further set of factors relating to female labour force participation which might also be included under this general head of 'household structure' relates to couples without children. There were only 3 childless couples in the sub-sample, all in Puerto Vallarta, all of whom were married and had both partners working. In one case the couple was in late middle age (María Auxilio is 59, her husband, Ines, 54). María Auxilio has only been able to dedicate a substantial amount of her time to income-generating activities since her sons left home and left her with a much-reduced load of domestic labour. In the other two cases the couples are young and planning their families in order that wives may continue working. This brings us on to considering cases where the situation is reversed i.e. when female labour force participation precedes and/or appears to be a catalyst for changes in household structure.

First, however, it is useful to note the existence of a small 'bridging' category of cases where it is extremely difficult to isolate the precipitating factor.

The most obvious example here is that of María, female spouse in a male-headed extended unit in Puerto Vallarta. María, 37 years old, has been married for five years to José (32 years) and has two young children – a little girl of 4 and a son of one-and-a-half. The family is extended though the co-residence of María's 39-year old sister, Graciela, who has lived with María all her life. They were both born in Puerto Vallarta and having lost their mother at a very young age, were raised and cared for by their father and two successive step-mothers until his death in 1974. Their father had been very strict, rarely let them out of his sight and forbade them to do such things as wear trousers, have boyfriends and work away from his surveillance. As a result, both girls' experience of the 'outside world' was fairly limited until their mid- to-late twenties. Graciela, of a rather shy and nervous disposition, with a number of physical ailments tended to stay at home helping her step-mothers with housework, while María had assisted in her father's shop, then in the family *cenaduría* (small home restaurant) and finally in a grocery store owned by a family friend. Although the death of their father was a blow to the sisters, at the same time María claimed that the pain of their bereavement was substantially lessened by a great sense of relief and freedom. Almost immediately after their father's death, María took a better-paid job selling swimwear and soon after moved with Graciela to the home of their married half-sister. Following that, the two girls moved into their own lodgings where they could be fully independent.

Then, at 31, María met José, a porter for a major Mexican airline, and married him a year later, having moved jobs yet again for a better paid one in a thriving souvenir shop. There was no question that Graciela would not live with them, and this of course has enabled María to continue working. Although José and María both spend alot of time with the children in the evenings and on their days off, it is unquestionably Graciela who is in charge of the bulk of child-care and the everyday running of the household. María doubts very much that she would have been able to continue with a full-time career had it not been for this assistance. Although José receives a good wage and tips at the airport and the family could conceivably survive on his earnings alone, María feels that a job is an essential part of her life and has no plans to give up work, even as her third pregnancy gets underway.

María's case demonstrates how difficult it often is to map the sequence of women's labour force participation and household structure, let alone to establish the direction of cause–effect relationships, however in many instances there is a time-lag between the two, and quite often household structure changes *after* women have entered the labour force. Having said that, just as when household structure changes prior to women's entry into the labour force, there are no grounds for assuming that one factor automatically leads to another. Moreover, fewer working women whose entry into the labour market has been followed by modifications in household structure rationalised their current labour force status in these terms. Few admitted to consciously manipulating household structure, in order to cope better with the everyday management of household life. This is perhaps hardly surprising given that in a society where kinship is of extreme social and symbolic importance, people are reluctant to rationalise mutual aid and obligation in terms of an explicit economic or contractual agreement. Women are unwilling to state categorically that their mothers, sisters, cousins and so on came to stay simply because it would be easier to run the home, even if they sometimes stress it as a contributory factor.

Female labour force participation: effects on household structure

Household extension

None the less, the sheer numbers of households in the sub-sample, both male- and female-headed, which have become extended following female entry into the labour force suggests a certain element of causality. Indeed not only did over one-quarter of households in which women were working experience extension shortly after women had entered the labour force, but in the majority of cases (5 out of 8), the extended appendage consisted of *female* rather than male kin. Assistance with domestic labour is obviously critically important for working women and in the Mexican context it is much more likely that women relatives will help out in the home (see also Benería and Roldan, 1987: 131), although in one case a female head had incorporated an elderly widowed father who looked after the children and did much of the cooking. In addition to the fact that households with working women may often provide a home for female relatives on this account (subconsciously or otherwise), it is also important to remember that a greater number of women relatives, especially if alone, are perhaps more likely than men to need to rely upon kin at certain stages of their lifecycle. In a sense then, there is both a greater demand for female helpers in certain households, *and* a greater supply. The case of Santos and her mother highlights both sides of this equation.

Santos, 41, lives in León in a male-headed extended household consisting of her husband (also 41), her mother (92), 4 daughters (aged 10–19 years, 3 of whom work), and a 12-year old son. Extension occurred in 1982 ostensibly because her mother was getting too old to live alone and had received no offers of assistance from her other children. One possible reason that Santos took on this responsibility is because she did not mind having another pair of hands around the house. Even though her mother is elderly, she hates being idle and is always doing something. Santos got married at 23 and except for a brief spell at the beginning of her married life, has always worked, mainly because her husband, a builder, has been ill a good deal of the time. Santos has usually had part-time home-based occupations such as taking in washing, child-minding, embroidery and so forth, and in the last two years has moved into piecework for a large shoe factory; this latter job involves distributing batches of moccasins for hand-stitching among herself and a small group of women in the neighbourhood. Santos acknowledges that even though her mother is elderly, it has been a great help to have her around, combined with the fact that her teenage daughters also assist with household chores when they are home from work.

Although Santos stresses that her mother came primarily because she had nowhere else to live and as a daughter she could not possibly have abandoned her, one wonders whether this same willingness would have applied if a brother or male relative had wanted to move in. Indeed even if family extension appears only to be incidental to women's work role, the fact that women have employment might be conducive to their willingess to provide a roof for other kin, particularly if female. Another crucial factor here is that once wives are earning, they also have a greater say in household decision-making and as such can exert more pressure upon their husbands to consent to sharing their homes with relatives (see also Chant, 1984, 1985a).

Another interesting case highlighting various dimensions of this argument is that of Elba, 30-year-old female spouse in a male-headed extended unit in Puerto Vallarta. Elba has never agreed to marry her partner, mainly because she feels that it would give him greater opportunity to exercise control over her activities – a reason cited by many other women in the city for staying single. Since setting up house with Teodosio at the age of 18 and giving birth to three children, she has consistently been in and out of the labour force in a part-time capacity. Although in the past she has often been forced to leave jobs on account of tiredness, pregnancies or inability to cope, Elba has always felt it very important to retain a source of independent means, and also to be able to contribute to household expenditure. In 1983 Elba moved away from pig-breeding, an activity carried out near home, and into a regular domestic service job involving five mornings a week in another part of town. Shortly afterwards her sister came to live with them from their nearby home village, primarily in order to pursue her studies, yet this arrangement also worked out very conveniently from Elba's point of view because by doing the afternoon shift at college her sister is able to look after the children in the mornings when she is at work. The arrival of their mother in 1984 has further strengthened the ability of Elba's household to manage productive and reproductive labour: despite working as a full-time domestic servant, she helps the daughters out with housework and child-care. Elba admits that co-residence is working very well and it is perhaps no coincidence that this is the first occasion she has actually stayed in the same job for over one year, let alone three. Therefore, whatever factor might come first – entry into the labour force or extension of the household – they certainly seem compatible, and indeed are often mutually reinforcing.

Extension of female-headed units is even more common. Paula, 39 years, in Bolaños, Querétaro, *de facto* head of such a family, convinced her husband Tereso in 1980 to let her take a cleaning job in the settlement primary school. Two years later in the height of the recession, Tereso went to the United States as an illegal immigrant. Continued devaluation of the peso against the dollar means that a relatively small proportion of his earnings, mainly from casual work on farms and in factories in southern Texas, goes a long way back home. Money is sent fairly regularly and he has made two return visits. However, since Tereso first left, Paula has had quite a job managing the home as well holding down a full-time position, especially since he had formerly played a major role in housework and looking after their five children now aged between 9 and 15 years. So when Paula's sister asked if she could move in in 1986, she was happy to accept. Despite the fact that Brenda is presently getting over a drug problem, she has been extremely helpful around the house and has therefore relieved Paula of a good deal of strain. Having adult company also appears to have lessened the loneliness resulting from Tereso's absence.

In some circumstances links between household extension and female labour force participation are made explicit in the sense that families acknowledge they could not have accommodated the workforce participation of wives without the assistance provided by female kin. Such is the case of María Asunción, 33-year-old spouse of a male-headed extended unit in Querétaro, whose unemployed husband's 15-year-old sister was purposely asked to come and stay with them to help out with the housework and child-care while María sets up a grocery business with Antonio's redundancy money. This arrangement is expected to last for at least a year after which the situation will be reviewed from both angles, the hosts' and the helper's.

Thus extension often follows on from the participation of women in the labour force, and frequently smooths out some of the problems associated with the management of family life. However sometimes female labour force participation promotes the opposite response in that couples *restrict* household expansion, i.e. they avoid having children or at least living with them.

Absence of children

Both these points are illustrated by the remaining two couples in Puerto Vallarta. In one case, that of Eva (22 years) and Hector (29 years), there has been a joint agreement not to have children until Eva has worked for a few more years. Having moved into business studies teaching after a fairly lengthy education and 4 years' experience as a secretary, Eva is unwilling to sacrifice her career so soon, although there is no question that she will leave work or at least go part-time in order to raise a family at a later stage. The other case is slightly more interesting whereby María Elena (23 years) and husband (24 years) have deliberately left their young daughter on a ranch in their home state, Sinaloa, in order that they can both work in Puerto Vallarta and '*juntar dinero*' (save money). Here household structure is being consciously manipulated in order to allow both parents to work.

Summing up the situation so far then, 25 out of 33 women with paid work in the sub-sample owe their present involvement in economic activities to some modification(s) in household structure before or after they entered the labour force. Obviously there are other reasons as well, which are discussed a little later. However, in order to encapsulate the importance of household structure in influencing women's labour force participation it is also instructive to consider the remaining group of 14 women without any form of paid work. To what extent is their *non-participation* in the labour force linked to household structure?

Non-participation of women in the labour force and household structure

In 44% of nuclear households in the sub-sample women were not working, compared with 33% in female-headed extended households, 21% in male-headed extended households and only 20% in one-parent households (See Table 5.2.)[8] Without exception these women attributed their non-participation to various aspects of household form and organisation, particularly to the fact that through extension or stage in the lifecycle there were other earning members in the home (thereby reducing their need to go out to work), or because they had no assistance in domestic labour and child-care. This latter point is in effect the converse of households where women have employment and highlights the critical importance of extra hands to manage domestic work in such circumstances. However, additional reasons for non-participation included inability to work through sickness, and, especially in nuclear households, male resistance or prohibition. Interestingly, not one woman explicitly attributed their non-employment to a lack of opportunities in the local economy, although most non-participants in fact resided in León and Querétaro where demand for female labour is considerably less than in Puerto Vallarta.[9] Moreover, not one woman who had been previously employed gave up their jobs *prior* to changes in household structure, which suggests that non-participation is a luxury *some* women cannot afford until their households have multiple earners and/or are relatively financially secure.

In the case of women-headed non-extended households, only 1 out of 5, Sabina in León, did not have paid work. Now aged 56, Sabina was a housewife throughout her entire married life and by the time she was widowed in 1980 her teenage sons were working and able to support her. Given that Sabina also has two much younger children who needed looking after, she did not see any point in getting a job after her husband's death. As far as female heads of extended households are concerned, the 3 without a job consisted of one who had damaged her arm and was taking time off; another had left work to look after her aged mother but was able to rely upon other earning members in the home; the other had withdrawn from her job once her sons were old enough to support her. In all cases here, the fact that other people in the household unit were earning an income had given these female heads the freedom to *leave* the labour force. In this respect, there are obvious connections between household structure and *non-participation* as well as participation. In the male-headed extended families only one of the three women without work had withdrawn recently from the labour force, in this case because her adult sons and daughters were able to provide for her. However in the two remaining cases, women had remained out of the labour force all their lives because their husbands did not want them to work. This last factor was even more common in the nuclear households where 5 out of 7 husbands actively prevented their wives from taking employment (see below). In the other two nuclear households women had their hands tied with dependent children.

One of these latter two, Berta in Querétaro, had in fact at one time played a major role in the home-based family toy-making business. In 1982 at the time of the first period of fieldwork the household was extended through the co-residence of the husband Antonio's sister. However, when her sister-in-law left in 1984 to work in Mexico City, Berta had to abandon her duties in the business in order to cope single-handedly with six young children. Her former post in the family enterprise has since been filled with a paid male worker. Here again there is an obvious link between household structure and female labour force participation in respect of domestic management. In the other case, a 39-year-old mother of 4 young girls, Gloria R., had worked for only 2 months in 1982 as her daughters (then aged between 7 and 12 years) did not seem able to look after themselves properly. Besides, neighbours began teasing her husband Emilio about not being able to maintain his wife. Popular views and peer-group commentaries on 'men who let their wives work' are often vital in promoting and reinforcing male restrictions on women's labour force involvement (see also Chapter 4) and prompts us to return to the question of why this should particularly be the case in nuclear structures. Indeed the fact that women facing restrictions from their husbands in non-extended units varied greatly in age, and there was some potential for all of them to take at least a part-time job, suggests that the nuclear household structure is most supportive of dominant gender ideologies, a rigid sexual division of labour and status within the household, and a correspondingly greater degree of male control over their wives' labour power. This issue has been discussed in some detail elsewhere on the basis of the earlier research in Querétaro (see, for example, Chant, 1985a; 1987b), but it is important to reiterate that a critical feature of most nuclear structures is that women are inevitably less able than in other units to share and/or delegate gender-assigned duties, which in turn has two major outcomes. First, male heads of nuclear families fear that if wives take employment, housework and child-care will be unacceptably neglected; second, and in part because of women's virtually inevitable total or primary assignation to domestic tasks, men are usually the sole breadwinners in the family unit and as such probably in a position to command more authority and control over their dependants than in households with multiple earners (see Chapter 4; see also Scott, 1990). Hence at one level men in nuclear households raise objections to women working on the grounds that there is no one else to take over their domestic responsibilities, and at another (especially if husbands are the sole generators of family income), have the economic power to enforce those objections.

Whatever general validity these observations may have, we may deduce from the above that in a range of Mexican cities sex of household heads in low-income families is a critical variable in determining women's propensity to move into the labour force. Just as much as being a female household head often requires women to take employment, as we saw earlier, a major barrier to a woman's freedom to choose is also removed when the man disappears. Indeed the majority of women in the male-headed households wanted to work, and could have found a job fairly compatible with their domestic responsibilities, but they were not *allowed* to do so.

In the above section an attempt has been made to pinpoint the kinds of ways in which household structure interrelates with female labour force participation. The two most common factors associated with female involvement in the workforce include presence or absence of the male head, and the ability of women in some households to delegate a range of household duties to female kin or offspring. A third factor is the absence of a heavy load of child-care which inevitably is much more likely at either end of the developmental-cycle spectrum. However, it would be misleading to suggest that female labour force participation arises from a single cause, or indeed only has one set of effects. Household extension, for example, does not exclusively result from the fact that working women need help around the home. As pointed out in Chapter 4 there are other reasons as well: housing shortages, economic pressure and/or income-maximising strategies, the inability or unwillingness of kin to live alone and so on (see also Chant and Ward, 1987). In León an additional factor relates to the labour requirements of small-scale domestic shoe production units. Moreover, a switch from male to female headship not only arises out of male desertion, but also widowhood, female-instigated separation and sometimes (particularly in Puerto Vallarta) because women choose not to marry or set up home with the father(s) of their children. Similarly, there are other 'supply' factors aside from household structure prompting women's entry into the labour force which merit brief attention here. In iterating these reasons it is important to note that several might occur in combination with one another, and frequently relate in some way to household structure.

Further reasons for female labour force participation

Husband's job loss

In a small number of cases women had entered the labour force during periods when husbands had lost their jobs, and could not or did not want to move into another occupation immediately (see also Benería and Roldan, 1987: 98). This is especially common in Querétaro where the crisis hit hardest, particularly in young nuclear households where the pool of potential labour is usually small (to be discussed in more detail in the next chapter). Nevertheless, it is important to note that women in nuclear households whose heads become unemployed do not usually go out to work straight away. Generally there is a time-lag during which the husband either tries to find another job and/or keeps going on whatever redundancy money might be at his disposal. Indeed in cases where women have been prevented from working throughout their married lives, men are frequently unwilling to permit their wives to enter the labour force except as a last resort, probably through a combination of pride, sexual jealousy and the fear that they will totally lose the esteem of of other household members, kin, friends and neighbours.[10] As one interviewee put it *'El hombre nunca se da por vencido'* (a man never admits defeat). The case of Josefina in Querétaro is typical here. Josefina (34 years) and her husband José Guadalupe (37 years) have three teenage children and in 1983 were a nuclear household. When I first interviewed them they were living on José's redundancy money; he had been sacked from his supervisor's job in a large agricultural machinery plant and could not find a similar opening elsewhere in the city. It was a full year before he managed to get another job (this time as a low-level clerical worker in the Police Department), and throughout the period refused point blank to let Josefina out to work; partly because the children were still quite young, and partly, one imagines, because this would have constituted a further dent to his pride. However, by 1985 a combination of increased economic pressure and the fact that the children were a little older forced him to renege on his original decision and Josefina moved almost immediately into an office-cleaning job protected by contract and eligible for the legal minimum wage. Roberto, their eldest son also began working around the same time and the family is presently much better off. Shortly after Josefina went to work Roberto got married and his wife, Graciela, moved in by invitation, partly so as not to lose Roberto's earning power, and partly to compensate for Josefina being away from home all day. Graciela now takes charge of the housework leaving Josefina more or less completely free when she comes in. Thus male job loss can often set in action a chain of events which lead, via female labour force participation, to a change in household composition.

Inability of women to rely on financial support from male partners

In some cases female labour force participation arises in order to counteract a partial or near total lack of financial support from male partners. Occasionally this is due to ill-health on the part of men, but more frequently because they are '*desobligado*' (uncommitted/irresponsible). Again this is more usually the case in nuclear households where instead of common budget contributed to, overseen and managed by a number of adults, there is often only one (male) wage earner (see Chapter 4). In some instances men still try to prevent their wives from working, although in others appear to reach a stage where they do not particularly care. An example of this is provided by María, spouse in a four-member nuclear household in Puerto Vallarta. María is only 29, but looks considerably older, and entered into a '*union libre*' (free union) with her partner, a self-employed car mechanic, at the age of 18. Although he makes a reasonable sum of money, it is apportioned in such a way that only one-third of it ends up in María's hands for the housekeeping. The rest is spent on drink and in recent months times have got so hard that María has had to go out to work as a domestic servant, simply in order to feed her 7- and 8-year-old children. In earlier days her partner would not have dreamed of letting her take employment, but is now so often drunk that he seems to have passed caring. Indeed María says that although he does not beat her, it is just as painful to be treated as as if she was not there. He shows no interest in his family, and spends most evenings out drinking. One of María's first purchases with her own money was a small black and white reconditioned television to fill up the hours during his nightly absences.

Tolerant attitudes on part of husband

On a more positive note concerning husbands however, a third reason cited by some working women as accounting for the fact they had jobs was that their husbands were 'understanding'. Indeed most thought that it was quite a bonus to live with someone who did not mind them working. It is obviously hard to speculate on why certain husbands are more tolerant than others, beyond accepting that there are inevitably differences among individuals and the relationships they have with one another. This problem is obviously accentuated when one considers only a small number of households However what can be said is that all five women who cited this as a major factor in explaining their labour force participation appeared to have particularly close and trusting relationships with their partners. In all cases the women tended to have strong, forceful personalities as well. In one instance, both husband and wife were highly educated and seemed aware of the advantages of mutual respect and cooperation, with both participating equally in household chores. In another two cases men had been brought up in single-parent families and were used to seeing their mothers working. In another case the man did not earn very much and accepted that his wife would have to help. The final husband had struck a bargain with his wife that she could take a part-time job provided he could go off occasionally and work in the United States! Location might also be a significant factor here, since all five of these women live in Puerto Vallarta (see below).

Child-care facilities (non-family)

A fourth and much less common reason helping to account for female labour force participation is the presence of child-care facilities over and above those provided by other people in the home (discussed in the earlier section on household structure). Generally speaking state-provided and/or subsidised child-care facilities are in such short supply however, that people do not expect them and other strategies such as household extension are utilised instead. Indeed even though factories in Querétaro are supposed to lay on creches by law if they employ a certain number of women, it is extremely rare for them to do so. As such it is not perhaps surprising that only one respondent, Rodalinda, a 31-year-old inhabitant of Puerto Vallarta, mentioned the importance of extra-domestic child-care facilities for her own labour force participation. With three children to support and a miserly unpredictable husband, Rodalinda has had to work for most of her married life yet this was always difficult without relatives in the city. When the children were very young for example, Roda took a job as a domestic servant but was only able to do so by having the good fortune to find them places in the heavily over-subscribed nursery attached to the regional health centre in Puerto Vallarta, notwithstanding that the cost of keeping them there took a disproportionate amount of her salary. Now she works as a chambermaid in a block of holiday apartments and is grateful for the fact that her boss allows the children to wait in the office for a couple of hours after school while Roda completes her shift. However, generally speaking such concessions on the part of employers are rare, and alternatives scarce. Regular child-minding by friends or even kin in the neighbourhood is something of a rarity, although some women in previous periods of workforce participation have paid local women to look after their children during the day.

Previous job experience

The fifth contributory factor explaining women's current labour force participation in the three cities includes experience of work, training and so on. From the discussion of the questionnaire data in Chapter 4 it appeared there was little connection between education and workforce involvement, although in the sub-sample it seems that a larger proportion of uneducated women were not in employment (21%) than those who were (15%). However, evaluating this in conjunction with work experience produces interesting results. All except 2 of the 33 women in work had some prior work experience, whereas a substantial number (36%) in the non-working group had no previous job experience at all. When one takes little or no education and job experience together, this appears to have a decidedly negative effect on current participation rates. Not only were a substantial number of women with limited or no education and/or work experience not working at present, but also indicated they were unlikely to do so. *Type* of work experience is also critical here. For example, Emilia, a 49-year-old mother of 5 in a nuclear family in León had only worked for 4 years of her life, as a domestic servant in Guadalajara, prior to her marriage at the age of 22. Aside from the fact that her husband had never wanted her to work, Emilia did not feel there was much point anyway. As far as she was concerned domestic service (the only thing she feels equipped to do) was not really a job. What was the point of doing someone else's housework for a pittance when one could sit at home and do something useful such as sewing or mending? In her opinion she had no skills which would ease her passage into the job market, and besides, the financial returns for what she could do were so negligible that it would not be worth her while.

Female job opportunities in the local economy

The sixth and final reason which seems to have a strong bearing on women's work is where they live. This is highly significant from the point of view of the present research and highlights the importance of a comparative study. In some places (notably Puerto Vallarta) women's labour force participation is consistently higher *regardless* of household structure and suggests that in some instances factors external to the household and its individual economic circumstances play an important part in stimulating the workforce involvement of women. Analysis of this issue is the main focus of the following section where an attempt is made to evaluate the relative strength of 'demand' and 'supply' factors in female labour force participation.

Determinants of female labour force participation: perspectives on nuclear households

As we have seen in this and previous chapters, women's labour force participation is higher in Puerto Vallarta than in León and Querétaro. The sub-sample reveals similar patterns with 85% of women in Puerto Vallarta having some form of income-generating activity compared with 50% in León and 55% in Querétaro (1986) (see also Table 4.12).[11] Moreover, while the labour force participation of women in *non-nuclear* households is high in all cities, relatively speaking the workforce involvement of women in *nuclear* households is considerably greater in Puerto Vallarta. In the sub-sample, 87.5% of women in nuclear households work in Puerto Vallarta, compared with 50% in León and only 16.7% in Querétaro. (In the questionnaire survey the figures were 55.31%, 42.9% and 16.7% respectively.)

At this stage, therefore, it is useful to just consider women in male-headed nuclear households. What explains their greater workforce involvement in Puerto Vallarta compared with the other two cities? Again use is made of the in-depth case study data. Table 5.3. summarises some of the basic household and employment characteristics of the relevant interviewees.

Table 5.3: Women in nuclear households in the sub-sample: some basic characteristics

City	Name	Age (years)	Education	No. of children at home	Age range of co-resident children	Husband/ partner's occupation	No. of household members earning income	Current work status
Puerto Vallarta	María de Carmen	23	4 years primary	2	1½, 3 years	Barman	1	Houseperson
	Eloisa	26	5 years primary	2	5, 18 months	Tailor	2	Part-time worker (home-based)
	Fidelina	27	6 years primary	2	1, 6 years	Janitor	2	Part-time worker (home-based)
	María	29	None	2	7, 8 years	Mechanic	2	Full-time worker (domestic servant)
	Rodalinda	31	2 years primary	3	6–9 years	Waiter	2	Full-time worker (chambermaid)
	Idalia	34	3 years primary	10	1½–18 years	Odd-job man	2	Full-time worker (restaurateur, home-based)
	Consuelo	36	2 years primary	2	6, 12 years	Mechanic	2	Part-time worker (home-based)
	Dolores	39	3 years primary	8	4–21 years	Bicycle repairer	4	Full-time worker (cook)
León	Celia	28	1 year secondary	3	6–12 years	Salesman (electrical firm)	2	Part-time worker (home-based)
	Emilia	49	None	5	10–19 years	Tanner	2	Houseperson
Querétaro	Laura	25	6 years primary	4	2–9 years	Photographer	1	Houseperson[a]
	Berta	30	4 years primary	6	2–12 years	Toymaker/seller	1	Houseperson
	Lourdes	33	6 years primary	2	4, 5 years	Factory operative	1	Houseperson
	Gloria	39	None	4	11–16 years	Master builder	1	Houseperson
	Francisca	40	2 years primary	8	7 mths–14 yrs	Soldier	2	Part-time worker (home-based)
	Rosa	44	1 year primary	6	7–20 years	Petty trader	3	Houseperson

Note: Laura occasionally helps out in husband's photographic business on an unpaid basis.

Source: Sub-sample Household Interview Survey, 1986.

Women and work in nuclear households, Puerto Vallarta

The only woman not working out of the eight nuclear units in the Puerto Vallarta sub-sample was María del Carmen. María is 23 years old and has two young children. Born and bred in Silao, Guanajuato in the central highlands, María married her childhood sweetheart Juvenal at the age of 19 and soon after they moved away from the countryside with ideas of improving their prospects in a thriving city. Juvenal has made significant career steps since their arrival in Puerto Vallarta. Having started as a corridor sweeper in a 4-star hotel and working his way up, he was promoted to barman a year ago and receives a good wage and gratuities. Relatively speaking the young couple are quite well-off. At present they are renting a room in a *vecindad* in Caloso but have recently bought a plot of land in a new settlement being promoted by *ejidatarios* on the far side of the airport. María has never worked except on the farm and wants a large family. Given that they are alone in the city and have no relatives close at hand, both think it is unlikely that María will take a job in the near future, even though Juvenal is not against it in principle and also recognises that there are lots of things women can do in Puerto Vallarta without any specific training.

As far as the working women in Puerto Vallarta's sub-sample of nuclear structures are concerned, 3 have decidedly casual or part-time income-generating activities, while 4 have jobs which occupy all or the bulk of the working week. Fidelina, one of those working part-time, is doing so behind her husband's back and cannot entertain the thought of taking something more regular or formal for fear of being discovered. Fidelina and her husband David, both 27, have 2 sons – one of 6 years and another of 12 months. Fide was born in Ixtlahuacán, Colima, and spent most of her childhood in Porvenir, Nayarit (about an hour by bus from Puerto Vallarta). At 14 years old she came to the city and found work as a live-in servant. During the two years she stayed in the job half her earnings regularly went to support her widowed mother who has since remarried. Work was easy to find in Puerto Vallarta according to Fidelina and she changed jobs twice after leaving her first position, on both occasions being able to improve her earnings – first as a domestic servant in a wealthy household where she made frequent visits to the United States with her employers, and then as a kitchen assistant in a small restaurant where she resided with the boss's family. It was during her time in this latter job that she met her husband. Five months after their first meeting she became pregnant (he threatened to leave her if she did not sleep with him), although she carried on working until she was 8 months pregnant, moving in with David just before the baby was born. Fide was 21 years old.

Their partnership got off to a very inauspicious start. Not only was her first child born out of wedlock, but they also moved into cramped lodgings with his brother, wife and three children with whom Fide did not get along at all well. Nevertheless, prospects seemed a little brighter when they got married a few months later and moved out to a rented room on their own. For three years they were relatively happy, but after the novelty wore off, David started seeing other women and money grew scarce. David, who has worked in the maintenance department of a large 4-star hotel ever since Fide has known him, is of the opinion that a wife has no right to know her husband's wage and has never disclosed how much he earns. Nevertheless, Fide estimates that it is well above the minimum salary and that she might receive an average of around one-quarter of it.

As times grew progressively lean in their fourth year of marriage, Fide took the plunge and secretly started a part-time cleaning job in a nearby doctor's surgery where she was able to take her infant son. However a neighbour informed David, who, in his anger, decided they would move to Caloso which given its isolated location would prevent her yielding to the temptation of doing the same kind of thing again. When Fide confronted her husband about why he was so strict, he claimed that it was because she was a '*puta*' (colloq. 'whore' – otherwise why would she have slept with him prior to their marriage?) and wanted to make sure that she would not get up to her 'same old tricks'. Fide feels that through levelling these kinds of accusations at her, he is trying to exonerate the guilt associated with his own extra-marital affairs. Indeed when he contracted a venereal disease he went as far as to place the blame on Fide. Beatings are now regular occurrence in her life and most of her time is spent trying to placate him.

Fide's fear of further violence and reprisals means that her employment options are very limited. She occasionally cuts hair and takes in a next-door-neighbour's washing, but has to be extremely discreet since her elder son has been threatened with the consequences of not giving his father a blow-by-blow account of his mother's activities during the day. Fidelina would like very much to leave David but cannot. First because she has no relatives she could stay with in Puerto Vallarta and there would be no work for her back in Porvenir. Second because she has two young sons and could not possibly get a live-in job in town . Third because she is determined not to lose her present accommodation. If she moved out, it would give David licence to install his present mistress and all Fide's hard work in terms of building and decorating their shelter would be gone to waste. The fact that the lot papers are in his name also makes her feel very vulnerable. So instead she stays, hopes that he will eventually be the one to move out, and in the meantime tries to make the best of it, working secretly when she can, and occasionally seeking professional help, primarily from the town priest and the family doctor. As it is, both of these individuals (men) have advised her strongly to stay with David. The doctor has put her on heavy tranquillisers, and the priest has encouraged her participation in intercessionary prayer meetings held specifically for women to pray for the souls of recalcitrant husbands and ask God to bring about changes in their characters. However, David has recently even denied her the right to go to church except on the rare occasions he happens to be going along as well.

The other two women in nuclear units with part-time work do not have similarly unhappy domestic situations; however, the very fact that they are working part-time in home-based activities stems in part from their partners' unwillingness for them to be away from the house all day.

In one case here, Consuelo, a 36-year-old mother of two (formerly three, but one child died from leukaemia at the age of 9), went out to work in the past in complete defiance of her husband's wishes. Ten years ago when her two eldest children were very young, her sister-in-law and husband came to live with them for a while. Taking advantage of the fact that her daughters would have someone reliable to keep an eye on them, Consuelo went out and got a job as a waitress. She and her husband Pedro have always had a very close, good-humoured relationship and his admonishments were not particularly severe. However, when their relatives moved out to their own accommodation, Consuelo had no choice but to leave work. Her only daughter now, Mayra, refuses to be left in charge of her younger brother, which means that Consuelo has to work from home. She makes a small income selling soft drinks from her living room and also works on commission selling clothes and shoes brought to her by a woman trader from Guadalajara. Her main clientèle are friends and neighbours who appreciate the opportunity to buy relatively well-made goods at favourable rates. In Puerto Vallarta such items are usually much more expensive because of tourist mark-up. However, Consuelo says that the main advantage of her part-time trade is the ability to save money on clothing her own family since she gets the goods at cost price. Consuelo occasionally complains to her husband about not being able to do a 'proper' job, but he feels she has quite enough to do in the home all day without wearing herself out completely. He also claims there is no need for her to work. He provides for all the household items and usually lets Consuelo spend her own earnings on 'treats/luxuries' for herself and the children.

The other woman working part-time, Eloisa (26 years), also from the home, combines embroidery with the provision of basic health care to neighbours. On arrival in the settlement Eloisa placed a notice above the door advertising injections and first aid. With so many children in the settlement and numerous minor accidents, mothers are always popping in for advice and help. Ideally Eloisa would like to finish an elementary nursing course started as an adolescent in her home town of Valle de Santiago, Guanajuato, so that she could set up a proper home clinic, however an appropriate course in Puerto Vallarta would involve five morning study sessions a week for one month and at present her husband is unwilling to let her do it. He claims he does not object to the principle of women working (although he feels most men only let their wives take a job out of economic necessity), but *does* worry about leaving their two infants with someone else, even Eloisa's sister who lives nearby. *'Para mí, lo importante es que los niños sean bién cuidados'* (for me, the important thing is that the children are well looked after). Eloisa, on the other hand, feels it would be worthwhile to leave the children on a short-term basis in view of the long-term gains. At the end of the day, however, his word is paramount.

The four women working full time include two we have already mentioned, María (the domestic servant) and Rodalinda (the chambermaid). The other two are Idalia who does *cenas* (suppers) three evenings a week and spends the rest of her time embroidering tea-towels, tablecloths, handkerchiefs and blouses. The other is Dolores, a cook in a small restaurant. In both these latter cases the women's husbands are not mean or irresponsible, merely badly-paid, and recognise the value of an extra source of income. In fact Dolores has been the economic backbone of the household all her life.

Dolores, 39 years, was married at the age of 15 to a man of 48. Now 72, her husband does what he can to contribute to the household budget, repairing bicycles in a leanto againt the house, but as Dolores said to me when I first met her, '*Yo soy el hombre y la mujer en esta casa – yo dirigo todo*' (I am both the man and the woman in this household, I'm in charge of everything). According to Dolores her husband was always a very weak, dependent individual. As an only child, he married to please his mother who wanted grandchildren. Dolores bore him 7 (6 of whom are still at home) but in the last 6 years has had 2 children by another man. Her husband was so grateful for Dolores's support and loves his children so much, that he was prepared to allow her to have a relationship with someone else. This is a very unusual occurrence, yet perhaps more likely to happen in Puerto Vallarta than in the other two cities, simply because women have fairly ample opportunities in the local labour market and husbands recognise they could lose their wives completely if they restrict them unduly.

It is obviously difficult to summarise the positions and experiences of women in the Puerto Vallarta nuclear household sub-sample. They have very diverse backgrounds and very different reasons for going to work (or not) at present. However, it may be concluded that the majority (5) of them go to work because they *have* to (either because their husbands do not earn enough or are financially uncooperative), and two because they feel it gives them a sense of achievement and of being useful (although need and want are not necessarily mutually exclusive factors here).

What is perhaps most interesting is that of the women working full-time, all 4 were either born in Puerto Vallarta or moved to the city as children (under 10 years of age). All their mothers were divorced or separated and had worked for most of their lives. Whereas of the 3 part-timers 2 only came to the city as married women, and one, Fidelina, as an adolescent. In only two cases here had their mothers worked María del Carmen, the housewife in the nuclear household sub-sample, had never been employed in her life; this is perhaps understandable given that she comes from a farm in Silao, Guanajuato where women have traditionally been confined to the home. Her own mother, for example, was a full-time housewife.

None of the 4 women currently working full-time (with quite a wide age range – 29–49 years; see also Table 5.3) had more than 3 years of primary education, and had started work at a very early age, ranging from 8 years in the case of Rodalinda and 13 in the case of María. Without exception their first jobs had been as domestic servants and/or childminders in private homes in the city. However, partly as a reflection of their relatively long time in Puerto Vallarta, all have considerable experience of different jobs in the tourist industry. María, the youngest, had 4 different occupations in her life – 3 before she set up home with her husband (1 as a childminder, 2 in domestic service), and her current domestic job, although she did have a 10-year period out of employment when she first set up home with her partner.

Rodalinda (31 years) and Idalia (34 years) have both had 8 jobs apiece. Rodalinda was a childminder, domestic servant and hotel chambermaid before marriage, and afterwards had two domestic service posts, one as a childminder and

Figure 5.1 *Cenaduría*, Puerto Vallarta

her current chambermaid position. Since the beginning of her working life she has only spent 3 years out of the labour force. Prior to marriage Idalia worked as a domestic servant, a laundrywoman in a large hotel and shop assistant. As a married woman her economic activities have been mainly part-time and home-based including embroidery (both for self-employment and as an outworker), shop-keeping, an agent for a mail order firm, and her current activity as a petty restaurateur (see Figure 5.1). Idalia with 10 children so closely spaced in age has obviously been less able than Rodalinda with only 3 to work outside the home. Yet Idalia has only dedicated herself entirely to the home for 6 months in the last 24 years, for 2 months when she was first married and tried to conform to family pressures to be a housewife and 4 months when she was still living at home and had to look after her mother's children.

Finally, Dolores the eldest, has had 11 jobs. Beginning work as a domestic servant at the age of 13, she has mainly taken employment in petty trading and catering, both as a cook and a waitress. She had a year out of the labour force work between 1982 and 1983 when her lover maintained her and the children. However, she says she is much happier to have returned to work and not to have to rely on 'handouts'.

As far as the part-timers are concerned, on the other hand, they appear to have rather different employment experiences; fewer jobs and more punctuated work histories than their full-time counterparts, even since moving to Puerto Vallarta.

Although any conclusions of the basis of such few cases are inevitably highly tenuous, it could perhaps be suggested that the experience of growing up in an environment where women are fairly accustomed to working (and at close range, for 6 out of the 7 mothers of working nuclear family spouses in Puerto Vallarta had been heavily involved in economic activities), and where there is a fairly varied and abundant range of opportunities for women in the local labour market, that this produces a much more generalised pattern of female labour supply than in cities where demand for female labour is much lower and/or confined to a narrower range of occupations (as in Querétaro for example). In other words, residence in a context where the perception and reality of women's work oppportunities is relatively positive could lead to a dilution of barriers, both practical and social, which bind women to the home in nuclear households elsewhere. Indeed the general consensus of women in this particular group of nuclear households in Puerto Vallarta was not only that work opportunities were much more varied than in other cities they knew, but also, more lucrative. Almost invariably when women had moved directly from one job to another it was in order to improve their salaries. Although women frequently mentioned chambermaiding, kitchen work and domestic service as the major occupations open to them in the 'formal' economy, there was also recognition of countless abilities to exploit the market with self-generated activities. Idalia suggested that one could sell *anything* in Puerto Vallarta, especially in the way of prepared foodstuffs because many working women did not have time to cook themselves. The same kind of principle applied to services. Eloisa, for example, pointed out that the city had grown so fast that conventional health facilities were in short supply; as a result one could use an elementary course in first aid or nursing to distinct advantage. Nevertheless, Rodalinda, while recognising that opportunities for women in Puerto Vallarta were much better than in other towns in Jalisco, also observed that this was not necessarily unconditionally positive for married women. While husbands in other parts of the country would normally object to their wives working, in Puerto Vallarta they do not; not because they are less *'macho'* according to Roda, but because they turn it to their own advantage.[12] When women earn, they tend to be penalised for it by receiving less financial support from husbands than they would otherwise. In fact when I first met Roda at the time of the initial house count, and in trying to establish the sex of the household head asked if she had a co-resident partner, the response was: *'Pues, tengo y no tengo - El trabaja nada mas por sus vicios, y yo trabajo por mantener a mis hijos'* ('Well I have and I haven't - He only works to support his vices whereas I work to support the children').

Indeed women's advantage in the local labour market appears in some cases to be counteracted by reduced economic cooperation from men on the home front. Even the Development Plan produced by the Commission for the Development of the Río Ameca Conurbation (COCODERA, 1980: 515–18) deems this worthy to note in their section on social evolution in the region, suggesting that in the past 15 years the female population in the city have become perceptibly 'liberated' through tourism development, not only because of unprecedented opportunities in the labour force, but also because of contact with foreign habits and behaviour (see also Lea, 1988: 70ff.). However, this greater economic and social freedom for women has been tempered by a lack of economic obligation on the part of men and in some instances made highly problematic by aggravating relations between the sexes. COCODERA (1980: 518–9) suggest that men who are used to being breadwinners and having dependent wives, find it extremely difficult to adjust in a town where women have an advantage in the labour market and may well be the only members of the household with a secure wage. The male reaction to this is predominantly aggressive, responding to a loss of economic dominance by intensifying so-called *'macho'* behaviour.[13,14]

Although there is some truth in this interpretation, and indeed it is interesting to find specific mention of a gender issue in such a document, I would not agree with the assertion that women in Puerto Vallarta have a *better* position in the labour market than men. On the whole they have access to fewer jobs, and also get paid less than men. This is also the opinion of many of the interviewees, although at the same time they acknowledged that a woman on her own need not starve in Puerto Vallarta, whereas in other parts of the country she might well do.

To what extent does the experience of women in nuclear households in Puerto Vallarta differ from that of their counterparts in the other two cities where demand for female labour is much lower?

Women and work in nuclear households, León

In León there were only two nuclear households in the sub-sample, one of the wives (Celia) worked, the other (Emilia) did not. Celia, 28, presently engaged in small-scale retailing of clothes and footwear, has been discussed earlier in the context of being able to take on an income-generating activity because her eldest daughter now minds the youngest child. Born in León and with one year of secondary education, this is the first employment Celia has had in her entire life. Celia feels that it is relatively easy to get work in León with an education, even if it is generally difficult for for most people in her class. However, she also mentioned that it may be easier for women to find work than men at present because they are often more flexible and prepared to accept part-time employment. In the other case, Emilia, 49, also mentioned earlier, worked for four years in Guadalajara between the ages of 18 and 22 before marriage. As a wife she has lived in several parts of Mexico and observes that León at present is one of the hardest places for both men *and* women to find work because of cut-backs in production. However, it is especially difficult for women because they are less likely to have skills. Aside from these rather negative perceptions of the current state of León's economy and the obvious difficulties women have in finding employment compared with Puerto Vallarta, a possible generational pattern is also discernible. It is perhaps no coincidence that both Celia's and Emilia's mothers were full-time housewives in male-headed households, and this distinguishes them clearly from the mothers of the women in nuclear households in Puerto Vallarta who were for the most part working and surviving alone.

Women and work in nuclear households, Querétaro

In Querétaro the only woman working in a nuclear household was Francisca, 40 years, and in 1982 she had been heading her own household unit. This is perhaps the most important single factor accounting for her current participation. Born in the municipality of El Marqués, Querétaro, Francisca came to the city at the age of 14 where she obtained a series of domestic service jobs. According to her there was little else a woman could do in those days. Francisca worked for 9 years until she married and then withdrew from the labour force in accordance with her husband's wishes. Five years into their marriage he had an affair with another woman and left home. Francisca was both emotionally and financially devastated. Having three young children at the time, and no one close at hand to help out, she had to stay at home and make what she could out of washing and ironing other people's laundry. However, the separation was short-lived. Her husband returned within the year and again she left the labour force for another three years until he died in 1980. During that period Francisca gave birth to a further 3 children. As a widow with six dependants to feed and clothe, Francisca had no choice then but to get what terms as a 'proper' job. Instructing the eldest child (only 8 years old at the time) to keep an eye on the younger ones and to make sure there was always someone looking after the baby, Francisca got work for the first 7 months after her husband's death as an assistant in a *tortillería*. However, the job was so poorly paid that she left and was fortunate enough move into a fruit-packing job at the local Clemente Jacques plant, working there until October 1982 when as a result of the crisis the factory had to shed a considerable fraction of its labour force and made her redundant. Her only option in such a generalised state of recession in local industry was to go back to the home and embark once again upon making a living from her own devices, this time making *tortillas*. Her son also began working part-time in a small grocery store to help out. In 1984 she entered into a second marriage with a 25-year old soldier, 15 years her junior. Her son has since been withdrawn from the labour force and sent back to school, but Francisca wants, and is permitted, to continue working. Her new husband apparently has no objection to this, possibly because he met her when she was economically self-sufficient and has thus had to accept her on her own terms. Additional factors explaining Francisca's strong position include the fact that they are living in her house, and that she has a certain degree of authority accruing from seniority.[15] Two further children have been born since their wedding.

The five non-working women in nuclear households range in age from 25 to 44 years. Two of them, despite having completed primary education, have never had paid work in their lives. One, Lourdes, 33 years old, with two young children and married to a factory worker was born in Querétaro and never allowed to work by her father or husband. The other, Laura, 25-year-old mother of four, who came to Querétaro with her parents at the age of 14, was not allowed to work by her father either, although now helps out occasionally on an unpaid basis in her husband's photographic business beneath the family's two-roomed rented flat.

Two others, Rosa and Gloria, have only ever had experience of domestic service jobs. Rosa, 44, is a native of Querétaro and had 3 different domestic service jobs before marriage, 2 in Querétaro and 1 in Mexico City. She married her husband, a petty tradesman, at the age of 20, and had six children, now aged between 7 and 20, all of whom live at home. Her eldest daughter, 20, with one year of secondary schooling is currently out of work and finding it hard to get a job.

Gloria, 39, with no education at all had been born in a rural part of Guanajuato into a very large family. Her father, an *ejidatario*, could not maintain all his children, especially with so many daughters, so at the age of 10 Gloria came with her aunt to Querétaro and got a live-in domestic service job in which she stayed for 8 years until she married. In 1983, as has already been mentioned in a previous section, Gloria went out to work on a part-time basis for a couple of months as a domestic servant but had to return home in order to look after her daughters properly and to stop Emilio being ridiculed by neighbours. Gloria feels that domestic service is the only job a woman with no education is likely to get in Querétaro in spite of slight recovery in industrial employment in recent years.

Finally, Berta, whom has also been discussed previously, only came to Querétaro as a married women. Before marriage, Berta had had a couple of domestic service/childminding posts in Cuernavaca and Mexico City, and then, as her husband was building up his manufacturing and retail business in fluffy toys, was paid to help out. The household was purposely extended for two years to let Berta have more time at the loom. However, since contracting once again to a nuclear unit she has had to retreat to full-time housework and child-care and has been replaced by a male worker.

One striking fact about all these women in Querétaro is that they have very undifferentiated work histories – mainly domestic service and child-minding. Another interesting point is that only two of the women – Berta and Francisca – had working mothers. What is also perhaps significant is that despite the fact that one of them, Rosa, experienced 10 years of living in a unit extended through the co-residence of her mother-in-law, she *still* did not work. Her husband was completely opposed to the idea that either his wife or mother should take a job. The rest of the households have been pretty stable in terms of structure. Nevertheless, it might suggest that a paucity of demand for female labour in the city may filter down and influence attitudes towards the sexual division of labour, and in turn the organisation of survival strategies at the household level. If the only occupations women can get are low-paid menial ones, then it is unlikely that the benefits will outweigh the costs of releasing them from their labour in the home. As such they remain housepersons and there is little need for family extension. Instead it is more likely that their daughters will go out to work (see Chapter 7).

Certainly all the Querétaro nuclear family interviewees felt that finding 'proper work' with a wage, contract, paid holidays and so on was very difficult in the city, particularly without an education. However, the fact that so many other households which were nuclear in 1982-3 are now extended and have high rates of labour force participation suggests that economic crisis has prompted an increased number to move into the labour force and relaxed the objections of husbands to their so doing. This issue is explored further in Chapter 6.

Women's labour force participation in the three cities: demand or supply?

To an extent we have already examined the major reasons for female labour force participation in non-nuclear households, and there is no need to reiterate them here. However, what is important in the context of the present discussion of supply and demand factors is to consider particular features of households which apply to the different cities, and also to examine perceptions and attitudes regarding local employment opportunities. In terms of *sequence* in all cities most women entered the labour force *after* household structure changed, rather than before, which might suggest that impulse to work is determined above all by household circumstances rather than the local economy, but this alone is not sufficient to inform us about the relative strength of different supply and demand factors, especially given that household form and organisation itself is likely to be strongly affected by local patterns of production. For example, we must consider the issue of what kinds of households arrive in the cities; is there anything significant about the composition and headship of migrant families which favours particular patterns of female labour force participation? Moreover, in our discussion of nuclear households it is apparent that in some cities (notably Puerto Vallarta) over half the women work (albeit part-time) with no change in family structure; this suggests that adaptations other than modifications to membership are also possible.

Female labour demand and household headship: inter-city differences

Probably the most distinctive factor differentiating Puerto Vallarta from the other two cities is that a much larger component of women household heads come to the city without a man. Indeed all four female heads of household in the Puerto Vallarta sub-sample had come to the city as single-parents anticipating that it would be relatively easy to find a job. Only one is not working at present because she is allowing herself to be supported by her sons for a while. In a sense then, those women who come on their own to the city or as heads of household (and who display the highest rates of labour force participation of all household structure sub-groups) are self-selecting. Whereas in León, the two female heads had only lost their husbands once in the city, one through widowhood, the other through desertion. In Querétaro too, about which more will be said in the next chapter, only 1 out of 8 female heads came to the city on their own (in this case to join her mother). All the others had come to the city as children or with their husbands and had become heads of household once there. Thus migration of women-headed units to these cities is rare, and women only work once their husbands have left home. Six out of 8 female heads work in Querétaro, and 1 out of 2 in León. High demand for female labour in the local economy (as in Puerto Vallarta) therefore, may not only have a positive effect on female labour force participation rates in *general*, but also exert a decisive influence on household structures in low-income communities: women household heads are those most likely to work, and at the same time the percentage of these structures is higher in such a city (19.6%, in Puerto Vallarta as against 10.4% in León, and 13.5% in Querétaro, 1982-3 – see Table 4.9), partly because a large number of them arrive already in this formation. In Puerto Vallarta, many women heads of household come specifically with the objective of finding work. This in turn feeds back into prospective household form in the sense that wage-earning gives gives them more control over their own lives, including the capacity to determine whether to enter further partnerships or not. Indeed 3 of the 4 women heads of household in Puerto Vallarta did not want nor expect to be economically dependent on men, partly one might argue because they have greater opportunities for independent survival here than in other places.

Another critical factor explaining high numbers of women-headed households and high rates of female labour force participation in Puerto Vallarta is the way in which seasonal variations in labour demand induce a number of men to spend some part of the year away from the city. Again it could be suggested that certain men are prepared to leave their families periodically *only* in places where their wives can find work.

Female labour demand and marriage: inter-city differences

Another important potential effect of local differences in demand for female labour which inevitably to some degree impinges on household structure concerns *marriage*. While the great majority of women are in formalised unions (civil and/or religious) in all three cities, a significant minority (both in female- and male-headed households) have never been married in Puerto Vallarta. For example, of all women currently in male-headed units in the three cities, the questionnaire survey reveals that 91.6% of spouses in Querétaro were formally married to first husbands, 97.1% in León, but only 79.7% in Puerto Vallarta. In addition, while 14.7% of women in male-headed units in Puerto Vallarta were in a *'unión libre'* (free union, common-law marriage), there were no such cases in León, and only 8.3% in Querétaro. These differences undoubtedly relate, at least in part, to inter-urban variations in labour demand and questions of female economic security and/or self-sufficiency. In places such as León and Querétaro, where women have fewer opportunities to obtain work, it is probably more advantageous to marry than to retain independent status, simply because a man is likely to be slightly more obliged to a wife than to a mistress.[16] However, in Puerto Vallarta, the situation is different. As we have already discussed, the fact that women *can* make a living on their own, sometimes has the effect of making men withhold economic support. As such, many women prefer to have the freedom to dissolve unsatisfactory partnerships, rather than to tie themselves to someone whom they might end up maintaining (see also Safa, 1981). Furthermore, marriage for many interviewees signifies a much greater degree of restriction over their lives than simple cohabitation. Women in Puerto Vallarta feel that as wives, they would lose alot of their former rights, and so prefer to continue working and not marrying. Of course other factors may come into the question of inter-city differences in marriage patterns. One relates to kinship. Querétaro, and particularly León, are much longer established cities than Puerto Vallarta, where the bulk of migrants have only arrived in the last decade (see Chapter 4). Since pressure from kin can sometimes result in young people marrying (especially where a pregnancy is involved) and in Puerto Vallarta several households have no relatives in the city at all, people here are perhaps freer not to conform to social norms associated with traditional concepts of family honour. Another point, touched upon earlier, includes the effects of extensive contact with foreigners in Puerto Vallarta and the possibility of 'Western' attitudes influencing those of local women. Certainly there appears to be much more above-board sexual freedom for women in Puerto Vallarta than in the more conservative cities of León and Querétaro. Indeed women in Puerto Vallarta were not at all reticent about declaring they were single, or in a *unión libre*, whereas in the few cases in León and Querétaro that marriages were not formalised, or babies had been born illegitimately, people seemed embarrassed and/or reluctant to disclose the fact. As a result, in Puerto Vallarta, there did not appear to be the same stigma attached to the idea of being a *madre soltera* (unmarried mother) than there was in the other two cities. Many women readily volunteered the information that they wanted to have children and were in the process of 'trying their partners out' before making a serious commitment to the fathers. Indeed the Development Plan referred to earlier sees fit to mention that single-parents are widely accepted in the city (COCODERA, 1980: 516). Conclusions which might be drawn from the above are that the nature of female labour opportunities in a given city influences not only the relative balance of male- and female-headed households, but also the marital status of women in general.

Female labour demand and household composition: inter-city differences

The effects of local patterns of labour demand on *compositional* aspects of household structure are less easy to identify, partly because the data from the questionnaire survey and the sub-sample are somewhat contradictory. Nevertheless certain provisional interpretations may be suggested. The first is that while nuclear households represent the single most important household structure in all three cities, they are least common in Puerto Vallarta (51.1% of the total) than in León (63.6%) or Querétaro (1982–3: 68.5%). In Puerto Vallarta this low figure is in part accounted for by the large proportion of female-headed households (both extended and non-extended), but also by the very high proportion of extended households (32.6%). The respective figures for León and Querétaro (1982–3) are 27.3% and 22.5%. Although it was originally imagined that extended households would be highest in León because of the need for small-scale workshops to incorporate kin, the fact that they are most numerous in Puerto Vallarta suggests that domestic production is not the primary factor. Indeed the critical element here appears to be that most adult women are working which in turn entails need for help with *reproductive* labour. Although inter-city differences in female labour force participation in extended structures vary substantially between the questionnaire survey and the sub-sample (rates in the latter are 71% in Puerto Vallarta, 100% in León and 67% in Querétaro, compared with respective figures of 57%, 71% and 45% [Querétaro, 1982-3] in the questionnaire survey), certain conclusions may be offered. The first is that in Puerto Vallarta as a whole, extended households are most frequent where there are highest *general* rates of female labour force participation, and nuclear households least common. The second is that a much higher proportion of women in extended households in León are working in comparison with their nuclear family counterparts (in the more repesentative questionnaire sample, over three-quarters of women in extended households in León have part- or full-time employment compared with only half the nuclear family spouses). A third factor, to be explored further in the following chapter, is the massive rise in extended households in Querétaro between 1982–3 and 1986 which has been unequivocally accompanied by an increase in women working over the same period. All these findings suggest that female labour force participation is highly integrated with household formation and reinforces the observation that nuclear households are probably least well equipped to cope with the movement of women into the workforce.

Additional observations relevant to composition include the greater diversity of households in Puerto Vallarta compared with the other two cities, for example, large numbers of married couples without children, and the case in the sub-sample where a young couple have left their child in their place of origin. Other types of household discovered in the initial house count included an arrangement where four teenage brothers and sisters were working in Puerto Vallarta but supporting parents in a rural part of Jalisco. There are also considerable numbers of single-person units, usually renting in the city yet tied in with a much larger network of dependent rural relatives. Puerto Vallarta also shows interesting trends in the configuration of women-headed units over time. One of the female heads of household for example came to the city with just two of her children in 1980, and the rest have gradually joined her as she has got established. Such trajectories are not found in case studies from either Querétaro or León, partly because very few women-headed households actually move to the city anyway, but also because it is very unlikely in these places for women to be in a position where they can wholly support dependent offspring.

Although the wide-ranging multiplicity of household structures in Puerto Vallarta relates in part to the fact that it is the only city in the study with a buoyant economy at present, one might also suggest that the comparatively greater number of opportunities for women in the local labour force have a role to play. Indeed if women did not have such opportunities there might not be the same amount of deviation from the conventional nuclear model; as noted above, the nuclear structure provides least flexibility for women to move away from the domestic responsibilities assigned to them through the sexual division of labour. Indeed a major point for consideration is the prospects for existing nuclear families in Puerto Vallarta where women engage in waged work. Given the strain imposed on the management of reproductive labour by women's involvement in the workforce, it might well be the case if present trends continue, and in the light of likely future in-migration of rural relatives, that the proportion of nuclear households in the city will decline still further.

Conclusions

A number of conclusions may be drawn from the material presented in this chapter. The first is that in the great majority of cases female labour force participation appears to be closely integrated with household structure. Changes in one sphere frequently have repercussions in another. Further detailed evidence of this from the diachronic study in Querétaro is provided in the next chapter. The sequence in which these events occur sheds some light on the relative importance of supply and demand factors in female labour force participation, but is not particularly reliable in itself; first, because people are much more likely to rationalise their current workforce status in terms of specific tangible/material household factors, rather than more general abstract conditions such as the nature of the local economy, particularly if they have no direct experience of employment; and second because separation in time does not actually imply that the first step (female entry into the labour force or a change in household structure) was *conceived* as independent of the other, or conversely, automatically led on to the next one.

Another issue here concerns the problem of demographic variations between cities, specifically the composition and headship of households on arrival in the city; this makes it somewhat difficult to ascertain the relative importance of supply and demand factors in female labour force participation *in situ*. Obviously women work in certain types of household because they have a greater need to do so (in female-headed units for example); from this perspective a strict interpretation might emphasise the overriding importance of 'supply' variables. Yet at the same time, if local economic circumstances did not favour female employment then there would probably be fewer of these households in the locality. In this respect demand is obviously crucial in shaping the overall structure of supply. The observations of Saskia Sassen-Koob (1984: 1,159) seem relevant here. In discussing immigrant women in the United States, Sassen-Koob suggests that there is strong 'interaction effect' between supply and demand factors in the sense that in places where there is a growing demand for low-wage female workers (mainly in producer and distributive services) , this is usually accompanied by a burgeoning supply of women workers, and those most likely to work, especially in the Mexican case, are those who head their own households (see also Fernández Kelly, 1983a; Safa, 1981).

Although it is often difficult therefore, to separate the two, I would suggest on the basis of the available evidence that the critical factor influencing female labour force participation in low-income communities is the structure of *demand* in the local economy. Not only does this influence the types of household which arrive in the city, as well as their subsequent evolution, but also affects the workforce participation of women in all units. In cities such as Puerto Vallarta, more women work in households which usually retain adult females in the home and more households where women have to work are attracted to the city. However, household structure still plays an important role in mediating the release of adult women into the labour force. Although women's workforce participation in nuclear households is relatively high in Puerto Vallarta, for example, it is still lower than in all but one of the other household types. In short, therefore, the main conclusion of this chapter is that women respond actively to labour market opportunities by adapting household structure within existing constraints, and at the same time, labour market conditions may act as both incentives and material facilitators for them to do so. Further discussion of the interactions among these variables is presented in the following chapter in a context of economic crisis.

Notes

1 As in the previous chapter, female household heads and spouses are the subject of discussion unless otherwise stated.

2 Fewer households were interviewed in the León sub-sample, partly because there was not the same diversity in women's occupations as there was in Puerto Vallarta and Querétaro, and partly because the original questionnaire survey in Piletas was smaller than that in Caloso. An additional four households were interviewed in Puerto Vallarta that are not listed in Table 5.1 for the reason that they did not conform with the dominant types of structure (see Appendix 1).

3 The fact that a very large number of nuclear households with working women appears in Puerto Vallarta is an incidental result of small size of the sub-sample, which was picked more or less at random. As it is, a much higher percentage of nuclear family wives in Puerto Vallarta have paid work compared with the other two cities (see Table 4.12).

4 'Changing household characteristics' refer primarily here to changes in the sex of the head of household, extension of the household unit (through the incorporation of additional kin), absence/departure of children, and also in a few cases, to progress through the 'developmental cycle' whereby children begin to take over some of their mothers' responsibilities in the home. These points are clarified and illustrated in the text.

5 All ages cited taken as of 1986 and referred to as current age.

6 The importance of other female household members able to take on domestic responsibilities in order to free adult women for income-generating activities has been noted by several other authors. See for example Achío and Mora (1988) and Ramirez Boza (1987) on Costa Rica, Ennew (1982) on Jamaica, and Moser (1989) on Ecuador. Interestingly however, in Moser's study of the impact of recession and structural adjustment over ten years in a low-income community in Guayaquil, it was found that the few women not working in the neighbourhood were generally from extended or women-headed households: in these units women tend to rely instead on the earnings of kin and children. A similar finding was made by Benería and Roldan (1987: 91) in Mexico City where they found that young recently-married women living in extended formations (usually with parents/parents-in-law) were often able to afford to move out of the labour force temporarily, although at the same time there are a number of women in such households who work due to the ability to leave child-care and domestic labour in the hands of female kin (ibid.: 31). This latter observation is much more in line with the findings of the present study where female heads and spouses in extended units normally work and pass on their reproductive duties to another kin member. Obviously much depends on the sex and age of co-resident kin. The critical point here appears to be, however, that few adult women can usually enter the workforce unless there is someone to take their place in the home.

7 This could explain why there did not appear to be a major effect exerted by women's own ages on their labour force participation. See Chapter 4

8 This is broadly consonant with the more representative figures of the larger questionnaire survey (see Table 4.12).

9 This relates to the point made earlier (in Chapter 4) where city-wide demand for female labour has important, if not directly measurable, effects on shaping household structure. These may influence personal and household decision-making about women's employment quite strongly, but not be specifically acknowledged as such.

10 Teresa Quiróz *et al.* (1984: 82) in their study of Costa Rica also found that unemployed husbands were reluctant to let their wives work, even where they needed the money.

11 It must be remembered that percentages calculated on the basis of sub-sample data are obviously not as 'representative' as those calculated from the questionnaire data. As such they must be evaluated in the light of the larger survey results presented in Chapter 4.

12 This point is highly relevant to Alison MacEwen Scott's (1990) observations about *machismo* in Peru. In her discussion of research which presents evidence of a relaxation of gender roles, especially among the urban middle classes, and expressed through such factors as rising participation of women in the labour force, in politics and so on, Scott points out that there is considerable debate over whether these changes have actually resulted in a 'diminution in *machismo* or merely a change in its form'.

13 In full, the relevant paragraph reads:

'El hombre y jefe de familia habituado a ser al sostén económico de su hogar, emigra a un pueblo donde la mujer tiene preferencia en la mano de obra, porque los servicios turísticos requieren de gente que pueda atender al turista y la mujer, de acuerdo al rol que ha venido desempeñando, está capacitada para desempeñarlo, así pues, el hombre tiene en su mujer a

su principal competidor y mientras que ella puede colocarse fácilmente, el tiene que esperar a capacitarse o adiestrarse o sub-emplearse como albañil, vendedor, pequeño comerciante etcétera por lo repentinamente se enfrenta una situación nueva para él; su mujer a quién consideraba dependiente e inútil para producir dinero, es quién se encuentra manteniendo a la familia con un sueldo seguro, mientras que el o no ha encontrado trabajo o está sujeto a eventualidades, se da cuenta que no es tan importante como el creyera y su imagen decrece ante sí mismo … Estas circunstancias producen un choque emocional en el hombre, el que contrarresta su sentimiento de impotencia e inferioridad, canalizándolo a través de una agresión sorda hacía la mujer y cuyo producto podríamos dividir en dos prototipos extremos al 'mantenido' y el 'macho', ambos manifestados en diversos grados y entremezcladas las actitudes' (COCODERA, 1980: 518–9).

14 Chaverría *et al*'s (1987) study of women members of production cooperatives in Guanacaste, Costa Rica also reveals that in certain cases men display a very negative response to their wives going out to work including refusal to cooperate, resistance to exhortations to help out a little more around the home and resorting to more aggressive behaviour. (Guanacaste is an area of Costa Rica where several working-class men are permanently un- and underemployed.)

15 Indeed Scott (1990) has argued for Lima that generally speaking senior men are those with most power in working-class households, which could explain the different balance of authority in Francisca's case.

16 For the case of black families in the Americas, MacDonald and MacDonald (1978) also observe that although many women are economically independent, most prefer to be married for greater economic and social security.

6

Economic crisis, women's work and household change: the case of Querétaro

Introduction

This chapter concentrates on the way in which households interviewed in Querétaro in 1982–3 and again in 1986 have responded to recession over three-and-a-half years. In what ways have households adapted their survival strategies in order to cope with increased hardship? General aspects of the recession in the Mexican economy and some of its major implications for Querétaro were discussed in Chapter 2, but it is important to reiterate that the crisis was particularly felt in cities heavily dependent upon large-scale modern manufacturing. Indeed between 1982 and 1983, around one-quarter of Querétaro's industrial workforce lost their jobs (see Chant, 1984). Although many firms in the 1986 Employer Survey noted that there had been some recovery by this latter period, they were not employing the same numbers as they had been prior to 1982. Many workers are currently hired on short-term contracts to make it easier for them to be laid off during downswings in production. Querétaro's economic decline has had serious effects on many groups of citizens, but particularly for those who had fewest resources to begin with. As such, local economic stagnation has called for several changes in the survival strategies of poor households. In this chapter a range of the most significant changes are examined with particular reference to household structure and female labour force participation. The main conclusion is that adjustments in either one, or generally both, these areas have helped the poor avoid outright destitution in the context of national economic crisis.

Household survival and economic crises: contemporary perspectives

Setting this work in context it is important to consider the findings of two key longitudinal studies of a similar nature: first, the work of Mercedes González de la Rocha (1988) on economic crisis, women's work and domestic reorganisation among low-income groups in Guadalajara, western Mexico, in the 1980s; and second, the work of Caroline Moser (1989) on responses of poor urban households in Guayaquil, Ecuador, to recession and structural adjustment over the period 1978–88. González de la Rocha's work is obviously more relevant to the present study in terms of both area and timing, and indeed certain aspects of the Mexican recession such as deteriorating real wage levels have affected low-income groups everywhere in the country. Although Guadalajara has a more diverse industrial base than Querétaro, with a plethora of small-scale enterprises that have probably kept more of a lid on open unemployment, on the whole it appears that the effects of increased poverty have been broadly similar

Ninety-five of the 100 households interviewed by González de la Rocha in 1982 were traced and re-interviewed in 1985, and again in 1987, although her 1988 article concentrates mainly on the changes between 1982 and 1985. The principal findings of the research are as follows. First, households increased their size between the two periods, particularly through the incorporation of other kin. Second, and related to this, while nuclear households were in the majority in both years, by 1985 they had declined at the expense of increasing proportions of both extended and multiple family households.[1] Third, there was an increase in the numbers of wage earners in households, particularly among women aged 15 years or more, and among boys under 14. Partly as a result of this last factor there was a decrease in household dependency (worker: consumer) ratios.

As far as household size was concerned, this increased from an average of 6.58 to 6.97 members during the three-year interval, and in some respects is associated with the rise in non-nuclear households. Nuclear households fell from 80% of the sample in 1982, to 74.7% in 1985 (González de la Rocha, 1988: 211–12). At the same time the average number of workers per household rose from 2.13 to 2.69 (ibid.: 212). Although there is no way of telling from her article whether female labour force participation increased in those households which had become extended in the period, it appears that households with women aged 15 years or more working rose from 63% of the earlier sample to 79% in the later one, and the labour force participation of female heads (by which she refers both to female heads and spouses) increased from 38% to 46.7%. Younger women were playing an important role in taking over from their mothers who now went out to work.

González de la Rocha also discusses household expenditure and consumption. Although there was a drop in real wages of the order of one-third to one-half, and the real salaries of male heads dropped by 35%, there was actually only an 11% fall in real per capita household income for those in the survey, largely because families were deploying more members into the labour force. Nevertheless, cuts in most parts of the family budget were inevitable. Although people tried to protect food consumption, they were eating less in the way of protein, and in per capita terms, expenditure on food had dropped by 13%. Very few households were saving money and less was being spent on education and health (ibid.: 216–19)

Moser's (1989) findings over a longer time span in Guayaquil, Ecuador, show remarkable similarities. Although Ecuador is poorer than Mexico, with substantially greater numbers of people in rural areas, as an oil producer it has also undergone the same kind of economic peaks and troughs experienced by Mexico during the last 15–20 years. High rises in public spending in the 1970s at the expense of a mounting external debt were followed by drastic cuts in the following decade associated with the oil price shocks of 1982 and 1986–7. As in Mexico, a massive stabilisation programme was set in operation in 1982–3, with severe curtailment in wage rises and public expenditure (see Moser, 1989).

At grassroots level, poor households of the neighbourhood Barrio Indio Guayas in the port of Guayaquil, Ecuador's second major city, have responded to recession in much the same way as Guadalajara. The principal effects noted by Moser are also increased numbers of workers in each household, with many women amongst those additional workers, and modifications in consumption patterns. Regarding workers, Moser observes that the proportion of households with only one wage earner fell from nearly one-half to one-third of all households in the period 1978–88. At the same time, those households with three or more workers rose from one-fifth to one-third of the total, and women's labour force participation increased from 40% to 52%. With respect to consumption, as in González's study, people were eating less in the way of high protein and/or nutritious foodstuffs such as milk, fish and fresh fruit juice, were eating smaller portions, and had fewer meals a day (many people cut out supper for example). In addition Moser observed an disturbing rise in domestic violence, particularly over cash and in households where women were not contributing to household income and thus having to ask their husbands for bigger handouts. Although this was not mentioned by González de la Rocha, she does note that the poor in Guadalajara are more tired and worn and have less time to relax than they used to (González de la Rocha, 1988: 220).

Many of the changes identified in both the above cities are also found in Querétaro to a greater or lesser degree.

Household survival strategies in Querétaro 1982–3 to 1986

Family size

As in González de la Rocha's study in Guadalajara, the average size of household units in Querétaro also increased over 3 to 4 years, but by an even bigger margin – from 6.8 in 1982–3 to 7.6 in 1986. However, it is also important to bear in mind that the sub-sample selected for interview in 1986 from the earlier survey had slightly different characteristics from the overall questionnaire survey, with an average size in 1982–3 of 7 persons. Even then, this was still a larger increase (8.5%) than in Guadalajara (6%) (González de la Rocha. 1988: 211).

Larger household size in Querétaro, as in Guadalajara, is mainly accounted for by the incorporation of new members: over one-third of the households which had been nuclear or one-parent in 1982–3 converted to extended formations in 1986 (see Table 6.1). Although 65% of households selected for the 1986 survey had been non-extended in 1982, this dropped to 40% by the latter period (see also Table 4.11).

Table 6.1: Actual changes in household structure in Querétaro 1982–3 to 1986

Original structure 1982–3		Structure by 1986				Total in 1986
	Stayed same	Nuclear	One-parent	Male-extended	Female-extended	original−losses+additions= total
Nuclear	****	n/a		***	*	8 − 4 + 2 = 6
One-parent	**	*	n/a		**	5 − 3 + 0 = 2
Male-extended	***	*		n/a	*	5 − 2 + 3 = 6
Female-extended	**				n/a	2 − 0 + 4 = 6
Net gain or loss of household type		−2	−3	+1	+4	

Source: Household Questionnaire Survey, Querétaro, 1986.

Numbers of workers and dependency ratios

Numbers of workers in Querétaro had also risen slightly, if only in absolute terms. In the larger questionnaire survey in Querétaro in 1982–3 the average number of workers per household was 1.6, and in the sub-sample, 2.1. In 1986 the average had risen to 2.3. Using the sub-sample figures which are more accurate for direct comparisons, the increase in numbers of workers is far less than that calculated by González de la Rocha: around 10% as against 65%. The slightness of the increase is even more apparent when set against household size and numbers of dependants. Although González de la Rocha (1988: 213) found that one waged worker supported only 2.59 household members in 1986 (compared with 3.09 in 1982), in Querétaro in 1986 one worker was still supporting an average of 3.3 persons in each household, only fractionally less (under one decimal point) than in 1982 (see Chant, 1984). What explains the fact that the poor in Querétaro have not significantly increased their numbers of workers in relative terms?

One contributory reason is probably that many schoolchildren in Querétaro, especially in female-headed one-parent units had been working part-time in 1982–3 and were accordingly registered as workers in the earlier survey. However, by 1986 some of these former part-time adolescent workers had left school, moved into full-time jobs and were thus bringing in higher wages (see below). With greater financial returns from these individuals, there was obviously less need to send other members out to work. It does indeed seem also that parents are holding onto children for longer. Aside from the fact that many in their late teens and early twenties are still single and thus living at home, it also seems that a significant number are staying with their parent(s) on marriage. Although a total of 6 sons and daughters from 5 households in the sample formed their own independent households with spouses during this period, a further 4 (from 4 different households) got married but continued living at home, in another case a son and his wife returned and in another case, even though a daughter had left home the father of a female head moved in and essentially took her place.

The same argument about existing workers receiving higher wages by 1986 probably also applies to female income-generators; although some women had entered the labour force in the previous three years, some had also moved into higher-paid jobs during that period. In the sub-sample of 20 households, exactly 50% of the female heads and spouses had been working in 1982–3. This had risen to 55% (or 60% if one includes a woman working on an occasional unpaid basis in her husband's photographic business) by 1986. This seemingly small change calculated from the sub-sample masks a great deal of actual movement: a large percentage of those working in 1986 were in fact new to the labour force, and correspondingly some of those working in 1982–3 had left by the latter period. This last group consisted of 3 women: 1 left work because of sickness, 1 because she was replaced by a male worker in her husband's small manufacturing enterprise when the household lost the extended component, and 1 because of a combination of inability to delegate her domestic work to daughters and because her husband was jeered at by neighbours for letting his wife 'out on the streets'. In contrast, 4 new women had taken up work, and 3 had changed their jobs. Two of this last group were female heads of household who had moved from part-time/ casual work in domestic service and garbage-picking in 1982–3 to better-paid positions as municipal roadsweepers by 1986.

This kind of movement could explain why the percentage of single-earning households had actually increased (30% of the sub-sample in 1982–3 to 35% in 986), although at the same time households with three or more workers had still increased quite substantially from 35% in 1982–3 to 50% in 1986 (cf. Moser's observed rise in such households in Guayaquil from one-fifth to one-third between 1978 and 1988).

Purchasing power, consumption and savings

As in Guadalajara and Guayaquil, strategies to cope with deteriorating real wage levels have partly offset the hard edge of recession. Between the second half of 1982 and 1986, consumer prices in Mexico rose by 981%, whereas the daily minimum wage rose by only 573%. At the household level in Querétaro, this loss of over one-third of the purchasing power of the minimum wage has been counteracted by a combination of sending more members into the workforce and by a number of pre-existing workers somehow moving into jobs with better remuneration. Average per capita income (based on earnings) of households in Querétaro in 1986 was 6,037 pesos, compared with 563.7 in 1982–3: thus an increase in the order of 971% has actually meant that households have almost managed to maintain their relative earning capacity. Overall households in Querétaro have only lost 1% of per capita income in real terms, whereas in Guadalajara per capita household income fell by 11%. While this is an average figure it means that some households in Querétaro at least are managing to insert their members into relatively well-paid jobs, in spite of recession. If anything, the worst of the crisis was felt in 1982 and 1983; most changes in family organisation ocurring in response to this came about in 1984 and 1985, and remained that way until 1986 by which time the economy had recovered slightly. Nevertheless, it is also important to remember that by 1982, wages had already lost about one-third of their purchasing power from the mid-1970s.

Unfortunately detailed data on expenditure and consumption such as that collected by González de la Rocha was not gathered in the present project: households were merely asked to comment on the way in which the crisis had most affected them. Some emphasised very specific changes in their consumption behaviour, others focused on work patterns, and a number even identified certain positive social impacts for women.

Changes in consumption

Somewhat surprisingly, very little was said about modifications to diet, seeming to confirm González de la Rocha's (1988: 217) observation that people had tried to protect food consumption above all their other outgoings: in her study households were only spending marginally less of their total budget on food in 1985 (58%) than in 1982 (60%), whereas that ear-marked for medical care and savings had dropped to virtually nothing. As such we can see a tendency for resources to be shifted away from long-term to short-term reproduction. In Querétaro, too, the key objective on people's minds was to ensure that they had as much to eat as possible, although one or two of the poorest households no longer buy meat and live on a meagre diet consisting of only beans, *tortillas* and occasionally eggs.

However, most people were cutting corners in other ways – in Bolaños, for example, where households have no piped water and still have to rely on costly tanker deliveries, people were washing clothes less frequently. In all settlements few people had invested money in housing improvements, despite the fact that general servicing levels in all three settlements had improved: Los Andadores now has piped water and sewerage and Bolaños and Las Américas, while still lacking these services, at least have paving of major thoroughfares. Expenditure on shelter was regarded as a luxury which should wait until such time as people began to feel more secure in their jobs and earnings, especially with inflation running at over 80% in 1986 (see also Chant, 1984: Chapter 7 on the effects of inflation on building materials). Several households had also stopped saving money; long-term perspectives which had been the prerogative of the more privileged households in 1982–3 had now been replaced by a much more day-to-day approach to survival. In 1982–3 nearly half the 244 households in the questionnaire survey in Querétaro were able to put aside small amounts of cash each week; by 1986 this had dropped to one-third of the families in the sub-sample, partly because household income was insufficient in many cases to cover more than the very basic necessities (food, clothing, rates, service charges and so on), and partly because people were highly sceptical about the utility of saving money when inflation could so easily erode its value, even in a high-interest bank account. (In 1982–3 most people [55%] had saved money at home or in the local *tanda* [an informal rotating credit arrangement among groups of neighbours in the community], and only 45% of households in a savings association or bank.) On average, saving households in 1986 had 30% more earnings per capita than non-savers.

Changes in women's work and status

Many households stressed that they had lived fairly comfortably on one wage prior to 1982, they now had to have two or three members working in order to maintain comparable standards of living, although this was not always seen as negative. For some women, for example, the crisis was seen as having had rather positive results for them personally, especially when they had ended up gaining their husbands' permission to go out to work. For working wives, employment was argued to have increased a sense of independence, power, and equality of status within the household. At the same time, work could be a major burden if they had no help to rely upon in the home. Indeed one respondent, Doña Lupe P., argued that although women's position in the labour force had improved slightly in Querétaro during the course of the crisis (partly as a result of an equal opportunities programme in public services promoted by the incoming State governor, Mariano Palacios Alcocer in 1985), women were still held back with their responsibility for organising and managing '*la vida hogareña*' ('domestic life'), even if some husbands were now beginning to help a little more around the home. Furthermore, those women (especially female heads of household) who already had long experience in the labour force and were accordingly more cynical about employment than those enjoying the first flush of freedom from possessive husbands, still maintained how difficult it was for women to get work in factories or the public sector. Socorro, for example, despite having benefited personally from the state government's equal opportunities programme (she was now a roadsweeper for the municipality) felt that this was tokenism, a mere showpiece at the start of Palacios Alcocer's six-year term. Furthermore, women were generally only recruited into inferior jobs, partly due to a lack of schooling: most women in their position could only find work as domestic servants. Some also commented on the negative effects female employment could have on children (see below).

Women's work during the crisis: supply or demand?

Regardless at this stage whether the rising numbers of women in paid work in Querétaro is positive or negative in the short and long term (about which more will be said in Chapter 7), the tendency is undoubtedly linked to economic crisis and mirrors the finding of both the Guayaquil (Moser, 1989) and Guadalajara (González de la Rocha, 1988) studies. Benería and Roldan (1987: 49) in their research on industrial homeworkers in Mexico City have noted a similar trend, and are careful to stress that it is not merely economic needs *within* households which have stimulated increased labour force participation of women during this particular period of Mexican development, but also the requirements of the wider economy; as such, the phenomenon is very much a joint product of both 'demand' and 'supply' factors. The two crucial 'demand' factors identified by Benería and Roldan are first, that employers facing declining profits need to exploit cheaper sources of labour to reduce production costs; here the employment of women is particularly relevant to labour-intensive *máquila* production carried out in the home on contract from large firms. Second, that the widespread recruitment of women in multinational enterprises, both in Mexico and elsewhere, is beginning to have a 'trickle-down' effect in the sense that Mexican employers are now beginning to imitate the example of their foreign counterparts (ibid.).

On the 'supply' side, the two most important stimuli identified by Benería and Roldan in releasing women into the labour force are one, that women's work outside the home is becoming more acceptable generally (although the authors do not really provide an explanation here). Most probably, it is a knock-on effect from their second designated supply factor, that in the course of the recession, women's income has become an increasingly vital component of household survival strategies. Although their discussion revolves mainly around homeworking they do stress that there is no reason to believe that the same strategy does not apply to work outside of the home (ibid.: 49).

Although Benería and Roldan are undoubtedly correct in identifying household economic needs as critical in explaining the rising numbers of female household members in the labour force, it is also important to note this so-called 'supply' factor is very much exogenously determined, i.e. were it not for economic recession at a national level, would the supply of female workers necessarily be the same? Moreover, with respect to their point about the relaxation of traditional mores surrounding the labour force participation of married women, to what extent is this aspect of 'social change' an inevitable response to strategies designed by households to accommodate more pressing financial needs? – again largely shaped by national crisis. In other words, Benería and Roldan's attribution of the above two processes to the 'supply' side of the labour market may not be entirely appropriate. The scheme used in the present study is that 'supply' factors are those more properly *internal* to households (see Chapter 1). Such definitional and classificatory problems and the separation out of supply and demand factors are taken up again in the final chapter of the book. However, here it is important to bear in mind that the evidence from Querétaro suggests that other 'supply' factors, whose origins are perhaps less easily attributed to external circumstances, are essential in determining the relative success of individual households in riding out the crisis, especially household structure.

Benería and Roldan (1987) do in fact identify in another part of their book the way in which certain kinds of family unit facilitate the labour force participation of women, noting for example that in young extended households counting on help from resident adult relatives for housework and industrial homework was fundamental in the work strategies of the majority of wives (ibid.: 31). They also go on to identify that degrees of assistance depend on a whole series of more specific factors such as the sex of the kin in question, whether the relative(s) are from the husband's or wife's side of the family, reasons for co-residence and so on. Male relatives on the husband's side for example tend not to take on any domestic activities at all, whereas sisters, aunts and mothers do (see also Chapter 5). However, they do not discuss at any length the general effects exerted by household structure as a major supply variable, and to what extent household structure undergoes modification as a result of women's entry into the workforce.

We have already seen in previous chapters that in all cities female labour force participation and family structure are often closely linked. Here attention is drawn more specifically to these interrelationships in Querétaro over three years of economic crisis.[2]

Female labour force participation, family structure and economic crisis: changes in Querétaro 1982–3 to 1986

As mentioned a little earlier in the chapter, women's overall labour force participation has risen between the two time periods, and workforce changes have often been accompanied by related shifts in household structure.

Remembering that there are altogether 20 households in the Querétaro sub-sample, a total of 70% (14) of these had experienced some change in household structure and/or the workforce position of the adult woman (whether entering or leaving the labour force or a qualitative shift in job status) within the three years between 1982–3 and 1986. In 9 of these 14 cases, women's changing employment characteristics had been in some way related to adjustments in domestic arrangements: 6 were linked directly to alterations in family structure, 2 to movement through the lifecycle (see also Chapter 5), and in the remaining case, although there had been no family extension as such, the woman in question had engaged a paid servant in order to let her out to work. Thus in over two-thirds of the households which had experienced changes in household composition or female employment between 1982–3 and 1986, there was a strong link between the two variables. Obviously a sample as small as this does not lend itself easily to generalisations, but an attempt is made below to pinpoint the main sources of changes and articulations of links.

Linkages between changes in women's work and changes in household structure

Regarding the 6 households where women's labour force entry or withdrawal or job change was associated with a shift in family structure, 3 changes in female employment followed on from modifications in household structure; in 2, changes in household structure came about as a result of women's entry into the labour force, and in 1, both events were planned to coincide.

The 3 cases where changes in women's employment arose from modifications in household structure (all mentioned in Chapter 5) include, first, Berta who was forced to withdraw from the family toy-making business when the household became nuclear in 1984 following the move of her husband's niece to Mexico City. Second, Francisca, the female head who had remarried in 1984 and instead of taking up an offer to go back to her previous job in factory (which she had previously intended to do), had decided to remain at home making *tortillas* for local sale. And finally Socorro, another female head who in 1982 had been surviving on the basis of casual domestic service jobs. Following the extension of the household with the arrival of her elderly father in 1985 who took on most of the domestic chores, Socorro was able to move into full-time formal employment as a municipal roadsweeper.

Of the two women whose labour force participation had prompted a change in household structure, the shift was in both cases from nuclear to extended. Josefina who had entered the labour force after her husband had been made redundant now has her newly-married daughter-in-law living with them who does most of the domestic labour. The other, Paula, who while actually starting work in 1980, has filled the gap left by the departure of husband as a migrant labourer to the United States in 1982 with a sister who is now largely in charge of the housework.

Finally, in the case of María Asunción (also mentioned in Chapter 5) who is now setting up a grocery business with her husband's redundancy money, a niece has come to help out in the home while she gets the business off the ground.

Overall, the four 'positive' changes in women's employment here (i.e. a move into the labour force or an upward shift in job status) have been associated with the transformation of a nuclear or single-parent unit into an extended structure; conversely, 'negative' changes (i.e. labour force withdrawal or retreat into a home-based informal occupation) have been associated with the change of a single-parent or extended household into a nuclear unit.

Of the two cases where women's changing labour force participation had been linked to progress through the lifecycle, one Guadalupe R., in an extended household has gone into full-time factory work and delegated the bulk of her domestic duties to two teenage daughters. The other, Ana Piña has been able to move from informal garbage-picking and petty commerce into municipal roadsweeping now there is only one child (a daughter of 14) still at school, who is old enough to fend for herself. Two sons, previously schoolboys with part-time jobs, now work full-time. In order to fit around these new work schedules, the family eats together in the evenings, rather than at 3pm as they used to.

Finally, one woman Laura since moving with her family to a flat above her husband's photogaphic business and beginning to help out part-time on an unpaid basis in the studio, has enlisted the help of a daily domestic so that all she has to do herself is cook the meals.[3] In time Laura expects to become much more involved in the business.

In all the above three cases, women have only been able to sustain a move into the labour force through passing some of their reproductive responsibilities to a daughter or to outside help – the same kind of process which occurs when families convert to extended formations *sensu strictu*.

Non-linked changes in women's work and household structure

What of the other five cases where a change in female employment *or* family structure but not both occurred during the crisis years? Three women had experienced changes in household structure, and two in workforce participation. One of these latter two interviewees had withdrawn from the labour force because of damage to her arm; here the household was already extended and the existence of other earners has largely compensated for the loss of her own contribution. The other, Gloria, spouse in a nuclear household already mentioned in Chapter 5, had worked briefly in 1982 as a domestic servant, but found it impossible to manage both domestic work inside and outside the home, especially as her daughters were not really mature enough to be left in charge. She had since resumed her role as full-time housewife.

In 2 of the 3 cases in which changes in household structure had not apparently affected women's employment, women were already working in 1982–3 and had the same occupations in 1986. One woman head of an extended unit had been widowed during that time. She had worked most of her life because her husband had a weak liver and was not allowed to over-exert himself . The other, Lupe, was head of a non-extended unit in 1982 whose married son had brought his wife to live with the family in 1985, who within a year had given birth to a baby girl. Although there is no direct link here, the arrival of a daughter-in-law has been extremely beneficial to Lupe, where 3 out of her 4 children are working full-time and she herself is temporarily laid off (on half-pay) with a work injury. With her daughter-in-law now doing the bulk of the housework, extension in this case could concievably be interpreted in part as a delayed reaction to female labour force participation.[4] In the remaining case, the formerly nuclear household of household of Doña Lupe P., has recently become extended with a daughter-in-law and grandchild. Neither woman is permitted to work by her husband, but neither is it particularly necessary with 4 adult male workers in a family of only 8 persons.

Summing up this sub-section, family extension occurred in situations where 2 out of 3 women had already been working in 1982 and continued to do so. In only one case had the conversion from nuclear to extended happened in a household where the adult woman was a full-time housewife. Of those women who had withdrawn from the labour force, one belonged to a nuclear unit which could not cope with the strain of releasing her from reproductive work, and the other where the existence of multiple earners within the household made it possible for her to retreat to the home.

Having scrutinised Querétaro more closely, similar factors seem to apply here as in the other cities discussed in Chapter 5, namely that working women need some assistance in domestic labour, and this is usually much more feasible when households adopt an extended structure.

No changes in work or household structure

Finally, what of the 6 cases where there had been *no* change in household structure or female labour force participation? In 2 instances, women belonging to a female-headed one-parent and a male-headed extended unit respectively were working in the same occupations in both periods. In another case, the female head of an extended unit had died and been replaced by her daughter: neither woman worked because there were several other earners in the household. Finally, of 3 women not working in either 1982–3 or 1986, 2 belonged to nuclear households and one to a male-headed extended unit. This latter household consisted of 13 members where there were three adult male workers and an adult female worker. The woman worker in question was the spouse's sister and in this instance the spouse herself did most of the child-care and domestic labour of the household unit.

Although it is obviously difficult to pick out general tendencies and factors from such a wide variety of experiences represented by the twenty households, the main ones apparent are first, that in order to cope with positive changes in female labour force participation, households usually have to make some adjustments on the domestic front – either by becoming extended or substituting the labour generally provided by the female head or spouse with the labour of daughters or paid help. When that assistance is impossible to obtain, it is rare that women's labour force participation can be sustained. A second, and related point, is that this is most often the case in nuclear households, hence Berta's and Gloria's withdrawal from the labour force. During the crisis it has been largely imperative that women keep working or enter the labour force (unless there are very good reasons for not doing so – such as in the four extended households in the sub-sample where the existence of at least two other household members in the workforce, mainly men, reduced the need for women to work).[5] As such, nuclear units which are less well-equipped to accommodate women's labour force participation are likely to be less able to protect income levels.

Indeed, recapping the date presented in Chapter 4 (Table 4.12), both female-heads of one-parent units worked; two-thirds of female heads of extended units (4 out of 6) and female spouses in male-headed extended households (4 out of 6), and only 1 out of 6 women spouses in the nuclear units. Alternatively, considering the issue from the angle of the sex of head of household, 75% of all female heads in Querétaro worked, compared with only 42% of spouses in male-headed families.

Do these differences in female labour force participation between households affect in any major way the poor's ability to shoulder the increased economic pressures imposed upon them by national recession? Does, for example, the inflexibility or resistance of nuclear units to the labour force participation of wives place these households at a significantly greater disadvantage than those in which women's remunerated work is an increasingly accepted and integral part of household survival strategies and facilitated by a more flexible sharing of reproductive labour? Certainly the data seems to suggest that this may be the case.

While we have already considered general trends in household income and employment patterns at the beginning of the chapter, it is now necessary to break down the analysis in such a way that different types of household structure may be compared. Since the object of the analysis is to consider the effects of *structure* on survival strategies, *categories* of household in 1982–3 are compared with like categories in the later period, rather than looking at individual household trajectories, many of which have already been discussed in Chapter 5. Comparisons in structures between the two time periods are based where possible on the specific conditions of the 1986 sample in 1982–3, rather than the larger survey. Thus, for example, overall averages of household size, numbers of working members and so on are calculated on the basis of the twenty households in the 1986 survey in their configurations in 1982–3 to give more accurate comparisons.

Household survival strategies 1982–3 to 1986: the influence of household structure

Family size, numbers of workers and dependency ratios

While average family size increased from 7 to 7.6 between 1982–3 and 1986, the only *type* of household which actually increased its membership was the nuclear unit (see Table 6.2). All other household structures actually experienced an overall decline in membership. Increased size of nuclear units was either the result of further children being born or because those which became extended between 1982–3 and 1986 and were thus taken out of the nuclear category in the latter period had been slightly smaller than those who remained. Conversely in extended units the decline in size is possibly due to the fact that five of the households which converted between 1982–3 and 1986 were nuclear and single-parent units (see also Table 6.1): recently–extended households are obviously less likely to be as large as those which have been extended for some time – over the years kin tend to be incorporated in an incremental manner, with births to young newly-weds and so on. However, even those households which remained extended during the whole period also declined in size from an average of 10.3 to 9.6 members, partly as a result of deaths in a couple of instances and partly, as discussed earlier in the chapter, because there were a few cases where sons and daughters formed independent households in the intervening years and one or two already had children, meaning that when they moved out moved out household size dropped considerably. Single-parent households became smaller still between the two time periods, possibly because the larger ones among this group in 1982–3 (and *ipso facto* those less likely to be able to rely on a single female wage) became extended by 1986.

Table 6.2: Household size in Querétaro between 1982–3 and 1986 according to household structure

Household structure	Household size		% Change
	1982–3	*1986*	
Nuclear	5.6 (8)[a]	7.0 (6)	+25%
One-parent	5.8 (5)	4.0 (2)	−31%
Male extended	8.6 (5)	8.1 (6)	−6%
Female extended	11.5 (2)	8.8 (6)	−23.5%
All households/ average	*7.0(20)*	*7.6(20)*	*+8.5%*

Note: [a] Numbers in brackets refer to number of cases.

Source: Household Questionnaire Survey, Querétaro, 1986; and sub-sample 1982–3 Household Survey.

Regarding changes in numbers of workers and dependency (i.e. worker: non-worker) ratios, we noted earlier that overall there had been only marginal changes. However, breaking this down by family structure we find that in single-parent units and male-headed extended households, the number of workers relative to household size has risen substantially in the group as a whole, thereby reducing dependency in these structures (see Table 6.3). In nuclear household units on the other hand, while there was a marginal increase in their workforce participation, each worker was actually supporting a greater number of dependents in 1986 than in 1982–3 (see Table 6.3). This also applied to female-headed extended households which although having slightly lower dependency ratios than nuclear households in 1986, actually had fewer workers than in 1982–3 in both absolute and relative terms. In part this could be attributed to the fact that one male-headed extended household had become female-headed through death (which automatically reduced labour resources when the woman herself had worked in both periods,[6] but it could also be due to the fact that family extension between 1982–3 and 1986 has actually arisen in female-headed units where women were already working but did not incorporate domestic assistance until *after* they had entered the workforce. As such the incorporation of relatives has not actually resulted in additions to the household workforce, but merely come about in an attempt to sustain the position of those who were already in employment, with no major consequent losses in household welfare.

Table 6.3: Numbers of workers and dependency ratios in Querétaro according to household structure 1982–3 to 1986

Household structure	No. of workers 1982–3	No. of workers 1986	Dependency ratio 1982–3	Dependency ratio 1986
Nuclear	1.5[a]	1.7	1:3.7	1:4.1
One-parent	2.0	2.0	1:2.9	1:2.0
Male extended	2.4	3.0	1:3.6	1:2.7
Female extended	4.0	2.2	1:2.9	1:4.0

Note: [a] Figures rounded up to nearest decimal point.

Source: Household Questionnaire Survey, Querétaro, 1986; and sub-sample 1982–3 Household Survey.

Household income

Indeed, considering per capita household income (earnings) it appears that female-headed extended households have not suffered from their relative rise in dependency ratios: if anything, they have substantially improved their financial position since 1982–3 (see Table 6.4). The most interesting set of figures from Table 6.4 however is that while nuclear households in 1982–3 were (in terms of wages per capita at least), the most well-off category of household, by 1986 they were the poorest by a substantial margin, earning only just over half that earned by female heads of single-parent units, and less than 90% of that of female-headed extended units. In many respects this suggests that those households which have either deployed women into the labour force or extended their membership, or as is usually the case, both, have been able to cope with the recession more adequately than nuclear families. (This is even more apparent when we consider household budgets and disposable income in Chapter 7.) Indeed, if we recall that consumer prices rose by 981% between late 1982 and 1986, then non-nuclear households have actually managed to increase their potential purchasing power between these dates, whereas each member of a nuclear unit now has over 20% less in wages at their potential disposal.

Table 6.4: Mean per capita earnings[a] in Querétaro according to household structure 1982–3 to 1986.

Household structure	Per capita earnings 1982–3 (pesos)	Per capita earnings 1986 (pesos)	% increase
Nuclear	585.6[b]	5,022.0	758
One-parent	579.8	9,250.0	1,495
Male-extended	516.9	6,075.0	1,075
Female-extended	387.3	5,776.0	1,391
Total	563.7	6,037.0	971

Notes: [a] Mean per capita earnings are calculated by summing the wages of all members with an income-generating activity in the household and dividing by household size. As such the figures show the amount of income actually generated by households on a per capita basis. This is not necessarily equivalent to the income which actually ends up in the household budget for the use and benefit of all household members (see Chapter 7).
[b] Figures rounded up to nearest decimal point.

Source: Household Questionnaire Survey, Querétaro, 1986; and sub-sample 1982–3 Household Survey.

Another very interesting finding is that female household headship is not the apparent sentence to relative poverty that it was in the early 1980s. In terms of per capita household earnings in 1982–3, women-headed households in general (extended and non-extended units) were poorer than their male counterparts (with only 90% of the per capita earnings of male-headed households: 515.6 as against 571.1 pesos), but this balance has now changed. Members of women-headed units now have *greater* earnings per capita (6,644 pesos) than male-headed units (5,596 pesos), meaning that the situation has become more or less reversed: earnings of male-headed households are only about 84% of those of female-headed structures.[7] Moreover, in terms of budgets and actual disposable income, differences are even more marked (see Chapter 7). In some senses then, the Mexican crisis has turned the table on male-headed households, especially nuclear structures, where women's labour power is not likely to be mobilised for the labour market and where there is often a rather arbitrary sub-optimum use of household income-generating resources (see also Chant, 1984, 1985a, 1985b).

Women's labour force participation in Querétaro 1982–3 to 1986

In Chapter 7 we go on to look in general terms at what women's labour force participation means for household survival in all three cities, but before concluding the present one, it is useful to briefly consider the major characteristics of female labour force changes in Querétaro between the early and mid 1980s. Since more female heads and spouses seem to working than before, and some have obviously moved into better paid jobs, does this indicate that there has been some improvement of women's position in the local economy?

In Chapter 4 it was noted that the gap between male and female wages among household heads and spouses was actually much less in Querétaro than in the other two cities, partly because proportionally greater numbers of women in the Querétaro sample worked full-time and/or had jobs in the formal sector. Certainly there had been a dramatic rise in the proportions of women engaged in formal employment in the Querétaro samples between the early and mid 1980s. Whereas domestic service and/or home-based retail and food production had employed the great majority of women workers in 1982–3 (collectively 87% of all working female heads and spouses), over half the women workers in 1986 had jobs in the formal sector (either in public services, service employment in registered private enterprise, or factory work). Only one woman was a domestic servant, two were home-based food producers, and two had quite lucrative commercial enterprises: one with her own shop, and the other with a long-running breakfast business based at a licensed stall in the Industrial Zone.

In 1986 women workers earned an average of 14,840 pesos. Although this was 30% more than the legal general minimum wage, it was still only 58% of average male earnings. Neverthless it was a substantial improvement on 1982–3 when women had earned well under half (40%) that of their male counterparts. The closing gap between male and female earnings cannot, however, be explained by greater parity of remuneration within the occupations traditionally held by both sexes. Women industrial workers in 1982–3, for example, were earning 75% of male wages, whereas this had dropped to 64% by 1986,[8] and in self-employment (home-based commerce, production and so on) men were still earning two to three times as much as women in the latter period. Neither can it be explained by a rise in earnings within exclusively female activities such as domestic service; pay here was still only about one-third of that in formal employment. Thus, the relative rise of women's earnings in general has to be accounted for by their movement into new areas of work, rather than an increase in wages or occupational status in their traditional and/or former branches of employment. Broadly speaking there had been a shift away from domestic service (which had employed one-third of all women workers in 1982–3, but only one-tenth in 1986) to public or registered private-service work (45% of workers in 1986). The increase in unskilled public-service work opportunities is undoubtedly due directly to Querétaro's equal opportunities programme. However, it is not only formal employment which accounts for higher wages: some self-employed women with businesses such as shops or permanent dining outlets in which there are higher investment levels than for example, door-to-door *tortilla*-selling or the retail of soft drinks from a kitchen fridge, are also making very reasonable incomes (see also Chapter 4).

What explains these changes in women's labour force participation in the space of three to four years of economic recession? Recalling the discussion of Benería and Roldan (1987) earlier in the chapter, their argument was that demand-led factors in women's rising employment include changing attitudes on the part of employers in the light of foreign examples and their need for cheaper sources of labour, and 'supply'-led factors such as greater social acceptance of married women working and a heightened need for low-income households to generate extra sources of income, I have already questioned the appropriateness of their attribution of such trends to the 'supply' or 'demand' dimensions of the labour market, and also suggested that one should take into account household structure as a critically important supply factor. While in Querétaro rising numbers of extended units has undoubtedly in some cases facilitated and in others been prompted by an upward trend in women's employment, further elaborations are needed.

For instance, although women's move into the labour force is often a catalyst of household change, the crisis has also given rise to modifications in household structure for other reasons; the fact that just over one-third of households in the sample became extended between 1982–3 and 1986 is not due to women's labour force participation alone. One such reason is an all-round increase in poverty and the need for low-income people to pool resources. In Socorro's case for example, her father was too old and too poor to continue to live alone and thus *needed* to come and live with his daughter, even if at the same time his incorporation within the household has allowed her to move into a full-time formal sector job and thereby give a major boost to family income. The rise in household extension, then, is to some extent motivated by the poor's need to join forces in times of increased hardship. Indeed, only one household in the entire sample reverted to a nuclear form from an extended unit; and the only other household which became nuclear was a former one-parent unit where a widow had remarried (see also Table 6.1).

Combined with the likelihood that household extension will allow women to move into the workforce, a small niche has also been opened up at the level of demand through the state government's equal opportunities programme in public services. Women roadsweepers, for example, are now being absorbed into what was a traditionally male occupation. Whether or not this concession to equal opportunities is largely to enhance the position of the new state governor in the early part of office is a question which cannot effectively be answered in the light of available evidence. In part, aside from political reasons, it may fit Benería and Roldan's suggestion that Mexican employers are now beginning to emulate the example of their foreign counterparts. What is strange however is that so far this phenomenon does not seem to have extended to the private sector in Querétaro. Benería and Roldan argued that women would be taken on increasingly by firms as a means of keeping wage costs low, and indeed the small amount of evidence on industrial pay in Querétaro suggests that women's rates of remuneration have fallen behind those of men in the period 1982–3 to 1986; nevertheless there are no major signs yet of a generalised feminisation of Querétaro's workforce. In part this may be due to differences in industrial structure between the cities: in Mexico City which has a wide range of industries, many of which are labour-intensive, women tend to be taken on increasingly as homeworkers, whereas the more restricted range of industrial establishments in Querétaro (predominantly large-scale, capital-intensive manufacturing plants) is perhaps less likely to lend itself to domestic sub-contracting or piecework arrangements which tend to utilise female labour.

Aside from state policy then, there are few employer-related demand factors in evidence to explain women's changing employment patterns in Querétaro. Women in this city still have more restricted access to formal-sector jobs than men, and their general position within the employment hierarchy does not seem to have altered substantially (although women are now employed in increasing numbers by the public sector, roadsweeping is still a very low-grade occupation). In accounting for women's greater involvement and remuneration in Querétaro my main conclusion on the basis of the evidence, is that the women themselves are pushing themselves (and various members of their households) harder in order to cope with economic crisis, i.e. women themselves are the main architects of observed changes in work patterns. One of the most effective ways of cushioning their families against recession is to enter the labour market *personally* – one obviously has more scope to control one's own income than commandeering the wages of another person. In order to do this they have either to exploit existing reserves of reproductive labour within the household unit (for example using daughters and/ or sons for domestic work), or, failing this, and to make domestic arrangments run smoother still, absorb the labour power of kin and extend their households.

Conclusions

In conclusion, the mobilisation of women's earning capacity, generally through a change in household structure or the exploitation of extant reproductive resources within the domestic unit, appears to be one of the critical strategies developed to shield families from the more deleterious effects of Mexican economic recession in the early to mid 1980s, notwithstanding that several households recognised that no matter what they did they could not cure the national crisis. Many were acutely aware that major improvements in their situation would not come about unless there were significant measures taken by the state over the national debt, political corruption, the diversion of public funds into private foreign bank accounts, and the amount of Mexico's trade and industry under multinational control. As such, most respondents realised that the crisis could not be overcome indefinitely by the mere mobilisation of resources at the household level, even if they had done their utmost to maximise earning power.

Having said that, shifts in women's workforce involvement and flexible approaches to household composition have served some households quite well, with most success apparent where households have not only maintained or encouraged women's labour force participation but also moved away from a restrictive nuclear model. The association between female labour force participation and the de-nuclearisation of household units has been more than incidental and confirms the argument of the previous chapter that there are usually very fundamental links between household structure and female employment. In the absence of evidence to support the idea that growth and change in female work patterns is primarily derived from the needs of Querétaro's employers during the crisis (with the possible exception of the state and municipal government), one is left to conclude that this is owed to low-income women themselves, who have pushed further towards the front-line of battle against poverty in the city via a fundamental restructuring of household labour supply patterns. The immediate consequences of this trend appear to be that those households which are exploiting the earning potential of adult women are best able, in a material sense at least, to face up to crisis. Indeed female heads of household, who have had traditionally greater freedom to move into areas of work prohibited to women with male partners, now appear to have overtaken the earning levels of their male-headed counterparts. However, what the longer-term and non-material consequences might be are open to question. A closer analysis of the implications of female labour force participation for household survival, both present and future, and in all cities, is provided in the following chapter.

Notes

1 González de la Rocha (1988: 212) defines extended households as those which consist of one conjugal unit and additional members which do not constitute a second conjugal unit, and mutiple households as those consisting of two or more conjugal units.

2 In many respects the Querétaro sample is most reliable on the issue of recent work histories since the data personally collected by the author in 1982–3 enables confirmation of respondents' own recall. Moreover, longer acquaintance with and knowledge of the interviewees undeniably aids in data verifiability. Most case studies in Querétaro itemised here have already been referred to in Chapter 5.

3 Laura is not counted as a worker in the 1986 sample generally because she was only helping out on a very occasional basis besides receiving no remuneration. However, her example still provides a useful point of reference, especially as she intends to play a larger part in the family business in the future.

4 In addition to the value of having a full-time houseworker to execute the reproductive tasks of so many income-generators, it is also likely that Lupe's son did not want to leave his mother. Many elder sons in female-headed households feel it is their duty to support the family. As such it is likely that Lupe's daughter-in-law was incorporated for a combination of reasons, including the fact that it meant her husband could continue to stay with his mother.

5   The average size of this particular group of extended households is 11.3 persons with a mean of 3.3 working members.

6   Inevitably small sample size inflates the significance of such changes.

7   It is interesting that data presented in Molly Pollack's study of urban poverty in Costa Rica between 1971 and 1982 shows that women-headed households here have also tended to improve their position relative to male-headed units among the poorest classes. Notwithstanding an overall decline in women-headed units from 20.2% to 15.7% of the national total during the period under consideration and that the former are generally more prevalent among the poor, in 1971 male-headed units constituted 52.8% of destitute households in Costa Rica, and women-headed households 47.2%, whereas by 1982 women were only 37.1% of this category, and men 62.9%. In poor households (those classed as an intermediate group between the destitute and non-poor) similar trends occurred, with women-headed households here falling from 24.7% to 17.7% of the total and male-headed households rising from 75.3% to 82.3%. Thus although the proportion of women-headed units in non-poor households also declined from 18.1% to 13.8% in the same period and men increased their share in this latter category from 81.9% to 86.2%, relatively speaking the increase of the latter in the best-off group was small (+5%) compared with that of +10% in destitute groups, and +7% in poor households.

8   Again this may be partly due to the very small size of the sample. Comparisons between weekly earnings of male and female industrial workers are made on the basis of only one woman and two men, although the results are broadly consonant with data on wages gathered in the Employer Survey (see Chapter 3).

7

Women's employment and household survival strategies

Introduction

Having in the course of the previous three chapters arrived at the conclusion that household structure and the local economy are both highly significant in interpreting women's workforce participation in urban Mexico we now move on to look more closely at some of the short- and longer-term implications of women's employment for the survival and welfare of low-income households in the study cities.

In particular, analysis revolves around four main questions. First, how successful is the deployment of women into the labour force as a strategy for survival? In the preceding chapter we noted that households in Querétaro with working women, usually non-nuclear units, have been among those best able to combat poverty, at least in terms of earnings. How far is this true for the other cities in the study and to what extent does it translate into qualitatively better living standards for other household members? How do the general economic characteristics of households where women are employed compare with those in which they are not, and what further variations arise from their insertion into different family structures? Comparisons are not only made between earnings, but also between income-allocation and budgeting. Are households where women work better-off in terms of earnings *and* disposable income (i.e. that income which ends up being used for the benefit of the household as a whole)? How much say do women have in household financial decision-making and does this effect expenditure priorities?

Second how do women evaluate their working roles? How do they feel about working for an income? More specifically, what personal benefits arise from waged work, what costs, if any, do women pay for entering the labour force, and what effects does the employment of female heads or spouses have on their power and status in the household?

Third, what are the implications of female labour force participation for other household members, particularly younger women? Does the workforce involvement of mothers affect male and female children differently? Does women's work rebound in a positive way upon the activities and aspirations of their daughters (through providing an alternative or at least modified role model to that of mother and housewife, for example), or does it place them at a disadvantage (through transference of a heavy burden of domestic tasks at a young age)? How do husbands react to wives' paid employment, and how may the general effects of women's work on other household members vary according to household structure?

Finally, while it appears on the surface that women's move into the labour force is positive in terms of increasing the poor's current capacity to cope with poverty, it is also important to consider what the longer-term effects might be. The final part of the chapter speculates on some of the possible future implications of women's employment for household structure, for low-income Mexican women in general, for gender roles, relations and divisions of labour. It also considers the prospects for long-term feasibility and effectiveness of women's labour force participation as an integral part of household survival strategies among the urban poor. In Querétaro, at least, it appears that the utilisation of female labour power has played a major part in protecting household income levels, how likely is this to continue, by itself, to be an adequate strategy for survival in the future?

Household survival compared: the role of women's employment and family structure in affecting living standards

How does women's employment affect household survival? We noted in Chapters 4 and 6 that generally speaking households where women work are better off in terms of per capita earnings, than those in which they are full-time housepersons; overall, households with adult female heads and spouses working have higher per capita earnings (6,803 pesos) than those where female spouses do not have employment (6,285 pesos) – a difference of nearly 10 per cent, notwithstanding the existence of certain anomalies (for example, per capita earnings of households where women are in part-time work are actually higher than those in which they have full-time jobs – see Chapter 4) . Indeed although various multiple regression analyses indicated that the most important factors accounting for variations in per capita household earnings included total number of income-earners in the family (a figure which inevitably incorporates women workers), number of dependants (negatively related), sex of head of household, household structure, and pay of male heads, the amount of income earned by women themselves also had a small, but statistically significant effect in explaining varying proportions of variance in per capita household earnings data.[1] None the less, critically important in any analysis of household survival is not so much the sum total of wages as the amount of income which actually ends up in a fund earmarked for the use of the household as a collective entity (see also Chant, 1985a, 1985b). Almost invariably total household earnings cannot be equated with the sum of disposable income available to all members of a family unit. Inequality of intra-household resource distribution has been recognised by several authors and in recent years has given rise to a growing body of literature on the subject (see, for example, Dwyer and Bruce's [1988] collection of Third World case studies). Before proceeding to examine specific data on household income contribution and allocation patterns in the study cities, it is important to note some of the more general conclusions which have arisen out of this kind of research in Mexico and other developing countries.

Household income contributions and expenditure: perspectives from the literature

Most case studies of household income and expenditure have shown that members vary widely in terms of the proportion of their wage they allocate to family budgets. In the great majority of households where both men and women work, women are usually expected to spend either all or most of their wages on household needs, while men often withold a substantial portion of their earnings for personal, and often non-essential, use (Bruce and Dwyer, 1988; Chant, 1984; Folbre, 1988; Jain *et al.*, 1982; Huston, 1979; Quiróz *et al.*, 1984). In South India, for example, evidence from a number of villages in the states of Kerala and Tamil Nadu shows that female informants dedicate an average of between 95 and 100% of their earnings to the household, whereas men's contibutions are usually lower and more variable, ranging from 93% among a richer income group in one village to as little as 57% in another. On average, in all income groups and all villages men contribute less than 80% of their wages (see Mencher, 1988: 112–3 Table 3B). In the families of female domestic outworkers in Mexico City, women also donate virtually all their income to household needs whereas men retain about one-quarter of their wages for 'pocket money' (Benería and Roldan, 1987: 118). The same applies to low-income households in Guadalajara (González de la Rocha, 1988: 219). Sometimes it is even difficult to work out the percentage of earnings withheld by men since many wives do not have any idea of their husbands' income. In a study of Yoruba households in Lagos, for example, 80% of women did not know how much their husbands earned (Fapohunda, 1988: 147), and in Mexico City Martha Roldan (1988: 233) discovered that 45% of her informants were also ignorant on this matter, especially when it came to knowledge of overtime payments, gratuities and bonuses.

Whether or not women actually know how much their husbands earn or how much of a proportion they pass onto the household, when women go out to work themselves this is sometimes construed by men as grounds for retaining even more of their income for personal use (Chaverría *et al.*, 1987; Munachonga, 1988; see also Chapter 5). Moreover, not only is it the case that women devote the bulk of their own earnings to family needs (see below), but also that they are *expected* to do so. Among poor urban households in Zambia, for example, Monica Munachonga (1988: 174) notes that women who fail to contribute all their income to the household run the risk of being forbidden to work by their husbands, whereas this stipulation rarely applies to men. Despite the fact that the withholding of even part of a man's wage can have serious survival implications for poor households, the practice of keeping a portion of money back is accepted as a male prerogative (see Hoodfar, 1988 on Cairo; and Roldan, 1988 on Mexico City). In some instances in South India, in addition to women paying the entire costs of household needs, they also have to 'top-up' the personal expenses of their husbands with their own funds (Mencher, 1988: 118).

Whether or not husbands are tolerated, expected or condoned in retaining part of their earnings, the income available for household needs is often spent in very different ways and/or accorded different priorities by male and female members.

Where women earn their own income and/or where there is some kind of 'fixed allowance' from their husbands (see below), this money is generally spent on routine necessities – food, transport, education and so on. Men, on the other hand, are more likely to invest their money in 'extras', or in more durable, luxury and/or visible consumption goods. Homa Hoodfar (1988: 137) for example, notes that low-income men in Cairo are much less likely to spend on items of little direct personal use or benefit to themselves such as gas cookers; instead it is much more probable that they will buy televisions or cassette players related to their own enjoyment.

Benería and Roldan (1987) observe that male–female differences over expenditure and contributions turn the idea of the unified harmonious household completely on its head: 'Husbands and wives differ in their definition of the basic necessities of the family complex, their consumption priorities, the way in which income should be distributed, and the proportion to be allocated to the common fund, if there is one' (ibid.: 122).

Allocative systems
This last point leads on to the fact that income is not necessarily pooled and controlled equally by household members. Evidently this partly derives from the fact that some household members (especially children) are too young either to contribute to, or exercise control over income. However, when it comes to adults, systematic inequalities in the control of household economic resources and their underlying reasons need to be considered.

A number of 'allocative systems' have been observed in different parts of the developing world. In Mexico City, Benería and Roldan (1987) found two dominant types: first, 'pooling' or the 'common fund', and second, the 'housekeeping allowance'. In the former, earnings of wives and a portion of their husbands' enter a joint fund which is used to pay for basic household necessities. This pattern tends to obtain in cases where husbands earn very low wages. In the second system, which usually characterises higher-income households where the man is the main breadwinner, a portion of the husband's earnings are given to the wife to cover basic necessities. If this is insufficient to cover minimum needs wives have to 'top-up' these funds with their own earnings. Within this second category there are various types of allowance according to whether or not a wife works (see Benería and Roldan, 1987: 116–18). In Lusaka, Zambia, Monica Munachonga (1988: 187–91) found an even more elaborate set of patterns. In addition to variants on the allocative systems categorised by Benería and Roldan in Mexico

City (pooling and allowance), there was (1) 'doling-out' whereby the husband keeps and controls all household finance and his wife has no spending money of her own; and (2) separate spending whereby earning wives and husbands spend their own money independently.[2]

The important feature about most of these systems is that women rarely have much control over expenditure, even when they earn their own wages. Indeed regardless of whether wives work or not, in male-headed households men dominate financial matters, and *ipso facto* women, through keeping their wives ignorant of how much they earn, in deciding to keep money back for personal use, in deciding how to hand it over to their spouses (in installments or a lump sum), through the fact that women are often required to contribute all their own money (leaving little over for themselves), and finally, by continuing to exercise influence over how their wives spend family income, even when it has already been passed over (Benería and Roldan, 1987: 113–22).

Household income contributions in the Mexican study cities
Weight is added to the above studies by the findings from Puerto Vallarta, León and Querétaro. As far as contributions are concerned for example, it appears that women consistently place a much higher portion of their wages into the family budget. In all cities together, working women's contribution to the household budget represented 106% of the earnings from their principal jobs (a number of women also had a minor sideline activity), whereas the corresponding figure for working men was only 67.5%. One must also bear in mind that male contributions might be exaggerated since only 69% of wives had actually been told exactly how much their husbands earned in the first place (although most were confident that their estimates were reasonably accurate – many women swopped notes with neighbours whose husbands were in similar kinds of jobs and so on).

Generally speaking, where women themselves were working, husbands were more likely (1) to tell their wives their earnings, and (2) to allocate more of their wage to the household budget. For example, in nuclear households where women did not have a job, only 49% of men contributed 75% of their wage or more to the household budget, whereas this applied to 57% of cases where women did have work. Obviously because more men have income-generating activities than women overall, women's general contributions to household budgets in male-headed units seem low. However, across all three types of male-headed households (nuclear, extended and couples without resident children), women contribute an average of 18% of total weekly household income (see Table 7.1).

Of particular interest in Table 7.1 is that while per capita earnings are lowest in nuclear structures, so too is the disposable income per person which ends up in the household budget. In male-headed extended households for example, people have 26% more income (in absolute terms) at their disposal than in nuclear households. In part this relates to the fact that male heads of extended households are less able to retain as much of their own wage than their counterparts in nuclear structures. Another interesting fact is that in all households where women work, per capita income is greater than that where they are not working, not only in absolute terms

Table 7.1: Average contributions to weekly household income according to household structure in the study cities

Household member	Household structure									
	Nuclear		One-parent		Male-extended		Female-extended		Couple	
	Income (pesos)	%[a]	Income (pesos)	%	Income (pesos)	%	Income (pesos)	%	Income (pesos)	%
Male head	13,568	66	–		14,875	46	–		12,356	76
Female head	–		9,657	39	–		7,484	26	–	
Female spouse	3,487	17	–		6,198	19	–		3,600	22
Children[b]	3,363	16	13,087	53	6,998	22	8,837	30	–	
Co-resident relatives	–		–		4,453	14	8,079	28	–	
Non-resident relatives[c]	318	2	2,300	9	22	.06	4,458	15	278	2
Mean household income	20,418		25,044		32,546		28,858		16,234	
Mean household size	6.5		5.5		8.2		8.1		2	
Mean per capita income[d]	3,156		4,526		3,978		3,563		8,117	
Mean per capita earnings	5,944		6,587		6,820		7,235		12,093	
Per capita income as % of earnings	53.1%		68.7%		58.3%		49.2%		74.5%	

Notes: [a] % of total weekly household income contributed by various members in respective household structures.

[b] children still residing at home.

[c] and one or two cases of income provided by rent.

[d] While mean household size has been rounded up to one decimal point in the table, actual division by size to produce per capita earnings and income figures have been based on average household size at two decimal points.

Source: Household Questionnaire Survey, 1986.

but also as a proportion of household earnings (see Table 7.2). This is undoubtedly due to the fact that in every type of family unit, adult women tend to dedicate a very high proportion, if not all, of their wage to household needs. Indeed multiple regression showed that while the single most important predictor of per capita income was per capita earnings (explaining most of the variance in household budget data), women's earnings were the second most important factor, followed by number of workers in the household.[3]

Table 7.2: Per capita earnings and income according to female labour force participation and household structure

Household Structure	Women not at work			Women at work			
	Per capita earnings (pesos)	Per capita income (pesos)	Income as % of earnings	Per capita earnings (pesos)	Per capita income (pesos)	Income as % of earnings	Average per capita earnings
Nuclear	5,399[a]	2,610	48	6,525	3,746	57	5,944
One-parent	6,288	2,776	44	8,332	5,162	62	6,587
Male-extended	7,708	3,790	49	6,342	4,075	64	6,820
Female-extended	8,347	3,485	42	6,578	3,633	55	7,235
Couple	9,250	5,750	62	15,883	10,370	65	12,093

Note: [a] Figures rounded up to nearest whole peso.

Source: Household Questionnaire Survey 1986

Control of household budgets

In the study settlements, most 'housekeeping' budgets cover basic household necessities – food, service costs, transport, school expenses and so on. Items such as new clothes, shoes, consumer durables and so on are sometimes regarded as 'extras', sometimes not. Given the problems over working out where control over major household finances actually lies, two main sets of questions were asked: (1) who controlled daily living expenses; and (2) who controlled overall financial matters in the family (see also Appendix 1). On the whole, women were mainly in charge of the former in all household types (see Table 7.3), bearing out Morris's (1988: 392) observation that women are more likely to be involved in routine management and budgeting than overall control.

Food figured as the key universal element in all basic household budgets, and across the board consumed an average of 37% of total household earnings, and 63% of the average household budget (pooled income). Obviously in poorer households a greater percentage of household income was spent on this particular item. Thus in nuclear households 67% of total household income went on food, compared with 50% of couples (the best-off category of household). Over and above this one might imagine that larger households do not have to spend as much on food per person because buying and cooking food for greater numbers of people might tend to work out more economically: as such the absolute amount of per capita income spent on food may be expected to decline with increased household size. However, although more was spent on food per person in women-headed one-parent units (which have the smallest household size next to couples) at 3,524 pesos per person per week, and less (2,155 pesos) in male-headed

Table 7.3: Control of routine housekeeping budget by family structure

Person in charge	Nuclear	One-parent	Family Structure Male-extended	Female-extended	Couple
Male head	2.9%(3)	–	2.3%(1)	–	0%(0)
Female head	–	100.0%(15)	–	84.2%(16)	–
Female spouse	92.2%(94)	–	84.1%(37)	–	88.9%(8)
Husband and wife	3.9%(4)	–	2.3%(1)	–	11.1%(1)
Daughter			4.6%(2)	5.3%(1)	–
Female kin member	–	–	4.6%(2)	0% (0)	–
No-one in particular/ collective control			2.3%(1)	10.5%(2)	
No budget	1.0%(1)				
Total	100%(102)	100%(15)	100%(44)	100%(19)	100%(9)

Note: Number in brackets refers to number of cases.

Source: Household Questionnaire Survey, 1986.

nuclear households which are larger, in extended households, which are larger still, a mean of 2,184 pesos was spent on food. It is likely therefore that greater food expenditure in non-nuclear units partly reflects higher household incomes, and also the amount of money under women's personal control for buying it.

Regarding overall decision-making on expenditure, women have much more say in nuclear households where they are working, and in the other households, decision-making is generally fairly democratically shared among earning and non-earning adults. Earning women in nuclear households also have much more influence over non-traditional aspects of budgetary allocation than those without work whose financial autonomy is generally limited to making routine decisions about which foodstuffs to buy. Indeed in 43% of nuclear families where women were full-time housewives, women had no scope to make expenditure decisions on anything but the barest essentials of household subsistence. Thus women without their own income in nuclear units are in a very restricted position, having to ask their husbands for specific handouts for most purchases, and often being refused. Clothing, entertainments, housing and consumer good expenditure then, tends to be the preserve of men in nuclear structures, except where women work, and in non-nuclear households.

Male-domination of financial decision-making often finds its way into very tangible expressions of general living standards. For example, among nuclear households (where this most applies) there were lower levels of home ownership than all other household types (73% as against an overall average of 78%), and amongst these owners, nuclear households where women were not working had lower levels of housing quality (or 'consolidation' as measured by a sum of numerical scores for dwelling structure and services – see Appendix 1) than those where they had employment. The idea that women's role in income-earning and decision-making is a critical factor in accounting for differentials in dwelling standards has been developed on the basis of the earlier research in Querétaro in some detail elsewhere (see, for example, Chant, 1984: Chapter 7, 1987b), and these and other findings of the present study serve to reinforce the fact that women's control over household resources is a major element in influencing the quality of household survival. Thus Benería and Roldan's (1987) suggestion that a wage does not necessarily empower women is only partly true in the context of the present study; indeed in all three cities in the survey here, financial independence was frequently cited as one of women's principal motivations in going out to work.

Women and labour force participation: emancipation or exploitation?

Leading on from the previous section, we now consider the kinds of differences labour force participation makes to women's lives. Research in both the developed and developing world suggests that women's employment is a critical variable in understanding changing gender roles and relations, especially in terms of their position in the family, the power they exercise over household decision-making, family size and so on (see, for example, Losh-Hesselbart, 1987; Papanek, 1976; Zosa-Feranil, 1984). The particular aim here is to examine the stated rationale for women working, and to pinpoint the major perceived advantages and disadvantages of women's work. The potential differences which household structure makes to how women view their employment are also explored.

Central to considerations of the implications of labour force participation for women is a perspective on why they work (or not), and whether they are happy to do so. A series of questions relating to the perceived advantages and disadvantages of employment was asked in the questionnaire survey (see Appendix 1) as well as a more general discussion in the semi-structured interviews. Non-working women were not asked in the questionnaire survey what they perceived as the major advantages and disadvantages of work, but those in the sub-sample were asked their feelings on the subject in in-depth discussions (see Chapter 5). The perceptions of those women who had recently worked or are working at present are summarised in Table 7.4.

On the whole work is regarded very positively by women. As is evident from Table 7.4 nearly two-thirds of workers felt there were no major disadvantages in having a job. Many see work as a route to greater independence, to having more freedom to spend money (instead of having to ask their husbands for hand-outs), and as leading to a much greater sense of self-worth. Despite the fact that so many women are in menial, poorly-paid jobs, they still feel that they are doing much more for their families than if they stayed at home. This of course, also reflects a

Table 7.4 Principal advantages and disadvantages of work as perceived by women in the study cities[a]

Rank order	Advantages	% of respondents	Disadvantages	% of respondents
1	Independence, personal satisfaction/enjoyment	42[b] (57)[c]	No disadvantages	60 (81)
2	Greater financial security for family	24 (32)	Exhaustion, no time for leisure activities	14 (19)
3	Satisfaction at contributing to family budget	10 (13)	Guilt at neglecting children children	10 (14)
4	Has had no option but to work	7 (10)	No time for housework	6 (8)
5	Getting away from home/domestic routine	5 (7)	Health problems e.g. stress, eye strain	5 (7)
6	Sociable, meets other people	4 (6)	Causes conflicts with husband	4 (6)
7	Learns new skills	4 (5)	–	
8	No advantages	3 (4)	–	
9	Allows her to maintain own parents/kin	1 (1)	–	
Total		*100(135)*		*100(135)*

Notes: [a] Table includes women in the questionnaire survey who are currently working or who have worked in the last six years.

[b] Percentages rounded up to nearest whole number.

[c] Numbers in brackets refer to number of cases.

Source: Household Questionnaire Survey, 1986.

very pervasive belief that housework and child-care are not particularly important activities. Despite the emphasis Mexican society places on being a 'good mother', domestic work is very undervalued and viewed as secondary in the league table of socially important tasks. In part, the feeling that housewives do not do very much also undoubtedly relates to the fact that there is little tangible evidence for a hard day's domestic labour: the real value of reproductive labour is rarely apparent, either in childcare (which takes several years to realise in terms of results) or housework, which in unconsolidated slum areas involves hours of drudgery in a losing battle against discomfort and uncleanliness associated with poor housing and environmental conditions (see Chant, 1984: Chapter 5).

By the same token, a few of the women who were not working because of lack of education or work experience, especially in Querétaro and León, and were only likely if they did enter the labour force to get work as domestic servants felt that they might just as well stay at home than be paid a pittance for doing the same labour in someone else's house (see also Chapter 5).

The major disadvantage faced by working women was their continued major share of household duties; meaning that they had very little time on their hands and were often worn out (see Table 7.4) – although 90% of women who did not work were principally (and often exclusively) in charge of domestic labour, as many as 75% of working women continued to have major responsibility for housework. This 'double-day' of labour for women in the Third World is widely documented (see for example Moser, 1989; Quiróz *et al.*, 1984). Tiredness and exhaustion were particularly common among working women in nuclear households who only had the help of daughters upon which to draw. In most extended households this burden was alleviated through the presence of other adult women. None the less, it cannot be denied that women often expressed some 'guilt' at going out to work, given their primary social role as mothers. Work was quite frequently viewed as a rather selfish pursuit, partly because many women recognised its value in breaking-up dreary domestic routines, and partly because it perhaps conveyed an impression to others that women wanted their own income for personal gain (even if all they earn is usually spent on other household members).

Effects of female employment on other household members

Leading on from the above, women's experience as workers is often tied-up with their families in a very contradictory way. At one level women's labour force participation is largely motivated by the idea of helping their households, yet at the same time it takes them away from their socially-legitimised roles of mother and housewife; as such many women feel 'unnatural' 'uncomfortable', 'guilty' and/or 'disloyal' when they become involved in income-generating activities, especially when their partners refuse to take over any domestic and child-care duties (see below). Given this general ambivalence felt by women themselves, it is also important to consider the more specific effects of their employment on other household members.

The effects of female labour force participation on children

It is rare that working women do not have some doubts as to their efficacy as parents, especially when they work full-time and away from home. Indeed some working mothers live on a knife-edge of guilt, worrying about whether their children will get into trouble, play truant, start drinking, drug-taking and so on, mainly because they would see themselves as the principal source of blame and would no doubt be attributed a major share of the fault by husbands and neighbours. Implicit in every younger mother's decision to enter the workforce is an uneasiness in putting at risk their children's development and safety. Only as time goes on and their children get older do mothers feel more comfortable in their working roles. Certainly in Guayaquil, Moser (1989: 154–7) notes that with the rise of women working in the 1980s, young children seem to receive less maternal attention, suffer greater nutritional problems, and older sons and daughters cut short their schooling. Maternal neglect in turn may lead boys to street gangs or drug addiction; girls to promiscuity and even prostitution (ibid.).

However, as it is, there is little evidence to suggest in the study cities in Mexico that children of working mothers suffer from social afflictions to any greater degree than children of women who stay at home.[4] Indeed virtually all working women make adequate alternative arrangements for them, whether in the form of leaving them with a female kin member in the home or neighbourhood, arranging to work shifts which dovetail with the hours they are at school, or (in nuclear households especially) leaving them in the care of an older sibling, almost invariably a daughter (see Chapter 5). On the surface at least, women's employment does not appear to seriously disadvantage the immediate daily care and supervision of children. Moreover, working mothers set aside the great majority of their time at home to the children – washing and ironing their clothes, helping them with their homework, listening to their problems. Rarely do working women spend their free time alone, unlike their husbands. The only possible qualification here is that women who have spent several hours at work are undoubtedly more tired and therefore perhaps less receptive to their children's needs than those who have been at home all day, although there was little evidence of this within the sample.

However, the issue of delegated child-care does affect some children more than others, notably those who end up with the responsibility for looking after their siblings and doing the housework when their mothers are out at work. In the case of working heads of single-parent families in Jamaica for example, Judith Ennew (1982: 560) notes 'When the mother has to be the father, it is inevitable that in many cases the children have to be the housewives.' In León, Querétaro and Puerto Vallarta it is the eldest or second eldest daughters in non-extended units who most often have to take over where their mothers leave off. This pattern has also been observed in other Mexican and Latin American cities (Benería and Roldan, 1987; González de la Rocha, 1988; Moser, 1989).

Moser (1989: 154–5) stresses the negative aspects of this transference of domestic labour for young girls. Those still at school for example, have to balance their academic loads with reproductive chores, frequently resulting in lower educational attainment, and in turn depressing their chances of obtaining good jobs in the future (see also Ennew and Young, 1981: 41). Certainly some daughters in the Mexican study cities had actually left school to run the home full-time. This issue highlights the immense pressures placed on women generally and the seemingly inveterate nature of gender divisions; in entering the labour force mothers can often only do so at the expense of casting their daughters into the unenviably premature role of mother–housewife, thereby reducing their future employment potential, and impressing a duty on younger women that fails to bring about any fundamental change in the gender-assignation of reproductive tasks. Strangely enough it is often working women who have the highest ambitions for their daughters, who want them to have a career and to be financially self-sufficient, but often by the time the youngest children have grown up it is too late for the older ones. The potentially positive effects of women working are likely to be confined to younger female siblings who escape the early yoke of reproductive responsibilities. Having said that, there were only marginal differences in levels of completed education between eldest sons and daughters in the home who had finished school[5]: 61% of girls had completed primary education or more, and 64% of sons, and indeed on average children of working mothers did slightly better – 65% of sons in this group had completed primary education or more and 63% of daughters. However, broken down by family structure some revealing differences emerge among daughters. For example, in nuclear households only 61% of eldest daughters in the home who had finished school and whose mothers were working full- or part-time had completed primary schooling, compared with many as 78% in male-headed extended households where wives were working (usually because tasks in these structures were taken over by a female relative instead of a daughter). By the same token, rates of completed primary education among eldest daughters at home and no longer studying in both these types of household were higher where women were full-time housewives: 80% in nuclear households and 100% in extended structures.[6] The data suggest quite strongly therefore that the partial or total transference of domestic tasks to daughters where women have employment has rather negative effects on their primary school completion rates, even if it is also the case that daughters are expected to help out around the home when women are full-time housewives too, and that there is little difference in the proportions of eldest girls still studying between all households in the sample where women work (60.6%) and where they do not (63.4%). Indeed, of all households which contain a daughter and where women are full-time housewives, only 4.7% of the oldest girls at home described themselves or were described by their mothers as 'housewives', whereas this applied to 15.5% of cases where mothers were in full-time employment, and 6.4% where they worked part-time. In part these figures could point to an association between lower levels of educational attainment and propensity to stay in the home on leaving school, at another level it could signify some continuity in daughters' activities: in other words, once girls become involved in household chores, as schoolgirls or teenagers, they are less likely to abandon those duties as time goes on. Lack of detailed longitudinal data on daughters here however prevents formulating a general conclusion on this topic.

What must be noted however, is that no matter how much women's employment may seem to prejudice their daughters' education and subsequent job prospects, when women do *not* have employment there is often just as much pressure for children to take time off their studies in order to get jobs themselves. This pressure could mean a permanent move out of education at an early age, or at least the finding of part-time work while they remain at school.[7] Indeed in households where women are full-time housewives 1 in 7 schoolchildren have part-time jobs, compared with 1 in 8 where women work part-time, and only 1 in 12 where women have full-time employment. In many respects then, and especially in non-extended households, children have to compensate for their mothers' involvement or non-involvement in the labour force in some way, either by taking on a greater share of domestic labour in the former case, or by taking a part-time job in the latter. Unfortunately the sex of working schoolchildren was not coded in the questionnaire survey so it is not known precisely how many schoolboys and girls had jobs. However, evidence from the sub-sample interviews suggest that boys predominate in this activity, as do the findings of Licia Valladares (1989) in the *favelas* of Rio de Janeiro, Brazil. As such one can see the same pattern of gender roles persisting with each model. When women do *not* work, their school age sons tend to play the part of supplementing the earnings of their fathers, thereby perpetuating the traditional custom for men to work and women to stay at home. When women *do* work, on the other hand, they often have to pass on their domestic responsibilities to daughters, which again fails to challenge existing sexual divisions of labour. The only possibilities for radical change in gender roles in this latter group of households applies to younger daughters whose services in the home are not needed if they have older sisters who have already taken responsibility, and to those (extended) households where adult kin leave young children freer of productive and reproductive labour in general.

Effects of women's work on husbands

If the gender division of labour remains essentially unchanged through the transference of 'women's' responsibilities to daughters, then this is generally reinforced by the failure of men to take on domestic chores in any substantial way to help their working wives. Although a few women observed that their husbands were doing more to help them around the home since entering the labour force (see also Chaverría *et al.*, 1987 on Costa Rica), for the most part men did not alter their behaviour in any way. Even where women felt their husbands had grown accustomed to the idea that they should work, and even had more 'respect' for them, this did not usually find practical expression in terms of men taking on a greater share of housework.

As noted previously, some men effectively penalised their wives for working, not only through refusing to help out in the home, but also by retaining more of their wages. Some men left their wives to pay the great majority of household expenses. As such when male control over their wives' labour power was no longer possible, they did their best to ensure that women's personal disposable income was so limited that they could not mount a major threat to male dominance. This was particularly the case in Puerto Vallarta where *machismo* appears to have found new ways of working around women's comparatively favourable position in the local economy (see Chapter 5).

Effects of women's labour force participation on kin

As far as other household members are concerned, the labour force participation of female heads and spouses obviously has the greatest direct effect on female relatives, particularly those assigned primary charge of domestic labour. This could sometimes be a little conflictive, especially where the relative in question also wanted to work, and was sometimes resolved through both women taking a part-time job. Nevertheless, most female kin were older women (mothers, aunts and so on) who wanted a chance to stay at home. This made even more sense when they were older, less healthy and/or less energetic and could not command equally high wages in the labour market.

Finally, it is important to note that female labour force participation can have very positive effects on non-resident kin. Working women felt justified in using some household income to support their own non-resident relatives, especially parents, even if only one actually cited it as her main reason for working (see Table 7.4)

Women's workforce participation: some speculations on future trends

In the final part of this chapter, attention is drawn to some of the longer-term implications of Mexican women's participation in the workforce. During the crisis years, in Querétaro at least, women's labour force participation has changed both quantitatively and qualitatively. Women's increased movement into the workforce and into new segments of the economy has to a large extent shielded low-income families from the more deleterious effects of declining real wages, and gradually become more accepted as an integral part of household survival strategies. Given lack of direct longitudinal work in Puerto Vallarta and León it is impossible to talk about trends in those cities with the same degree of reliability, although earlier census figures (see Chapter 4) and six-year retrospective work profiles of women in the questionnaire survey, both indicate that over time women's labour force participation has increased. For example, in León it appears that twice as many women entered or re-entered the labour force in the years between 1980 and 1986 as those who had left; and in Puerto Vallarta the net rise was in the order of 20%.

Given Mexico's continuing debt problem and the likelihood that wages will fall still further behind prices in the foreseeable future, it is not unreasonable to suppose that within the next ten years, women will form an increasingly larger component of the urban workforce. The question of what repercussions this might have upon women themselves, their households and the gender division of labour and status in society in general is obviously very complex. Within this question it is also important to consider whether women's entry into the labour force is sufficient in itself to stem the tide of immiseration threatening to engulf increasingly larger numbers of the Mexican urban poor.

Possible trends in household structure

We have noted in previous chapters that women's labour force participation is often associated with the de-nuclearisation of family units. More specifically, it is related on one hand with the formation of female-headed households, and on the other with family extension. As far as family extension is concerned this often arises as a direct response to female labour force participation through its role in partially, if not totally, alleviating the burden of domestic labour of the female head or spouse (see Chapter 5). In some cases, then, family extension occurs as a direct response to women's need for extra help around the home. Indeed in Querétaro in only three to four years, several households converted from either a nuclear or a simple single-parent structure to more complex extended arrangements as a direct or indirect result of women's move into the workforce. As such further decline in nuclear families could well occur if female labour force participation continues rising, although an inter-generational perspective should also be borne in mind here – new households are still forming (see Chapter 6) and it is possible that young households may pass through a relatively protracted stage of being nuclear if they do leave home to establish their own units on or soon after marriage.

The relationship of female household headship to female labour force participation is more difficult to establish. In most cases in the study it seems that women become household heads *before* they go to work: women who find themselves heading their own households are in a position where they either can or must get a job (see Chapter 5). In turn, female household heads tend to be common in areas where local demand for female labour is high; cities with a large tertiary sector, for example, are likely attract more migrant female household heads than centres of male-dominated manufacturing employment. Of course, female household headship may also arise as an outcome of women's financial autonomy, and although there is less evidence in the case study data to indicate this pattern it was apparent in Puerto Vallarta that some women at least could afford the prerogative of living alone with their children of their own free will. Whatever, the combined effects of greater financial pressures on households in contemporary Mexico and a more positive attitude towards female recruitment in firms, could conceivably lead to more women heading their own households in time. Female-headed households may thus increase as women begin to squeeze themselves into new segments of the urban economy. We saw in Chapter 3, for example, that in Puerto Vallarta some employers are recognising the value of recruiting women workers into 'non-traditional' branches of employment such as bar and restaurant work, and in Querétaro, state policy has opened up opportunities for women in public services. Working on the argument of Benería and Roldan (1987: 49) that a growing number of Mexican businesses are beginning to follow the example of multinationals, it could well be the case that in the next ten years low-income women have greater opportunities in the formal sector than they do at present. This process could be intensified if women's recruitment at supervisory and managerial levels also follows an upward trend since greater representation of women at these levels tends also to increase the numbers of women workers on the shop floor (see Chapter 3). With this putative rise in economic opportunities more Mexican women may opt out of marriage, particularly if it makes little economic sense to tie themselves to a partner who is unlikely to commit himself wholeheartedly to family life. However, the idea that more jobs for women may necessarily lead to the ability or desire to establish or maintain independent households should be tempered by two main considerations. The first is that jobs opened up for working class women might not be sufficiently well-paid to allow them the freedom to live comfortably without the additional wage of an adult male. Women workers still earn far less than their male counterparts, and if one major rationale for employing women lies in their relative cheapness for capital, then it is unlikely that the 'gender gap' in wages will close significantly.

The second major qualification is the possibility that an increased incidence of employment among married women may produce a situation in which they begin to command more respect from husbands that assists in cultivating a sense of joint responsibility for household welfare. In other words the sharing of productive labour and economic interdependence in dual-earning households may lead to more harmonious relationships than those which obtain when men monopolise the generation and allocation of finance. As such, relations between the sexes could conceivably become more egalitarian and less conflictive in future. Certainly Caroline Moser (1989) observes that the only households in Guayaquil where the incidence of domestic violence does not appear to have escalated with recession are those in which women earn money on a regular basis and are respected by their menfolk. Similarly, in the study cities, working women usually have better relationships with their spouses than those confined to the home, and in the former households men tend to hand over more of their income to wives. Thus if male acceptance of married female labour force participation increases there is possibly less likelihood that women will *want* to establish independent households. Nevertheless, at present it would seem that major changes in gender roles and relations in male-headed families are a long way off; and in the absence of such changes what is more likely is that nuclear households will also decline at the expense of female-headed units.

Of course female labour force participation's influence on household headship and composition is not the only factor that may turn nuclear units into a minority group. Continued downward pressure on real wages, for example, growing shortages of land and housing and so on may well force kin to adopt more communally-based living arrangements. Whatever, the net effect of all these processes could be that nuclear households prove increasingly unviable among the urban poor by the turn of the century.

If nuclear units become less viable economically, it is also possible that non-nuclear units may be less stigmatised socially. We noted earlier in the book how non-nuclear households – especially female-headed ones – are often viewed as 'deviant', 'problematic' and so on. As such they tend to get treated very differently by society to conventional two-parent households, and this negative treatment may well reinforce whatever vulnerability a single-parent household might have from lack of parental, financial and legal resources (see for example Gongla and Thompson, 1987; Macklin, 1987). In Jamaica, for instance, Ennew (1982: 559) notes that women are made to feel 'failures' if they do not have a male partner with whom to form a nuclear household. When so many Jamaican women are heads of household it is perhaps surprising that more positive evaluations of women-headed structures have not come to the fore. Nevertheless, the greater the trend away from nuclear families, especially if it begins to affect middle-class people as much as it has low-income groups, the likelier it perhaps is that women-headed and/or extended households may come to be accepted as entirely 'respectable' forms of social organisation. Indeed positive evaluations of non-nuclear families are already beginning to appear. Research in the developed world, for example, has shown that single-parent households are less hierarchical, inequitable and authoritarian than 'conventional' two-parent households (see Macklin, 1987: 329), and in Mexico certainly, domestic violence appears to be rarer in non-nuclear units (Chant, 1985b). Aside from these advantages, it is also important to recognise that the deliberate adoption of non-nuclear household structures among the poor is often a considered and positive strategy for material survival.

Possible implications for female status and the gender division of labour

Highly interrelated with conjectured changes in household structure are undoubtedly certain qualitative shifts in women's roles and status (see also Brydon and Chant, 1989: 151–8). In the previous section, for example, I mentioned that some men begin to show more respect for their wives once they start contributing to family budgets, and that over time this may be accompanied by an increased general acceptance of married women working. As this kind of trend begins to replace former patterns, the status of women in the household could well improve alongside their position in the labour market, thereby mitigating the inequalities inherent within the gender division of labour and setting the stage for more harmonious relations between the sexes. But this optimistic scenario is subject to several qualifications. One concerns the fact that in the short-term future at least, conflict could arise from women invading economic territory which has customarily been the domain of men, not only in the home (in terms of sharing responsibility for breadwinning), but also in the labour market (women moving into 'male' jobs for example). In some instances, we noted that when women enter the labour force, men withdraw some of their financial support. Moreover, conflict could also arise in the workplace: male-dominated trades unions have often worked to keep women out of jobs and enterprises (see Brydon and Chant, 1989: 184–5). The likelihood that conflict will preside over cooperation depends very much on the importance attached by men and women to sustaining the ideal of a two-parent household. If Marianne Schmink's point is correct that 'household survival strategies' are often little more than the 'uneasy aggregate of individual survival strategies' (Schmink, 1984 cited in Bruce and Dwyer, 1988: 8), then the fragmentation of household units could well increase over time, with no direct consequences for confrontation of gender divisions at the domestic level.

Another important qualification to the idea that women's employment may pave the way for improved female status and a more egalitarian division of labour lies in the fact that at present adult women seem only able to move into the labour force when another woman takes their place in the home. When the women concerned are daughters this raises all sorts of questions as to whether the future will actually look different for Mexican women at all. Those girls who leave school early and prejudice their studies in the economic interests of their parents and siblings are not likely in later life, one imagines, to move into anything but unskilled menial occupations with limited career mobility and financial rewards. In addition their assumption of domestic chores frees male siblings to follow the examples of their fathers, to get ahead of women in obtaining human capital, and to avoid taking any role in domestic labour. In all respects here then it is unlikely that the gender division of labour will be qualitatively transformed. Moreover, if daughters are pressurised into sacrificial roles at an early stage, burying their own ideals and aspirations for the sake of their families, the psychological potential for abnegation in later life is perhaps more accentuated than that of their brothers.

By the same token, it should be remembered that *some* daughters are spared the yoke of reproductive chores and and many mothers these days appear to have high ambitions for both girls and boys. Working mothers themselves may provide positive role models for daughters, and in women-headed households in particular the often necessary assignation of domestic chores to sons means that in those households the seeds of change might grow to fruition in years to come. However, a rapid, generalised and fundamental transformation of gender roles and status is unlikely in the immediate future.

An additional factor in need of mention here is that the increased resources of wives conjectured to lead to the diminution of patriarchal power and equalisation of status and power vis-a-vis decision-making (see for example Benería and Roldan, 1987; Lee, 1987) can have very positive effects on the material quality of household survival. At the same time however, although it is usually the case that women are more altruistic finanancially and spend most or all of what they have on other household members, how much is this a function of limited command over resources? Nancy Folbre (1988: 261) in her discussion of altruism among kin, and the particular sacrifices made by women, suggests that as women spend more time in paid work and increase their bargaining power in the home, they may become more egoistic. There is no evidence in the present study to support this hypothesis as yet, but Folbre's point possibly bears thinking about for the future.

Women's work and household survival

Finally, while the labour force participation of adult women has proved positive in combatting extreme poverty among low-income groups up until now and might well continue to do so in the near future, how long is this pattern likely to be feasible and/or adequate in itself?

Women who work generally continue to bear the major responsibility for domestic labour, and even in households where women have assistance from kin or a daughter, still usually participate themselves. Obviously this combination of paid and unpaid work consumes several hours and many women end up exhausted (see Anker and Hein, 1986; Quiróz *et al.*, 1984). Furthermore, sometimes women's contribution to household income is not sufficient in itself to fend off crisis. The combined effects of this is that several women and their households have no guarantee that they will be able to carry on as they are doing now. Nevertheless, many development agencies in recent years have come to the conclusion that women are the key to household survival, under the illusion that women always can and do work for the benefit of their families. However, Moser (1989: 159) also points out that 'Not all women can cope under crisis and it is vital that the romantic myth of their infinite capacity to do so be debunked'. Moser subdivides her Ecuadorian interviewees in Barrio Indio Guayas into three main groups: 'women who are coping', those who are 'burnt-out', and those who are 'hanging on' (ibid.: 160). The 'copers' represent only one-third of the community and are usually women who have stable partnerships, multiple sources of family income and who are able to share reproductive work with other household members. The 'hangers-on' are a mixed group, making up just over half the cases who in a sense are taking out an 'overdraft' on family credit, making adjustments to the crisis at present which are very likely to prejudice their potential for upward social and economic mobility in the longer term. In Moser's words 'These women are using up future resources in order to survive today, sending their sons out to work, or keeping their daughters at home to take over domestic responsibilities' (ibid.: 160).

The remaining group which Moser labels the 'burnt-out' are often female household heads in later stages of the lifecycle who receive no financial support from partners and/or whose children have a high drop-out rate from school and so on. Interestingly, women-headed households have proved to be disproportionately represented among the 'survivors' in the Mexican case, possibly because in Puerto Vallarta especially, women do have a fairly wide range of opportunities in the lower end of the formal labour market. Guayaquil is a port where most low-income women appear to end up slotted into casualised and/or informal tertiary occupations such as domestic service, cooking or laundrywork where one imagines that the scope for providing adequately for dependants is somewhat limited (see Moser, 1989: 142).

It is obvious from Moser's work that as well as prompting an increase in the labour force participation of adult women, economic crisis and structural adjustment in Ecuador have also led to the often premature entry of sons into the labour market. The same was also found by González de la Rocha's (1988) in Guadalajara.[8] Both these authors also found that young girls were being retained in the home for domestic labour, however González de la Rocha (1988: 220) notes that if recession in Mexico continues, the next group to be plucked out of the home and sent to work will probably be the adolescent daughters. What this implies for the satisfactory execution of reproductive tasks is potentially critical. If the combined earnings of heads, wives and sons are not enough, and daughters also go out to work, the quality of domestic life may well deteriorate to the point that households cannot sustain themselves at all. Considerable amounts of labour are needed in urban slums to translate low incomes into better living conditions, to maintain minimum levels of hygiene and comfort, to eke out nutritious and varied diets on limited budgets, and to adequately protect, supervise and care for children. If there is no one to look after these jobs, it is difficult to imagine how households will be able to experience anything but the crudest and most vulnerable existence. It must also be noted that since young girls, especially those with a limited level of education, are likely to earn least in terms of wages, more household members may be pushed into the labour force over time with ever-diminishing returns. At some point the buck must stop. The key question for the future is at what point the line will be drawn where Mexican households shift their efforts away from exploiting their own resources, to demanding that the state provide them with more satisfactory and dignified means of survival.

Notes

1   The principle of multiple regression is explained in detail Chapter 4 (Note 5). In this particular case various combinations of factors expected to influence per capita household earnings were entered into a number of multiple regression equations such as numbers of workers in the household, numbers of household dependants, numbers of co-resident children, migrant status, earnings of women and so on. Depending on the number and nature of the variables (and the extent to which they are interrelated) fed into the equation, one gets different results. However, factors consistently coming up as significant were numbers of workers, numbers of dependants as a proportion of household size, sex of the head of household, household structure, earnings of male heads and earnings of all women heads and spouses (obviously these were zero where women were not working). The best explanation of per capita earnings came from a calculation whereby the following nine independent variables were regressed against per capita household earnings: number of workers, earnings of women, pay of male head, number of household dependants, age of women (as a crude indicator of stage in the family life-cycle), household structure, sex of the household head, number of schoolchildren and household size. Together these factors explained 54.5% of the variance in per capita earnings data with the proportion of dependants in the household accounting for 62% of this (the greater the proportion of dependants, the lower the per capita earnings of households). All factors other than this were positively related with pay of male heads accounting for a further 11% of the variance explained, sex of household head 9%, earnings of all women 7.5%, and number of workers 5%.

2   See also Lobo (1982: 103–6) and Pahl (1983) for further discussions of variations in family budgeting arrangements.

3   The best explanation of per capita household income was produced with a regression equation that included nine independent variables: per capita household earnings, number of dependants as a proportion of household size, women's activity category (houseperson, full-time worker etc), earnings of all women, household structure, sex of head of household, number of workers, household size and number of co-resident children. Here the R-sq value was 66.6% and the adjusted value 64.7%, meaning that nearly two-thirds of the variance in per capita budget data was explained by the above variables. As much as 86% of this variance was explained by per capita earnings, a further 6.5% by women's earnings, 2% by the number of workers, slightly over 1% by sex of the household head, and slightly under 1% by household structure.

4   The work of Licia Valladares (1989) on the youth of Rio de Janeiro's *favelas* echo the findings of the present study, namely that the children of working mothers do not appear to have any particular difficulties or 'negative' behaviour patterns. Unlike Moser's study, Valladares' research suggests that there are no major socially pathological problems associated with 'maternal neglect' in Brazil. Indeed even where mothers are out of the *favela* all day, they establish domestic routines for children which allow them to know what

children are up to at certain times of the day and where they can be found if necessary (ibid.: 21)

5   Information here relates to eldest sons and daughters living at home at the time of the interview who had actually completed their schooling. *Ipso facto* the data does not include sons and daughters who may have already left home. Indeed for all households an average of 1.3 children had left home. By household structure this breaks down as follows: an average of 0.6 children had left home in nuclear families, 1.1 in one-parent families, 1.9 in male-headed extended families and 2.7 in female-headed extended families. It should also be stressed that neither does the analysis take into account the educational levels reached by eldest children in the family who are still studying.

6   On average two children had already left home in male-extended families and only 0.5 in nuclear families where women were full-time housewives. This means that we are likely to be looking here at younger daughters in extended households who might have received more education than their older sisters. By the same token there was still virtually the same number of children living at home in extended households as nuclear units (4.0 as against 4.4). Moreover in households where women were working there was little difference in the mean number of children who had left home (0.7 in nuclear households and 0.8 in extended households). For this latter group therefore we can assume with a reasonable level of accuracy that eldest daughters in extended households generally have greater primary school completion rates than their counterparts in nuclear structures, notwithstanding that the analysis excludes those still studying.

7   While pressure on children to take part-time jobs might also prejudice schooling, Licia Valladares (1989) has a different conception. In her research on casual work of young boys in the *favelas* of Rio de Janeiro, she concludes that neighbourhood-based part-time work is not only very common, but also very positive in the sense that it allows school, work and leisure to be easily combined in an 'integrative triangle' (ibid.: 13). She further notes that by getting sons to work at an early age, mothers are effectively protecting them: keeping them busy with domestic or casual jobs in the local area means that they are more likely to remain in the neighbourhood and not venture into the inner city to join street gangs and the like. Judith Ennew and Pansy Young (1981) in their study of child labour in Jamaica also point out that children are often quite willing to adapt to multiple forms of labour as a means of improving their situation, rather than be unemployed or turn to crime. Furthermore, despite the fact that the self-reliance and independence Jamaican children develop through the early shouldering of household responsibilities tends to deprive them of their childhood, as proto-adults they are also eminently 'adept at surviving in the midst of poverty and unemployment' (ibid.: 59).

8   Rodgers (1989: 20) also notes for Latin America and Southeast Asia generally that 'the response of households to poverty involves changes in labour supply strategies, predominantly women, but also male children and older workers'. He also notes that 'The success of these strategies obviously depends on issues of labour market access ... and secondary workers are subject to particularly intense discrimination'. See also Ennew and Young (1981) on the exploitation of child labour in Jamaica.

8

Conclusion

In the previous chapter a series of suggestions were put forward as to possible trends in family structure, female labour force participation and household survival among the urban poor in the three study cities. This final chapter has two main aims. First it brings together the major findings of the research, identifying how they relate to the conclusions of other studies and how they might inform future analyses of gender, households and economic development. Second, there is a brief concluding comment on social and economic prospects for low-income Mexican women as the twentieth century draws to a close.

Women, work and household structure in Mexican cities: a summary

The major conclusion of this book is that women's work in Mexican cities has highly complex, dynamic and interactive relationships with local characteristics of labour demand (patterns of gender recruitment in the urban economy) and local characteristics of labour supply (primarily household structure). In addition, both these latter factors display strong interrelationships with one another which in a significant number of cases are articulated through the economic activity of women. It is undoubtedly the case, in Querétaro, León and Puerto Vallarta at least, that women's labour force participation is not only an outcome of the intermeshing of labour supply and labour demand factors, but also a motor of change in itself, especially in stimulating modifications to household organisation that allow low-income people to be more responsive to local opportunities or pressures. A further conclusion is that female labour force participation and facilitative (usually non-nuclear) household structures are positive insofar as they seem to result in more equitable patterns of sharing of resources and responsibilities within the domestic unit and also to guarantee generally higher standards of well-being.

While the above is a broad summary of the research results, a definitive answer to the principal question posed in the book, namely whether women's labour force participation is more strongly influenced by local demand for female labour or local supply, remains elusive. Indeed the only possible conclusion here is that the relative importance of these factors is likely to vary from place to place and time to time. Although it has been shown that women are much more likely to engage in paid work when local employers require above-average numbers of female workers, as in Puerto Vallarta where many jobs within the tourist industry are gender-typed as 'female', it is also apparent that the increased participation of women in economic activity and rising numbers of households such as women-headed and extended units which accommodate it more easily, may also occur in situations where there is no obvious shift in local patterns of labour demand. In Querétaro, for example, growth in women's work and the de-nuclearisation of household units over three years of economic crisis took place in a situation where employment opportunities in general stayed roughly stable, or more probably declined. In this instance, the growing economic participation of women stemmed largely from household needs to find further sources of income in the face of diminished purchasing power of existing real wages, rather than any discernible expansion in female employment opportunities, echoing Rodgers' (1989: 20) assertion that 'arguably the most general influence of poverty on the labour market is the influence of extreme need on patterns of labour supply and production'. Another point made by Rodgers is also relevant here in its emphasis on the difficulty of separating 'the influence of poverty from other household determinants of labour supply, and from the broader issue of access to the labour market' (ibid.). Economic recession obviously affects both supply and demand sides of the local economy, and in the case of the latter, usually by cutting jobs, particularly in the 'formal sector'. However, this may not necessarily affect women more than men and indeed may affect them less because of their smaller representation in the sector to begin with. In the early stages of recession therefore, men may lose ground to women in the labour market on account of their disproportionate concentration in formal activity and could be one reason over and above the effect of greater pressure on household resources that women's work in the present context has actually increased in the face of economic crisis. However, we must also remember that *within* the formal sector women are probably equally, if not more, likely to lose their jobs in conditions of slump. If we take this argument further, it may even suggest that gender selectivity of local labour demand in the formal sector might not always be as relevant as it first appears to explain differential rates of female labour force participation in a given locality. Thus although the comparative analysis of the three cities in the earlier part of the book showed that women had much greater likelihood of working in areas where female job opportunities were relatively abundant, either because of the nature of local activity or because of an excess of demand over supply (as in Puerto Vallarta), examination of three years of recession in Querétaro alone in the latter part of the volume revealed that economic stagnation, which in all probability led to an excess of labour supply over demand, was still accompanied by positive shifts in women's involvement in the workforce. This not only underlines the point that demand in itself is inadequate to explain women's involvement in paid work, but also that its influence on female labour force participation may occur in very different ways and for very different reasons depending on the period under examination.

Critical to understanding whether positive or negative aspects of general demand for labour will prevail in influencing women's work at any given moment in time are a wide range of circumstantial factors of which two of the most important are probably the following: (1) the nature of female labour supply in the locality and particularly household responses to short and long-term economic trends; and (2) the capacity for informal self-generated economic activities to emerge in particular labour market situations. Both these factors are likely to be highly interrelated and to be linked to a large degree through a third critical element – *time*.

Household structure and female labour supply

Regarding first the issue of labour supply, we noted throughout the book that whatever the circumstances of demand, women are likely to have more direct involvement in economic activity if they belong to households where they are freer to make the decision to enter the workforce, whether on account of absence of male control (as in women-headed units) or due to opportunities to spread responsibility for domestic labour and child care (as in extended or late stage nuclear families). We also noted that while in many cases the emergence of such households was prompted by women's economic activity *per se*, changes could also arise for several other reasons, some occurring by design and others by default. Associated with such changes, however, is also a need at the bottom line, for household units to survive in their new forms. Thus even in cases where modifications to household structure are unplanned – women are abandoned by men against their will or households become extended through obligation rather than by choice – the poor's position at the bottom of the urban economic hierarchy means they must often move quickly in order to avoid deterioration in income levels. As such, even if households are forced rather than elect to adopt new structures, they often make rapid adjustments in their survival strategies and internal divisions of labour in order to resist poverty, with such adjustments often involving the reallocation of female labour power from from home to workplace.

In terms of the influence this has on labour supply it means that certain types of household (notably non-nuclear units) will probably have consistently high needs *and* opportunities to send women out to work. Since women's entry into the labour force so often proves beneficial to the urban poor, households may then be concerned to maintain their involvement by ensuring that structures are kept in forms that continue to enable it. In a sense then, while female labour force participation might initially be an effect of involuntary or *ad hoc* changes in household structure, it may subsequently come to be a major *cause* for keeping household membership in non-nuclear configurations, even in the face of changes in wider patterns of labour demand. When local economies are hit hard by national recession (as in Querétaro) for example, the evidence shows that if anything households maximise their opportunities by keeping their pools of available labour high, and indeed often resort deliberately to the absorption of additional household members to free-up women for economic activity. But even dis-regarding the positive aspects for households of releasing women into the labour force, the crucial factor here is that existing balances of different types of household in a given city may to a large extent 'fix' the numbers of people who need to work, in spite of upward or downward trends in jobs available.[1] As such, any analysis of the effects of changes in the wider economy must take into account the way in which labour supply is already structured, and especially the fact that the latter may well temper the ways in which cities as a whole are affected by economic crisis in terms of their generation of a range of informal activities (see below).

Time, of course, is of the essence here, not only in the way that it affects households' perceptions of their own duration in a particular configuration and with a particular mode of survival in a given location, but also, and perhaps more importantly, in terms of the way it is used analytically to study such phenomena. The work of Alison MacEwen Scott (1988a) is particularly relevant to this latter point in its emphasis on the way in which selection of the time span over which, in this case female labour force participation, is analysed can radically affect the ways in which different types of trends and *ipso facto* interpretations of those trends are identified and developed respectively.[2] In relation to female employment, Scott notes that this usually declines in the early stages of industrial development, but is later reconstituted as a secondary workforce in labour-intensive branches of industry and services. Following this, women's employment is often further casualised as part of the reserve army of labour (ibid.). Evidently choice of time period is crucial in its influence over the rather arbitrary separation and classification of short- and long-term trends. With respect to the specific concerns of the present study we basically have a snap-shot of women's work, household structure and urban economies in the mid 1980s in which explanation, especially of the differences between the three cities, have been based on inferences about fairly long-term convergence between local labour demand and labour supply. Even in Querétaro, the period of direct longitudinal study is only 3–4 years during which apparently extreme movements in female labour force participation and household structure may well constitute a short-term anomaly in the light of longer-term historical trends. In time to come, if modern manufacturing is retained as Querétaro's principal economic sector, continues to favour male workers, and is eventually able to bring wages to their former levels, it is entirely possible that low-income women may retreat once more to the home. This is perhaps particularly likely when intergenerational prospects for women's labour force participation are considered. In Chapter 7, for example, we noted that the price of increased economic activity among adult women at present, may be paid in the future by daughters, especially those having to assume a major share of domestic labour at a young age: lacking education and job experience as adolescents, when these girls grow up and have their own children, their conjectured disadvantage in the labour market could well lead to a situation where, in spite of shifts in the sexual division of labour forged during their mothers' generation, they have little option but to comply with more traditional roles. A crucial task for future research will be to see what happens to granddaughters and great granddaughters. Only with much longer periods of hindsight will it be possible to ascertain the general direction of social and economic change.

With regard to households' opinions of their own duration, while inevitably association with the life-cycle means that household structure can never be regarded as an inherently stable or permanent phenomenon, most of the evidence suggests that people have a reasonably open-ended and/or long-term view of changes to their units. In only one case in the in-depth survey, for example, did households acknowledge becoming extended for a specified period of time – that of Antonio and María Espinosa who had asked a niece to come and live with them for a year while María set-up shop on the domestic premises (see Chapter 5). Moreover, a large number of female heads who had migrated to Puerto Vallarta had done so precisely because they wanted to work themselves and did not envisage being in the position, or indeed wanting, to set up a household with another man in the foreseeable future. The key issue here is that whether or not households adopt a particular structure and division of labour in response to a particular set of opportunities at a particular point in time, patterns of employment of various household members initiated during these periods may then endure despite wider economic trends or further changes in household membership. For example, if tourism in Puerto Vallarta was to enter a period of slump as a result of depression in the United States, it is entirely possible that women would not automatically withdraw from the labour force and indeed might even increase their participation, albeit in more informal segments of the local economy. This latter issue brings us on to the second point qualifying the influence of labour demand on women's work, namely the capacity for informal self-generated forms of employment to carve a permanent niche for themselves in local labour markets.

Growth of informal economic activities and labour demand

The analysis of labour demand in the present book has largely focused on patterns of gender selectivity at the level of the 'formal' sector, but it is also important to note that rising activity rates among the poor as a result of shifts in the nature of labour supply may contain the seeds of potential long-run modifications in the nature of urban economies and their patterns of labour demand. When households push more of their members into income-generating activities in order to cushion themselves against the effects of economic recession, this in turn may create new sectors of activity within the local economy. While small-scale production, commerce and services are unlikely to become major forces as far as national accounting is concerned, at a local level certain types of activity may become integral parts of the city-wide economy. For example, businesses that offer breakfast to factory operatives who have no facilities to eat on the premises may become a desirable alternative for industrialists wishing to save money on the installation of infrastructure catering for the reproductive needs of workers. Thus if low-income people, as they so often have done, find niches where they can develop activities that accommodate their own labour within the local economy, over time these might become an integral and permanent part of local production. Certainly it would appear that in most countries in Latin America and Asia for example, labour markets have responded to recession by a burgeoning informal sector (Rodgers, 1989: 24). Women in particular are those most often in the position of devising their own means of making money: as these activities expand and develop direct or indirect linkages with other sectors of the economy it is entirely possible they will become more firmly instituted and thus ensure demand for female labour in future. The capacity for the poor themselves to influence the structure of local economic activity and *ipso facto* labour demand may be limited compared with large-scale heavily capitalised initiatives, but should almost certainly not be discounted. Another relevant point is that raised by Susan Joekes (1987: 114) who suggests an increase in numbers of workers to the informal sector in situations of crisis is likely to mean a disproportionate drop in wages compared with formal employment. However, in turn this could actually lead to a greater demand for services provided by female labour as a result of their cheapness. Nevertheless it must also be remembered that informal activities are often heavily dependent upon the formal sector and decline in the latter could well force down wages and profits in small-scale employment to such a level that they are ultimately unviable.

Bringing the above issues together, changes in women's labour force participation, household structure and local economic development, just as much as they have been shown to be linked in the current context, are in turn likely to have very important influences upon each other in future, with the major point in need of emphasis here being that changes initiated by the poor themselves in terms of household organisation and divisions of labour may begin to reshape the nature of urban employment. In other words, there is probably considerable capacity for social and economic restructuring from the 'bottom up', and *ipso facto* important implications for demand originating at the level of supply. With this in mind, it now remains to comment on the utility of analysing women's employment through the lenses of 'supply' and 'demand' factors in particular places, and to identify ways in which future studies of women's work can be moved forward.

Ways forward for the analysis of gender, households and economic development

Labour demand factors explaining female labour force participation have conventionally been associated with trends in the 'economy', whereas labour supply factors have been more closely associated with social and cultural factors which revolve around the construction of gender roles and relations in family units. Some authors, such as Beechey (1987) and Walby (1985) have equated these phenomena with 'workplace' and 'family'; others such as Benería and Roldan (1987) have seen demand factors as belonging in the sphere of system or national level economic conditions, and supply factors as those pertaining to the individual needs of women and their households. In most cases then , 'demand' variables are interpreted as expressions of the wider concept of 'mode of production' (usually capitalism), and 'supply' factors as reflecting culture and ideology.

However, in many respects as several of the above authors acknowledge, separation of these various concepts is merely a heuristic device. As mentioned in the Introduction, we disaggregate society into separate elements in order to understand it, but it presents itself to us as a totality, and it is the totality of influences that we must explain. As authors such as Scott (1988a) have pointed out, patriarchy is firmly embedded in capitalist practices and as such difficult to draw out and treat in any way as an autonomous phenomenon. Similarly, the material basis of life is so critical in affecting ideologies that shape culture and gender that it cannot really be divorced from social issues (Barrett, 1986). In short, we put distance between various types of influences on women's labour force participation that in reality are much more closely linked. As such, the end product of examining women's work as the outcome of dialectical relationships between supply and demand, should probably be to pinpoint their principal axes of convergence. Linda Lim (1983: 78) for example has identified patriarchy as being the crucial force in welding them together: 'both the demand for and supply of female labour are determined by the culture of patriarchy, which assumes women's role in the family as natural and consigns her to a secondary and inferior position in the capitalist wage labour market'.

While I am reluctant to attribute undue importance to patriarchy *per se*, it is undoubtedly one of the more significant variables in understanding the intermeshing of supply and demand factors in the present study. However, what is also interesting to consider is its potential transformation through current changes at the level of the household and the labour market which are both influencing and being influenced by rising rates of female labour force participation. Writers such as Scott (1990) have warned against the dangers of attributing a universal or transhistorical nature to patriarchy, and one major contribution of the present study has been to indicate how, at the level of individual households and the local labour market, women have been challenging various aspects of their subordination, both as a class and as a gender, whether through deciding to head their own households, taking or creating their own economic opportunities, and/or using the resources gleaned from these activities to try and improve the lives of both male and female children. The key notion here then is that of *process*: changes in household structure, women's workforce involvement, and the emergence of self-generated activities within the local economy, may all contribute to eroding the bases on which male–female inequality have conventionally been derived, notwithstanding that residual elements of male dominance may well exert considerable control over the shape and pace that any transformation takes. In short, however, while *gender roles and relations* are obviously going to be important in the analysis of social and economic change in Mexico for some time to come, they could well be of a *different* kind to that prescribed by the stereotypical patterns of patriarchy generally accepted as the norm at present (see also Scott, 1990).

'Family' in its institutional as well as its pragmatic/material guises (particularly the household), is the other major variable which assists in shedding light on the articulations between demand and supply as they affect women's status and involvement in the labour market. The organisation of society into small units of reproduction linked by kinship which at both normative and practical levels requires certain members to stay at home, and others to go out to work, is critically important in determining notions of familial responsibility and in turn, employer recruitment practices. Evidence from the present study suggests that normative assumptions about family form and obligations on the basis of gender, age and so on, are often paramount in limiting women's, especially married women's, access to jobs. However, the apparent tendency in urban Mexico for low-income households to move away from a nuclear model towards more flexible structures that allow their constituent members to break with narrowly specialised roles and to share responsibilities with others, may well begin to influence employers' perceptions. Indeed there is some evidence of this already, with certain enterprises (especially if they have female personnel managers) beginning to recognise that women, particularly single parents, need an income just as much as men, and responding by exercising positive discrimination.

In conclusion then, while 'supply' and 'demand' are useful analytical devices insofar as they provide a means of grouping different types of factors as they affect women's position, the first critical point is that recognition must be made of their inherent dynamism. The second is that efforts must be directed towards understanding how they interrelate, and probably one of the most valid ways of doing this is by studying them through in-depth empirical analyses of the household. With a 'household approach' that pays attention to diversity and detail, one not only analyses a unit of social organisation where key relations of production and reproduction meet (Brydon and Chant, 1989: 10), but also has a basis for testing the validity of a wide range of theoretical formulations about society in general. Detailed study of the household can assist, for example, in improving our analyses of women's work which have tended in the past to rely on stereotypical conceptualisations of patriarchy (Scott, 1990), and beyond this, in gaining more meaningful perspectives on other aspects of social and economic change. While several authors have argued for such an approach, it is perhaps best summed up by Elizabeth Kuzesnof (1989) in her review of family history in Latin America, where although not talking directly about the household, maintains that the family is the 'central complex of relationships' which helps make sense out of various phenomena – an entity which 'reflects, refracts and interfaces the Latin American political economy and the ideals, values and strategies of Latin American society' (Kuzesnof, 1989: 169). Probably the most fruitful 'way forward' for studies attempting to understand the links between gender, households and economic development then, is to look very closely at the specific ways in which individual households are tied to different local labour markets (see Scott, 1990), and in so doing to make very few assumptions about the roles that their constituent members, on the basis of age, gender and so on, are likely to play within that framework.

Mexican women and the future: a comment

The call for a minimum of normative assumptions about gender relations and households is perhaps particularly apparent in the Mexican case where economy, society and politics in the 1990s are in a considerable state of flux. On the political front, there is currently much debate as to whether the PRI will actually rebuild itself as a 'real political party' and maintain power until the next elections, or whether opposition from within and outside the party, particularly from the left, may lead to its eventual demise. Mexico's political future is intrinsically bound up with economic conditions beyond the control of the Mexican state, and at present, eminently difficult to predict (see Cornelius *et al.*, 1989: 45). President Salinas seems to have started his term with a major attempt to get the economy moving again, mainly in the form of opening up Mexico to further foreign investment, liberalisation of trade, closure or privatisation of various unprofitable state industries, reduction of dependence on oil exports, increased manufacture of non-traditional products, and, somewhat contradictorily, further decentralisation (Philip, 1989; Roberts, 1990; Seyde and Hobbs, 1989). Whether the above set of developments is likely to benefit the poor, and women in particular, is highly debatable. Certainly, further expansion of key sectors of economic growth such as in-bond manufacturing and tourism may well boost women's access to the labour market, if only because they continue to be a more exploitable source of labour.[3] It must also be remembered that gender-typing of jobs into which women move tends to depress their social and occupational status and in turn to constrain their prospects for achieving equality with men. Nevertheless, evidence from the present study also shows that whatever economic activity low-income women have, it often provides, at a bottom line, a critical basis of independence and/or some means with which to challenge existing powers and privileges of their male counterparts. Indeed, those households with less rigid gender divisions of labour and greater egalitarianism between the sexes, are those most likely to survive in current conditions, especially when one considers 'secondary' household members. Trends towards increased levels of female labour force participation at present seem largely due to women themselves taking initiatives to gain greater control over their own and their families' welfare in the face of wider economic pressures: the key task now for the 'sisters of the shaking earth' will be turn their contributions during the crisis years to their longer-term advantage, and particularly to pass on to their own sons and daughters the idea that it is not only possible, but positive for men and women to have more equal shares of household responsibilities and resources.

Notes

1   In turn this may influence the shaping of employer recruitment patterns by presenting firms in the locality with a particular pool of labour (see Purcell, 1988: 164).

2   With respect to trends in female labour force participation particularly, data can

present a major problem , with a distinct lack of reliable sources, especially for the pre-war period. Census enumerations for example are frequently prone to gross inaccuracy, especially in the registering of women's economic activities (see Brydon and Chant, 1989).

3   Even here there is no guarantee that women will continue to be employed. For the case of the *maquiladora* industries in the northern border region which have tended to employ disproportionately large numbers of female workers in the past, Bryan Roberts (1990) notes that men are now beginning to play a larger part in these operations, particularly with the expansion of hi-tech in-bond industries such as computer manufacturing that are much more capital-intensive than the more traditional border plants.

Appendix 1

Household Survey

The overall objective of the Household Survey was to gather basic socio-economic data on poor households in each city with particular reference to household structure and women's employment. The material gathered in this aspect of the research forms the basis of the analysis in Chapters 4 to 7.

Before going on to outline the methodology more specifically, it is important to outline basic background to the analysis of households and household structure in Mexico and to clarify in more detail the terms introduced in Chapter 1.

Section 1: background to the Household Survey

1 Defining 'households'

In the present study, households were defined as groups of people who shared a common residence and common budgeting and consumption activities (see also Section 2[a]).

2 Defining 'household structure'

Household structure as defined here embraces two major criteria: sex of the household head and household composition. Household composition describes the constitutent members of the household unit and can basically be classified into two categories: households which consist of parent(s) and children only, and those which include affinal or consanguineal kin (i.e. in-laws or blood relatives). Defining the 'head of household' however is somewhat more problematic (see below).

3 Defining 'household heads'

In general terms, where the adult woman in a household has a resident male partner, the latter is designated as 'head', by the household members themselves and by the state (for example, for census purposes). This is especially the case in patrilineal and/or patriarchal societies where adult men are vested with varying degrees of authority over and responsibility for wives and children (Harris, 1981; Lerner, 1986). Only when a woman has no resident male partner (through death, desertion, divorce and so on) is she referred to as the household head. However, many writers, especially feminist researchers, refer to both partners in a couple as 'heads' in order to dispense with the notion that a man is necessarily responsible for other household members. Others prefer to tie the definition to something more instrumental, such as who earns the principal wage, who makes the major decisions and so on. On the whole however, there are few explicit definitions and this complicates the issue of making links between studies. This problem is probably even more apparent with official sources of data. Youssef and Hetler (1983), for example, discuss the findings of a United Nations Review of Census Documents published in 1973 which shows that only thirty-six countries actually stated what they meant by headship of which there were three types: first, those who reported themselves or were reported by others as household heads; second, those with most authority in the household; and third, the main breadwinner. To an extent the problems associated with this instrumental approach have been circumvented in the United States by a change in terminology: in 1980 the US Bureau of the Census substituted 'householder' for 'head of family', with householder being the first person listed on the census questionnaire (Wilkinson, 1987: 189).

Notwithstanding the problems of classification in themselves, another difficulty arises with the inconsistency of classifications from country to country and from time to time: non-comparability of data sets makes it extremely hard to establish trends in the incidence of different types of household unit. For example, many studies talk of a global increase in women-headed households, when in fact there is little substantive evidence. Large numbers of women-headed households have only really been 'discovered' and/or 'exposed' by 'gender-aware' researchers in the last twenty or so years, and we are thus limited in terms of reliable estimates for longer time periods. Even recent census data are often notoriously inadequate in this respect. For example, while the Mexican census of 1970 includes a table showing sex of heads of household, the same table does not appear in 1980. As such, the basis of suppositions on trends of different types of household is confined to a rather restricted time span, notwithstanding the huge amount of subjectivity in defining households and household heads.

Another related problem arises from the fact that there are several different *types* of female head. Youssef and Hetler (1983: 232) propose a five-fold classification of *de jure* and *de facto* women-headed households where *de jure* essentially refers to cases where there is no man in the household at all or only on a very temporary basis, and *de facto* to cases where there is usually a man or men present, but women play the dominant economic role. More specifically their categories are as follows:

(a) No male present, e.g. single mothers, divorced or separated women, widows etc (*de jure*).

(b) Man only present as a transient resident providing no economic support to the household (*de jure*).

(c) Man is temporarily absent because of local labour market conditions, but continues to provide some support (*de facto*).

(d) Man present but minimal support because of unemployment or long-term illness/disability (*de facto*).

(e) No male spouse present, but other adult male residents (*de jure* and/or *de facto*).

In the present study, however, women are only referred to as heads if they have no resident male partner and are therefore *de jure* heads. The *de facto* definition was not used (1) because only two households in the entire survey consisted of women who were receiving occasional remittances from men living away from home, and (2) because even where resident Mexican husbands are unemployed and in this sense might allow women to assume a dominant position in the family, they usually continue to exercise considerable (if not absolute) control over the activities of their wives and children.

Section 2: implementation and content of the Household Survey

The Household Survey fell into two main parts:

[a] *Household Questionnaire Survey* where questionnaires were applied to a series of households selected randomly from a sampling universe derived from complete lists of households compiled by the author in two or three settlements in each city (see below); and

[b] *Sub-sample in-depth semi-structured interviews* where a smaller number of households in each city were interviewed using an open-ended format that embraced the detailed reconstruction of women's employment histories.

[a] *Household Questionnaire Survey*

The Household Questionnaire Survey was applied to a total of 189 households (92 in Puerto Vallarta, 77 in León and 20 in Querétaro) between January and December 1986. Only 20 households were interviewed in Querétaro since a major study of 244 households had already been carried out by the author in 1982–3 in connection with a doctoral research programme on low-income housing (see Chant, 1984). The 20 households interviewed in 1986 were picked from the three low-income settlements in the 1982-3 survey (Bolaños, Los Andadores and Las Américas) and thus fulfilled a dual function of documenting some of the changes that had occurred in a cross-section of households during three years of national economic crisis. The bulk of this data is used in Chapters 4, 6 and 7.

Respondents in the 1986 questionnaire survey in the other two cities were drawn at random from a census compiled by the author of two low-income settlements in Puerto Vallarta (Caloso and Buenos Aires), and two in León (Piletas and Lomas de Jerez), much as the original 1982–3 survey in Querétaro had been (see Chapter 4). The initial housecount recorded address (or description of the lot and house), tenure, name of household head and type of household structure, notwithstanding that household structure, especially if extended and/or women-headed, is often difficult to obtain reliable information on in a preliminary visit. For example, it is sometimes problematic to establish whether households are fully extended (where everyone lives as part of the same functional and reproductive unit), or only partly extended as is the case with nuclear compound households where although two or more related households share the same plot of land they actually form distinct domestic nucleii (see below). In order to get around this particular problem it was asked if the household concerned shared the lot with kin, and if so whether they shared expenses and cooked together (see also Chant, 1984: Appendix 1). Regarding preliminary classification of female-headed households, it is sometimes hard to get women heads of household to admit that they do not have a resident male partner. In order to convey the impression that there is a man around, some women give the name of their son as household head. In order to work around this difficulty women were asked with whom they lived and if they had a husband or partner residing there at the moment; the latter question was asked in such a way that there was no implication that there *should* be a partner. From these lists a sampling universe was drawn by pinpointing households which belonged to five main categories of household unit which are generally the most common in low-income Mexican neighbourhoods:

1 *nuclear households*: consisting of a married or cohabiting couple and their immediate offspring.
2 *Female/women-headed one-parent households*: consisting of a mother and her children.
3 *Male-headed extended households*: consisting of a nuclear family core that resides with relatives other than their own children, such as aunts, uncles, cousins and so on and who share economic and domestic functions and resources on the same basis as parent–child households. As such they are very different to what have been termed 'nuclear compound' households where two or more related families share the same plot of land, but do not pool finances nor cook or eat together on a regular basis. Nuclear compound households therefore consist of families who live in the same dwelling environment but function as separate units, even though their might be a certain amount of reciprocity between them. These were excluded from the questionnaire survey for the reason that there is so much variation in their forms, functions and interdependence that meaningful comparisons with other types of household would have been impossible in the light of relatively small sample size.
4 *Woman-headed extended households*: core women-headed unit with additional relatives as in (3).
5 *Couples* (childless): these describe male–female unions where there are no children at all, or no children resident in the home, as is the case where children are brought up by someone else or have left home to form their own households.

Households rejected from the sampling universe consisted of infrequently occurring types of unit such as nuclear–compound households, male-headed one-parent households, single-person households and households where adolescent siblings resided without parents (see also Chapter 4). All tenure categories (owners, renters and sharers) were interviewed in 1986. Renters were classified as those who did not own their plot or house and were paying rent; sharers as those people who were living on land or in a property owned by someone else (often a relative), and owner-occupiers as those who whether or not in legal possession of the plot were set to become owners through expropriation at a future date, in the meantime were not paying any rent or sharing with kin, and/or had paid or were in the process of paying for regularisation. In Querétaro only owner-occupiers had formed the basis of the 1982–3 survey and accordingly no non-owners were interviewed in the later period. In all cases interviews were directed to the adult woman at the core of the household unit (either the female-head in women-headed extended and non-extended units or the female spouse in male-headed units [nuclear, male-extended and couples]). The author carried out all the interviews, read out the questions to respondents and wrote down their replies. Generally speaking it was preferred to interview women in the questionnaire survey on their own – when women's husbands were around they tended to take over and/or appeared to hamper women's willingness to talk. This was not the case however, with all instances of semi-structured interviews (see below).

The Household Questionnaire fell into nine main sections:

(A) *Migration*
Here information on the birthplace and previous residence of the female head or spouse was elicited, including the year she arrived in the city and in her present house, reasons for the move to the city, and by whom she had been accompanied at time of arrival (e.g. parents, husbands, children etc).

(B) *Family structure*
This section collected basic details of household composition, age, sex, main activity (e.g. paid work, domestic labour, education) of household members, marital status of woman, age at marriage of respondent and partner, number of unions, number of children who had left home, age at which they left home and their main reasons for moving out. It was also tried to build up a picture of changes in household composition over the previous six years by asking who had left, their relation with the household female head or spouse, and who had moved in. People were also asked whether they found it economically beneficial to live with kin.

(C) *Paid work*
The third section gathered data on paid work of household members, including job type, size of enterprise in which they worked, pay, hours, conditions, access to social security and so on. Further details were elicited on the occupation of the principal earner in the household such as the years they had spent in their present job, where their work was situated, travel costs and so on. In this section it was also

asked if the household had other sources of income aside from wages from main occupations, such as income from second/odd jobs, rent, interest on savings, or financial support from non-resident kin. Within this section there was also a sub-section aimed at examining women's current activity and her work history over the previous six years. Details were asked on the types of jobs they had had and for how long, pay, hours, earnings at the time, the advantages and disadvantages of working and so on. The same was done in the final sub-section on schoolchildren with part-time jobs who were not classified as workers in the main section on paid work.

(D) *Domestic labour*
The fourth section of the questionnaire dealt with domestic labour, members participating in different household tasks, frequency of washing, cooking and cleaning, time spent in these various activities, and the problems associated with different domestic chores arising from low levels of housing consolidation and poor-quality community services. Information was also gathered on consumer durables possessed by the household such as electric irons, gas stoves and washing machines.

(E) *Family budgets*
This section dealt with family housekeeping budgets and spending patterns including who managed spending, items included in weekly housekeeping budgets, contributions to pooled income from various household members and non-resident kin, decision-making on expenditure on different items (e.g. clothing, food, service charges), the amount of money sent to non-resident relatives (e.g. in rural areas), forms of saving money (where relevant), and reasons for saving. Given the difficulties of establishing decision-making patterns on spending people were asked who was in charge of routine expenditure (e.g. who bought the food, handed out bus fares to the children and so on), and who was involved in decision-making on specific items such as clothes, housing improvements, consumer durables and so on.

(F) *Housing characteristics and land tenure*
This section dealt with rent (where applicable), size of lot and house, mode of acquiring land (in the case of owner occupiers) and payments connected with tenure regularisation in cases where the authorities had intervened. Some measure of housing quality was derived from recording the materials used for walls, roofs and floors, and evaluating levels of such services as water supply and electricity and summarising them by means of a 'consolidation score' index developed by Peter Ward in his study of slum housing in Mexico in the mid 1970s (see Ward, 1976), and modified and used by the author in her earlier study of Querétaro in 1982–3 (see Chant, 1984: Chapter 7), and again in 1986.

(G) *House consolidation and improvement*
Here an exploration was made of how families had gone about building their houses, number of rooms, the nature of labour used in building different aspects of the dwelling (e.g. outside labour, family labour, friends and kin), usual times of day or the week when household members themselves generally worked on the construction of the dwelling, and major problems with house-building in the settlement.

(H) *Costs of consolidation and services*
Questions here related to the costs of installation of various domestic and community services and amenities, monthly charges for different types of service (formal and informal), rates, problems associated with non-formal supply of services (e.g. tanker deliveries of water by private companies, public standpipes), and present costs of land in the settlement.

(I) *Problems of community life*
The final section was concerned to pinpoint the main problems of community life as perceived by residents and their key priorities for settlement improvements. Some questions were also asked as to the effectiveness of and people's participation in neighbourhood organisations, and whether people envisaged staying in the community or whether they had plans to move elsewhere and why.

Analysis
The interview responses were coded onto computer forms within forty-eight hours of the interview taking place and areas of confusion were remedied by re-visiting the household as soon as possible thereafter. Cross-tabulations, frequencies, means, and various statistical tests (e.g. correlation, multiple regression and chi-square) were used on the data with the package MINITAB on the Vax computer (initially at Liverpool University and subsequently at the London School of Economics). Copies of the questionnaire (in Spanish) and coding guide are available from the author on request.

[b] *Semi-structured Interviews*

A sub-sample of 47 households were selected for in-depth semi-structured interviews from the original questionnaire survey, with an additional four households which had been listed in the original house count but not included in the general survey because they were rather uncommon as household types. These four households were in Puerto Vallarta and included a male- and female-headed nuclear compound structure, a male-headed one-parent household and a single male renter. Altogether 24 households were interviewed in-depth in Puerto Vallarta, seven in León and twenty in Querétaro. The information gleaned from this branch of the household survey is discussed mainly in Chapters 5 and 6. All in-depth interviews in Querétaro were done with the 20 people who had also been selected for the 1986 questionnaire survey, mainly to strengthen the data base for longitudinal analysis on what had happened to a range of households since 1982–3, most of whom had also been interviewed in-depth in the earlier period. Households selected for the sub-sample were chosen for various reasons, with the prime objective overall of capturing a range of household types and experiences. Thus within the sub-sample there was a broadly representative range of structures, sizes, ages, income-levels and female labour force involvement. Where possible selection was made of households who were particularly informative, and/or did not mind or actually wanted me to return to their houses.

The semi-structured interviews, as their name suggests, were interview formats which allowed a relatively free-ranging discussion within broad categories identified by the the author as key aspects of the research (see below). Above all they were concerned with examining the reasons for, and the outcome of, female labour force participation (or lack of) for household structure and to build-up in-depth profiles of women's work experiences as they related to household composition and headship, place of residence, family history, educational qualifications, job experience, stage in the lifecycle and so on.

There were few set questions as such, only topic areas. This was to allow the interviewee a degree of freedom in letting issues come to the fore that were personally important to them. Sometimes semi-structured interviews were carried out on a single occasion (taking between 2 to 4 hours), but more often two 'formal' and a series of 'informal' ('drop-in') visits were made in connection with this part of the fieldwork. On at least one of the visits associated with the in-depth interviews it was tried to call when most of the family, and at least the husband where relevant was at home in order to gain a perspective on how people interacted with one another, who tended to dominate conversation and what the views of other household members were. A few interviews were taped on a cassette recorder and later transcribed, but more often than not there was too much background noise to make this feasible, so that notes were jotted down and written up in full soon afterwards.

Most material collected in the semi-structured interviews was used either as illustrative case-study material or closely content-analysed. For the most part responses were full and informative, especially in Querétaro where the author had long acquaintance with interviewees from the earlier fieldwork in 1982–3 and correspondence with several in the intervening period.

There were five main topic areas in the semi-structured interviews:

(A) *Life history*
Here detailed data was gathered on women's life histories with particular reference to household structure and work experience over time. Attention was also paid to marriage, the amount of time women had known their partners prior to living with them, their reasons for getting married (or not), present household divisions of labour and decision-making, and periods of greatest happiness and periods of greatest crisis. The bulk of the data on women's employment, household cirumstances and places of residence through the life cycle was subsequently transcribed into a format which allowed fairly ready examination of

factors precipitating female entry or exit into the labour force at various points in time, by entering the data on the following (abbreviated) sample form (Figure A1.1):

(B) *Kinship and family structure*
This section explored attitudes towards living with kin, the reasons for changes in household composition over time and how it related to women's employment

Figure A1.1

Employment profile						
Age/ Period	*Marital status*	*Position in household*	*Household size and structure*	*Occupation*	*Place of residence (i.e. town/village)*	*Comments*

Name ....   Education...........................   Age...........................

Total number of jobs........   Age at starting work..........   Type(s) of job.............

Main reason for working/type(s) of employment and job changes/entry or exit into labour force ....
....
....

Total number of children........   Resident children..........Children who have left home.....

(where relevant) , and proximity to kin and frequency of contact (some households may not be extended *sensu strictu* but have various reciprocal arrangements with neighbouring households).

(C) *Women's work and the local economy*
This section explored in detail women's perceptions of work opportunities in the local economy and how they differed to their places of origin and other places of residence. It also explored family attituds to women working and to gender roles and relations in general. It was also inquired as to the plans parents had for male and female children regarding work and education.

(D) *Economic crisis and household responses*
This section examined the way that households felt about the Mexican recession and any steps they had taken in order to offset the declining value of real wages. For example, had the household resorted to any forms of domestic self-provisioning in the 1980s? Did they think that the Mexican economy would pick up again and how did they envisage their situation ten years from now? This section was particularly relevant when examining in detail the changes in household structure and survival strategies in Querétaro between 1982–3 and 1986 (see Chapter 6).

(E) *Women-headed households*
This section concentrated on the particular problems faced by female-headed households, including reasons why women were living alone, what advantages and disadvantages accrued to living with or without a partner, and the ways in which they were treated by kin, neighbours, employers and so on.

Participant observation
In addition to formal interviews, participant observation was undertaken by joining in various individual and community social events, talking generally in local shops and markets, and holding discussions with leaders, local teachers and priests. In addition, friendships that arose with various people in the community allowed a deeper and more rounded perspective on various aspects of the research.

Appendix 2

Employer Survey

The Employer Survey was carried out with a total of 49 employers across the 3 study cities (21 in Puerto Vallarta, 14 in León and 14 in Querétaro). The aim of the survey was to build up a profile of labour demand in enterprises characteristic of the local economy, to gather detailed information on different types of job and corresponding rates of remuneration, and above all to explore the question of levels of male and female representation in different sectors/occupations and to evaluate employers attitudes towards gender. The bulk of this information is synthesised and discussed in Chapter 3 ('Gender and local labour demand').

Twenty-one employers were interviewed in Puerto Vallarta in order to capture the range of different establishments involved in tourist activity (hotel, catering and commercial establishments) at different levels (small-, medium- and large-scale). Only 14 firms were interviewed in León however since most of the workforce is employed in shoe manufacturing or a related activity. Here the bulk of interviews were carried out in different sizes of shoe production units, with one or two in support businesses in areas such as sole-manufacturing, cardboard box-making and rubber sheet production. In Querétaro 3 or 4 firms were selected from the 4 dominant industrial sectors in the city: capital goods, food and drink manufacture, metal-mechanical production and chemicals and parachemicals (see Chapter 3).

The Employer Survey was carried out in all cities *after* the Household Survey had been done, and in some cases firms were chosen when it was known they employed some of the household interviewees. Others were selected from local industrial or tourist directories. In the case of León, small family home-based shoe production workshops, which are hard to identify from the street, were selected from within one of the surveyed neighbourhoods.

In all cases it was attempted to interview a broad cross-section of the dominant types of local enterprise. In only one instance was the author refused an interview (a large shoe firm in León). Names of firms are not disclosed in the text for reasons of confidentiality – indeed assurance of complete discretion was often a precondition of being granted an interview in the first place.

Interviewees from the firms were personnel directly involved in recruiting workers, either personnel managers, or in smaller enterprises, owners or general managers.

All respondents were asked the same questions on the basis of a structured questionnaire where the author noted down comments and responses.

The questionnaire fell into seven main sections:

(A) *Firm/enterprise description*

This section covered type of firm, nature of product or service, nature of management (e.g. direct [owner] or delegated management [e.g. managers, supervisors]), size, source of capital, age of firm and total number of employees/ workers. It also asked for a breakdown of jobs within the firm, the numbers in different posts, average salaries/wages in different occupations, percentage of casual workers as against 'permanent' workers in different occupations, break- down of the sex of workers in different occupations, and hours/shifts. There were also questions relating to nature of the long-term stability of the labour force, such as the length of time in employment of the longest-serving worker and the date at which the last worker had been taken on.

(B) *Recruitment policy*

This section was concerned to establish how the firm went about recruiting workers, concentrating particularly on modes of advertising vacancies, entrance requirements for different types of jobs, and perspectives on what jobs were equally open to both sexes, or only to men or women and why. Further questions in this section attempted to identify method of entry into a job (e.g. via interviews, personal references, tests, probationary periods and so on).

(C) *Labour turnover*

This section explored personnel managers' perceptions of labour turnover in different types of job within the firms, how often they had to contract workers, how long people stayed (if their contracts were indefinite), whether most people tended to leave voluntarily or when they came to the end of a (short-term contract), and the reasons behind workers' voluntary departures, including whether the same reasons applied to men and women. It was also inquired as to the grounds for dismissal, and whether sackings were more common among male or female workers.

(D) *Internal occupational mobility*

Here investigation was made of the opportunities for career mobility within firms, including training provided by the firm, frequency of promotions at different levels and in different sections of the enterprise, and key criteria for promotion. It was also asked about gender differences in promotion characteristics and how often people themselves actually asked for salary rises, transfers, promotions, upgrading and so on. Other questions in this section explored fringe benefits attached to different types of job (housing benefits, pension schemes, profit-sharing etc) and whether these increased with length of service.

(E) *Pay and legislation*

This section included a series of questions as to regularity and forms of payment of different groups of workers within the firm (e.g. monthly salary, weekly wage, piece rates and so on), patterns of allocating tips, gratuities, bonuses in various service occupations, commission rates (in sales jobs), and the overall percentages of firms' outgoings and profits spent on wages. Further questions here related to the proportion of the workforce who were insured and/or had access to social security, including firms' policies regarding maternity leave, sickness benefit, paid holiday (and whether this increased over time) and rates for public holidays. Exploration was also made of workers' amenities within the firm such as creches, nurseries, retail outlets and banking/saving facilities.

It was also asked whether workers were permitted to belong to unions, to which unions they belonged, and to which groups of workers this applied. (In Mexico generally only manual workers are unionised; white-collar workers alternatively are referred to as '*empleados de confianza*' [trusted employees] where union membership does not apply).

(F) *Gender and divisions of labour within the firm*

While various questions about gender differences were asked in previous sections of the questionnaire, in order to round off the examination of this topic, a series of questions were asked as to the entry requirements for women workers in different types of job within the firm, such as age, education and marital status, and whether the same stipulations applied to men seeking the same or similar positions. It was also inquired why certain posts in the enterprise were dominated by women and others by men and to explore the rationale for any horizontal (sectoral) and vertical (hierarchical) segregation by gender.

(G) *General comments*

Finally, there was a section for additional observations where attention was paid to what managers had to say in general about labour recruitment in the firm itself and in the city at large, including whether personnel managers themselves felt that their own sex might influence who was recruited into different posts.

On the whole there was little difficulty obtaining answers under any of the headings, except when it came to justifying gender segregation within the firm. Here employers seemed to have some difficulty explaining why men and women were recruited into different jobs, except where there were obvious grounds of physical strength. This tends to underline how assumptions and practices are so deeply embedded in dominant cultural and ideological structures that they are very difficult to explain or rationalise at an instrumental level.

Copies of the Employer Survey questionnaire (in Spanish) are available from the author on request.

Bibliography

Abu, Katherine 1983. The Separateness of Spouses: Conjugal Resources in an Ashanti Town. In Christine Oppong (ed.) *Female and Male in West Africa*, George Allen and Unwin: London, 156–68.

Achío, Mayra and Mora, Patricia 1988. La Obrera Florista y la Subordinación de la Mujer. In *Revista de Ciencias Sociales* (Universidad de Costa Rica) 39, 47–56.

Aguiar, Neuma 1980. The Impact of Industralization on Women's Work Roles in Northeast Brazil. In June Nash and Helen Safa (eds) *Sex and Class in Latin America*, Bergin: New York, 110–28.

Aguiar, Neuma 1986. Research Guidelines: How to Study Women's Work in Latin America. In June Nash and Helen Safa (eds) *Women and Change in Latin America*, Bergin and Garvey: Massachusetts, 22–33.

Aguilar-Barajas, Ismael and Spence, Nigel 1988. Industrial Decentralisation and Regional Policy, 1970–1986: The Conflicting Policy Response. In George Philip (ed.) *The Mexican Economy*, Routledge: London, 183–228.

Alba, Carlos 1983. Jalisco: Un Caso de Desarrollo Contradictorio. *CEPES* (Jalisco) 2, 56–61.

Albert, Michèlle 1982. *Sex Selectivity in Internal Migration: An Exploratory Study of Costa Rica*, Working Paper No. 827, Institute for International Development and Co-operation, University of Ottawa.

Allen, Sheila 1981. Invisible Threads. In *Bulletin* 12.3, Institute of Development Studies, University of Sussex, 41–7.

Anderson, Michael 1980. *Approaches to the History of the Western Family*, Macmillan: London.

Anker, Richard and Hein, Catherine 1986 (eds) *Sex Inequalities in Urban Employment in the Third World*, Macmillan: Houndmills, Basingstoke.

Arias, Patricia 1980. La Consolidación de Una Gran Empresa en un Contexto Regional de Industries Pequeñas: El Caso de Calzado Canadá. In *Relaciones: Estudios de Historia y Sociedad*, 1:3, El Colegio de Michoacán: Zamora, 171–253.

Arizmendi, Fernando 1980. Familia. Organización Transicional. Estructura Social. Relación Objetal. In Carlos Corona (ed.) *Antropocultura*, Universidad de Guadalajara: Guadalajara, 68–87.

Arizpe, Lourdes 1977. Women in the Informal Labour Sector in Mexico City. In Wellesley

Editorial Committee (eds) *Women and National Development: The Complexities of Change*, University of Chicago: Chicago, 24–37.

Arizpe, Lourdes 1978. *Etnicismo, Migración y Cambio Económico*, El Colegio de México: México DF.

Arizpe, Lourdes 1982a. Women and Development in Latin America and the Caribbean. In *Development Dialogue*, 1/2, 74–84.

Arizpe, Lourdes 1982b. Relay Migration and the Survival of the Peasant Household. In Helen Safa (ed.) *Towards a Political Economy of Urbanization in Developing Countries*, Oxford University Press: New Delhi, 19–46.

Armstrong, Warwick and McGee, T. G. 1985. *Theatres of Accumulation: Studies in Asian and Latin American Urbanization*, Methuen: London.

Babb, Florence 1986. Producers and Reproducers: Andean Marketwomen in the Economy. In June Nash and Helen Safa (eds) *Women and Change in Latin America*, Bergin and Garvey: Massachusetts, 53–64.

Banck, Geert 1980. Survival Strategies of Low-Income Urban Households in Brazil. In *Urban Anthropology*, 9:2, 227–42.

de Barbieri, Teresita 1982. Familia y Trabajo Doméstico. Paper presented at the seminar 'Domestic Groups, Family and Society', Colegio de México: México DF, 7–9 July.

Barrett, Michèle 1986. *Women's Oppression Today: Problems in Marxist Feminist Analysis*, Verso: London (fifth impression).

Beechey, Veronica 1987. *Unequal Work*, Verso: London.

Benería, Lourdes and Roldan, Martha 1987. *The Crossroads of Class and Gender: Industrial Homework, Subcontracting and Household Dynamics in Mexico City*, University of Chicago Press: Chicago.

Beuchler, Judith-Maria 1986. Women in Petty Commodity Production in La Paz, Bolivia. In June Nash and Helen Safa (eds) *Women and Change in Latin America*, Bergin and Garvey: Massachusetts, 165–88.

Birkbeck, Chris 1979. Garbage Industry and the 'Vultures' of Cali, Colombia. In Ray Bromley and Chris Gerry (eds) *Casual Work and Poverty in Third World Cities*, John Wiley: Chichester, 161–83.

Bisilliat, Jeanne and Fiéloux, Michèle 1987. *Women of the Third World: Work and Daily Life*, Associated University Presses: Cranbury, New Jersey.

Blumberg, Rae Lesser 1976. Fairy Tales and Facts: Economy, Family, Fertility and the Female. In Irene Tinker, Michèle Bo Bramsen and Mayra Buvinić (eds) *Women and World Development*, Praeger: New York: 12–21.

Blumberg, Rae Lesser 1978. The Political Economy of the Mother–Child Family Revisited. In André Marks and René Römer (eds) *Family and Kinship in Middle America and the Caribbean*, University of the Netherlands Antilles and the Department of Caribbean Studies, Royal Institute of Linguistics and Anthropology: Leiden, Netherlands, 526–75.

Blumberg, Rae Lesser with García, Maria 1977. The Political Economy of the Mother–Child Family. In Luis Leñero-Otero (ed.) *Beyond the Nuclear Family Model: Cross-Cultural Perspectives*, Sage: London, 99–163.

Bock, E. Wilbur, Iutaka, Sugiyama and Berardo, Felix 1980. Urbanization and the Extended Family in Brazil. In Man Singh Das and Clinton Jesser (eds) *The Family in Latin America*, Vikas: New Delhi, 161–84.

Bolaños, Bernardo and Rodríguez, Hannia 1988. La Incorporación de la Mujer en el Proceso Productivo de Flores en Costa Rica. In *Revista de Ciencias Sociales*, 39, 57–68.

Bolles, A. Lynn 1986. Economic Crisis and Female-Headed Households in Urban

Jamaica. In June Nash and Helen Safa (eds) *Women and Change in Latin America*, Bergin and Garvey: Massachusetts, 65–83.

Boyle, Catherine 1986. Images of Women in Contemporary Chilean Theatre. In *Bulletin of Latin American Research*, 5:2, 81–96.

Brambila, Carlos 1986. *Migración y Formación Familiar en México*, El Colegio de México/ UNAM: México DF.

Bridges, Julian 1980. The Mexican Family. In Man Singh Das and Clinton Jesser (eds) *The Family in Latin America*, Vikas: New Delhi, 295–334.

Bromley, Ray 1982. Working in the Streets: Survival Strategy, Necessity or Unavoidable Evil? In Alan Gilbert in association with Jorge Hardoy and Ronaldo Ramirez (eds) *Urbanization in Contemporary Latin America: Critical Approaches to the Analysis of Urban Issues*, John Wiley: Chichester, 59–77.

Browning, Harley and Roberts, Bryan 1980. Urbanization, Sectoral Transformation and the Utilization of Labour in Latin America. In *Comparative Urban Research*, 9:1, 86–104.

Bruce, Judith and Dwyer, Daisy 1988. Introduction. In Daisy Dywer and Judith Bruce (eds) *A Home Divided: Women and Income in the Third World*, Stanford University Press: Stanford, California, 1–19.

Bruner, Edward 1982. Models of Urban Kinship. In Helen Safa (ed.) *Towards a Political Economy of Urbanization in Developing Countries*, Oxford University Press: New Delhi, 105–18.

Bryceson, Deborah Fahy 1985. Women's Proletarianization and the Family Wage in Tanzania. In Haleh Afshar (ed.) *Women, Work and Ideology in the Third World*, Tavistock: London, 128–52.

Brydon, Lynne 1979. Women at Work: Some Changes in Family Structure in Amedzofe-Avatime, Ghana. In *Africa*, 49:2, 97–111.

Brydon, Lynne and Chant, Sylvia 1989. *Women in the Third World: Gender Issues in Rural and Urban Areas*, Edward Elgar/Gower: Aldershot and Rutgers University Press: New Brunswick, New Jersey.

Butterworth, Douglas and Chance, John 1981. *Latin American Urbanization*, Cambridge University Press: Cambridge.

Buvinić, Mayra and Youssef, Nadia 1978. *Women-Headed Households: The Ignored Factor in Development Planning*, International Center for Research on Women: Washington DC.

Calleja, Margarita 1984. Dependencia y Crecimiento Industrial: Las Unidades Domésticas y la Producción del Calzado en León, Guanajuato. In *Relaciones: Estudios de Historia y Sociedad* (El Colegio de Michoacán) 5:17, 54–85.

Cámara de la Industria del Calzado del Estado de Guanajuato. 1985. *Annual Report*, León.

Cámara Nacional de la Industria de Transformación (CANACINTRA) 1984. *Directorio Industrial*, Querétaro.

Cammack, Paul 1988. The 'Brazilianisation' of Mexico. In *Government and Opposition*, 23:3, 304–320.

Canton Moller, Miguel 1974. Equality of Employment Opportunities in Mexico. In International Labour Office *Equality of Opportunity in Employment in the American Region: Problems and Policies*, ILO: Geneva, 50–60.

Carr, Barry 1989. The Left and its Potential Role in Political Change. In Wayne Cornelius, Judith Gentleman and Peter H. Smith (eds) *Mexico's Alternative Political Futures*, Monograph Series 30, Center for US–Mexican Studies, University of California: San Diego, 367–87.

Carrillo, Jorge and Hernández, Alberto 1981. *La Industria Maquiladora en México:*

Bibliografía, Directorio e Investigaciones Recientes, Monograph Series 7, Center for US–Mexican Studies: University of California, San Diego.

Carter, William and True, William 1978. Family and Kinship Among the San José Working Class. In André Marks and René Römer (eds) *Family and Kinship in Middle America and the Caribbean*, University of the Netherlands Antilles and the Department of Caribbean Studies of the Royal Institute of Linguistics and Anthropology: Leiden, Netherlands, 227–50.

Carvajal, Manuel and Geithman, David 1985. Income, Human Capital and Sex Discrimination: Some Evidence from Costa Rica 1963 and 1973. In *Journal of Economic Development*, 10:1, 89–115.

Censo Industrial 1976. *Resumen General*, México DF.

Chant, Sylvia 1984. 'Las Olvidadas': A Study of Women, Housing and Family Structure in Querétaro, Mexico. Ph.D. dissertation, Department of Geography: University College London.

Chant, Sylvia 1985a. Family Formation and Female Roles in Querétaro, Mexico. In *Bulletin of Latin American Research*, 4:1, 17–32.

Chant, Sylvia 1985b. Single-Parent Families: Choice or Constraint? The Formation of Female-Headed Households in Mexican Shanty Towns. In *Development and Change*, 16, 635–56.

Chant, Sylvia 1987a. Family Structure and Female Labour in Querétaro, Mexico. In Janet Momsen and Janet Townsend (eds) *Geography of Gender in the Third World*, Hutchinson: London, 277–93.

Chant, Sylvia 1987b. Domestic Labour, Decision-Making and Dwelling Construction: The Experience of Women in Querétaro, Mexico. In Caroline Moser and Linda Peake (eds) *Women, Human Settlements and Housing*, Tavistock: London, 33–54.

Chant, Sylvia and Ward, Peter 1987. Family Structure and Low-Income Housing Policy. In *Third World Planning Review*, 9:1, 5–19.

Chaverría, Carmen; Elizondo, María Elena; García, Carmen and Martínez, María del Rosario 1987. Algunas consideraciones sobre la familia de mujeres guanacastecas organizadas: análisis de tres grupos femininos productivos. Thesis for licenciado en trabajo social, Universidad de Costa Rica, Centro Universitario de Guanacaste: Liberia.

Chester, Robert 1977. The One-Parent Family: Deviant or Variant? In Robert Chester and John Peel (eds) *Equalities and Inequalities in Family Life*, Academic Press: London, 149–61.

Clarke, Colin 1986. *Livelihood Systems, Settlements and Levels of Living in 'Los Valles Centrales de Oaxaca' Mexico*, Research Paper 37, Department of Geography: University of Oxford.

Cobos, B. 1974. Mexico. In International Labour Office *Equality of Opportunity in Employment in the American Region: Problems and Policies*, ILO: Geneva, 66–73.

Cockcroft, James 1983a. *Mexico: Class Formation, Capital Accumulation and the State*, Monthly Review Press: New York.

Cockcroft, James 1983b. Immiseration, not Marginalization: The Case of Mexico. In *Latin American Perspectives*, 10: 2/3, 86–107.

Comisión Co-ordinadora del Desarrollo de la Desembocadura del Río Ameca (COCODERA) 1980. *Programa de Ordenación de la Zona Conurbada de la Desembocadura del Río Ameca*, Puerto Vallarta.

Comisión Nacional de los Salarios Mínimos 1975. *Salarios Mínimos 1974–1975*, Mexico DF.

Connolly, Priscilla 1981. El Desempleo, Subempleo y la Pauperización Urbana: Crítica a las Interpretaciones Corrientes. Paper presented at the third reunion of the Grupo Latinamericano de Investigación: México DF, 23–31 July.

Cornelius, Wayne 1975. *Politics and the Migrant Poor in Mexico City*, Stanford University Press: Stanford, California.

Cornelius, Wayne 1986. *The Political Economy of Mexico under de la Madrid: The Crisis Deepens 1985–1986*, Research Report Series 43, Center for US–Mexican Studies, University of California: San Diego.

Cornelius, Wayne and Craig, Ann 1988. *Politics in Mexico: An Introduction and Overview*, Reprint Series 1, second edition, Center for US–Mexican Studies, University of California: San Diego.

Cornelius, Wayne; Gentleman, Judith and Smith, Peter H. 1989. Overview: The Dynamics of Political Change in Mexico. In Wayne Cornelius, Judith Gentleman and Peter H. Smith (eds) *Mexico's Alternative Political Futures*, Monograph Series 30, Center for US–Mexican Studies, University of California: San Diego, 1–51.

Cross-Beras, Julio 1980. The Dominican Family. In Man Singh Das and Clinton Jesser (eds) *The Family in Latin America*, Vikas: New Delhi, 270–94.

Cubitt, Tessa 1988. *Latin American Society*, Longman: London.

Cunningham, Susan 1987. Gender and Industrialization in Brazil. In Janet Momsen and Janet Townsend (eds) *Geography of Gender in the Third World*, Hutchinson: London, 294–308.

Dankelman, Irene and Davidson, Joan 1988. *Women and Environment in the Third World: Alliance for the Future*, Earthscan: London.

Das, Man Singh 1980. Introduction to Latin American Family and Society. In Man Singh Das and Clinton Jesser (eds) *The Family in Latin America*, Vikas: New Delhi, 1–11.

Das, Man Singh and Jesser, Clinton 1980 (eds) *The Family in Latin America*, Vikas: New Delhi.

De la Peña, Guillermo. 1986. Mercados de Trabajo y Articulación Regional: Apuntes sobre el Caso de Guadalajara y el Occidente Mexicano. In Guillermo De la Peña and Agustín Escobar (eds) *Cambio Regional, Mercado de Trabajo y Vida Obrera en Jalisco*, El Colegio de Jalisco: Guadalajara, 47–88.

De los Ríos, Rebeca 1989. Mujer, Pobreza y Estrátegias de Sobrevivencia Familiar. In *Mujer*, 5 (CEFEMINA, San José) 103–12.

Deere, Carmen Diana 1986. Rural Women and Agrarian Reform in Peru, Chile and Cuba. In June Nash and Helen Safa (eds) *Women and Change in Latin America*, Bergin and Garvey: Massachusetts, 189–207.

Delphy, Christine and Leonard, Diane 1986. Class Analysis, Gender Analysis and the Family. In Rosemary Crompton and Michael Mann (eds) *Gender and Stratification*, Polity Press: Cambridge, 57–73.

Dex, Shirley 1988 Gender and the Labour Market. In Duncan Gallie (ed.) *Employment in Britain*, Basil Blackwell: Oxford, 281–309.

Duncan, Simon 1989. Uneven Development and the Difference that Space Makes. In *Geoforum*, 20, 131–9.

Duncan, Simon and Savage, Mike 1989. Space, Scale and Locality. In *Antipode*, 21:3, 179–206.

Durán, Esperanza 1988. Mexico's 1986 Financial Rescue: Palliative or Cure? In George Philip (ed.) *The Mexican Economy*, Routledge: London, 95–109.

Durrani, Lorna Hawker 1976. Employment of Women and Social Change. In Russell Stone and John Simmons (eds) *Change in Tunisia*, State University of New York Press: Albany 57–72.

Eckstein, Susan 1977. *The Poverty of Revolution: The State and the Urban Poor in Mexico*, Princeton University Press: New Jersey.

Edholm, Felicity; Harris, Olivia and Young, Kate 1982. La Conceptualización de la Mujer. In Secretaría de Programación y Presupuesto (SPP) (ed.) *Estudios Sobre la Mujer 1. El Empleo y la Mujer. Bases Teóricas, Metodológicas y Evidencia Empírica*, SPP: México DF, 349–73.

Edwards, Michael 1982. Cities of Tenants: Renting among the Urban Poor in Latin America. In Alan Gilbert in association with Jorge Hardoy and Ronaldo Ramirez (eds) *Urbanization in Contemporary Latin America: Critical Approaches to the Analysis of Urban Issues*, John Wiley: Chichester, 129–58.

Eisenstein, Zillah (ed.) 1979. *Capitalist Patriarchy and the Case for Socialist Feminism*, Monthly Review Press: New York.

Elmendorf, Mary 1976. The Dilemma of Peasant Women: A View from a Village in Yucatan. In Irene Tinker, Michèle Bo Bramsen and Mayra Buvinić (eds) *Women and World Development*, Praeger: New York, 88–94.

Elmendorf, Mary 1977. Mexico: The Many Worlds of Women. In Janet Zollinger Giele and Audrey Chapman Smock (eds) *Women: Roles and Status in Eight Countries*, John Wiley: New York, 127–72.

Elson, Diane 1982. The Differentiation of Children's Labour in the Capitalist Labour Market. In *Development and Change*, 13:4, 479–97.

Elson, Diane and Pearson, Ruth 1981. 'Nimble Fingers Make Cheap Workers': An Analysis of Women's Employment in Third World Export Manufacturing. In *Feminist Review*, 7, 87–107.

Engels, Frederick 1972. *The Origin of the Family, Private Property and the State*, Lawrence and Wishart: London. (originally published in 1884.)

Ennew, Judith 1982. Family Structure, Unemployment and Child Labour in Jamaica. In *Development and Change*, 13, 551–63.

Ennew, Judith and Young, Pansy 1981. *Child Labour in Jamaica*, Child Labour Series No. 6, Anti-Slavery Society: London.

Enriquez, Rosario 1988. The Rise and Collapse of Stabilising Development. In George Philip (ed.) *The Mexican Economy*, Routledge: London, 7–40.

Escobar, Agustín 1988. The Rise and Fall of an Urban Labour Market: Economic Crisis and the Fate of Small-Scale Workshops in Guadalajara, Mexico. In *Bulletin of Latin American Research*, 7: 2, 183–205.

Escobar, Agustín; González, Mercedes and Roberts, Bryan 1987. Migration, Labour Markets and the International Economy: Jalisco, Mexico and the United States. In Jeremy Eades (ed.) *Migrants, Workers and the Social Order*, Association of Social Anthropologists Monograph N. 26, Tavistock: London, 42–64.

Estrada, Margarita 1980. Condiciones de la Reproducción Social: La Familia de los Obreros del Calzado en la Ciudad de León, Guanajuato. Thesis for licenciado en antropología social, México DF.

Fapohunda, Eleanor 1988. The Non-pooling Household: A Challenge to Theory. In Daisy Dwyer and Judith Bruce (eds) *A Home Divided: Women and Income in the Third World*, Stanford University Press: Stanford, 143–54.

Fernández-Kelly, Maria Patricia 1983a. *For We are Sold, I and My People*, State University of New York Press: Albany, New York.

Fernández-Kelly, Maria Patricia 1983b. Mexican Border Industrialization, Female Labour Force Participation and Migration. In June Nash and Maria Patricia Fernández-Kelly (eds) *Women, Men and the International Division of Labour*, State University of New York Press: Albany, New York, 205–23.

Fideicomiso Puerto Vallarta 1985. *Cuaderno Básico de Estadísticas*, Puerto Vallarta.

Flandrin, Jean-Louis 1979. *Families in Former Times: Kinship, Households and Sexuality*, Cambridge University Press: Cambridge.

Flora, Cornelia Butler and Santos, Blas 1986. Women in Farming Systems in Latin America. In June Nash and Helen Safa (eds) *Women and Change in Latin America*, Bergin and Garvey: Massachusetts, 208–28.

Folbre, Nancy 1988. The Black Four of Hearts: Towards a New Paradigm of Household Economics. In Daisy Dwyer and Judith Bruce (eds) *A Home Divided*, Stanford University Press: Stanford, 248–62.

Fortes, Meyer 1958. Introduction. In Jack Goody (ed.) *The Developmental Cycle in Domestic Groups*, Cambridge University Press: Cambridge, 1–14.

Fortes, Meyer 1970. Time and Social Structure. In Meyer Fortes (ed.) *Time and Social Structure and Other Essays*, Athlone Press: London, 1–32.

García, Brígida; Muñoz, Humberto and de Oliveira, Orlandina 1982. *Hogares y Trabajadores en la Ciudad de México*, El Colegio de México/UNAM: México DF.

García, Brígida; Muñoz, Humberto and de Oliveira, Orlandina 1983a. *Familia y Mercado de Trabajo: Un Estudio de Dos Ciudades Brasileñas*, El Colegio de México/UNAM: México DF.

García Brígida; Muñoz, Humberto and de Oliveira, Orlandina 1983b. Familia y Trabajo en México y Brasil. *Estudios Sociológicos*: 1: 3 El Colegio de México, DF, 487–507.

Garrido, Luis 1989. The Crisis of Presidencialismo. In Wayne Cornelius, Judith Gentleman and Peter Smith (eds) *Mexico's Alternative Political Futures*, Monograph Series 30, Center for US–Mexican Studies, University of California, San Diego, 417–34.

Garro, Nora 1983. Discriminación Sexual en la Industria: El Caso de la Cuidad de México. In Análisis Económico (UAM at Azcapotzalco), 2: 1, 311–29.

Garza, Gustavo 1980. *Industrialización de las Principales Ciudades de Mexico*, El Colegio de México/UNAM: México DF.

Gilbert, Alan 1983. The Tenants of Self-Help Housing: Choice and Constraint in the Housing Markets of Less Developed Countries. In *Development and Change*, 14, 449–77.

Gilbert, Alan (ed.) 1989a. *Housing and Land in Urban Mexico*, Monograph 31, Center for US–Mexican Studies, University of California: San Diego.

Gilbert, Alan 1989b. Housing During Recession: Illustrations from Latin America. In *Housing Studies*, 4: 3, 155–66.

Gilbert, Alan and Gugler, Josef 1982. *Cities, Poverty and Development: Urbanization in the Third World*, Oxford University Press: Oxford.

Gilbert, Alan and Varley, Ann 1989. From Renting to Self-Help Ownership? Residential Tenure in Urban Mexico since 1940. In Alan Gilbert (ed.) *Housing and Land in Urban Mexico*, Monograph 31, Center for US–Mexican Studies, University of California: San Diego, 13–37.

Gilbert, Alan and Ward, Peter 1981. Public Intervention Housing and Land Use in Latin American Cities. In *Bulletin of Latin American Research*, 1: 1, 97–104.

Gilbert, Alan and Ward, Peter 1982. *Public Intervention, Housing and Land Use in Latin American Cities*, Final Report submitted to the Overseas Development Administration: London, September.

Gilbert, Alan and Ward, Peter 1985. *Housing, the State and the Poor: Policy and Practice in Three Latin American Cities*, Cambridge University Press: Cambridge.

Gobierno del Estado de Guanajuato/H Ayuntamiento del Municipio 1981. *Plan Director de Desarrollo Urbano de León, Guanajuato*, Guanajuato.

Gobierno Constitucional de los Estados Unidos Mexicanos/Gobierno del Estado de Querétaro 1986 *Plan Querétaro*, Querétaro.

Goddard, Victoria 1981. The Leather Trade in the Bassi of Naples, *Bulletin*, 12: 3, Institute of Development Studies, University of Sussex, 30–35.

Gongla, Patricia and Thompson, Edward H. 1987. Single-Parent Families. In Marvin Sussman and Suzanne Steinmetz (eds) *Handbook of Marriage and the Family*, Plenum: New York, 397–418.

Gonzalez, Gloria 1980. Participation of Women in the Mexican Labour Force. In June Nash and Helen Safa (eds) *Sex and Class in Latin America*, Bergin: New York, 183–201.

González de la Rocha, Mercedes 1984. Urban Households and Domestic Cycles in Guadalajara, Mexico. Ph.D. Dissertation, Faculty of Social and Economic Studies, University of Manchester.

González de la Rocha, Mercedes 1986. *Los Recursos de la Pobreza*, El Colegio de Jalisco: Guadalajara.

González de la Rocha, Mercedes 1988. Economic Crisis, Domestic Reorganization and Women's Work in Guadalajara, Mexico. In *Bulletin of Latin American Research*, 7: 2, 207–23.

González de la Rocha, Mercedes; Escobar, Agustín and De la Peña, Guillermo 1985. Crisis Económica y Pobreza, Vecindad y Organizaciones Populares en Guadalajara en los Años 1981–1985. Research project presented by the Centro de Estudios Regionales, Colegio de Jalisco in collaboration with the Centro de Estudios Superiores en Antropología Social (CIESAS): Mexico DF.

Goode, William 1963. *World Revolution and Family Patterns*, The Free Press: New York.

Goody, J. R. (ed.) 1958. *The Developmental Cycle in Domestic Groups*, Cambridge University Press: Cambridge.

Gudmundson, Lowell 1986. *Costa Rica Before Coffee: Society and Economy on the Eve of the Export Boom*, Louisiana State University Press: Baton Rouge and London.

Gugler, Josef 1982. Employment in the City. In Alan Gilbert and Josef Gugler, *Cities, Poverty and Development: Urbanization in the Third World*, Oxford University Press: Oxford, 65–80.

Hackenberg, Robert; Murphy, Arthur and Selby, Henry 1981. The Household in the Secondary Cities of the Third World. Paper prepared for Wenner-Gren Foundation Symposium 'Households: Changing Form and Function'. New York, 8–15 October.

Hall, Carolyn 1985. *Costa Rica: A Geographical Interpretation in Historical Perspective*, Dellplain Latin American Studies 17, Westview: Boulder.

Hamilton, Nora 1986. State-Class Alliances: Issues and Actors in the Mexican Economic Crisis. In Nora Hamilton and Timothy Harding (eds) *Modern Mexico: State, Economy and Social Conflict*, Sage: London and Newbury Park, 148–74.

Hansen, Roger 1971. *The Politics of Mexican Development*, Johns Hopkins: Baltimore.

Harris, Christopher and Morris, Lydia 1986. Households, Labour Markets and the Position of Women. In Rosemary Crompton and Michael Mann (eds) *Gender and Stratification*, Polity Press: Cambridge, 86–96.

Harris, Nigel 1983. *Of Bread and Guns: The World Economy in Crisis*, Penguin: Harmondsworth.

Harris, Nigel 1986. *The End of the Third World: Newly-Industrializing Countries and the Decline of an Ideology*, Penguin: Harmondsworth.

Harris, Olivia 1981. Households as Natural Units. In Kate Young, Carol Wokowitz and Roslyn McCullagh (eds) *Of Marriage and the Market*, CSE: London, 48–67.

Harris, Olivia (ed.) 1982. *Latin American Women: An Overview*, Minority Rights Group: London.

Hart, Keith 1973. Informal Income Opportunities and Urban Employment in Ghana. In

Richard Jolly, Emmanuel De Kadt, Hans Singer and Fiona Wilson (eds) *Third World Employment: Problems and Strategy*, Penguin: Harmondsworth, 66–70.

Hein, Catherine 1986. The Feminisation of Industrial Employment in Mauritius: A Case of Sex Segregation. In Richard Anker and Catherine Hein (eds) *Sex Inequalities in Urban Employment in the Third World*, Macmillan: Houndmills, Basingstoke, 277–311.

Hernández Aguila, Helena de la Paz 1988. Mujer y Trabajo: Las Adornadoras del Calzado en Guadalajara. In Luisa Gabayet *et al.* (eds) *Mujeres y Sociedad: Salario, Hogar y Acción Social en el Occidente de México*, El Colegio de Jalisco: Guadalajara, 17–33.

Heyzer, Noeleen 1981. Towards a Framework of Analysis. In *Bulletin*, 12: 3, Institute of Development Studies, University of Sussex, 3–7.

Hirschman, Albert 1986 *The Political Economy of Latin American Development: Seven Exercises in Retrospection*, Copublications Series No. 3. Center for US–Mexican Studies. University of California: San Diego.

Hoodfar, Homa 1988. Household Budgeting and Financial Management in a Lower-income Cairo Neighbourhood. In Daisy Dwyer and Judith Bruce (eds) *A Home Divided: Women and Income in the Third World*, Stanford University Press: California, 120–42.

Humphrey, John 1985. Gender, Pay and Skill: Manual Workers in Brazilian Industry. In Haleh Afshar (ed.) *Women, Work and Ideology in the Third World*, Tavistock: London, 214–31.

Huston, Perdita 1979. *Third World Women Speak Out*, Praeger: New York.

Hutter, Mark 1981. *The Changing Family: Comparative Perspectives*, John Wiley: New York.

IAP Querétaro/SEDUE 1986. *Ciudades Medias: Programa Estratégico/Prioridades Territoriales y de Centros de Población*, Querétaro.

Iglesias, Norma 1985. *La Flor Más Bella de la Maquiladora: Historias de Vida de La Mujer Obrera en Tijuana, Baja California Norte*, SEP/CEFNOMEX: México DF.

Institute of British Geographers, Women and Geography Study Group (IBG) 1984. *Geography and Gender: An Introduction to Feminist Geography*, Hutchinson: London.

Jain, Devaki; Singh, Nalini and Chand, Malina 1982 India. In Rounaq Jahan (ed.) *Women in Asia*, Minority Rights Group Report No. 45, (reprinted 1982 edition), London 8–10.

Jelin, Elizabeth 1977. Migration and Labour Force Participation of Latin American Women: The Domestic Servants in the Cities. In Wellesley Editorial Committee (eds) *Women and National Development: the Complexities of Change*, University of Chicago: Chicago, 129–41.

Jones, Gavin W. (ed.) 1984. *Women in the Urban and Industrial Labour Force: Southeast and East Asia*, Development Studies Centre Monograph No. 33, The Australian National University: Canberra.

Joekes, Susan 1985. Working for Lipstick? Male and Female Labour in the Clothing Industry in Morocco. In Haleh Afshar (ed.) *Women, Work and Ideology in the Third World*, Tavistock: London, 183–213.

Joekes, Susan 1987. *Women in the World Economy: An INSTRAW Study*, Oxford University Press: New York.

Jud, G. Donald 1974. Tourism and Economic Growth in Mexico since 1950. *Inter-American Economic Affairs*, 19–43.

Jules-Rosette, Benetta 1985. The Women Potters of Lusaka: Urban Migration and Socioeconomic Adjustment. In Beverly Lindsay (ed.) *African Migration and National Development*, Pennsylvania State University: Pennsylvania, 82–112.

Kaufman, Robert 1977. Mexico and Latin American Authoritarianism. In José Luís Reyna and Richard Weinert (eds) *Authoritarianism in Mexico*, Institute for the Study of Human Issues: Philadelphia, 193–232.

Kaufman Purcell, Susan 1975. *The Mexican Profit-Sharing Decision: Politics in an Authoritarian Regime*, University of California Press: Berkeley.

Kaufman Purcell, Susan 1988. Mexico in Transition. In Susan Kaufman Purcell (ed.) *Mexico in Transition: Implications for US Policy*, Council on Foreign Relations: New York, 3–17.

Kemper, Robert 1977. *Migration and Adaptation: Tzintzuntzan Peasants in Mexico City*, Sage: Beverly Hills.

Kennedy, Janet; Russin, Antoinette and Martínez, Amalfi 1978. *The Impact of Tourism Development on Women: A Case Study of Ixtapa-Zihuatanejo, Mexico*, Draft Report for Tourism Projects Department, World Bank: Washington.

Keren, Donna 1982. Procesos y Contradicciones del Crecimiento Industrial de Querétaro. Paper presented at the Centro de Investigaciones Sociológicas, Universidad Autónoma de Querétaro, Querétaro, March.

Kishwar, Madhu and Vanita, Ruth (eds) 1984. *In Search of Answers: Indian Women's Voices from Manushi*, Zed: London.

Knight, Alan 1989. Comment. In Wayne Cornelius, Judith Gentleman and Peter H. Smith (eds) *Mexico's Alternative Political Futures*, Monograph Series 30, Center for US–Mexican Studies University of San Diego, 453–63.

Kouyoumdjian, Armen 1988. The Miguel de la Madrid Sexenio: Major Reforms or Foundation for Disaster? In George Philip (ed.) *The Mexican Economy*, Routledge: London, 78–94.

Kuzesnof, Elizabeth 1980. Household Composition and Headship as Related to Changes in the Mode of Production: São Paulo 1765–1836. In *Comparative Studies in Society and History* , 22, 78–108.

Kuzesnof, Elizabeth 1989. The History of the Family in Latin America: A Critique of Recent Work. In *Latin American Research Review*, 24: 2, 168–86.

Lailson, Sylvia, 1980. Expansión Limitada y Proliferación Horizontal: La Industria de la Ropa el Tejido de Punto. In *Relaciones: Estudios de Historia y Sociedad*, (El Colegio de Michoacán) 1: 3, 48–102.

Land, Hilary 1977. Inequalities in Large Families: More of the Same or Different? In Robert Chester and John Peel (eds) *Equalities and Inequalities in Family Life*, Academic Press: London, 163–76.

Laslett, Peter 1972. *Household and Family in Past Time*, Cambridge University Press: Cambridge.

Laslett, Peter 1977. *Family Life and Illicit Love in Earlier Generations*, Cambridge University Press: Cambridge.

Latin American and Caribbean Women's Collective (LACWE) 1980. *Slaves of Slaves: The Challenge of Latin American Women*, Zed: London.

Lea, John 1988. *Tourism and Development in the Third World*, Routledge: London.

Leacock, Eleanor 1972. Introduction to the Origin of the Family, Private Property and the State. In Frederick Engels *The Origin of the Family, Private Property and the State*, Lawrence and Wishart: London, 7–67.

Lee, Gary 1987. Comparative Perspectives. In Martin Sussman and Suzanne Steinmetz *Handbook of Marriage and the Family*, Plenum: New York, 59–80.

Lerner, Gerda 1986. *The Creation of Patriarchy*, Oxford University Press: New York and Oxford.

Lim, Linda 1983. Capitalism, Imperialism, and Patriarchy: the Dilemma of Third-World Women Workers in Multinational Factories. In June Nash and Maria Patricia Fernández Kelly (eds). *Women, Men and the International Division of Labour*, State University of New York Press: Albany, 70–91.

Loaeza, Soledad 1988. The Impact of the Economic Crisis on the Mexican Political System. In Susan Kaufman Purcell (ed.) *Mexico in Transition*, Council on Foreign Relations: New York, 43–52.

Lobo, Susan 1982. *A House of My Own: Social Organisation in the Squatter Settlements of Lima, Peru*, University of Arizona Press: Tucson.

Lomnitz, Larissa 1977. *Networks and Marginality – Life in a Mexican Shanty Town*, Academic Press: New York.

Looney, Robert 1983. Mexican Economic Performance During the Echeverría Administration: Bad Luck or Poor Planning? In *Bulletin of Latin American Research*, 2: 2, 57–68.

Losh-Hesselbart, Susan 1987. Development of Gender Roles. In Marvin Sussman and Suzanne Steinmetz (eds) *Handbook of Marriage and the Family*, Plenum: New York and London, 535–64.

Lu, Yu-Hsia 1984. Women, Work and the Family in a Developing Society: Taiwan. In Gavin Jones (ed.) *Women in the Urban and Industrial Workforce: Southeast and East Asia*, Development Studies Centre Monograph No. 33, Australian National University: Canberra, 339–67.

MacDonald, John Stuart 1979. Planning Implementation and Social Policy: An Evaluation of Ciudad Guayana. In *Progress in Planning*, 11: 1/2, 1–211.

MacDonald, John Stuart and MacDonald, Leatrice 1978. The Black Family in the Americas: A Review of the Literature. In *SAGE Race Relations Abstracts*, 3: 1, 1–42.

Machado, Leda 1983. Low-income Housing in Brazil and Women: Evaluation of the PROFILURB Project in Terms of its Capacity to Define and Reach Female-Headed Households as a Target Group. Unpublished Masters Dissertation. Development Planning Unit, University College London.

Mackintosh, Maureen 1979. Domestic Labour and the Household. In Sandra Burman (ed.) *Fit Work for Women*, Croom Helm: London, 173–91.

Mackintosh, Maureen 1981. Gender and Economics: The Sexual Division of Labour and the Subordination of Women. In Kate Young, Carol Wolkowitz and Roslyn McCullagh (eds) *Of Marriage and the Market*, CSE: London, 1–15.

Macklin, Eleanor 1987. Non-traditional Family Forms. In Marvin Sussman and Suzanne Steinmetz *Handbook Of Marriage and the Family*, Plenum: New York, 317–54.

McGee, Terry 1987. Mass Markets–Little Markets: a Call for Research on the Proletarianization Process, Women Workers and the Creation of Demand. In Janet Momsen and Janet Townsend (eds) *Geography of Gender in the Third World*, Hutchinson: London, 355–88.

McKee, David 1988. *Growth, Development and the Service Economy in the Third World*, Praeger: New York, Westport, Connecticut, London.

Mencher, Joan 1988. Women's Work and Poverty: Women's Contribution to Household Maintenance in South India. In Daisy Dwyer and Judith Bruce (eds) *A Home Divided: Women and Income in the Third World*, Stanford University Press: Stanford, 99–119.

Mernissi, Fatima 1985. *Beyond the Veil: Male–Female Dynamics in Modern Muslim Society*, Al Saqi Books: London.

Merrick, Thomas and Schmink, Marianne 1983. Households Headed by Women and Urban Poverty in Brazil. In Mayra Buvinić, Margaret Lycette and William McGreevey (eds) *Women and Poverty in the Third World*, Johns Hopkins: Baltimore, 244–71.

Meza, Manuel 1982. Desarrollo Industrial en el Estado. In *PRI: Consulta Popular en las Reuniones Nacionales: Querétaro*, PRI/IEPES: Mexico DF, 22–4.

Mitterauer, Michael and Sieder, Reinhard 1982. *The European Family*, Basil Blackwell: Oxford.

Molyneux, Maxine 1984. Mobilisation Without Emancipation? Women's Interests, State and Revolution in Nicaragua. In *Critical Social Policy*, 10, 4: 7, 59–75.

Momsen, Janet and Townsend, Janet (eds) 1987. *Geography of Gender in the Third World*, Hutchinson: London.

Mondragón, Margarita. Se me han ido las horas. In Armando Rodríguez (eds) 1980. *Antología de la Poesía Latinoamericana*, Editorial Mexicanos Unidos: México DF, 163.

Morris, Lydia 1988 Employment, the Household and Social Networks. In Duncan Gallie (ed.) *Employment in Britain*, Basil Blackwell: Oxford, 376–405.

Moser, Caroline 1978. Informal Sector or Petty Commodity Production: Dualism or Dependence in Urban Development? *World Development*, 6: 9/10, 1,041–64.

Moser, Caroline 1981. Surviving in the Suburbios. In *Bulletin*, 12: 3 Institute of Development Studies, University of Sussex, 19–29.

Moser, Caroline 1987. Women, Human Settlements and Housing: A Conceptual Framework for Analysis and Policy-Making. In Caroline Moser and Linda Peake (eds) *Women, Human Settlements and Housing*, Tavistock: London, 12–32.

Moser, Caroline 1989. The Impact of Recession and Structural Adjustment Policies at the Micro-Level: Low-Income Women and their Households in Guayaquil, Equador. In UNICEF (ed.) *Invisible Adjustment Vol. 2*, UNICEF Americas and Caribbean Regional Office: New York, 137–62.

Moser, Caroline and Chant, Sylvia 1985. *The Participation of Women in Low-Income Housing Projects*, Gender and Planning Working Paper No. 5, Development Planning Unit, University College London (final draft of training module commissioned by the United Nations Centre for Human Settlements (HABITAT) Nairobi.

Moser, Caroline and Young, Kate 1981. Women of the Working Poor. In *Bulletin*, 12:3, Institute of Development Studies, University of Sussex, 54–62.

Munachonga, Monica 1988. Income Allocation and Marriage Options in Urban Zambia. In Daisy Dwyer and Judith Bruce (eds) *A Home Divided: Women and Income in the Third World*, Stanford University Press: Stanford, California, 173–94.

Murray, Colin 1987. Class, Gender and the Household: The Developmental Cycle in Southern Africa. In *Development and Change*, 18, 235–49.

Nacional Financiera 1981. *La Economia Mexicana en Cifras*, México DF.

Nash, June 1980. A Critique of Social Science Roles in Latin America. In June Nash and Helen Safa (eds) *Sex and Class in Latin America*, Bergin: New York, 1–21.

Nash, June 1986. A Decade of Research on Women in Latin America. In June Nash and Helen Safa (eds) *Women and Change in Latin America*, Bergin and Garvey: Massachusetts, 3–21.

Nelson, Nici 1987. Rural–Urban Child Fostering in Kenya: Migration, Kinship, Ideology and Class. In Jeremy Eades (ed.) *Migrants, Workers and the Social Order*, Association of Social Anthropologists Monograph No. 26, Tavistock: London, 47–58.

Ortiz Monasterio, Fernando and Schmink, Marianne 1986. Women and Waste Management in Urban Mexico. In Judith Bruce and Marilyn Köhn (eds) *Learning about Women and Urban Services in Latin America and the Caribbean*. The Population Council: New York, 163–83.

Padilla, Cristina 1978. Marginados o Asalariados: El Trabajo Domiciliar de Máquila en una Colonia Popular. Thesis for licenciado en Antropología Social, Universidad Iberoamericana: México DF.

Pahl, Jan 1983. The Allocation of Money and the Structuring of Inequality within Marriage. In *Sociological Review*, 31, 235–62.

Pahl, Ray 1984. *Divisions of Labour*, Basil Blackwell: Oxford.

Papanek, Hannah 1976. Women in Cities: Problems and Perspectives. In Irene Tinker, Michèle Bo Bramsen and Mayra Buvinić (eds) *Women and World Development* Praeger: New York, 54–69.

Pasternak, Burton 1976. *Introduction to Kinship and Social Organization*, Prentice-Hall: New Jersey.

Pearson, Ruth 1986. Latin American Women and the New International Division of Labour: A Reassessment. In *Bulletin of Latin American Research*, 5: 2, 67–79.

Peattie, Lisa Redfield 1968. *The View from the Barrio*, Ann Arbor: Michigan.

Pedredo, Mercedes and Rendón, Teresa 1982. El Trabajo de la Mujer en México en los Setentas. In Secretaría de Programación y Presupuesto (SPP) (ed.) *Estudios sobre la Mujer 1: El Empleo y la Mujer. Bases Teóricas, Metodológicas y Evidencia Empírica*, SPP: Mexico DF, 437–58.

Peek, Peter 1978. Family Composition and Married Female Employment. In Guy Standing and Glen Sheehan (eds) *Labor Force Participation in Low-Income Countries*, ILO: Geneva, 51–73.

Peil, Margaret 1975. Female Roles in West African Towns. In Jack Goody (ed.) *Changing Social Structure in Ghana*, International African Institute: London, 73–90.

Peil, Margaret with Sada, Pius O. 1984. *African Urban Society* John Wiley: Chichester.

Pescatello, Ann 1976. *Power and Pawn: The Female in Iberian Families, Societies and Cultures*, Greenwood Press: Westport, Connecticut.

Pessar, Patricia 1988. The Constraints on the Release of Female Labour Power: Dominican Migration to the United States. In Daisy Dwyer and Judith Bruce (eds) *A Home Divided*, Stanford University Press: Stanford, 195–215.

Philip, George 1988. Introduction. In George Philip (ed.) *The Mexican Economy*, Routledge: London, 1–6.

Philip, George 1989 Mexico. In World of Information (ed.) *Latin America and Caribbean Review 1989*, World of Information: Saffron Waldon, 82–6.

Phillips, Anne 1983. *Hidden Hands: Women and Economic Policies*, Pluto: London.

Pollack, Molly 1989. Poverty and the Labour Market in Costa Rica. In Gerry Rodgers (ed.) *Urban Poverty and the Labour Market: Access to Jobs and Incomes in Asian and Latin American Cities*, ILO: Geneva, 65–80.

Pollard, Frank and Wilburg, J. 1978. Family Organization in a Squatter Settlement in Guyana. In André Marks and René Römer (eds) *Family and Kinship in Middle America and the Caribbean*, University of the Netherlands Antilles and the Department of Caribbean Studies of the Royal Institute of Linguistics and Anthropology, Leiden, Netherlands, 431–45.

Purcell, Kate 1988. Gender and the Experience of Employment. In Duncan Gallie (ed.) *Employment in Britain*, Basil Blackwell: Oxford, 157–86.

Queen, Stuart and Habenstein, Robert 1974. *The Family in Various Cultures*, J.B. Lippincott: Philadelphia.

Quiróz, Teresa; Osorio, Rodolfo; León, Carmen Violeta and Vasquez, Rita 1984. *La Mujer en Costa Rica y Su Participación Politica-Económica en el Desarrollo del País*, Avances de Investigación No. 51. Instituto de Investigaciones Sociales, Universidad de Costa Rica: San José.

Raczynski, Dagmar 1977. *El Sector Informal Urbano: Controversias e Interrogantes*, Corporación de Investigaciones Económicas para Latinoamérica: Santiago de Chile.

Radcliffe, Sarah 1986. Gender Relations, Peasant Livelihood Strategies and Migration: A Case Study from Cuzco, Peru. In *Bulletin of Latin American Research*, 5: 2, 29–47.

Ramirez Boza, Mario 1987. *Limitaciones y Obstáculos que tiene la mujer de dos sectores populares para su integración al mercado laboral*, Avances de Investigación No. 62. Instituto de Investigaciones Sociales, Universidad de Costa Rica: San José.

Resources for Action 1982a. *Women and Shelter in Honduras* United States Agency for International Development, Office of Housing: Washington DC.

Resources for Action 1982b. *Women and Shelter in Tunisia: A Survey of the Shelter Needs of Women in Low-Income Areas*, United States Agency for International Development, Office of Housing: Washington DC.

Reyna, José Luís 1977. Redefining the Authoritarian Regime. In José Luís Reyna and Richard Weinert (eds) *Authoritarianism in Mexico*, Institute for the Study of Human Issues: Philadelphia, 155–71.

Rivas, Sergio 1985. La Industria Maquiladora en México: Realidades y Falacias. *Comercio Exterior*, 35: 11, 1,071–84.

Roberts, Bryan 1978. *Cities of Peasants: The Political Economy of Urbanization in the Third World*, Edward Arnold: London.

Roberts, Bryan 1990. Economic Crisis, Social Change and Political Reform in Mexico. Seminar presented at Institute of Latin American Studies, University of London, 14 March.

Roberts, Kenneth 1985. Household Labour Mobility in a Modern Agrarian Economy: Mexico. In Guy Standing (ed.) *Labour Circulation and the Labour Process*, Croom Helm: London, 358–31.

Robertson, Claire 1976. Ga Women and Socioeconomic Change in Accra, Ghana. In Nancy Hafkin and Edna Bay (eds) *Women in Africa: Studies in Social and Economic Change*, Stanford University Press: Stanford, California, 111–33.

Rodgers, Gerry 1989 Introduction: Trends in Urban Poverty and Labour Market Access. In Gerry Rodgers (ed.) *Urban Poverty and the Labour Market: Access to Jobs and Incomes in Asian and Latin American Cities*, ILO: Geneva, 1–33.

Rogers, Barbara 1980. *The Domestication of Women: Discrimination in Developing Societies*, Tavistock: London.

Roldan, Martha 1988. Renegotiating the Marital Contract: Intrahousehold Patterns of Money Allocation and Women's Subordination among Domestic Outworkers in Mexico City. In Daisy Dwyer and Judith Bruce (eds) *A Home Divided: Women and Income in the Third World*, Stanford University Press: Stanford, 229–47.

Ronfeldt, David 1988. Questions and Cautions about Mexico's Future. In Susan Kaufman Purcell (ed.) *Mexico in Transition*, Council on Foreign Relations: New York, 53–66.

Ros, Jaime 1987. Mexico from the Oil Boom to the Debt Crisis: An Analysis of Policy Responses to External Shocks, 1978–85. In Rosemary Thorp and Lawrence Whitehead (eds) *Latin American Debt and the Adjustment*, Macmillan in association with St Antony's College Oxford: Houndmills, Basingstoke, 68–116.

Roxborough, Ian 1988. The Economic Crisis and Mexican Labour. In George Philip (ed.) *The Mexican Economy*, Routledge: London, 110–28.

Rubin-Kurtzman, Jane 1987. *The Socioeconomic Determinants of Fertility in Mexico: Changing Perspectives*, Monograph Series 23, Center for US–Mexican Studies, University of California: San Diego.

Safa, Helen 1964. From Shanty Town to Public Housing: A Comparison of Two Urban Neighbourhoods in Peurto Rico. In *Caribbean Studies*, 4: 1, 3–12.

Safa, Helen 1980. Class Consciousness among Working Class Women in Latin America: Peurto Rico. In June Nash and Helen Safa (eds) *Sex and Class in Latin America*, Bergin: New York, 69–85.

Safa, Helen 1981. Runaway Shops and Female Employment: The Search for Cheap Labour. In *Signs: Journal of Women in Culture and Society*, 7: 2, 418–33.

Safa, Helen 1983. El Empleo Feminino y la Reproducción Social en la Clase Obrera Puertorriqueña. In *Estudios Sociológicos*, 1: 3 El Colegio de México: México DF, 459–86.

Safa, Helen 1986. Female Employment in the Puerto Rican Working Class. In June Nash and Helen Safa (eds) *Women and Change in Latin America*, Bergin and Garvey: Massachusetts, 84–105.

Safilios-Rothschild, Constantina 1984. The Role of the Family in Development. In Sue Ellen Charlton *Women in Third World Development*, Westview: Boulder and London, 45–51.

Saffioti, Heleieth 1980. Relationships of Sex and Social Class in Brazil. In June Nash and Helen Safa (eds) *Sex and Class in Latin America*, Bergin: New York, 147–59.

Saffioti, Heleith 1986. Technological Change in Brazil: Its Effects on Men and Women in Two Firms. In June Nash and Helen Safa (eds) *Women and Change in Latin America*, Bergin and Garvey: Massachusetts, 109–35.

Salazar, Hector 1984. *La Dinámica de Crecimiento de Ciudades Intermedias de México: Los Casos de León, San Luís y Torreón (1960–1980)*, El Colegio de México/UNAM: México DF.

Sassen-Koob, Saskia 1984. From Household to Workplace: Theories and Survey Research on Migrant Women in the Labor Market. Notes on the Incorporation of Third World Women through Immigration and Offshore Production. In *International Migration Review*, 18: 4, 1, 144–67.

Schaefer, Kalmann 1976. *São Paulo: Urban Development and Employment*, ILO: Geneva.

Schmink, Marianne 1986. Women and Urban Industrial Development in Brazil. In June Nash and Helen Safa (eds) *Women and Change in Latin America*, Bergin and Garvey: Massachusetts, 136–64.

Schteingart, Marta 1989. The Environmental Problems Associated with Urban Development in Mexico City. In *Environment and Urbanization*, 1: 1, 40–50.

Scott, Alison MacEwen 1986a. Women in Latin America: Stereotypes and Social Science. In *Bulletin of Latin American Research*, 5: 2, 21–7.

Scott, Alison MacEwen 1986b. Industrialization, Gender Segregation and Stratification Theory. In Rosemary Crompton and Michael Mann (eds) *Gender Stratification*, Polity Press: Cambridge, 154–89.

Scott, Alison MacEwen 1986c. Women and Industrialisation: Examining the 'Female Marginalization' Thesis. In *Journal of Development Studies*, 22.4, 649–80.

Scott, Alison MacEwen 1988a. Capitalist Development and Women's Marginalization from Production: Theoretical and Methodological Problems. (Mimeo: Department of Sociology, University of Essex).

Scott, Alison MacEwen 1988b. Informal Sector or Female Sector? Gender Bias in Urban Labour Market Models. In Diane Elson (ed.) *Male Bias in the Development Process*, Manchester University Press: Manchester (forthcoming).

Scott, Alison MacEwen 1990. Patterns of Patriarchy in the Peruvian Working Class. In Sharon Stichter and Jane Parpart (eds) *Women, Employment and the Family in the International Division of Labour*, Macmillan: London, 198–220.

Scott, Joan and Tilly, Louise 1982. Women's Work and the Family in Nineteenth-Century Europe. In Elizabeth Whitelegg *et al.* (eds) *The Changing Experience of Women*, Martin Robertson: Oxford, 45–70.

Scott, Robert E. 1959. *Mexican Government in Transition*, University of Illinois Press: Urbana.

Seager, Joni and Olson, Ann 1986. *Women in the World: An International Atlas*, Pluto: London.

Seccombe, Wally 1980. Domestic Labour and the Working Class Household. In Bonnie Fox (ed.) *Hidden in the Household: Women's Domestic Labour Under Capitalism*, The Women's Press: Toronto, 25–99.

Secretaría de Asentamientos Humanos y Obras Públicas (SAHOP) 1980. *Plan Director de la Ciudad de Querétaro, Querétero*, Mexico DF.

Secretaría de Desarrollo Urbano y Ecología (SEDUE)/Gobierno del Estado de Jalisco. 1985. *Plan Municipal de Desarrollo Urbano: Centros de Población, Puerto Vallarta*, Puerto Vallarta.

Secretaría de Hacienda y Crédito Público (SHCP)/SEDUE 1982. *Programa de Estímulos para la Desconcentración Territorial de las Activades Industriales*, Mexico DF.

Secretaría de Patrimonio y Fomento Industrial (SECOFI) 1980. *Programa de Industrialización para el Estado de Guanajuato*, Dirección General de Industría Mediana y Pequeña: México DF.

Selby, Henry; Murphy, Arthur; Cabrera, Ignacio and Castañeda, Aida 1981. Battling Urban Poverty from Below: A Profile of the Poor in Two Mexican Cities. Paper prepared for Wenner-Gren Foundation Symposium on 'Households: Changing Form and Function', New York, 8–15 October.

Selby, Robert 1979. Women, Industrialization and Change in Queretaro, Mexico. Ph.D dissertation, Department of Anthropology, University of Utah. Reprinted by Ann Arbor: Michigan.

Seyde, Federico and Hobbs, Jeremy 1989 Economic and Political Change under De La Madrid and Salinas. Seminar presented at Institute of Latin American Studies, University of London, 13 December.

Sharma, Ursula 1986. *Women's Work, Class and the Urban Household: A Study of Shimla, North India*, Tavistock: London.

Sheahan, David 1987. *Patterns of Development in Latin America: Poverty, Repression and Economic Strategy*, Princeton University Press: Princeton, New Jersey.

Sinclair, Stuart 1978. *Urbanization and Labour Markets in Developing Countries*, Croom Helm: London.

Singhanetra-Renard, Anchalee 1984. Effects of Female Labour Force Participation on Fertility: The Case of Construction Workers in Chaing Mai City. In Gavin W. Jones (ed.) *Women in the Urban and Industrial Labour Force: Southeast and East Asia*, Development Studies Centre Monograph No. 33, Australian National University: Canberra, 325–35.

Siraj, Mehrun 1984. Islamic Attitudes to Female Employment in Industrializing Countries: Some Notes from Malaysia. In Gavin Jones (ed.) *Women in the Urban and Industrial Workforce: Southeast and East Asia*, Development Studies Centre Monograph No. 33, Australian National University: Canberra, 163–73.

Sklair, Leslie 1988. Mexico's Maquiladora Programme: A Critical Evaluation. In George Philip (ed.) *The Mexican Economy*, Routledge: London, 286–327.

Smith, Margo 1978. The Female Domestic Servant and Social Change, Lima, Peru. In Richard P. Schaedel and Jorge Hardoy (eds) *Urbanisation in the Americas from its Beginnings to the Present*, Mouton: The Hague, Paris, 569–86.

Smith, Peter H. 1979. *Labyrinths of Power: Political Recruitment in Twentieth Century Mexico*, Princeton University Press: Princeton.

Smith, Peter H. 1989. The 1988 Presidential Succession in Historical Perspective. In Wayne Cornelius, Judith Gentleman and Peter H. Smith (eds) *Mexico's Alternative*

Political Futures, Monograph Series 30, Center for US-Mexican Studies, University of California: San Diego, 391–415.

Smith, Raymond T. 1988. *Kinship and Class in the West Indies: A Genealogical Study of Jamaica and Guyana*, Cambridge University Press: Cambridge.

Smith, Stanley 1981. Determinants of Female Labour Force Participation and Family Size in Mexico City. In *Economic Development and Cultural Change*, 30: 1, 129–52.

Standing, Guy 1981. *Unemployment and Female Labour: A Study of Labour Supply in Kingston, Jamaica*, Macmillan: London.

Standing, Hilary 1985. Resources, Wages and Power: The Impact of Women's Employment on the Urban Bengali Household. In Haleh Afshar (ed.) *Women, Work and Ideology in the Third World*, Tavistock: London, 232–57.

Stansfield, David 1980. The Mexican Tourist Industry. In *Bolsa Review*, 14: 4/80, 226–32.

Stern, Claudio 1982, Industrialisation and Migration in Mexico. In Peter Peek and Guy Standing (eds) *State Policies and Migration: Studies in Latin America and the Caribbean*, Croom Helm: London, 173–205.

Stevens, Evelyn 1973. Marianismo: The Other Face of Machismo in Latin America. In Ann Pescatello (ed.) *Female and Male in Latin America*, University of Pittsburg Press: Pittsburg, 89–102.

Stivens, Maila 1987. Family and State in Malaysian Industrialisation: The Case of Rembau, Negeri Sembilan, Malaysia. In Haleh Afshar (ed.) *Women, State and Ideology: Studies from Africa and Asia*, Macmillan: Houndmills, Basingstoke, 89–110.

Stone, Elizabeth (ed.) 1981. *Women and the Cuban Revolution*, Pathfinder Press: New York.

Taylor, Harry and Fesenmaier, Daniel 1980. Spatial Patterns of Age–Sex Structures in Costa Rica – A Study in Demographic Modernization. In *Malaysian Journal of Tropical Geography*, 2, 35–44.

Teachman, Jay; Polonko, Karen and Scanzoni, John 1987. Demography of the Family. In Marvin Sussman and Suzanne Steinmetz (eds) *Handbook of Marriage and the Family*, Plenum: New York and London.

Thomson, Marilyn 1986. *Women of El Salvador: The Price of Freedom*, Zed: London.

Tienda, Marta and Ortega, Sylvia 1982. Las Familias Encabezadas por Mujeres y la Formación de Nucleos Extensos: Una Referencia a Perú. In Secretaría de Programación y Presupuesto (SPP) (ed.) *Estudios Sobre la Mujer 1. El Empleo y la Mujer. Bases Teóricas, Metodológicas y Evidencia Empírica*, SPP: México DF, 319–44.

Townsend, Janet and Momsen, Janet 1987. Towards a Geography of Gender in the Third World. In Janet Momsen and Janet Townsend (eds) *Geography of Gender in the Third World*, Hutchinson: London, 27–81.

Twomey, Michael 1989. A Falta de Pan, Tortillas: Mexican Economists on the Current Crisis. In *Latin American Research Review*, 24: 3, 240–9.

Unikel, Luis 1982. Regional Development Policies in Mexico. In Alan Gilbert in association with Jorge Hardoy and Ronaldo Ramirez (eds) *Urbanization in Contemporary Latin America: Critical Approaches to the Analysis of Urban Issues*, John Wiley: Chichester, 263–77.

Urry, John and Warde, Alan 1985. Introduction. In The Lancaster Regionalism Group (ed.) *Localities, Class and Gender*, Pion: London, 1–12.

Uthoff, Andras and Gonzalez, Gerardo 1978. Mexico and Costa Rica: Some Evidence on Women's Participation in Economic Activity. In Guy Standing and Glen Sheehan (eds) *Labor Force Participation in Low-Income Countries*. ILO: Geneva, 43–50.

Valladares, Licia 1989. Family and Child Labour in the Favela. Paper presented at the

International Symposium on Third World Urbanisation, Swedish Council for Research in Humanities and Social Sciences, Stockholm, June.

Vance, Irene 1985. *Women's Participation in Self-Help Housing: The San Judas Barrio Project, Managua, Nicaragua*, Gender and Planning Working Paper No. 4, Development Planning Unit, University College London.

Vatuk, Sylvia 1982. Changing Patterns of Marriage and the Family in an Urbanised Village in Delhi, India. In Helen Safa (ed.) *Towards a Political Economy of Urbanisation in Developing Countries*, Oxford University Press: New Delhi, 119–50.

Villareal, Rene 1977. The Policy of Import-Substituting Industrialisation, 1929–1975. In José Luís Reyna and Richard Weinert (eds) *Authoritarianism in Mexico*, Institute for the Study of Human Issues: Philadelphia, 67–107.

Walby, Sylvia 1985. Theories of Women, Work and Unemployment. In The Lancaster Regionalism Group (ed.) *Localities, Class and Gender*, Pion: London, 145–60.

Wall, Richard in collaboration with Robin, Jean and Laslett, Peter 1983 (eds) *Family Forms in Historic Europe*, Cambridge University Press: Cambridge.

Ward, Peter 1976. In Search of a Home: Social and Economic Characteristics of Squatter Settlements and the Role of Self-Help Housing in Mexico City. Unpublished Ph.D. dissertation, Department of Geography, University of Liverpool.

Ward, Peter 1982. Land for Low-Cost Housing: A Suitable Case for Treatment. Paper presented at 'Land for Housing the Poor: Towards Positive Action in Asian Cities'. International Seminar of the Asian Institute of Technology, Bangkok, 18–31 January.

Ward, Peter 1986. *Welfare Politics in Mexico: Papering over the Cracks*, Allen & Unwin: London.

Ward, Peter 1989. Government Without Democracy in Mexico City: Defending the High Ground. In W. A. Cornelius, J. Gentleman and P. H. Smith (eds) *Mexico's Alternative Political Futures*, Monograph Series No. 30 Center for US–Mexican Studies, University of California, San Diego, 308–23.

Webster, Andrew 1984. *Introduction to the Sociology of Development*, Macmillan: Houndmills, Basingstoke.

Weiss, A. 1984. Tradition and Modernity in the Workplace: A Field Study of Women in the Pharmaceutical Industry of Lahore. In *Women's Studies International Forum*, 7: 4, 259–64.

Wilkinson, Doris 1987. Ethnicity. In Marvin Sussman and Suzanne Steinmetz (eds) *Handbook of Marriage and the Family*, Plenum: New York, 183–210.

Wilson, Adrian 1985. *Family*, Tavistock: London.

Wolf, Eric 1959. *Sons of the Shaking Earth*, University of Chicago: Chicago.

World Bank 1988. *World Development Report 1988*, Oxford University Press.

Young, Kate 1978. Modes of Appropriation and the Sexual Division of Labour: A Case Study from Oaxaca, Mexico. In Annette Kuhn and Ann Marie Wolpe (eds) *Feminism and Materialism*, Routledge & Kegan Paul: London, 125–54.

Young, Mei Ling and Salih, Kamal 1987. Structural Change and Transformation – A Research Proposal. In Janet Momsen and Janet Townsend (eds) *Geography of Gender in the Third World* Hutchinson: London, 347–54.

Youssef, Nadia 1972. Differential Labour Force Participation of Women in Latin American and Middle Eastern Countries. In *Social Forces*, 51, 135–53.

Youssef, Nadia and Hetler, Carol 1983. Establishing the Economic Condition of Women-Headed Households in the Third World: A New Approach. In Mayra Buvinić, Margaret Lycette and William McGreevey (eds) *Women and Poverty in the Third World*, Johns Hopkins: Baltimore, 216–43.

Yudelman, Sally 1989. Access and Opportunity for Women in Central America: A

Challenge for Peace. In William Ascher and Ann Hubbard (eds) *Central American Recovery and Development: Task Force Report to the International Commission for Central American Recovery and Development*, Duke University Press: Durham and London, 235–56.

Zosa-Feranil, Imelda 1984. Female Employment and the Family: A Case Study of the Bataan Export Processing Zone. In Gavin Jones (ed.) *Women in the Urban and Industrial Workforce: Southeast and East Asia*, Development Studies Centre Monograph 33, Australian National University, Canberra, 387–403.

Index

Gender & Society

~~chaos~~ ~~margaret~~

ANDERSEN MARGARET

SAGE Publications

LONDON 1993